SIXTY SUMMERS

SOMERSET CRICKET SINCE THE WAR

SIXTY SUMMERS

SOMERSET CRICKET SINCE THE WAR

David Foot and Ivan Ponting

FOREWORD BY MARCUS TRESCOTHICK

FAIRFIELD BOOKS

Fairfield Books

17 George's Road, Fairfield Park, Bath BA1 6EY

Tel 01225-335813

Copyright © David Foot and Ivan Ponting

Page and jacket design by Niall Allsop

First published 2006

ISBN 0 9544886 3 6

Printed and bound in Great Britain by

Bath Press Ltd, Bath

FOREWORD BY MARCUS TRESCOTHICK

I may have been born at Keynsham, just outside the Bristol boundary, and not so far from the Gloucestershire County Ground but in spirit I have always been a Somerset lad. My loyalty shouldn't be too hard to trace; I grew up with glamorous names like Ian Botham and Viv Richards ringing in my ears. Beefy in particular was my hero and inspiration.

Somerset is in my blood. Dad played for the county's Second XI when not opening for Keynsham. Mother helped with the teas. My boyish dream was of me playing for Somerset; there was no other county. When Ian Botham came to Keynsham to play in a benefit match, I watched in awe, too shy to speak to him, though I believe I got his autograph. I told myself that one day I would bat for Somerset.

Cricket and Somerset dominated my life. Someone – perhaps on reflection it was me – worked out that I actually scored 4,000 runs one season. The fact was that I never turned down the chance of a game, whether it was on Saturday, Sunday or in the evening. I would play with equal enthusiasm for my school, for one of Keynsham's junior sides, to make up the numbers for a nearby village or for a friend's makeshift XI. My first hundred was for Avon Boys; I think I was eight. When I was 14 I scored my maiden ton at senior level. I was playing alongside Dad, and it was a special thrill.

Most of my idols in the Somerset club went for their shots. My natural game is, with the right degree of care, to do the same; I've never liked to give the bowler the chance to get on top. I'm a team man. I've always felt, right from my early schoolboy matches, that team spirit is essential. And I know that spirit will be there in the Taunton dressing room when my England days are over and I can return full-time to my beloved county.

Trophies have not come easily to Somerset. We are still waiting for our first championship. But just thumb through these pages, so many players stir a memory. I only wish I'd played with more of them.

INDEX OF ADDITIONAL ITEMS

EXPLANATORY NOTE

The player profiles in this book appear under the seasons in which each man made his debut for Somerset. Abbreviations used in the statistical notes at the end of each entry are as follows:

SFC: Somerset first-class matches.

OD: all one-day matches except Twenty20 Cup.

GC: Gillette Cup.

NW: NatWest Trophy.

C&G: Cheltenham and Gloucester Trophy.

B&H: Benson and Hedges Cup.

TT: Twenty20 Cup.

LOI: Limited-overs internationals.

RHB: right-hand bat.

LHB: left-hand bat.

RF: right-arm fast bowler.

RFM: right-arm fast-medium.

RMF: right-arm medium-fast.

RM: right-arm medium.

RSM: right-arm slow-medium.

OB: off-break bowler (right-arm).

LBG: leg-break and googly bowler (right-arm).

LF: left-arm fast.

LFM: left-arm fast-medium.

LMF: left-arm medium-fast.

LM: left-arm medium.

SLA: slow left-arm.

WK: wicket-keeper.

HS: highest score.

BB: best bowling analysis for innings.

HT (following entries on runs or wickets): highest total in a season.

0 wickets signifies the player did bowl but without success; where there is no mention of wickets he did not bowl at all.

MoM: Gillette Cup/NatWest Trophy/Cheltenham and Gloucester Trophy man of the match award.

GA: Benson and Hedges gold award.

* denotes not out.

Club statistics refer to Somerset careers only. International statistics refer to entire careers.

PUBLISHER'S FOREWORD

This book started out in 1993 as a 128-page paperback: 'Somerset Cricket – A Post War Who's Who'. Then early in 2005 the authors, David Foot and Ivan Ponting, approached me in the hope that I might publish an updated version. Somehow, twelve months later, in our enthusiasm we seem to have transformed it into a larger-format 320-page hardback, brimming with additional features.

David has brought up to date his pen portraits of the 219 cricketers who represented Somerset up to 1993, and he has added a further 59 who have arrived since then. The majority are accompanied by photographs, and these have been collected by Ivan Ponting, with especial help from the *Bristol Evening Post*, in particular Phil Lickaty, from Andy Cowie of Colorsport and from the Museum at Somerset County Cricket Club, where Tony Stedall and Peter Yates have been most helpful.

The individual players are arranged chronologically, appearing in the year in which they first played for the county. At the start of each year there is a summary of that season, written by David, and – for those who like to see the figures – the Somerset first-class averages.

The statistics have been compiled by Ivan Ponting, and in this task he has received great help from the website CricketArchive. All Somerset figures are correct to the end of 2005, with international appearances taken to the conclusion of the Australia-South Africa Test series on 6 January 2006.

In addition to all this, I have collected quotations to sit alongside each of the season summaries and some of the players' portraits. Some are from books, magazines and newspapers, some from interviews. I think that they add a little fun to the mix.

There are old photographs of five of the grounds – Taunton, Bath, Weston, Glastonbury and Yeovil – and we are very grateful to Bill Smith, F.R.P.S., for allowing us to use these.

We have also asked several players past and present to choose dream teams to represent Somerset, and these too are sprinkled about the book. I thank them for their time – especially Marcus Trescothick, whose foreword was written in a break between tours of Pakistan and India.

To complete the acknowledgements, I must thank Niall Allsop for his clear and attractive page design and Susanna Kendall for her perceptive editing and work on the photographs.

All in all, the book is intended as a treasure trove for lovers of Somerset cricket, a chance to look back across the past sixty summers, to remember all those who have represented the county and to live again some of the golden days – and the disappointments!

For anybody who wants to update this book in years to come, I have two wishes: that they will have the same fun in compiling it and that they too will be able to start at 1946 and say 'since the war'.

Stephen Chalke

INDEX OF PLAYERS

1946

Captain: E.F. Longrigg

First-class cricket was back. Familiar faces were to be seen in the dressing room; some of the older players, returning from the war, were a little less agile or subservient. Brig E H Lancaster had done his best to keep things ticking over for the previous six years. Now the white paint had been splashed on at Taunton and expectations were refreshingly high. Eight professionals had been re-engaged, a few of them doubtlessly not pleased at the offered contracts. But the natural sense of camaraderie largely made up for that.

Longrigg was the captain once more, just as he had been in 1939. Pulled muscles and rustiness were inevitable – and Somerset lost their opening four matches. This was, however, a deceptive prelude to a season which was their best overall since gaining first-class status in 1891. From late June to August 21, they were unbeaten for 16 games, 12 of which were won. They finished fourth in the championship, winning more games than ever before – in 1892 they ended in third position but then only 16 matches were played.

Nothing was more memorable, of course, than the almost insouciant way in which they beat the Indians by an innings at Taunton. The vaunted tourists were dismissed for 64 on the first day, as Andrews and Buse swung the ball like Test players themselves. By this stage of the summer Somerset had acquired the ebullient habit of scoring more than 500 in an innings. Gimblett was the leading batsman by some distance, carrying on where he had left off before the war. Middlesex were beaten by an innings, too, and Gimblett's 231 was his first double-century. Wellard, who hadn't lost his distinctive leap while now offering a more liberal sprinkling of off-breaks, headed the bowling.

Somerset had a genuine *team* look about them. Luckes, the efficient wicketkeeper, created a county record with his 51 catches and 26 stumpings. Lawrence, from Yorkshire league cricket, was an instant hit as he mixed leg-break with googly. The new amateurs, Walford and Langdale, announced their arrivals with hundreds. It was all better than the county had dared to hope.

Once we had settled down and the initial freshness had worn off, the majority of those who had played pre-war found that playing continuously for six days a week was proving to be far more strenuous than anticipated.

Frank Lee

COUNTY CHAMPIONSHIP 4th

Played 26   Won 12   Drawn 8   Lost 6

OTHER MATCHES

Played 2   Won 2

BATTING

	M	I	NO	Runs	HS	Ave	100	50	ct	st
M.M. Walford	7	10	1	472	141*	52.44	2	1	7	–
H. Gimblett	25	41	2	1947	231	49.92	7	8	24	–
R.J.O. Meyer	9	12	0	496	98	41.33	–	5	4	–
G.R. Langdale	8	13	1	355	146	29.58	1	2	2	–
H.T.F. Buse	28	42	8	909	59*	26.73	–	5	16	–
F.S. Lee	28	46	0	1180	169	25.65	1	5	7	–
E.F. Longrigg	21	31	5	633	74	24.34	–	4	12	–
W.T. Luckes	28	37	13	580	56	24.16	–	3	50	26
H.E. Watts	9	15	1	330	56	23.57	–	1	3	–
J. Lawrence	28	47	5	966	88	23.04	–	7	19	–
N.S. Mitchell–Innes	5	10	0	218	55	21.80	–	1	3	–
F. Castle	13	18	1	311	60*	18.29	–	1	4	–
A.W. Wellard	21	32	2	531	74	17.70	–	4	15	–
C.J.P. Barnwell	15	24	0	392	64	16.33	–	2	3	–
H.L. Hazell	23	28	10	201	43	11.16	–	–	27	–
W.H.R. Andrews	25	32	7	260	65	10.40	–	1	2	–
A.T.M. Jones	5	8	0	44	13	5.50	–	–	3	–
W.C. Caesar	3	4	1	14	7	4.66	–	–	3	–

(2 matches)   J.W. Seamer 0, 13, 6 (2 ct)   H.D. Burrough 15, 0, 0 (3 ct)
G.E.S. Woodhouse 70, 0, 13* (1 ct)

(1 match)   R.C. Peters 3, 2*

BOWLING

	Overs	Mdns	Runs	Wkts	Ave	5wi	10wm
G.R. Langdale	52.4	15	97	7	13.85	1	–
H.L. Hazell	430.4	125	940	54	17.40	4	1
A.W. Wellard	941	229	2216	119	18.62	10	2
J. Lawrence	431.5	85	1359	66	20.59	–	–
H.T.F. Buse	661.5	157	1573	77	20.42	2	–
W.C. Caesar	87	20	214	10	21.40	–	–
R.J.O. Meyer	235	61	522	21	24.85	–	–
W.H.R. Andrews	637.3	123	1721	68	25.30	3	–

F. Castle 13.1–1–43–1   R.C. Peters 6–1–18–0   F.S. Lee 5.4–0–39–0
E.F. Longrigg 5–2–11–0   M.M. Walford 5–0–17–0 C.J.P. Barnwell 4–0–13–0
H. Gimblett 3–1–17–0   A.T.M. Jones 3–0–21–1   H.E. Watts 1–0–6–0

1946

WALLY LUCKES 1924 – 1949

It may have been West Country allegiance, but Horace Hazell always used to reckon there wasn't a better wicketkeeper in the country. 'If you'd only shouted louder, Wally, you'd have played for England.'

Indeed, Luckes was unobtrusive in everything he did, though the stumpings were executed with remarkable sharpness and agility for someone who was hampered by a heart condition. Indeed, only Harold Stephenson has outstripped his total of wicket-keeping victims for Somerset.

The constant threat of ill health caused Wally to bat lower in the order than his vigilant skills deserved. His sole hundred came against Kent, maybe assisted a trifle in the end by the generosity of fellow gloveman Les Ames and one or two of the bowlers.

WALTER THOMAS LUCKES Born London, 1.1.01. Died 27.10.82. RHB, WK. Cap 1927. SFC: 365 matches; 5710 runs @ 16.22; 1 century; HS 121* v Kent, Bath, 1937; HT 662 in 1947; 828 dismissals (588 ct, 240 st).

> Like all wicket-keepers worth the name, he is fond of the lonely appeal; Duckworthian in his insistence, but more ventriloquial; turning sometimes, with accusing eye, towards a blameless long-leg.
> In the dog days you can tell him, like father in the song, by his hat. A white and shapeless affair.
> R.C. Robertson-Glasgow

'BUNTY' LONGRIGG 1925 – 1947

Back to lead Somerset again after the war, he deserved considerable credit for the fact that they finished fourth. In 1930 he had taken a double-hundred off Leicestershire, watched by his somewhat intimidating father, the Major, later to be county president.

'Bunty', a left-hander, played the spinners well and was apt to look vulnerable against genuine pace. At short leg, with jutting jaw and sleeked-back dark hair, he cut a patrician figure. The Bath law practice had first claims on him after the war but he was county president in the late 1960s, a difficult time.

EDMUND FALLOWFIELD LONGRIGG Born Bath, 16.4.06. Died 23.7.74. LHB. Cap 1926. Captain 1938-46. SFC: 219 matches; 8329 runs @ 24.56; 10 centuries; HS 205 v Leicestershire, Taunton, 1930; 1000 runs twice; HT 1567 in 1930; 0 wickets.

> Under his leadership the Somerset side was roused from its lethargy. We became conscious of a new team spirit invading the side, each one of us began to feel the necessity of 'putting our backs into it' and to giving everything we had to the game.
> Frank Lee

ARTHUR WELLARD 1927–1950

In 1938 he took 172 first-class wickets, more than anyone else in the land. He did it with a much-imitated leap just before releasing the ball, genuine pace and consistent swing away from the batsman. Yet, in the perverse way of cricketing lore, the majority of the stories about Arthur Wellard concern his batting.

For he was a slogger, glorious, with a pragmatic method distilled from the muscular orthodoxy of a hundred Somerset meadows, though he hailed from Kent himself. He would also claim that his many sixes, which in total made up virtually a quarter of all his runs for the county, were for the most part straight and scientifically dispatched. In truth, they described a wildish arc, threatened to get lost in the clouds and ended up – as authentically detailed – in distant allotments or passing trains.

Wellard first turned up in Somerset, with what then seemed like a Cockney accent and a flashy suit, to become an instant idol among the less sophisticated members of the staff. They admired his varying skills with ball and bat, just as they did the way he could regularly win a trick at cards or follow the right dog at the evening meeting straight after the close of play. His image was made for Somerset. In return he served them well and a more sensitive county would have kept him on for another year or so at the end.

He played only two Tests, against New Zealand in 1937 and Australia the following summer. He'd have gone to India but for the war. Later, as some of the venom went out of his bowling, he turned more to his off-breaks. He was still able to take those blinding catches at silly mid-off.

Doting third-formers came to chuckle at his exploits, and return the ball from the French beans. Rowing boats were at hand to retrieve from the adjacent Tone. Harold Pinter eulogised him in print and even persuaded an ageing Arthur to play for the showbizzy Gaieties CC.

ARTHUR WILLIAM WELLARD Born Southfleet, Kent, 8.4.02. Died 31.12.80. RHB, RFM/OB. Cap 1929. 2 Tests 1937-38. SFC: 391 matches; 11432 runs @ 19.34; 2 centuries; HS 112 v Surrey, Oval, 1934, and v Lancashire, Old Trafford, 1935; 1000 runs twice; HT 1232 in 1935; Double twice in 1933, 1935; 1517 wickets @ 24.32; BB 8-52 v Worcestershire, Bath, 1947; 100 wickets 8 times; HT 169 in 1938.

> Born and bred in Kent, he played several times against Kent Club and Ground but, when he inquired about the possibility of being taken on the staff, he was told he had much better go and be a policeman. The story will seem improbable only to those who have never tried to judge a young cricketer.
> R.L. Arrowsmith

FRANK LEE 1929 – 1947

Here was the ideal foil for Gimblett. The style was one of unwavering vigilance; right leg down the wicket and straight bat. Frank Lee scorned the histrionics of run-making. The Somerset innings, punctuated by cavaliers and wayward technicians, needed the Londoner's undisturbed calm. Eight times, all the same, he scored 1,000 runs; there were 23 centuries, and he kept wicket efficiently in an emergency.

On occasions, no doubt to his surprise, his gentle medium-paced seamers were introduced. He once completed an unlikely five-wicket haul against Warwickshire, an achievement that resulted in an even more unlikely appearance with the new ball in the next fixture. A modest man, he realistically down-played his rare bowling stints and knew that he was of much more value as a studious opener.

Everything Frank did carried an aura of dignity, a quality still apparent during his 29 Tests as an umpire.

FRANK STANLEY LEE Born Marylebone, London, 24.7.05. Died 30.3.82. LHB, RM. Cap 1931. SFC: 328 matches; 15243 runs @ 27.96; 23 centuries; HS 169 v Nottinghamshire, Trent Bridge, 1946; 1000 runs 8 times, incl 2000 runs once; HT 2019 in 1938; 23 wickets @ 32.56; BB 5-53 v Warwickshire, Taunton, 1933. Middlesex 1925. Fc umpire 1948-63.

A good, ordinary chap. He used to say, 'Make the first 20 runs for yourself and all the rest for the team.'
Eric Hill

DICKIE BURROUGH 1927 – 1947

Not all amateurs, by any means, were worth their places. Burrough, the Bath solicitor, was, emphatically so, and he proved it with his four centuries. Dickie, whose father had played for Somerset before him, was an enthusiast and popular with the pros, not least because he was prepared to do his stint of chasing in the outfield. As a batsman he went in anywhere from opener to middle order; but that was Somerset. Burrough's sporadic career spanned just over 20 years.

HERBERT DICKINSON BURROUGH Born Wedmore, Somerset, 6.2.09. Died 9.4.94. RHB. Cap pre-war. SFC: 171 matches; 5316 runs @ 20.92; 4 centuries; HS 135 v Northamptonshire, Kettering, 1932; 1000 runs once; HT 1007 in 1933; 0 wickets.

BILL ANDREWS 1930 – 1947

WILLIAM HARRY RUSSELL ANDREWS Born Swindon, Wiltshire, 14.4.08. Died 9.1.89. RHB, RFM. Cap pre-war. SFC: 226 matches; 4833 runs @ 15.59; HS 80 v Lancashire, Old Trafford, 1937; 1000 runs twice; HT 1141 in 1937; double – twice in 1937, 1938; 750 wickets @ 23.38; BB 8-12 v Surrey, Oval, 1937; 100 wickets 4 times; HT 143 in 1937.

I had to speak after him at a dinner in my benefit year. It was like trying to follow Morecambe and Wise. I was a very sad act. Dear old Bill. He's the only person I've known who could sell a pair of wicket-keeping gloves to an off-spin bowler.
Peter Robinson

The county never had a more impetuous devotee. He took on successive secretaries and committee members. He said his piece – with stammer and unequivocal fervour – and at times he was regretting it afterwards. Apart from the starchier elements within the club ('that bloody barrack-room lawyer, Andrews …') the county was soon embracing him again. He loved Somerset with an undimmed passion, and although fired four times – twice as a player and twice as a coach – kept coming back for more. Some would argue that he was the greatest character Somerset ever had. His funeral, complete with lurking TV cameras and hundreds of admirers, was that of a celebrity, just as Sammy Woods' had been before the war.

As a cricketer, one inevitably recalls him in tandem with his great friend, Arthur Wellard. Bill bowled the in-swingers, so well in fact that he took 100 wickets during four seasons in succession. It is possible that he would have played for England but for the war. He had a theory that Wally Hammond vetoed his chance. Twice he completed the double, so he was no mean all-rounder. At least he played for an England XI in festival matches.

Few equalled the sheer range of his cricket. His claims that he played professionally in Wales and Scotland also are well documented. He played in the leagues, in Minor Counties, and was finally back captaining his beloved Weston-super-Mare. And whatever the snubs, he was always around to offer the county advice.

Bill was a marvellous coach, of schoolboys in particular. Many, according to him, were potential Len Huttons; all were influenced by his undiluted zest for the game. He spoke at hundreds of village cricket dinners; he told countless stories, the majority of which were endearingly slanderous. He could exasperate but also was much loved by all who shared his unbridled instincts for the game. For someone so gregarious, it was sad to note the reclusive nature that went with depression in his late years.

BERTIE BUSE 1929 – 1953

The mannerisms were part of the fun. Preparing to bowl an over, from the moment he handed his faded cap to the umpire, it was a ritual to amuse the crowds that treated him so warmly. There was his studious contemplation, his stuttering approach, the touch of acceleration and the undisguised smile when the batsman failed to counter the late swing. The ball moved naturally away from the right-hander but Bertie was quite capable of bringing it back the other way.

Everything about the Buse appearance was prim and punctilious, as you would expect from someone who worked behind a ledger in a solicitor's office. The batting stance was ungainly; there was rather too much posterior, accentuated when he stretched suddenly to dab a personalised square-cut. For the most part he was obdurate. He was not by nature in a great hurry and, in any case, Somerset in those days – before and after the war – badly needed someone to shore up a teetering innings.

His first match for the county was as an 18-year-old amateur. He turned pro in the late 1930s and became one of that cherished coterie of honest journeymen within the team.

Bertie, though not a swift or graceful fielder, was a useful all-round sportsman. He played full-back for Bath Rugby Club; he excelled at table-tennis, billiards and snooker. When his county cricket was over he coached in Johannesburg and also ran a pub in Dorset before helping out in the office of the Bath evening newspaper.

Born in Bristol he may have been, but Bath, his spiritual home, was where he originally worked, enjoyed his best matches in summer and winter . . . and shuddered in despair when his benefit match was over in a day.

HERBERT FRANCIS THOMAS BUSE Born Ashley Down, Bristol, 5.8.10. Died 23.2.92. RHB, RM. Cap 1934. SFC: 304 matches; 10623 runs @ 22.69; 7 centuries; HS 132 v Northamptonshire, Kettering, 1938; 1000 runs 5 times; HT 1279 in 1948; 657 wickets @ 28.77; BB 8-41 v Derbyshire, Taunton, 1939; HT 81 in 1939.

In one of my early matches there was a big hit. It went up in the air not far from Bertie at long-on, and he let it bounce. He didn't move.

At the end of the over I said, 'Why the hell didn't you go for that catch?' 'Oh,' he said. 'It was a bit awkward, you know. And if you put one down, they always put it in the paper.'

Eric Hill

He gives himself a courteous nod and commences his run with the decorous tread of a butler anxious not to awake echoes from a stone or wooden floor; he puts down his feet with elaborate care.

John Arlott

HORACE HAZELL 1929 – 1952

All Horace Hazell wanted to do as a schoolboy was to play for Gloucestershire. He used to walk the four miles from his home in Brislington, on the outskirts of Bristol, just to watch Wally Hammond. Demoralisingly, when he was old enough for a trial, the county weren't terribly impressed.

However, his local club recommended him to Somerset instead. They didn't really need another slow left-armer as Jack White had no intention of leaving himself out. But Horace was sent to an indoor school in London, whence the report came back: 'As a bowler he's too slow, but he might make it as a batsman.'

Hazell's reputation was, of course, to be based on the precision of his bowling; so accurate, in fact, that he once bowled 105 successive deliveries to Tom Graveney and company at Taunton without conceding a run.

The post-war cricket writers noted how he kept topping the county's bowling averages. They described him as round and jovial. So he was, enlivening many a mournful dressing room, sharing in the Saturday night escapades when the team were playing away.

The players called him 'H'. They enthused about the way he held on to the catches in the slips and off his own bowling. They dubbed him 'The Crisis King' for the valued phlegm he could display as a number-11 batsman.

Somerset possessed some excellent left-arm slow bowlers in their history, and Hazell takes his rightful place with them. 'Yet I couldn't spin the bloody ball, my fingers weren't big enough,' he would say with true modesty. Somerset got rid of him a season or two before they should have done. How often have we heard that indictment?

HORACE LESLIE HAZELL Born Brislington, Bristol, 30.9.09. Died 31.3.90. LHB, SLA. Cap 1932. SFC: 350 matches; 2280 runs @ 8.17; HS 43 v Gloucestershire, Bristol, 1946; 957 wickets @ 23.97; BB 8-27 v Gloucestershire, Taunton, 1949; 100 wickets twice; HT 106 in 1949.

His avuncular appearance never remotely suggested a professional sportsman. I once asked him what he did in winter, and he came back with the perfect answer: 'I never get up before twelve.'
Trevor Bailey

NORMAN MITCHELL-INNES 1931 – 1949

Lucky he may have been to be chosen, when still an undergraduate, to play for England – and unlucky to be discarded soon afterwards. He got his chance because Plum Warner vividly remembered 'Mandy's' jaunty 168 for Oxford against the South Africans that May. In the Trent Bridge Test he flopped but was retained for Lord's. He had to withdraw because of chronic hay fever and was never asked again. Ironically, coinciding with the Lord's match, he suppressed his sneezes, batted down the order and scored a fine hundred again for Oxford.

His duties in the Sudan Political Service restricted his cricket for Somerset, though he was one of the county's many captains in 1948. He was a mature, stylish batsman who, if he had been able to stay in this country, might have been quite an influence on the county game. Apart from his cricket, he was a gifted golfer.

NORMAN STEWART MITCHELL-INNES Born Calcutta, India, 7.9.14. RHB, RFM. Cap pre-war. Joint Captain 1948. 1 Test 1935. SFC: 69 matches; 2835 runs @ 24.23; 3 centuries; HS 182 v Worcestershire, Kidderminster, 1936; HT 499 in 1936; 31 wickets @ 35.67; BB 4-65 v Sussex, Eastbourne, 1934. Oxford University 1934-37.

JAKE SEAMER 1932 – 1948

Son of a Somerset clergyman, Jake had a beaky ecclesiastical look himself. He was also quite a character as perhaps you would expect from someone with boyhood ambitions to go on the stage. There were colourful anecdotes from him – like his memory of one match abroad when he scored a century before breakfast – to enliven evenings during away fixtures for his county.

Appearances for the county were limited to leave periods from the Sudan Political Service. But he was one of the numerous skippers during 1948, when he endeared himself to most of the pros, for his persona rather than mere sporting ability. While at Oxford he once progressed spectacularly to near 200 against Minor Counties. Seamer liked going for his shots, though in county cricket he always seemed to find himself as the willing and admiring foil to the muscular Arthur Wellard.

JOHN WEMYSS SEAMER Born Shapwick, Somerset, 23.6.13. RHB. Cap pre-war. Joint Captain 1948. SFC: 59 matches; 1405 runs @ 15.61; HS 70 v Derbyshire, Taunton, 1932; HT 291 in 1938; 0 wickets. Oxford University 1933-36.

JOHN BARNWELL 1935 – 1948

He personified the old school, a debonair amateur who deputised occasionally as Somerset's skipper, and the county sounded him out to do the job on a more permanent basis, but he couldn't find the time. Rightly proud of his nimbleness in the covers – and of the four boundaries in a row he once took so audaciously off Bill Voce at Trent Bridge. Possessing Repton pedigree and with no lack of social aplomb, he was the secretary of the ex-Somerset County Cricketers Association when it was formed in 1982.

CHARLES JOHN PATRICK BARNWELL Born Stoke-on-Trent, Staffordshire, 23.6.14. Died 4.9.98. RHB. Cap pre-war. SFC: 69 matches; 1592 runs @ 15.16; HS 83 v Hampshire, Taunton, 1939; HT 396 in 1939; 0 wickets.

TREVOR JONES 1938 – 1948

Talk of the romance of cricket and you talk of 18-year-old Jones's walk to the wicket at Leicester. Somerset were close to an innings defeat. This diffident youth, batting at number nine, made 106, marvellously supported by Wally Luckes. After the war, despite some brilliant innings in high-class Bristol club cricket, some of the spark had gone. At county level, that ice-cool defiance against Leicestershire was never repeated. Still, Trevor was very near to becoming a full-time cricketer. Somerset had many worse. A fine bridge player, he was close to international status and for a time managed the Cornish team.

ARCHIBALD TREVOR MAXWELL JONES Born Wells, Somerset, 9.4.20. Died 6.05. RHB, LBG. SFC: 21 matches; 399 runs @ 11.40; 1 century; HS 106 v Leicestershire, Leicester, 1938; HT 281 in 1938; 3 wickets @ 44.00; BB 1-3 v Glamorgan, Newport, 1939.

HUGH WATTS 1939 – 1952

Who said that Somerset stuck to three captains during the bizarre leadership merry-go-round of 1948? Watts was number four – against Hants at Bath – and there were others. Hugh, whose spectacles gave him a studious appearance, used to be a history master at Downside and was dubbed 'The Abbot' by some of the pros because of it.

War wounds curbed his talent as an all-rounder. He was a popular teammate and, at times, a most attractive left-hander whose only championship hundred came against Glamorgan when Len Muncer got in a bit of a strop because of criticism from Wilf Wooller, his skipper, and started bowling full tosses as Watts moved into the 90s.

HUGH EDMUND WATTS Born Stratton-on-the-Fosse, Somerset, 4.3.22. Died 27.12.93. LHB, RLB. SFC: 61 matches; 2511 runs @ 25.11; 1 century; HS 110 v Glamorgan, Weston-super-Mare, 1949; HT 543 in 1947; 0 wickets. Cambridge University 1947.

JOHN HENSLEY CAMERON Born Kingston, Jamaica, 8.4.14. Died 13.2.2000. RHB, OB/LBG. 2 Tests 1939. SFC: 48 matches; 1373 runs @ 18.55; 3 centuries; HS 113 v Sussex, Eastbourne, 1937; HT 574 in 1937; 45 wickets @ 43.66; BB 6-143 v Glamorgan, Downside, 1934; HT 17 in 1937; Cambridge University 1934-37; Jamaica, West Indies, 1946-47.

JOHN CAMERON 1932 – 1947

In his early days with Somerset, John Cameron was known as either 'Monkey' or 'Snowball', insensitive by today's standards, and one wonders how he felt about such nicknames. He was a much sadder and more complex figure than was generally supposed as he trundled up to the wicket and bamboozled county batsmen with his wrist-spin. In private moments the small, stocky West Indian would confide his unhappy experiences at the wrong end of the colour bar. There was at least one period when he was desperately depressed.

Cameron was the son of a doctor and was sent to Taunton School, where he was encouraged – with a minimum of distracting coaching – to bowl leg-spinners and googlies. In 1931 he played at Lord's for The Rest against the cream of the Public Schools and in a little more than 19 overs he took 10-49. Not only *The Times* became instantly excited. Somerset homed in on this precocious local talent and he was playing for them by the age of 18.

At his best, Cameron was brilliant, but he lost the bewildering knack. His spinning fingers got too chubby. Old sweats on the circuit, less than enchanted by the emergence of an exceptional teenage leg-spinner, gripped their handles and single-mindedly got to work on him. He took some demoralising punishment at times. There was a perceptible shift in his value to the county and two of his three hundreds were scored in 1937.

In the last season before the war his career was given a timely lift when he was named as vice-captain of the West Indian touring team to this country. His final game for Somerset was in 1947 – and there was surely a poignant hint in the way he offered himself, unsuccessfully, as the county's secretary, and even as skipper, a few years later.

JACK MEYER 1936 – 1949

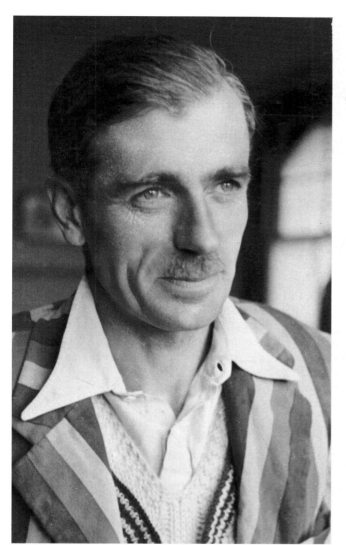

Innovative, experimental, eccentric: those three adjectives will do to begin with in conveying the flavour of this tall, lean man who founded Millfield School. As an educationalist, he was an unorthodox visionary. Often he operated on a 'Robin Hood' principle, stinging wealthy parents and enabling promising young sportsmen from humbler homes to have a comparatively inexpensive schooling. As a result, a formidable list of boys made it from the Millfield First XI to Somerset.

Meyer's own appearances for the county were necessarily limited; by the time he was captaining them, for a summer in 1947, he was bent double by lumbago. Inevitably he led the team of slightly cynical pros with an endearing quirkiness that, in matters of field-placing for instance, could be quite bewildering.

He was, nonetheless, a fine cricketer. His batting brought him one double-century, clinched allegedly by an offer of a donation to the opposing beneficiary's fund. His bowling could be a nightmare to any wicket-keeper; he spun the ball at brisk medium pace, was proud of his late swing and liked to trifle with half a dozen variations in an over.

He seldom went to bed, sleeping for a few hours instead in the headmaster's study. He liked placing a bet and kept a racing form-book with his academic tomes. In London he was known to spend all night at the gaming tables, alas at times with disastrous results.

ROLLO JOHN OLIVER MEYER Born Ampthill, Bedfordshire, 15.3.05. Died 9.3.91. RHB, RM. Cap pre-war. Captain 1947. SFC: 65 matches; 2929 runs @ 28.16; 2 centuries; HS 202* v Lancashire, Taunton, 1936; HT 853 in 1947; 158 wickets @ 28.31; BB 7-74 v Northamptonshire, Weston-super-Mare, 1947; HT 43 in 1947. Cambridge University 1924-26; Bombay, Western India and Europeans, all in India, 1926-35.

> RJO Meyer was a near genius. He was capable of bowling everything except left-arm fast. He could bat a bit, too. But I fear a painful back and an eccentric approach turned him rather into a figure of ridicule. I admired him so much, yet I wondered what was happening much of the time he was captain.
> **Maurice Tremlett**

HAROLD GIMBLETT 1935 – 1954

News of his presence at the wicket cleared the market of the farmers across the road from the County Ground at Taunton, or removed the holiday-makers from the seafront at Weston. In the doting, still unsophisticated and innocent days, before the might of Richards and Botham, Harold Gimblett was mesmeric.

What was more, here was a farmer's son from Bicknoller who had hitched a lift to Frome for his unplanned debut and then scored a century in 63 minutes. First-class cricket has rarely, if ever, come up with a romantic schoolboy tale to rival it.

He wasn't even being kept on after his trial with the county. Suddenly opinions were being revised. Gimblett went on to carry Somerset's batting for years and to play for his country.

At his best, the style was touched with genius. The off-drives could be as sweet as Wally Hammond's. Crusty wiseacres told him not to hook; he still did so, twice in the opening over if the opportunity was there. He also liked to crash a few straight drives into the sightscreen first bounce, before the scorers had sharpened their pencils.

Harold went to a minor public school but didn't have much time for the game's establishment. He never tried to hide his simmering complexes: over the hierarchy at Lord's or a succession of Somerset officials. He could be tetchy, a man of moods and disconcerting vacillations. His team-mates admired his considerable talent and the way he so often held their innings together. But they also knew when to leave him alone with his private thoughts and torment in the corner of the dressing room.

He was hounded remorselessly by depression, though the majority of the spectators who came to worship at the County Ground had no idea. In fact, the demons in his head wouldn't leave him. In time he came to hate Somerset and the game of cricket.

In search of a life utterly divorced from his native county and even sporting conversation, he moved with his wife to a mobile home in the New Forest. And there, burdened with added fears of insecurity and with acute arthritis, he took his life.

HAROLD GIMBLETT Born Bicknoller, Somerset, 19.10.14. Died 31.3.78. RHB, OB. Cap 1935. 3 Tests 1936-39. SFC: 329 matches; 21142 runs @ 36.96; 49 centuries; HS 310 v Sussex, Eastbourne, 1948; 1000 runs 12 times, incl 2000 runs twice; HT 2134 in 1952; 41 wickets @ 50.09; BB 4-10 v Gloucestershire, Bath, 1935.

A well-known writer on cricket has remarked of Harold Gimblett: 'Perhaps he is too daring for the grey-beards.'
But my own view is that he is also too daring for the majority of the black-beards, the brown-beards, the no-beards, and the all-beards, who sit in judgment on batsmen; in short, too daring for those who have never known what it is to dare in cricket.
Raymond Robertson-Glasgow

JOHNNY LAWRENCE
1946 – 1955

He tossed his leg-breaks up into the clouds, causing merriment and consternation. He chatted as he bowled, warning the batsman that the googly was coming. But opponents and team-mates alike knew what a practical joker Johnny Lawrence was.

His conversation, coloured by Yorkshire vowels, bubbled away, whether he was saving the game with the deadest of bats, relying on an intuitive stumping from Harold 'm'real partner in crime' Stephenson, or picking up catches at short-leg. Twice he took 100 wickets in a season, once he was desperately near to the double.

Little Johnny didn't approve of strong drink or strong language. His Nonconformist beliefs caused him to reject Sunday matches in his benefit year. For all that, he wasn't remotely a killjoy. His sheer enthusiasm for the game was conveyed ebulliently to the hundreds of lads who attended his cricket schools in the North.

JOHN LAWRENCE Born Carlton, Yorkshire, 29.3.14. Died 10.12.88. RHB, LBG. Cap 1946. SFC: 281 matches; 9094 runs @ 20.43; 3 centuries; HS 122 v Worcestershire, Worcester, 1955; 1000 runs 3 times; HT 1128 in 1955; 791 wickets @ 24.88; BB 8-41 v Worcestershire, Worcester, 1950; 100 wickets twice; HT 115 in 1950.

He was a jolly, kindly man, and perhaps the biggest contribution he made to Somerset cricket was his laughter and comradeship in the dressing room, at a time when things were generally going badly.
Alan Gibson

MICKY WALFORD 1946 – 1953

MICHAEL MOORE WALFORD Born Stockton-on-Tees, County Durham, 27.11.15. Died 16.1.2002. Cap 1946. RHB, SLA. SFC: 52 matches; 3395 runs @ 40.90; 7 centuries; HS 264 v Hampshire, Weston-super-Mare, 1947; HT 942 in 1947; 1 wicket @ 71.00; BB 1-18 v Lancashire, Weston-super-Mare, 1952. Oxford University 1935-38.

> Cricket was something I loved – but as a holiday pursuit.
> **Micky Walford**

Now here was undeniable class. Walford would arrive in August, straight from his teaching duties at Sherborne, to compile his centuries and play with a stylish orthodoxy and grace that brought murmurs of jealousy from one or two established heroes.

His fiercely competitive nature probably stemmed from his North County roots; he wasn't gregarious and was seen by some of the pros as a cold fish. But his eloquence at the wicket was a rare and cherished joy. Surely, if he had been available more often for county cricket, he'd have walked into the Test team.

Micky scored a hundred, undefeated, on his Somerset debut. The vacations coincided with Weston, and that was where he fashioned six of his centuries. His technique, with the sweetest of strokes off the front and back foot through the covers, was a delightful lesson to every schoolboy who came to watch.

In a ham-fisted and tactless approach, for reasons that are not apparent, Somerset finally asked him if he'd be prepared to surrender his special registration so they could use it for someone else. He would have gone on for another season or two.

Micky could have played part-time for Warwickshire. But after a meeting with RJO Meyer and an exchange of letters, he chose Somerset instead, because of its proximity to Sherborne. In turn, Walford recommended Harold Stephenson to the county.

A fine all-round sportsman, quite apart from his considerable gifts as an opening bat, he was an outstanding centre-three-quarter who played in final England rugby trials and in wartime internationals, in addition to representing his country at hockey.

GEORGE LANGDALE 1946 – 1949

He arrived a virtual stranger, this studious looking schoolmaster, and scored a hundred on his home debut. The jauntily struck 146 (92 of them in boundaries) came against his home county of Yorkshire, whose famous skipper, Brian Sellers, when asked for an unofficial reference, had joked: 'He'll probably be good enough for you.' On the strength of that qualified praise, Langdale went in at number eight, and made his point. The left-hander was quickly handed his cap, though the runs failed to come so easily again.

He never played for Yorkshire, though there were four games for Derbyshire before the war. Later he turned out for Berkshire, once taking all ten wickets for them with his off-breaks, and Norfolk.

GEORGE RICHMOND LANGDALE Born Thornaby, Yorkshire, 11.3.16. Died 24.4.2002. LHB, ROB. Cap 1946. SFC: 20 matches; 616 runs @ 19.87; 1 century; HS 146 v Yorkshire, Taunton, 1946; HT 357 in 1946; 20 wickets @ 37.80; BB 5-30 v Warwickshire, Edgbaston, 1946. Derbyshire 1936-37.

BILL CAESAR 1946

It could only happen in Somerset where, after all, the great Tom Richardson left his Bath pub to play one game for the county in 1905. Bill Caesar was the surprise choice for the side in the year after the war. He was an amateur, no more than military medium and of comfortable build by then. To compound the shock of his selection, it was discovered that the 45-year-old bowler, now living in Somerset, had played once for Surrey . . . in 1922.

For his second county he played three matches and took ten wickets. Between innings he kept his team-mates engrossed with tales of his unlikely soccer career – he'd been an England amateur international, had played for Dulwich Hamlet and several league clubs, including Fulham and Brentford.

WILLIAM CECIL CAESAR Born Clapham, London, 25.11.1899. Died 5.4.88. RHB, RM. SFC: 3 matches; 14 runs @ 4.66; HS 7 v Leicestershire, Melton Mowbray, 1964; 10 wickets @ 21.40; BB 4-59 same match. Surrey 1922.

RICHARD PETERS 1946

Just one match, after being well recommended at a time of selection uncertainties in the first season after the war, but the call was not apparently repeated.

RICHARD CHARLES PETERS Born Chew Magna, Somerset, 12.9.11. Died 26.10.89. RHB, RF. SFC: 1 match; 5 runs @ 5.00; HS 3 v Leicestershire, Melton Mowbray, 1946; 0 wickets.

FRED CASTLE 1946 – 1949

If he hadn't been a headmaster in Bath, Fred Castle could easily have ended up a professional cricketer with Somerset (or his native Kent, who had already sounded him out). Or maybe a professional footballer with Crystal Palace – and that's only half of it. He was a fine conjuror and a thoroughly passable baritone in Gilbert and Sullivan. But sport was probably his favourite hobby; he was a natural at most ball games, representing both Kent and Somerset at hockey.

Castle's high-scoring consistency in club cricket at Bath brought him the inevitable invitation to play for Somerset. It was never easy getting time off. He'd spend a few hours at school in the morning and then, for Bath matches, chase to the Recreation Ground in time for the first over. The holiday fixtures were far less complicated.

Fred was a stylish bat who never quite found his best form during intermittent appearances for the county. But his pupils, on the boundary, treated him as a hero.

FREDERICK CASTLE Born Elham, Kent, 9.4.09. Died 17.5.97. RHB, LBG. Cap 1946. SFC: 23 matches; 686 runs @ 20.78; HS 60* v Surrey, Weston-super-Mare, 1946; HT 311 in 1946; 1 wicket @ 43.00; BB 1-16 v Cambridge University, Bath, 1946.

GEORGE WOODHOUSE 1946 – 1953

He was Somerset's youngest captain, at 23, when he first shared the duties in 1948. Then, with quiet efficiency, he did the job on his own for a whole season before devoting his time and energies to the family brewery business.

George Woodhouse played wartime rugby and cricket for Cambridge. But after his brief, happy spell with Somerset, he accepted that there had to be priorities outside the game. He was chairman of the Blandford-based Hall & Woodhouse up to the time of his death from a heart attack. In his time he was High Sherriff and Deputy Lieutenant of Dorset. He was a life member of Somerset and also served as president of Dorset CCC.

Much earlier, there had been glimpses of his true batting capabilities when he composed his sole century, at Leicester.

GEORGE EDWARD SEALEY WOODHOUSE Born Blandford, Dorset, 15.2.24. Died 19.1.88. RHB, RM. Cap 1947. Joint Captain 1948, Captain 1949. SFC: 58 matches; 1903 runs @ 20.68; 1 century; HS 109 v Leicestershire, Leicester, 1947; HT 841 in 1949; 1 wicket @ 8.00; BB 1-8 v Sussex, Eastbourne, 1948. Cambridge University.

1947

Captain: R.J.O. Meyer

RJO (Jack) Meyer was the captain, taking leave for the summer from his duties as headmaster of Millfield School. He was, as usual, full of cerebral and unorthodox ideas when it came to field placings, batting order and kidology. But he just wasn't fit enough, at times bent almost double with his back trouble. Initially it had seemed that his innovative approach and dressing-room influence were what Somerset needed. The team went off to Lord's for the opening match and, in a wonderful, much-quoted encounter, they beat Middlesex by one wicket. The debutant Tremlett not only took eight wickets but also scored the winning runs in *Boys' Own* fashion. The Middlesex players lined up to applaud him and his imperturbable partner, Hazell, off the field. Here, it was being said, was Somerset's future star: he bowled straight and fastish, he batted with a dashing style. Before long, he was being taken in the England party to the West Indies.

Somerset's breezy start at cricket's headquarters was not sustained. There followed a depressing losing sequence. In June, the county were wretchedly beaten in a day by Derbyshire at Chesterfield. it was the first time a county had been defeated in a day since 1925, and that, too, was Somerset when they had been annihilated by Lancashire.

In the Chesterfield game, George Pope took 13 wickets for 50, bowling unchanged, yet he conceded 24 runs before his first wicket. That was bad enough; then Somerset made the short journey to Bristol to take on their West Country neighbours and rivals over the bank holiday. This time they were bowled out for 25 in their second innings. Lee scored 17 out of that pitiful total. Tom Goddard, all bounce and off-break, did the hat-trick while taking five wickets in seven deliveries. Despite the reverses, Somerset managed to maintain their reputation for surprises. They beat the eventual champions, Middlesex, twice and at Frome they inflicted the only defeat of the summer on Lancashire.

Scene: a local match in aid of Frank Lee's Benefit.

Teams: a Somerset XI and a local XV.

The county side mustered 180 and the opponents lost their fourteenth wicket with 100 on the board. The issue seemed fairly decided but, as the county XI were leaving the field, the home skipper rushed out from the pavilion and said: 'Wait a bit – we've sent into the village for five more players.'

Playfair Cricket Annual

COUNTY CHAMPIONSHIP 11th

	Played 26	Won 8	Drawn 6	Lost 12

OTHER MATCHES

Played 2	Drawn 1	Lost 1

BATTING

	M	I	NO	Runs	HS	Ave	100	50	ct	st
M.M. Walford	8	16	2	942	264	67.28	2	6	3	–
N.S. Mitchell–Inmes	7	14	2	444	74	37.00	–	4	12	–
H. Gimblett	26	47	2	1539	118	34.20	2	10	19	–
J.H. Cameron	3	4	1	95	38*	31.66	–	–	–	–
H.E. Watts	12	21	0	543	71	25.85	–	6	6	–
G.E.S. Woodhouse	12	19	1	380	109	21.11	1	1	3	–
R.J.O. Meyer	25	43	2	853	88	20.80	6	9	–	–
M. Coope	19	38	2	720	113	20.00	1	3	6	–
J. Lawrence	27	49	3	904	76	19.65	–	4	35	–
H.T.F. Buse	25	47	10	718	65	19.40	–	2	12	–
W.T. Luckes	25	44	9	662	57	18.91	–	1	42	19
F.S. Lee	17	32	1	548	77	17.67	–	1	5	3
M.F. Tremlett	23	42	7	599	85*	17.11	–	3	10	–
D.P.T. Deshon	3	6	1	73	21	14.60	–	–	1	–
E. Hill	5	10	1	128	38	14.22	–	–	1	–
A.W. Wellard	22	40	0	521	46	13.02	–	–	24	–
W.H.R. Andrews	10	17	3	154	52*	11.00	–	1	2	–
H.L. Hazell	23	35	17	195	28	10.83	–	–	19	–
G.W.L. Courtenay	4	7	0	66	34	9.42	–	–	–	–
A. Vickery	3	6	1	44	21	8.80	–	–	–	–

(2 matches) G.R. Langdale 0, 0, 10   E.F. Longrigg 0, 6, 3   F. Castle 58, 11, 1 (2 ct)
L. Angell 4, 2*, 6 (2 ct)

(1 match) H.D. Burrough 0, 3

BOWLING

	Overs	Mdns	Runs	Wkts	Ave	5wi	10wm
H.L. Hazell	715.4	217	1597	72	22.18	6	–
A.W. Wellard	856.4	182	2187	93	23.51	8	1
H.T.F. Buse	598.4	141	1720	61	28.19	3	–
R.J.O. Meyer	417.1	71	1263	43	29.37	2	–
W.H.R. Andrews	249	46	718	24	29.91	1	–
M.F. Tremlett	659	103	1964	65	30.21	2	–
J. Lawrence	428.1	58	1488	42	35.42	1	–

G.R. Langdale 39–7–123–3   J.H. Cameron 32–7–101–1   M. Coope 25–0–158–2
H. Gimblett 28–8–91–1   M.M. Walford 2–0–8–0

MAURICE TREMLETT 1947 – 1960

Here was Somerset's first professional captain: a social as well as a sporting statement. He did the job particularly well for much of the time. Few over the post-war decades had a more acute tactical awareness than Maurice Tremlett. He kept games nicely balanced and always tried to persuade the opposition to remain interested.

Countering this was an easy-going, even lackadaisical nature. He was often one of the boys, a popular member of the team and much liked around the boundary. But on the occasions when club politics got perniciously to work and he sensed that other candidates for his role might be advocated by some of the committee, he went into a shell.

Born in Cheshire but a Somerset lad in every sense, Tremlett started as the office boy at Taunton and quickly acquired something of a golden-boy image when he made his heroic entry at Lord's, to beat Middlesex almost on his own, soon after the war. The premature praise embarrassed him; he was never a conceited man.

He was taken to the West Indies, where Gubby Allen persuaded him to lengthen his run-up and experiment with his action in a search for added pace. It was a disaster. The bowler went miserably into decline. At home, he lost length, line and confidence – and simply got on with his batting.

The stroke-making could be clean, straight and excitingly lofted, even if inconsistent. He took a fearful blow on the forehead and almost lost an eye when fielding at silly mid-off at Bath. The balance was never the same again.

Yet the record reminds us that this fair-haired batsman could score 2,000 runs in a season. He was one of the finest, and most pleasing to the eye, in Somerset's history.

MAURICE FLETCHER TREMLETT Born Stockport, Cheshire, 5.7.23. Died 30.7.84. RHB, RFM. Cap 1947. Captain 1956-59. 3 Tests 1948. SFC: 353 matches; 15195 runs @ 25.93; 15 centuries; HS 185 v Northamptonshire, Northampton, 1951; 1000 runs 9 times, incl 2000 runs once; HT 2071 in 1951; 326 wickets @ 29.04; BB 8-31 v Glamorgan, Weston-super-Mare, 1948; HT 83 in 1948. Central Districts, New Zealand, 1951-52.

From time to time his glorious lofted straight drive, the regal purple of cricket, bursts out, to lift a hard-fought cricket to a memorable moment. The batsman himself is at rest, bat hanging from his hand, before the mighty arc of the hit is ended beyond the ring.
John Arlott

If Maurice had possessed top-class bowlers, he could have been one of the best leaders in the country. He was completely unflappable and, if we were having a rough day, he would say, 'Well, lads, we can't push this brick wall over. But keep on trying.'
Bill Alley

ERIC HILL 1947 – 1951

He became the elder statesman of the Taunton press box, his reserve. He spoke, and wrote, from experience, and with courage.

The experience came from his days with the county as an opening batsman; tall, correct and often unlucky. The courage was revealed when, with two fellow journalists, he took on a complacent and toffee-nosed establishment in 1953.

Even though the scales were weighted unfairly against the three unlikely rebels, Somerset cricket was positively shaken up. Hill became skipper of the Second XI; he served on the committee, and offered gentle words of help, when asked, to successive intakes of fledgling cricketers. Through it all, Eric's affection for Somerset never lessened.

ERIC HILL Born Taunton, 9.7.23. RHB. Cap 1949. SFC: 72 matches; 2118 runs @ 15.92; HS 85 v Northamptonshire, Kettering, 1948; HT 731 in 1948; 1 wicket @ 55.00; BB 1-25 v Surrey, Oval, 1949.

LES ANGELL 1947 – 1956

Older villagers at Norton St Philip, with an affection for cricket, were almost as quietly proud of this local boy as they were of their famous and ancient inn, The George. As a club batsman for Lansdown, Les was as prolific as he was unassuming, but when he he arrived at Somerset he was never going to establish himself in the way of predecessor Frank Lee.

He was neat, correct and perhaps a trifle too wary as he countered the new-ball men at county level. He was understandably in awe of his opening partner, Harold Gimblett (though just once he dared to outscore him), and in his less diffident moments could pull out a few lovely cover drives of his own. Team-mates were delighted when this popular fellow collected his sole first-class hundred, against the Pakistani tourists.

FREDERICK LESLIE ANGELL Born Norton St Philip, Somerset, 29.6.22. RHB. Cap 1950. SFC: 132 matches; 4596 runs @ 19.15; 1 century; HS 114 v Pakistanis, Taunton, 1954; 1000 runs once; HT 1125 in 1954; 0 wickets.

Les Angell (left) with Harold Gimblett

MILES COOPE 1947 – 1949

One brackets him with that other little Yorkshireman, Johnny Lawrence. Coope, despite an exquisite late cut and an adequate repertoire of shots that at times he showed a reluctance to parade, was the less talented of the pair. He stayed for three seasons, leaving us with a memorable cameo or two. Lack of consistency was his undoing.

MILES COOPE Born Gildersome, Yorkshire, 28.11.16. Died 5.7.74. RHB, LB. Cap 1947. SFC: 70 matches; 2718 runs @ 20.90; 2 centuries; HS 113 v Middlesex, Taunton, 1947; 1000 runs once; HT 1172 in 1948; 8 wickets @ 59.87; BB 3-29 v Yorkshire, Taunton, 1948.

GEOF COURTENAY 1947

This former Sherborne School boy made his debut at Taunton. Somerset were in trouble and he, at number five, soon found himself partnering Harold Gimblett. His 34 that day turned out to be his best in a mere quartet of outings for the county. He also played for Dorset and Scotland.

GEOFRY WILLIAM LIST COURTENAY Born Castle Cary, Somerset, 16.12.21. Died 17.10.80. RHB. SFC: 4 matches; 66 runs @ 9.42; HS 34 v Sussex, Taunton, 1947. Scotland 1955-57.

TONY VICKERY 1947 – 1948

The medical profession had first call on him. That was the county's loss. Here was a solid, technically skilful batsman, never seen at anything like his best during his sporadic post-war appearances.

ANTHONY VICKERY Born Taunton, 26.8.25. RHB. SFC: 6 matches; 89 runs @ 8.09; HS 21 v Worcestershire, Worcester, 1947.

DAVID DESHON 1947 – 1953

Something of a schoolboy star at Sherborne, he seldom seemed to fail as a forceful batsman and once scored a hundred before lunch in a wartime public schools' representative match at Lord's. He was to become a major in the Army, captaining the service at cricket. He collapsed and died at Heathrow airport.

DAVID PETER TOWER DESHON Born London, 19.6.23. Died 18.1.92. RHB. SFC: 4 matches; 82 runs @ 11.71; HS 21 v Middlesex, Taunton, 1947.

1948

Captains: N.S. Mitchell-Innes
         J.W. Seamer
         G.S. Woodhouse

This was the season that Somerset, searching unavailingly for so long for an amateur captain, ended up with three of them taking over the role in turn. At least two others also did the job, as well as several more who, in an emergency, found themselves as skipper for the occasional afternoon. Mitchell-Innes, Seamer and Woodhouse were the official choices, each to be captain for a third of the summer when they were available from their other professional or overseas duties. It was a chummy compromise but hardly an exercise in continuity. Cynics might say the county did well to finish in 12th position, especially as they didn't pick up a point from their first five matches. At Bath they were beaten by Oxford University, a reverse that galvanised them to outplay Notts and win by an innings in the next fixture.

The season did offer highlights. Gimblett went to Eastbourne to make 310. He calculated that he was on the field for nearly 18 hours during the match and claimed that a suggestion from Wellard that there should be a ground collection back in Taunton to recognise the triple-hundred was brusquely turned down by the secretary. A month earlier, in a nostalgic return to Frome, scene of his historic debut, he had hit a fine century off Leicestershire's attack. That was a game in which Woodhouse, in his first appearance as captain, shaped an impressive innings, and the phlegmatic Buse even lashed ten fours and two sixes in a notable undefeated 89, full of alien aggression. The rest was left to Lawrence's bewitching fingers and wrist.

It was good that season to see Coope, talented if inconsistent, reach his 1,000 runs. His fellow Yorkshireman, Lawrence, pulled out all his tricks against his native county. He took six first innings wickets, four of them in five balls, including the hat-trick.

Hazell took 100 wickets for the first time – at the age of 39 – and finished high in the national averages. There was no doubt that he was without superior among bowlers of his type at this stage in post-war cricket and more than one national critic, in bemoaning the lack of first-class youngsters among the slow left-handers, would comment 'If only Hazell were ten years younger …'

Ron Roberts

COUNTY CHAMPIONSHIP 12th

Played 26   Won 5   Drawn 7   Lost 14

OTHER MATCHES   Played 3   Lost 3

BATTING

	M	I	NO	Runs	HS	Ave	100	50	ct	st
H. Gimblett	23	43	1	1798	310	42.80	4	10	11	–
F. Castle	5	9	2	203	59*	29.00	–	1	2	–
M.M. Walford	4	7	0	184	71	26.28	–	1	2	–
H.T.F. Buse	28	51	2	1279	98*	26.10	–	8	14	–
G.E.S. Woodhouse	14	26	4	520	75	23.63	–	3	6	–
N.S. Mitchell-Innes	5	10	0	222	65	22.20	–	1	6	–
M. Coope	29	54	1	1172	89	22.11	–	8	6	–
M.F. Tremlett	28	50	4	958	96*	20.82	–	3	27	–
H.E. Watts	10	19	1	346	75	19.22	–	2	3	–
E. Hill	22	42	0	731	85	17.40	–	3	10	–
J.W. Seamer	11	19	5	238	51*	17.00	–	1	6	–
A.W. Wellard	21	37	5	530	60	16.56	–	1	25	–
G.R. Langdale	4	7	0	113	36	16.14	–	–	2	–
J. Lawrence	24	41	2	617	73	15.82	–	4	18	–
W.T. Luckes	27	43	16	403	36*	14.92	–	–	30	27
H.W. Stephenson	8	12	0	166	44	13.83	–	–	2	2
P.A.O. Graham	6	11	2	82	33	9.11	–	–	3	–
S.S. Rogers	7	13	0	117	23	9.00	–	–	3	–
A. Vickery	3	6	0	45	14	7.50	–	–	2	–
H.L. Hazell	29	44	15	215	31	7.41	–	–	14	–

(2 matches)   F.L. Angell 10, 25, 0 (3 ct)   A.T.M. Jones 9, 8, 3, 2 (1 ct)
R.J.O. Meyer 0, 30, 10, 12 (1 ct)   J. Redman 5, 8, 5

(1 match)   C.J.P. Barnwell 22, 5   J.E. Buckland 0*, 17* (2 ct)   M.A. Sutton 0, 13* (1 ct)

BOWLING

	Overs	Mdns	Runs	Wkts	Ave	5wi	10wm
H.L. Hazell	986.4	324	2077	105	19.78	7	–
J. Lawrence	586.5	95	1729	78	22.16	6	1
M.F. Tremlett	752.4	153	2174	83	26.19	4	–
A.W. Wellard	715.3	157	1767	62	28.50	1	–
G.R. Langdale	62	7	229	7	32.71	–	–
H.T.F. Buse	518.1	104	1396	35	39.88	–	–
P.A.O. Graham	91.2	14	316	7	45.14	–	–

R.J.O. Meyer 43–4–185–3   M. Coope 40–4–228–5   J. Redman 33–4–141–5
J.E. Buckland 17–3–55–3   M.A. Sutton 17–4–44–1   E. Hill 6–0–30–0
H. Gimblett 4–0–18–0   G.E.S. Woodhouse 4–0–8–1   M.M. Walford 3–0–12–0
H.E. Watts 3–0–15–0   J.W. Seamer 2.1–0–9–0

JIM REDMAN 1948 – 1953

Frome produced its moments of personal glory, as the county's record books reveal. Jim's came there, against Derbyshire. He'd never conjured so much movement and was at times almost unplayable as he took his seven cheap wickets. For the most part, he was an artisan seamer, persevering but unmemorable. There were also some useful bowling stints for Wiltshire.

JAMES REDMAN Born Bath, 1.3.26. Died 24.9.81. RHB, RMF. Cap 1951. SFC: 65 matches; 1012 runs @ 12.34; HS 45 v Essex, Brentwood, 1951; HT 472 in 1951; 117 wickets @ 35.63; BB 7-23 v Derbyshire, Frome, 1951; HT 50 in 1951.

JOE BUCKLAND 1948

This left-arm fastish bowler's only appearance was at Newport, where his three wickets weren't enough to persuade the county to come up with a full contract.

JOSEPH EDWIN BUCKLAND Born Lingfield, Surrey, 24.9.16. LHB, LF. SFC: 1 match; 17 runs (no average); HS 17* v Glamorgan, Newport, 1948; 3 wickets @ 18.33; BB 2-35 same match.

PETER GRAHAM 1948

One of the relatively unknown amateurs who popped up, at times at the behest of chums or school intermediaries, in the tentative years after the war. His reputation at Tonbridge had been built as a quick bowler. For the county he took seven wickets from six matches.

PETER ARTHUR ONSLOW GRAHAM Born Kurseong, India, 27.12.20. Died 2.3.00. RHB, RF. SFC: 6 matches; 82 runs @ 9.11; HS 33 v Glamorgan, Newport, 1948; 7 wickets @ 45.14; BB 3-47 same match.

MICHAEL SUTTON 1948

An Oxford blue just after the war and some useful hauls as an off-spinner were enough to earn him a solitary county appearance, against Oxford, as it happened.

MICHAEL ANTHONY SUTTON Born Weymouth, Dorset, 29.3.21. RHB, OB. SFC: 1 match; 13 runs @ 13.00; HS 13* v Oxford University, Bath, 1948; 1 wicket @ 44.00; BB 1-34 same match. Oxford University 1946-47.

STUART ROGERS
1948 – 1953

The question used to be: where do we find an old-style amateur to be captain, one with time on his hands and an affection for cricket? Rogers' appointment took most West Countrymen by surprise. They didn't necessarily disapprove of his loose, lively and technically naive batting, but they soon realised that his tactical sense was suspect.

He filled the captaincy gap for three years; in that time he scored three hundreds and leaned a bit on his senior pros like Horace Hazell, taken off in the skipper's flashy sports car occasionally for an evening meal and strong claret (until then an alien drink for the earthy spinner). Rogers' approach could be attractively cavalier, but some of the younger professionals wished he'd got to know them better.

STUART SCOTT ROGERS Born Muswell Hill, London, 18.3.23. Died 6.5.69. RHB. Cap 1949. Captain 1950-52. SFC: 118 matches; 3607 runs @ 19.08; 3 centuries; HS 107* v South Africans, Taunton, 1951; 1000 runs once; HT 1127 in 1950; 2 wickets @ 63.00; BB 2-13 v Nottinghamshire, Trent Bridge, 1950. Madras Europeans, India, 1946-47.

In the long view it is not the arithmetical performances of this or that player, nor merely the times of success and failure that strike the historian of Somerset cricket. It is rather the spirit – the spirit which win or lose has always been a happy compound of humour and independence.
Raymond Robertson-Glasgow

HAROLD STEPHENSON 1948 – 1964

He stands, statistically alone, as Somerset's finest wicketkeeper, and only Brian Langford has played more games for the county. Yet one is saddened that Test recognition slipped insensitively past 'Steve', maybe because he served an unfashionable side or, more realistically, because of the exceptional wealth of the competition. Somehow the Commonwealth tour to India and Ceylon in 1950-51 wasn't quite the same.

Harold came down from the North on the canny word of Micky Walford, quickly proved himself as consistent a keeper as any in England and, as a bonus for the West Country crowds, specialised gleefully and with consummate skill in the suicidal single during his characteristic pursuit of quick runs. Indeed, he scored 1,000 runs four times, aided by the youthful alacrity with which he bounded out of his ground.

As he crouched behind the stumps, the pads invariably looked too big for him. But he was a great technician, with the anticipation and intuition to take the sorcery and unpredictable variants of Johnny Lawrence.

Stephenson was a pragmatic rather than daring captain during his five years in charge. Under him Somerset came third in the table, their highest ever finish at that point, and weren't so far off the pennant. The parting carried certain pangs. He continued to live in Taunton but didn't return too often to the County Ground.

Subsequently keeping wicket for Dorset, there was still enough agility in him to suggest that the back was playing him up less and that Somerset needn't have been quite so ready to hunt for a successor.

He liked a drink, liked to make quick runs in the evening sunshine and liked to win without too much hassle. His loyalty to fellow pros was apparent; he was inclined to bristle when officials implied that it was time to bring in wet-behind-the-ears vacation players.

HAROLD WILLIAM STEPHENSON Born Haverton Hill, County Durham, 18.7.20. RHB, WK. Cap 1949. Captain 1960-64. SFC: 427 matches; 12473 runs @ 20.02; 7 centuries; HS 147* v Nottinghamshire, Bath, 1962; 1000 runs 4 times; HT 1085 in 1953; 0 wickets; 1006 dismissals (694 ct, 312 st). OD: 1 match; 4 runs @ 4.00; 1 dismissal (1 ct).

His greatest performance that I remember was against Gloucestershire at Bristol in 1959 on a thickish day, when Ken Biddulph moved his in-swing considerably at faster than medium. 'Steve' stood up to the stumps all the time, taking calmly and cleanly balls that whipped out of his sight across the batsman's body and often touched pads on the way. For good measure he threw in a leg-side stumping.

It was a fantastic performance so effortlessly executed that at one time I said to him: 'Why don't you let one go and show them how difficult it is?'

That's the trouble with wicket-keeping. If you do your job properly, nine out of ten people don't notice you, unless you are flinging yourself about and laying on the dramatic gestures. But drop one, and the whole world suddenly knows you are there.

Colin McCool

1949

Captain: G.E.S. Woodhouse

Somerset couldn't have had a worse start. They lost five games in a row, even if in the first of them Northants – struggling to make 64 to win – lost eight wickets in the process, seven to Buse's medium-paced accuracy and guile. There was some temporary improvement, with four victories in late May and early June, before another lamentable spell when the county suffered ten successive defeats in a demoralising run. These disasters were partly offset by dear old, capricious Clarence Park, Weston-super-Mare, where all three matches were won. It helped, too, that the schoolmasters, Walford and Watts, had turned up in their vacations to buckle their pads and introduce a new resolve.

Once again Gimblett had enlightened the gloom by scoring more than 1,800 runs. It could be reasonably be argued that he appeared at times to carry the team. When Hampshire came to Taunton in late May, the Bicknoller farmer's son fashioned a century in each innings for the first time in his productive career. As for the bowlers, Hazell wheeled away manfully with flawless precision and more flight than spin. He passed 100 wickets to head the county averages. Lawrence deservedly reached that landmark for the first time, teasing batsmen out, while the portly Hazell waited, laughter never far obscured behind those good-natured eyes, for opponents' patience to snap. They were convivial days; at Hazell's benefit game against Lancashire at Taunton, Wellard heaved a six through the press box window and exchanged a grin with a few of his drinking mates.

It was goodbye at last to Luckes, most conscientious and tidy of keepers, and welcome to Stephenson, recruited from Durham on the word of Walford.

Frome, with its short boundaries, was renowned for batting feats. This season, too, Sussex were guided spiritedly to their nine-wicket win with an opening second-innings stand of 148 in 80 minutes by John Langridge and David Sheppard, the last-mentioned not long out of Sherborne School and heading for Test and ecclesiastical honours.

> Somerset are a team of characters who look in some indefinable way as though they could not belong to any other county club but Somerset. Perhaps it is an air of easy-going tolerance to the game. The ambling mass of 47-year-old Arthur Wellard, sunburnt from many years of the summer game; rotund Pickwickian Horace Hazell; the solid Harold Gimblett; diminutive Lawrence; the scholastic Bertie Buse; the tall, broad figure of Maurice Tremlett. Laugh and jest flow through their cricket.
>
> **Wilfred Wooller**

COUNTY CHAMPIONSHIP 9th

Played 26 Won 8 Drawn 3 Lost 15

OTHER MATCHES

Played 3 Drawn 2 Lost 1

BATTING

	M	I	NO	Runs	HS	Ave	100	50	ct	st
M.M. Walford	9	16	2	763	120	54.50	1	4	3	–
H. Gimblett	26	50	3	2063	156	43.89	5	12	24	–
H.E. Watts	8	13	0	483	110	37.15	1	3	2	–
M.F. Tremlett	24	43	1	1012	104	24.09	1	4	26	–
H.T.F. Buse	27	48	3	1020	117	22.66	2	4	17	–
S.S. Rogers	13	20	2	400	61	22.22	–	4	3	–
M. Coope	22	42	1	826	102*	20.14	1	3	8	–
G.E.S. Woodhouse	26	49	7	841	59	20.02	–	2	6	1
H.W. Stephenson	24	43	4	735	88	18.84	–	3	39	44
E. Hill	20	40	1	718	60	18.41	–	2	6	–
F. Castle	3	6	0	102	52	17.00	–	1	–	–
W.T. Luckes	5	8	4	66	30*	16.50	–	–	8	13
G.R. Langdale	6	10	1	138	63*	15.33	–	1	1	–
A.W. Wellard	26	46	3	603	54	14.02	–	1	28	–
J. Lawrence	29	49	7	583	45	13.88	–	–	38	–
H.L. Hazell	25	39	23	185	29	11.56	–	–	15	–
N.S. Mitchell-Innes	7	14	0	157	42	11.21	–	–	10	–
F.L. Angell	9	18	2	160	45	10.00	–	–	5	–
J. Redman	6	10	3	45	12	6.42	–	–	2	–

(2 matches)   W.R. Genders 3, 22, 0, 4 (1 ct_

(1 match)   R.J.O. Meyer 14, 11   R. Smith 0, 40

BOWLING

	Overs	Mdns	Runs	Wkts	Ave	5wi	10wm
H.L. Hazell	923.1	303	2065	106	19.48	8	2
M.F. Tremlett	490	116	1324	61	21.70	2	–
J. Lawrence	771.3	123	2433	107	22.73	9	1
H.T.F. Buse	729.2	163	2017	79	25.53	4	–
A.W. Wellard	1021.1	223	2725	87	31.32	4	1
J. Redman	153.1	16	498	11	45.27	–	–
G.R. Langdale	78	9	307	3	102.33	–	–

R.J.O. Meyer 47-10-150-3   H. Gimblett 20-4-60-1   M. Coope 17-1-93-1

R. Smith 7-1-29-0   W.R. Genders 4-2-6-0   E. Hill 3--0-25-1

ROY SMITH 1949 – 1955

Not enough happened in the painstaking, unspectacular career of local boy Smith, whose left-arm slows were accurate enough but didn't give experienced batsmen too much trouble.

His best summer was 1953: that was when he scored his only hundred, at Frome (not quite in the Gimblett style there). He went on to complete 1,000 runs and earn his county cap.

As a batsman he could be the most stubborn of grafters, as the Aussies were to discover, but with the ball he was a disappointing successor to Horace Hazell. Later Roy played for Devon.

ROY SMITH Born Taunton, 14.4.30. RHB, SLA. Cap 1953. SFC: 96 matches; 2600 runs @ 17.10; 1 century; HS 100 v Worcestershire, Frome, 1953; 1000 runs once; HT 1176 in 1953; 19 wickets @ 57.00; BB 4-91 v Leicestershire, Leicester, 1952; HT 14 in 1952.

Roy Smith's hundred at Frome

Reg Perks was seaming and swinging the ball all over the place. And Roy couldn't get a bat on it. Gimblett came down the wicket. 'Come here, son. Are you having a bit of a problem down there? … I'll tell you what. I'll look after Perksy for a few overs. You come down this end.' Then, after Gimblett had hit him for three or four fours, he said, 'There you are, son. He might be a bit easier for you now.'

Ken Biddulph

ROY GENDERS 1949

Three counties – Derbyshire, Worcestershire and Somerset – and an amateur to boot. His first-class cricket was all crammed into the late 1940s.

WILLIAM ROY GENDERS Born Dore, Derbyshire, 21.1.13. Died 28.9.85. RHB. SFC: 2 matches; 29 runs @ 7.25; HS 22 v Cambridge University, Bath, 1949; 0 wickets. Derbyshire 1946; Worcestershire 1947-48.

Somerset crowds like Somerset best, and they are ready enough to point out Somerset virtues to visitors. Most players enjoy the experience, because a lifeless and indifferent crowd does take away some flavour from the match. Perhaps technical knowledge does not go deep, but honest endeavour always extracts appreciation and a spell of successful bowling, particularly fast bowling, or a hard-hitting innings can be relied upon to call forth admiration.
Norman Yardley, Yorkshire and England

A change of sport
Horace Hazell shakes hands with a supporter
The back row includes Roy Smith, Eric Hill, Arthur Wellard, Maurice Tremlett and Harold Stephenson
The front row is Harold Gimblett, Stuart Rogers and Johnny Lawrence

1950

Captain: S.S. Rogers

Somerset continued to agonise over the captaincy. Where was the amateur with indulgent parents, or someone able to take time off from his business career? Rogers, a handsome ex-Chindits major, was arguably appointed by default. He was painfully inexperienced in terms of first-class cricket, though that was a criticism that could be levelled at one or two other stopgap skippers at that time. His batting was technically suspect, but he possessed a pleasant, forceful style and at times he could pull out bold, entertaining shots. To the surprise of some of the older pros, he squeezed past his 1,000 runs for the season. The first of his three centuries came at Frome.

It took a long time for Somerset to run into any kind of decent, consistent form; then, true to their penchant for endearing unpredictability, they won eight matches. Lawrence, stump-tall, failed by a mere 19 runs to complete the double. Nothing was better than his bamboozling 8-41 at New Road, Worcester in August; he was a genuine all-rounder. In partnership with Hazell or Robinson, he demanded respect from the most distinguished of opposing batsmen. As for the West Country crowds, they loved the sheer enjoyment he brought to the game, whether producing prodigious turn or tumbling like a boy for a catch at short-leg

Tremlett, for his part, excited the spectators with those steepling sixes over long-on and long-off. Sadly the fans were also shaking their heads at the riddle of what had happened to that good-looking, assertive bowling of his. The theories were plentiful. Had too much advice been given him on that Caribbean tour?

A fine bowler on the way up appeared for Lancashire at Bath. He was 20 and his name was Brian Statham. Somerset were all out for 72. He took the first five wickets, those of Gimblett, Angell, Irish, Buse and Tremlett, in a 5-5 spell. The potential was palpable.

In 1950, after four years at Bromsgrove School, I wanted to play more than my teaching duties allowed. One day in the masters' common room, a colleague told me that he had seen an advert he thought might interest me – Captain/Secretary of Somerset County Cricket Club. I applied but returned after an extraordinary interview before a committee of 43 – or so I was told. I neither had the time nor the inclination to count them, but there seemed no way I could work with them.

Charles Palmer, later of Leicestershire and England

COUNTY CHAMPIONSHIP 7th

OTHER MATCHES								

Played 28   Won 8   Drawn 12   Lost 8

Played 2   Drawn 1   Lost 1

BATTING

	M	I	NO	Runs	HS	Ave	100	50	ct	st
M.M. Walford	9	13	1	511	114	42.58	1	5	–	–
H. Gimblett	26	47	1	1782	184	38.73	2	12	6	–
M.F. Tremlett	30	51	2	1311	132	26.75	3	5	20	–
H.T.F. Buse	30	50	3	1208	92	25.70	–	6	10	–
S.S. Rogers	30	49	5	1127	101	25.61	1	8	7	–
A.F. Irish	16	29	4	629	76	25.16	–	4	5	–
J. Lawrence	30	52	7	981	88	21.80	–	4	28	–
F.L. Angell	26	49	4	933	74	20.73	–	3	11	–
H.W. Stephenson	29	49	10	751	82	19.25	–	3	31	38
J. Redman	10	16	3	170	21	13.07	–	–	4	–
E.P. Robinson	30	44	11	369	40	11.18	–	–	30	–
R. Smith	8	14	1	138	32	10.61	–	–	2	–
H.E. Watts	4	6	1	52	21	10.40	–	–	–	–
G.E.S. Woodhouse	3	6	0	57	15	9.50	–	–	–	–
A.W. Wellard	5	6	1	47	19*	9.40	–	–	5	–
H.L. Hazell	30	41	19	165	22	7.50	–	–	11	–
E. Hill	6	11	1	67	26	6.70	–	–	3	–
W.J. Conibere	4	5	0	16	8	3.20	–	–	4	–

(2 matches)   G.G. Tordoff 37, 2, 5 (1 ct)
(1 match)   F.G.K. Day 29*, 4 (4 st)   M.R.G. Earls-Davis 4

BOWLING

	Overs	Mdns	Runs	Wkts	Ave	5wi	10wm
J. Lawrence	788	158	2174	115	18.90	9	–
H.L. Hazell	1027.2	339	2297	96	23.92	5	–
A.W. Wellard	145.2	31	311	10	31.10	–	–
W.J. Conibere	74	19	220	7	31.42	–	–
E.P. Robinson	909.3	203	2388	74	32.27	3	–
J. Redman	183.1	31	620	16	38.75	1	–
H.T.F. Buse	779.4	149	2057	53	38.81	2	–
M.F. Tremlett	262	46	683	12	56.91	–	–
A.F. Irish	55	10	206	3	68.66	–	–

H. Gimblett 11-3-41-0   R. Smith 9-1-32-0   S.S. Rogers 5.5-0-26-2
M.R.G. Earls-Davis 5-1-18-0

ELLIS ROBINSON 1950 – 1952

It was perhaps too much to expect his spinning fingers to contain the same wizardry for Somerset as they did for Yorkshire before and after the war. Yet Ellis Robinson's consistent off-breaks could still bring him 100 wickets in a season after coming West and once, at Weston, he returned match figures of 15-78.

He remained a North Countryman by nature, not wholly approving of differing attitudes in Somerset. He went on tour to Jamaica with Yorkshire in the mid 1930s; some felt he deserved greater recognition in the years that followed.

ELLIS PEMBROKE ROBINSON Born Denaby Main, Yorkshire, 10.8.11. Died 10.11.98. LHB, ROB. Cap 1950. SFC: 89 matches; 867 runs @ 8.17; HS 40 v Lancashire, Bath, 1950; HT 369 in 1950; 256 wickets @ 28.55; BB 8-47 v Sussex, Weston-super-Mare, 1951; 100 wickets once; HT 107 in 1951. Yorkshire 1934-49.

> Ellis Robinson was a somewhat temperamental off-break bowler, complete with a woebegone face, stoop and the conviction that the gods were not on his side.
> **Trevor Bailey**

KEN DAY 1950 – 1956

Bristol club cricket had few more accomplished wicketkeepers. He was also a Somerset lad and it seemed logical, when Harold Stephenson was unfit, for Day to take over. He did it seven times, his trusted reflexes accounting for eight stumpings. In different circumstances he could well have established himself at county level. As a batsman he took few risks, scoring more than 30 centuries for Knowle CC as a reward for that diligence.

FREDERICK GORDON KENNETH DAY Born Yatton, Somerset, 25.6.19. Died 9.12.91. RHB, WK. SFC: 7 matches; 201 runs @ 18.27; HS 56* v Lancashire, Old Trafford, 1956; 15 dismissals (7ct, 8 st).

FRANK IRISH 1950

He had an impressive cricketing pedigree for Devon and in club matches down there, so Somerset appeared to show enterprise in recruiting him as a pro. For his part he gambled, in the short term, by putting his business commitments on hold. His early form for the county suggested that a new career might be opening up. But the runs dried up and Somerset seemed to lose interest rather too prematurely. When they dangled a contract for the following year, Frank said: 'No thanks.'

ARTHUR FRANK IRISH Born Dudley, Worcestershire, 23.11.18. Died 17.7.97. RHB, RMF. SFC: 16 matches; 629 runs @ 25.16; HS 76 v Glamorgan, Cardiff, 1950; 3 wickets @ 68.66; BB 2-5 v Leicestershire, Bath, 1950.

GERRY TORDOFF
1950 – 1955

By some means or other, Tordoff's partial release was obtained from the Royal Navy for a season, so that he could lead Somerset. It was a bad appointment, though the blame should be levelled more at the committee than the skipper.

He was a useful left-hand bat, with some powerful shots and three centuries in the first-class game. More experienced players used to say that he was too loose with his batting and would profit from a tighter technique.

He passed 1,000 runs with one memorable fighting innings against Gloucestershire in his year as captain. But it was unreasonable to expect him to come in and lift an undistinguished side, and Somerset stayed on the bottom. Probably Tordoff enjoyed his carefree cricket with the Combined Services and Berkshire far more.

GERALD GEORGE TORDOFF Born Whitwood, Yorkshire, 6.12.29. LHB, RM. Cap 1952. Captain 1955. SFC: 54 matches; 2417 runs @ 25.44; 3 centuries; HS 145* v Gloucestershire, Taunton, 1955; 1000 runs once; HT 1132 in 1955; 26 wickets @ 46.03; BB 4-43 v Northamptonshire, Glastonbury, 1952. Cambridge University 1952.

JACK CONIBERE 1950

In the Wiveliscombe area his sporting reputation was assured. As a club cricketer, his left-arm pace brought plenty of success. He savoured his one first-class visit to Edgbaston and came away with four honest wickets. Probably he was a better rugby player, representing his county with typical zeal.

WILLIAM JACK CONIBERE Born Wiveliscombe, Somerset, 11.8.23. Died 19.8.82. RHB, LMF. SFC: 4 matches; 16 runs @ 3.20; HS 8 v Hampshire, Bournemouth, 1950; 7 wickets @ 31.42; BB 4-66 v Warwickshire, Edgbaston, 1950.

MICHAEL EARLS-DAVIS 1950

Another product of Sherborne School, popular source of Somerset amateurs. Blue at Cambridge in 1947, and his single, unproductive appearance for the county came three years later.

MICHAEL RICHARD GRATWYCKE EARLS-DAVIS Born Hampstead, London, 21.2.21. LHB, RM. SFC: 1 match; 4 runs @ 4.00; HS 4 v Worcestershire, Worcester, 1950; 0 wickets. Cambridge University 1947.

1951

Captain: S.S. Rogers

The county lost 15 matches and that was a matter of serious concern: for the team, the committee and the members. Harry Parks was brought in from Sussex as the new coach.

Gimblett was not at his best, although still he scored 1,403 runs in the championship. He looked out of sorts and it was agreed he should take a short break. Back he came, seemingly refreshed, to help himself most attractively to three hundreds in August. But Tremlett was really the outstanding batsman. He passed 2,000 runs, compensating for the decline in his bowling. Walford was clearly missed; instead of playing for Somerset, he chose to go on an MCC tour of Canada.

The Yorkshire exile, Robinson, canny, wise and occasionally cussed, paraded the uncomplicated art of off-spin and, now in his second season with Somerset, topped 100 wickets. There were several fine performances by him at Weston-super-Mare where, against Sussex, he finished with 15-78, the best of his 17-year career.

Back at Taunton in late August, Worcestershire needed six off the last ball. Buse was bowling, aiming for a yorker. Bob Wyatt, captaining his side, guessed what it would be, rapidly improvised and sent the ball soaring into the old pavilion. The crowd cheered the blow. Their relish of the tense finish overcame any regret that a sublime 174 by Gimblett had been nullified.

During the season, the county played for the first time at Johnson Park, Yeovil, though the town was not a new venue. A waterlogged pitch ruled out play on the last day. But eager, cricket-starved fans had at least seen the most elegant of hundreds from Joe Hardstaff.

For Wells, it was a final county fixture, against Warwickshire. Twice before the war, Wellard had had the students from the theological college ducking as he slammed five sixes in an over. But there was not much excitement from Somerset on their valedictory visit to the cathedral city. They lost by an innings, mainly to Eric Hollies, who took ten wickets.

The attack was without a bowler of genuine pace, and the batting was so ingloriously uncertain that number eleven had to be padded up before 3 p.m. on the first day more than once.

Ron Roberts, Playfair Annual

COUNTY CHAMPIONSHIP   14th

| | Played 28 | Won 5 | Drawn 8 | Lost 15 |

OTHER MATCHES

| | Played 2 | | Drawn 1 | Lost 1 |

BATTING

	M	I	NO	Runs	HS	Ave	100	50	ct	st
M.F. Tremlett	30	55	0	2071	185	37.65	2	15	10	–
G.G. Tordoff	3	6	1	185	87*	37.00	–	2	–	–
H.E. Watts	6	12	1	386	84*	35.09	–	2	–	–
H. Gimblett	25	46	2	1453	174*	33.02	4	5	20	–
J. Lawrence	30	54	4	1067	89	21.34	–	5	36	–
F.L. Angell	27	50	2	975	84	20.31	–	4	15	–
H.T.F. Buse	30	54	8	927	58*	20.15	–	4	3	–
S.S. Rogers	30	54	1	936	107*	17.66	1	2	14	–
H.W. Stephenson	30	53	9	772	62	17.54	–	2	34	31
E. Hill	19	35	2	474	66	14.36	–	1	6	–
J. Redman	27	44	10	472	45	13.88	–	–	8	–
R. Smith	17	29	4	287	47*	11.48	–	–	10	–
E.P. Robinson	30	46	5	257	30	6.26	–	–	21	–
H.L. Hazell	22	35	11	109	29	4.54	–	–	8	–

(2 matches)   J.P. Sainsbury 0, 0, 0, 16
(1 match)   M. Hanna 0   Khan Mohammad 0, 10*

BOWLING

	Overs	Mdns	Runs	Wkts	Ave	5wi	10wm
M.F. Tremlett	79.2	23	192	11	17.45	1	–
E.P. Robinson	1041.2	270	2707	107	25.29	10	–
H.L. Hazell	723.4	215	1765	63	28.01	1	–
H.T.F. Buse	767.3	188	1886	65	29.01	1	–
J. Lawrence	676	106	2060	71	29.01	3	1
J. Redman	531	96	1688	50	33.76	2	–

Khan Mohammad 28-5-104-5   R. Smith 15-5-45-0   S.S. Rogers 11-2-46-0
G.G. Tordoff 2-0-8-0   H.E. Watts 0.4-0-2-0

1951

MICHAEL HANNA 1951 – 1954

Stepped in for just a couple of games behind the stumps when Harold Stephenson was unavailable. Tidy, adequate, and seldom made a crucial mistake, just as in his winter career as a Bath and Somerset scrum-half.

MICHAEL HANNA Born London, 6.6.26. RHB, WK. SFC: 2 matches; 5 runs @ 2.50; HS 4* v Northamptonshire, Northampton, 1954.

KHAN MOHAMMAD 1951

He played in 13 Tests for Pakistan, just once for Somerset in 1951, when his handsome bowling action led to misplaced hopes of an extended career with the county while he was studying at Bristol University. Three years later he was plucked out of the Lancashire League to join the Pakistan touring team.

Somerset's loss became clear in October 1956 when at Karachi, in Pakistan's first ever Test against Australia, he and Fazal Mahmood secured a thrilling victory, taking all twenty wickets as the visitors were bowled out for 80 and 187.

KHAN MOHAMMAD Born Lahore, India, 1.1.28. RHB, RFM. 13 Tests (Pakistan) 1952-58. SFC: 1 match; 10 runs @ 10.00; HS 10* v South Africans, Taunton, 1951; 5 wickets @ 20.80; BB 3-74 same match. Northern India 1946-47; Indian Universities 1947-61.

JOHN SAINSBURY 1951

A county rugby player, but made only two nominal appearances for his native Somerset at cricket. His best form was revealed for Clifton and club sides.

JOHN POPHAM SAINSBURY Born Axbridge, Somerset, 8.1.27. Died 9.04. RHB, LM. SFC: 2 matches; 16 runs @ 4.00; HS 16 v Sussex, Weston-super-Mare, 1951.

BRIAN LANGFORD'S XI
from the years in which he played

Harold Gimblett
Graham Atkinson
Roy Virgin
Viv Richards
Peter Wight
Bill Alley
Ken Palmer
Harold Stephenson
Tom Cartwright
Brian Langford
Fred Rumsey

I consider myself privileged to have played in a tremendous Somerset team in the 1960s, and I make no apology for including eight of them in this line-up, even though my time with the county stretched back to 1953 and on to 1974.

Apart from those eight, I'm picking a great batsman from either end of my career, the fantastic Harold Gimblett and Viv Richards, and a brilliant bowler from my later years, Tom Cartwright, who knew more about cricket than anybody else I've met.

I felt it was right to limit myself to one overseas player, who had to be Viv. Therefore for the purposes of this exercise, Peter Wight and Bill Alley can be treated as honorary Englishmen.

I don't think there's much wrong with the balance of my side. If my first four batted to anything like their potential, then I wouldn't expect the rest to get a knock very often, even on uncovered wickets and certainly not on a flat track like we have at Taunton now.

We'd bat very deep with Harold Stephenson, a fine player of spin who scored plenty of centuries for Somerset, at number eight. Coming in at ten, I don't think I'd have been batting very often, though if I did I'd have a few not-outs with Fred Rumsey following me!

As for the bowling, the new ball has got to knock people over, and I'm confident that Fred and Kenny Palmer could do that. Then I've got Cartwright, the best bowler I ever played with, and Alley at medium pace. Finally, I couldn't resist picking myself as the spinner because I'd be so desperate to play in such a marvellous side.

1952

Captain: S.S. Rogers

How could it be? Somerset were on the bottom of the championship – and destined to stay there for four years – to the consternation of the committee and against a background of boundary murmurs. Yet they could still head for Bath and surprise a sceptical festival crowd by beating Middlesex, spinning them out for 52 in the second innings. This was a great match for the slow bowlers, especially Hazell, so it was sad that 'Nutty', despite being top of the averages again, would soon be on his way.

There were only two wins for Somerset, both at Bath. Too often, the team lacked balance or a belief that they could come out on top. Nor did fielding lapses help

Gimblett scored a timely hundred in his benefit game at Glastonbury. He reckoned that he emerged with a net profit of £8, upset that his original request for the Gloucestershire fixture at Taunton had been turned down. This was a good season for him, however. There were two hundreds against Derbyshire and he finished with a new county record of 2,134 runs, topping Tremlett's total of the previous summer. Stephenson's maiden hundred was at Swansea, where he had been elevated in the batting order. Lawrence, taking guard at number nine, jauntily hit his first century, and against the Indians; his partner in a late stand had been Dean, another Yorkshireman, who had come to Taunton on Lawrence's recommendation. Harris, later to become a first-class umpire, was briefly brought into the county side. Hopes that Smith, as a slow left-arm bowler, might be a worthy successor to Hazell, weren't materialising.

There was still Weston-super-Mare to come, always a riddle, spiteful or duplicitous, and invariably well supported. On the last day against Glamorgan, 24 wickets fell in under five hours. Then against Notts, in a drawn match, Robinson had a 4-0 spell. The visit of Lancashire produced another draw. This time it was Roy Tattersall who outwitted the last six Somerset batsmen at a cost of three runs. The best of the batting, hardly for the only time, had come from Cyril Washbrook.

> I shall always remember one shot Harold Gimblett made against us. It was a wettish wicket, and he hit a good-length straight ball from one of our fast bowlers, on the up, and sent it for six over the mid-wicket boundary.
>
> 'That's a shot I carry round with me in my bag,' he said. He always talked while he batted.
>
> He was as high-strung as you like but boy, what a creative player!
>
> **Dickie Dodds, Essex**

COUNTY CHAMPIONSHIP 17th   Played 28   Won 2   Drawn 14   Lost 12

OTHER MATCHES   Played 1   Drawn 1

BATTING

	M	I	NO	Runs	HS	Ave	100	50	ct	st
H. Gimblett	29	55	1	2134	169	39.51	5	11	24	1
G.G. Tordoff	11	20	1	636	101*	33.47	1	5	3	–
M.F. Tremlett	29	54	4	1530	100	30.60	1	9	16	–
J. Lawrence	29	48	13	885	111	25.28	2	3	18	–
H.T.F. Buse	27	49	8	988	102	24.09	1	3	8	–
H.E. Watts	8	13	0	295	93	22.69	–	1	2	–
F.L. Angell	16	31	0	619	90	19.96	–	3	4	–
H.W. Stephenson	27	49	0	958	114	19.57	1	1	40	30
S.S. Rogers	29	50	2	908	102*	18.91	1	4	14	–
R. Smith	15	28	4	413	58	17.20	–	1	3	–
B.G. Brocklehurst	7	12	0	195	40	16.25	–	–	2	–
M.M. Walford	8	14	1	194	61	14.92	–	1	10	–
J. Redman	17	26	6	270	29	13.50	–	–	4	–
D.L. Kitson	8	15	1	177	33	12.64	–	–	1	–
E.P. Robinson	29	41	9	241	29	7.53	–	–	24	–
H.L. Hazell	22	30	16	97	14	6.92	–	–	18	–
C.G. Mitchell	4	6	4	7	6*	3.50	–	–	–	–

(1 match)   M. Walker 6, 0 (1 ct)   J.H. Harris 18   W.H. Dean 21, 0*   J. Baker 1*

BOWLING

	Overs	Mdns	Runs	Wkts	Ave	5wi	10wm
H.L. Hazell	632	232	1341	63	21.28	5	1
R. Smith	127	32	320	14	22.85	–	–
M.F. Tremlett	200	33	636	22	28.90	–	–
E.P. Robinson	945.4	262	2214	75	29.52	3	–
J. Lawrence	843.2	156	2377	78	30.47	3	–
H.T.F. Buse	653.5	162	1706	54	31.59	–	–
J. Redman	358.1	62	1167	33	35.36	1	–
G.G. Tordoff	168.5	20	531	11	48.27	–	–
C.G. Mitchell	93	12	292	5	58.40	–	–

J.H. Harris 21-3-60-0   J. Baker 17-4-40-0   M. Walker 15-4-52-3
M.M. Walford 11-1-34-1   W.H. Dean 10-4-17-0   S.S. Rogers 9.5-0-54-0
H. Gimblett 8-2-18-0   H.E. Watts 3-0-8-0   F.L. Angell 3-0-10-0

BEN BROCKLEHURST
1952 – 1954

From farmer to cricket magazine proprietor; and in between, he was captain of Somerset for two seasons. Each time they finished bottom – but that sort of indignity wasn't exactly a rarity in the lustre-less days of the 1950s.

Brocklehurst wasn't a memorable skipper, while his own form with the bat was nondescript. But he shouldn't take too much blame for Somerset's plight. The club was in trouble financially, the rumblings of disquiet threatened at times to bring down the ceilings of the committee rooms, and the great Gimblett was at his most tormented. In the post-war years the county was going through captains at an alarming rate. If Brocklehurst, the martinet, was a failure, so were four or five others.

BENJAMIN GILBERT BROCKLEHURST Born Knapton, Norfolk, 18.2.22. RHB, RM. Cap 1953. Captain 1953-54. SFC: 64 matches; 1671 runs @ 15.61; HS 89 v Pakistanis, Taunton, 1954; HT 802 in 1954; 1 wicket @ 36.00; BB 1-3 v Warwickshire, Bath, 1954.

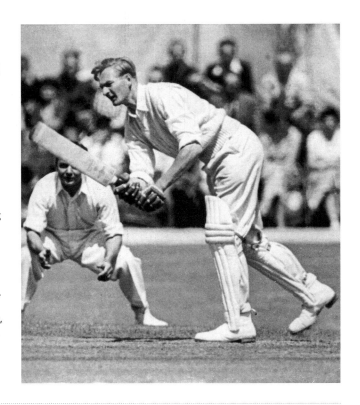

DAVID KITSON 1952 – 1954

One of the growing number that came down from the North in the 1950s. He arrived from Yorkshire with a sound pedigree but his batting progress with Somerset over three years was unspectacular. As a bowls player, he was later to earn just as much quiet acclaim and, no doubt, derive as much pleasure.

DAVID LEES KITSON Born Batley, Yorkshire, 13.9.25. Died 17.5.2002. RHB. SFC: 32 matches; 886 runs @ 15.54; HS 69 v Leicestershire, Leicester, 1953; HT 589 in 1953.

JOHN HARRIS 1952 – 1959

He was such a promising 16-year-old, playing in school and club cricket around his native Taunton, that he was invited to make his first appearance for Somerset at that tender age. He didn't get much quicker as a bowler, nor did he grow much more, and there were only another 14 appearances spread over eight summers. For a few seasons after that he played Minor Counties for Suffolk and Devon, later putting in a lengthy stint as a first-class umpire.

JOHN HENRY HARRIS Born Taunton, 13.2.36. LHB, RFM. SFC: 15 matches; 154 runs @ 11.00; HS 41 v Worcestershire, Taunton, 1957; 19 wickets @ 32.05; BB 3-29 v Worcestershire, Bristol, 1959; HT 12 in 1959. Fc umpire 1983-2000.

MALCOLM WALKER 1952 – 1958

Like one or two other off-spinners, this Yorkshireman was unlucky to be around when Brian Langford was making his impact. The frustrating result was that he played fewer than 30 times for his adopted county. Malcolm was no slouch with the bat, opening for the Second XI and grafting his way to a championship hundred against Essex. His untimely death came in a motor-cycle accident.

MALCOLM WALKER Born Mexborough, Yorkshire, 14.10.33. Died 8.86. RHB, OB. SFC: 29 matches; 574 runs @ 11.71; 1 century; HS 100 v Essex, Romford, 1955; HT 251 in 1956; 28 wickets @ 34.85; BB 5-45 v Gloucestershire, Bristol, 1955; HT 12 in 1955.

WILLIAM DEAN 1952

This Yorkshireman headed south for a trial on the recommendation of fellow Tyke Johnny Lawrence. He made a circumspect 21 against the Indians in 1952, and that was it. The North Country proved quite a nursery in those barren days.

WILLIAM HENRY DEAN Born Leeds, Yorkshire, 25.11.28. RHB, RFM. SFC: 1 match; 21 runs @ 21.00; HS 21 v Indians, Taunton, 1952; 0 wickets.

COLIN MITCHELL 1952 – 1954

This amiable amateur, who enjoyed a stint as captain of the Second XI, once took six wickets for the county side at Frome. He was fast by club standards but he had work to think of, apart from cricket, back in Bristol. An outstanding local footballer, a left-winger with a prolific scoring record, he played for Gloucestershire FA for a number of years.

COLIN GERALD MITCHELL Born Brislington, Bristol, 27.1.29. RHB, RFM. Cap 1953. SFC: 30 matches; 186 runs @ 7.44; HS 26* v Worcestershire, Frome, 1953; 53 wickets @ 38.39; BB 6-62 same match; HT 47 in 1953.

JOHN BAKER 1952 – 1954

Just a handful of appearances over three seasons, as an amateur. Sound record in club cricket. Also played for Combined Services and Dorset.

JOHN BAKER Born Weston-super-Mare, 18.5.33. RHB, RM. SFC: 9 matches; 105 runs @ 10.50; HS 26* v Northamptonshire, Taunton, 1953; 1 wicket @ 204.00; BB 1-10 v Warwickshire, Edgbaston, 1954. Oxford University 1955.

1953

Captain: B.G. Brocklehurst

Two Somerset wins and 19 defeats: oh dear. Those chilling statistics summed up the confidence and fortunes of the county side. But the season will also be remembered for one of the most eventful of all Bath festivals. It began with Buse's benefit match in his native city. Largely because of Tattersall's off-break proficiency and an evil track – it would never have been remotely close to meeting today's stringent requirements – the match was all over in a day. It left Buse miserably to calculate the costs, while the county were close to panic. There were still two county matches to come; would they last long enough to entice the spectators? Surgery on the pitch was clearly a priority. The groundsman was summoned from Taunton and he resorted to drastic and unconventional means, with a trip to the local abattoir for some bull's blood.

It worked and more cheerful features superseded that awful one-day teatime finish. In the next match, Langford, a 17-year-old off-spinner soon leaving for his National Service, took 14 wickets. His total of victims from the three games at Bath was 26. Centuries by Gimblett and Buse, against Kent, suggested that not everything had gone the spinners' way after all. In that same match, Tremlett, fielding at silly mid-off, was seriously injured when struck above the eye. He was never the same player again.

The Australians were here, relaxed after the Tests had finished, and now taking on the bottom county. Lindsay Hassett and Alan Davidson scored hundreds; so did Wight who, on his debut for Somerset, had been out for a duck in the first innings.

Smith batted resolutely in a season when he reached his only century, at Frome, and was awarded his cap.

In the autumn, three Taunton journalists boldly questioned the way the club was being run. It led to public meetings and acrimonious words. Somerset's cricket establishment closed ranks and did its best to out-manoeuvre the brave rebels. At least the episode led to some improvement.

The committee were sound blokes in their own fields – and perfectly well-meaning. But they reckoned they knew about cricket when they didn't. They were the sort of men who liked to say they were on so many committees – the Conservatives, the British Legion, that sort of thing: 'giving up my time when I could be at home doing the crossword or listening to the wireless.' They were extremely good at passing votes of thanks at the end of the year.

Eric Hill

COUNTY CHAMPIONSHIP 17th Played 28 Won 2 Drawn 7 Lost 19
OTHER MATCHES Played 1 Drawn 1

BATTING

	M	I	NO	Runs	HS	Ave	100	50	ct	st
H. Gimblett	25	49	4	1836	167*	40.80	4	10	27	–
R. Smith	27	51	6	1176	100	26.13	1	7	11	–
M.M. Walford	7	14	0	329	134	23.50	1	1	3	–
H.W. Stephenson	29	52	2	1085	98*	21.70	–	6	33	20
J. Lawrence	28	52	1	1015	89	19.90	–	6	22	–
H.T.F. Buse	24	42	3	767	102	19.66	1	3	9	–
G.G. Tordoff	5	9	0	173	48	19.22	–	–	6	–
D.L. Kitson	19	35	2	589	69	17.84	–	4	2	–
M.F. Tremlett	11	20	3	275	57	16.17	–	2	7	–
B.G. Brocklehurst	28	49	3	674	62	14.65	–	2	14	–
G.H.D. Evans	8	14	0	180	42	12.85	–	–	5	–
T.A. Hall	22	38	7	383	69*	12.35	–	1	7	–
C.F. Davey	8	15	3	129	30	10.75	–	–	2	–
J. Baker	5	8	2	64	26*	10.66	–	–	–	–
B.A. Langford	18	33	12	219	29*	10.42	–	–	5	–
S.S. Rogers	9	14	1	119	22	9.15	–	–	4	–
C.G. Mitchell	24	36	16	179	26*	8.95	–	–	8	–
J. Redman	3	6	1	37	27*	7.40	–	–	1	–
M. Walker	9	13	2	74	16	6.72	–	–	5	–

(2 matches) J.H. Harris 3, 0*, 16
(1 match) P.B. Wight 0, 109* Yawar Saeed 48 (1 ct) G.E.S. Woodhouse 13, 9
J.D. Stenton 18, 1 P.H. Fussell 5, 5 (1 ct) B.E. Collingwood 15, 1 (1 ct)
J.D. Currie 4, 13 D.P.T. Deshon 0, 9

BOWLING

	Overs	Mdns	Runs	Wkts	Ave	5wi	10wm
B.A. Langford	484.3	134	1329	51	26.05	4	2
H.T.F. Buse	595	152	1479	48	30.81	3	–
J. Lawrence	759.1	159	2224	70	31.77	1	–
T.A. Hall	553	72	1883	58	32.46	–	–
C.G. Mitchell	544.1	110	1696	47	36.08	2	1
M.F. Tremlett	120	20	399	8	49.87	–	–
M. Walker	127	29	500	9	55.55	–	–
G.G. Tordoff	68	10	226	4	56.50	–	–
R. Smith	188.3	39	657	5	131.40	–	–

J. Baker 36-13-132-0 J. Redman 18-6-55-2 Yawar Saeed 17-0-94-2
P.B. Wight 12-2-61-1 J.H. Harris 9-0-30-1 G.H.D. Evans 8-1-22-0
P.H. Fussell 6-0-26-1 J.D. Stenton 6-0-44-1 H. Gimblett 2-0-7-0
B.G. Brocklehurst 1.4-0-27-0

BRIAN LANGFORD 1953 – 1974

Only Jack White and Arthur Wellard have taken more wickets for Somerset, and nobody has come remotely close to his total of 504 first-class appearances for the county.

As a fair-haired teenager, without a presentable pair of boots to call his own, Langford signalled his intent in sensational style at Bath. Aided by a capricious strip, he twisted his supple fingers ingenuously in three matches for a 26-wicket haul. Fourteen of them came against Kent. Here was a new name, an off-spinner, for the national sports pages; and was it really true that he'd been bowling acceptable little seamers until fairly recently?

He went off to do his National Service and it wasn't certain that he'd be coming back to Somerset, as he surveyed the slow-bowling competition around in his absence. But he remembered the kindly words he had originally been offered by Wally Luckes, who lived just down the road from his childhood home in Bridgwater.

The return to Somerset was a prelude to a career which was to bring 'Langy' the captaincy, if not the chance to represent his country that his figures suggest he deserved. He really did spin the ball, and his accuracy served him well. At Yeovil, when the John Player Sunday League was still in its infancy, he bowled his allotted eight overs against Essex without conceding a run. It's a record that, of course, can never be beaten.

Once proud of his batting – at Dr Morgan's School and Bridgwater CC, for whom he opened the innings – he accepted that bowling must become his preoccupation, though he was always capable of coming up with some timely late runs.

Controversy didn't completely pass Langford by. For instance, in the 1960s he was one of the pay rebels who advocated a fairer structure. Then, while he was captain, the crowd once demonstrated and turned on him at Weston in the match with Tom Graveney's Worcestershire – later it was agreed that there was equal fault on the other side.

Later still, as chairman of Somerset's cricket committee, he was awkwardly placed in the Richards-Garner rumpus. But Brian Langford will be remembered most vividly for heading the national bowling averages at the age of 17, and for remaining so long as one of the most precise and guileful off-spinners in England.

BRIAN ANTHONY LANGFORD Born Birmingham, 17.12.35. RHB, OB. Cap 1957. Captain 1969-71. SFC: 504 matches; 7513 runs @ 13.58; HS 68* v Sussex, Hove, 1960, and 68 v Kent, Gillingham, 1963, and 68* v Glamorgan, Taunton, 1972; HT 638 in 1962; 1390 wickets @ 24.89; BB 9-26 v Lancashire, Weston-super-Mare, 1958; 100 wickets 5 times; HT 116 in 1958. OD: 66 matches; 441 runs @ 12.97; 65 wickets @ 24.24.

Taunton is a hard school for 'natural' spinners, but Langford goes on learning. He would not have to improve much to become a likely successor to Jim Laker.
Trevor Bailey, 1961

His greatest asset was his control. In 1974 Brian Close sent for 'Langie' when Tom Cartwright was injured. Immediately, after no practice, he was able to drop on an impeccable length and to bowl long, accurate spells.
Vic Marks

TOM HALL 1953 – 1954

This convivial fellow was a wholehearted fast-medium bowler, whether with Derbyshire or Somerset. He enjoyed some fine matches and was rightly proud of claiming Len Hutton twice in one contest.

But as a county cricketer, this good-looking amateur ran out of opportunities. He played also for Combined Services, once for the Gents against the Players, for Norfolk and the Free Foresters.

Sadly, we also think of the uncertain circumstances of his demise. His boat-building business was faring badly – and he fell from an express train. Hypertension was given as the partial cause of death.

THOMAS AUCKLAND HALL Born Darlington, County Durham, 19.8.30. Died 21.4.84. RHB, RFM. Cap 1953. SFC: 23 matches; 398 runs @ 12.43; HS 69* v Northamptonshire, Taunton, 1953; HT 383 in 1953; 63 wickets @ 32.26; BB 4-77 v Nottinghamshire, Weston-super-Mare, 1953; HT 58 in 1953.

JOHN STENTON 1953

Another Yorkshireman who turned up at Taunton, with just one match to show for it. The fact that he bowled left-arm spinners was part of the appeal, but his single wicket wasn't sufficient to bring a renewed call.

JOHN DEREK STENTON Born Sheffield, Yorkshire, 26.10.24. RHB, SLA. SFC: 1 match; 19 runs @ 9.50; HS 18 v Surrey, Taunton, 1953; 1 wicket @ 44.00; BB 1-18 same match.

CLIVE DAVEY 1953 – 1955

Solid record as a club cricketer led to 13 games for Somerset in the mid 1950s, but he made minimal impact before returning to his roots.

CLIVE FREDERICK DAVEY Born North Petherton, Somerset, 2.6.32. RHB. SFC: 13 matches; 261 runs @ 12.42; HS 46 v Leicestershire, Bath, 1955.

JOHN CURRIE 1953

Remembered more for his rugby, of course. The big Clifton and Bristol forward played 25 times for England, a formidable adversary in the line-outs because of his height and build. As a cricketer, he was a batsman with powerful shoulders, though a blue eluded him at Oxford; and he wasn't around long enough at the crease, on his solitary outing for Somerset, to make much of a mark at Bath.

JOHN DAVID CURRIE Born Clifton, Bristol, 3.5.32. Died 8.12.90. RHB. SFC: 1 match; 17 runs @ 8.50; HS 13 v Leicestershire, Bath, 1953. Oxford University 1956-57.

PHILIP FUSSELL 1953 – 1956

Farming had to come first when he had the chance to extend his limited late-season with the county. As a club player with the likes of Lansdown and Frome, Fussell was an all-rounder to be respected. But there were other pursuits to be enjoyed. He became a champion at clay-pigeon shoots, a skilled enthusiast at squash and salmon fishing.

PHILIP HILLIER FUSSELL Born Rode, Somerset, 12.2.31. RHB, RM. SFC: 2 matches; 10 runs @ 2.50; HS 5 v Nottinghamshire, Weston-super-Mare. 1953; 1 wicket @ 71.00; BB 1-26 same match.

YAWAR SAEED 1953 – 1955

Well-connected in cricketing terms back home. His application was irresistible to Somerset as they sustained their sporting links with the sub-continent. Yawar was slightly above medium pace with the appearance of being faster. He went home to play for Punjab and became a member of the Pakistan Test selection panel, returning to Taunton more than forty years after playing for the county, as manager of the Pakistan touring team.

YAWAR SAEED Born Lahore, India, 22.1.35. RHB, RM. Cap 1954. SFC: 50 matches; 1358 runs @ 15.60; HS 64 v Northamptonshire, Northampton, 1954, and v Middlesex, Bath, 1955; HT 731 in 1955; 78 wickets @ 35.73; BB 5-61 v South Africans, Taunton, 1955; HT 43 in 1955. Punjab, India, 1953-59.

BORIS COLLINGWOOD 1953

Once only: at Clarence Park. The middle-order bat came on the strength of his Cambridge blue and reputation on the field.

BORIS ESMOND COLLINGWOOD Born Lewisham, London, 8.1.20. Died 18.11.68. RHB. SFC: 1 match; 16 runs @ 8.00; HS 15 v Nottinghamshire, Weston-super-Mare, 1953. Cambridge University 1948.

DAVID EVANS 1953

As an amateur cricketer – he earned his living as an accountant at Weston-super-Mare – Evans was brought into a county side struggling for shape and improvement in 1953. He failed to reproduce his club form, despite one useful innings in front of his friends at Clarence Park. His emphasis on fitness ensured that he was at least as agile as any of the pros, and he played for Wales at hockey. He died, aged 62, after a heart attack at work.

GEORGE HERBERT DAVID EVANS Born Bristol, 22.8.28. Died 20.6.91. RHB, RM. SFC: 8 matches; 180 runs @ 12.85; HS 42 v Essex, Weston-super-Mare, 1953; 0 wickets.

PETER WIGHT 1953 – 1965

Who said he didn't relish fast bowling? You should have seen him take on the speed merchants in 1960. Well yes, he did occasionally appear to have a problem or two against Fred Trueman, and some observers even interpreted it as fear. But this slim, almost delicate batsman could parade an exquisite and seemingly intrepid repertoire of forcing shots, often when one of the openers had gone and the shine wasn't off the ball. Peter had come to England from Georgetown to be an engineer. He played some league cricket for Burnley, and he was a natural for the transition to the county game.

Those 27 hundreds were laden with the riches of his crisp driving, or the square-cutting when he went up on to his toes. He could hit on the up with a distinctive freedom.

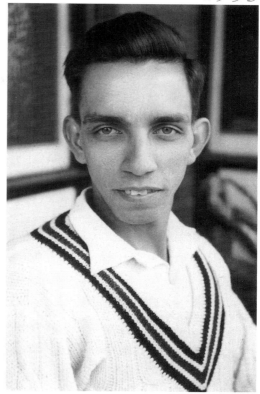

His first match for Somerset had been against the Australians, who very quickly got him caught in the slips in the opening innings. Wight was rarely a man of obvious emotion but he was privately imagining that his first-class career was coming to the hastiest of conclusions when Richie Benaud said: 'Cheer up, you'll get a hundred in the second innings.' And he did.

In the dressing room he could look nervous and morose, worrying about suspect health and fitness. All signs of such neuroses were forgotten once he got to the crease.

At his best Peter was a brilliant bat; he might have turned into a successful off-spinner with more overs (and the confidence to go with them). Once at Chesterfield, skipper Harold Stephenson threw the ball to him and he picked up a perfunctory six wickets.

After his playing days came the success of his indoor cricket school at North Parade, Bath, not far from his home, and some 30 seasons of first-class umpiring.

PETER BERNARD WIGHT Born Georgetown, British Guiana, 25.6.30. RHB, OB. Cap 1954. SFC: 321 matches; 16965 runs @ 32.75; 27 centuries; HS 222* v Kent, Taunton, 1959; 1000 runs 10 times, incl 2000 runs twice; HT 2316 in 1960; 62 wickets @ 33.24; BB 6-29 v Derbyshire, Chesterfield, 1957; HT 12 in 1958. OD: 6 matches; 56 runs @ 9.33. British Guiana, West Indies, 1950-51; Canterbury, New Zealand, 1963-64. Fc umpire 1966-95.

> Peter Wight was the best player at Somerset in the years I was there.
>
> There was always a lovely ring to his bat. If he'd gone out with an old chair leg, there'd still have been a nice ring to it.
>
> He was a quiet guy; his bat did the talking. I used to stand at the other end and drool at the shots he played.
>
> **Graham Atkinson**

1954

Captain: B.G. Brocklehurst

The playing staff was increased, with Lomax, Hilton, McMahon and Yawar Saeed coming in. But still Somerset were beaten 18 times, often seen by other counties as a soft touch. Gimblett, for so long the mainstay, decided he'd had enough after the game with Yorkshire in May when Fred Trueman dismissed him twice. He walked out of county cricket for good, weighed down by the mental demons and the slights, real and imagined, that had constantly tormented him. After Trueman had softened up the home batsmen, Bob Appleyard (7-16) ran through Somerset's second innings with his off-breaks on a damp pitch. All out for 48: and Gimblett gone.

There were glimmers of encouragement. The county's win against Notts was their first at Taunton since 1950. This season, Angell justified his recall. Atkinson, 16, shaped like a real prospect with North Country stubbornness. Wight discovered, in his first full campaign, that conditions were very different from what he was used to at home, but the strokes were elegant and he was starting to look the part. Little Lawrence, near to the double, was the latest professional to have his benefit, against Surrey, ruined by the weather. His receipts came to only £300 and the county agreed to cover all his expenses. With Merlin-like dexterity, Stephenson kept brilliantly again, particularly in tandem with Lawrence. Some of the stumpings were like optical illusions. Lomax's maiden hundred, off the Northants bowling in August, was well earned, not least because he achieved it with an injured elbow.

In every sense, though, this was a pretty miserable season, hardly helped by frequently losing the toss. For the first time since the war, the county lost all three matches at Bath. At Yeovil, Derbyshire's Les Jackson and Edwin Smith rolled them over for 60. Against Worcestershire, ill at ease when confronted by a fiery Reg Perks, they were dismissed for 68 and 79 at Clarence Park. Yet they came close to success at Weston against Essex. The rain came when, with all ten wickets standing, they needed only 62.

I went out to the wicket and tried – I really tried. But I got caught off my gloves when Trueman was bowling. I came in and said I couldn't take any more. I was finished. It was my last game for Somerset. I knew I shouldn't have played. I packed my bags and went home. I moped about the house. Soon I was to return to hospital as a voluntary patient.

Harold Gimblett

COUNTY CHAMPIONSHIP   17th   Played 28   Won 2   Drawn 8   Lost 18

OTHER MATCHES   Played 1   Drawn 1

BATTING

	M	I	NO	Runs	HS	Ave	100	50	ct	st
C.G. Tordoff	4	8	0	247	110	30.87	1	–	2	–
P.B. Wight	27	49	1	1327	81	27.64	–	7	12	–
H.W. Stephenson	28	48	4	1054	109	23.95	1	5	50	36
M.F. Tremlett	29	52	3	1131	118*	23.08	1	6	19	–
F.L. Angell	27	51	2	1125	114	22.95	1	4	4	–
J. Lawrence	29	52	8	929	95	21.11	–	6	27	–
J.G. Lomax	29	52	1	983	101	19.27	1	6	33	–
B.G. Brocklehurst	29	55	6	802	89	16.36	–	4	10	–
R. Smith	23	40	6	474	53*	13.94	–	1	3	–
Yawar Saeed	25	44	2	579	64	13.78	–	3	6	–
D.L. Kitson	5	10	0	120	54	12.00	–	1	–	–
J. Baker	3	5	1	40	18*	10.00	–	–	1	–
J. Hilton	24	42	9	275	36	8.33	–	–	16	–
J.W.J. McMahon	29	46	21	130	18	5.20	–	–	16	–

(2 matches)   H. Gimblett 29, 5, 0, 5 (1 ct)   G. Atkinson 4, 9*, 2*, 1 (2 ct)
C.G. Mitchell 0, 0, 0 (1 ct)
(1 match)   M. Hanna 4*, 1   T.A. Hall 15

BOWLING

	Overs	Mdns	Runs	Wkts	Ave	5wi	10wm
J. Lawrence	609.4	112	1922	93	20.66	3	1
J.W.J. McMahon	970.2	301	2336	85	27.48	7	1
M.F. Tremlett	478.1	82	1581	57	27.73	2	–
J. Hilton	450.2	94	1191	42	28.35	2	–
J.G. Lomax	476.2	88	1496	46	32.52	1	–
Yawar Saeed	336.2	42	1229	33	37.24	1	–
P.B. Wight	175.5	45	483	10	48.30	–	–

T.A. Hall 39-6-150-5   C.G. Tordoff 32-4-114-2   J. Baker 15-5-32-1
C.G. Mitchell 14-2-47-1   B.G. Brocklehurst 2.5-1-9-1   F.L. Angell 1.2-0-21-0
G. Atkinson 1-0-5-0   H.W. Stephenson 1-0-10-0

GRAHAM ATKINSON 1954 – 1966

Graham Atkinson arrived in the West as a 16-year-old and in 1961 he became the youngest Somerset player to score 2,000 runs in a season. When he repeated the feat in 1962, his name began to crop up in speculation about the Test team.

In the West Country, in particular, his claims for England recognition were advocated. But national pundits argued that he lacked a full range of shots on both sides of the wicket and, just as unfairly, that he was not agile enough in the field.

A fine on-side player, Atkinson revelled in taking on the fast bowlers at his own studious pace. Occasionally he might have scored more quickly, but in retrospect one realises what a sound, maybe under-praised, opener he was.

Some felt that he should have captained Somerset; most felt that the terms he was finally offered, causing him to leave the county, were less than generous.

Yorkshire-born, and a real pro in the Wakefield tradition, he surprised many observers by his move to Lancashire, a switch which could perhaps, for emotional reasons, be only a partial success.

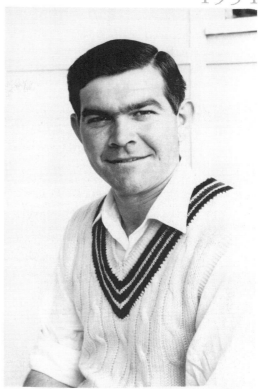

Was too much expected of him? Was someone of his natural talent assertive enough? Graham knew his worth and had the courage to plead his case. Looking back, it appears unfair that he left without the benefit he deserved, yet he returns to Taunton reunions with genuine pleasure, any erstwhile slight long forgotten.

GRAHAM ATKINSON Born Lofthouse, Yorkshire, 29.3.38. RHB, OB. Cap 1958. SFC: 271 matches; 14468 runs @ 32.07; 21 centuries; HS 190 v Glamorgan, Bath, 1960; 1000 runs 9 times, incl 2000 runs twice; HT 2035 in 1962; 4 wickets @ 59.00; BB 4-63 v Hampshire, Taunton, 1960. OD: 10 matches; 297 runs @ 29.70. Lancashire 1967-69.

On his 190 against Glamorgan at Bath, 1960

I was sat in the only bath in that old pavilion at the Rec, feeling quite pleased with myself. Then McCool, who'd gone in after me, came in and gave me a bollocking: first of all for getting him in with only about a quarter of an hour to go: 'What do you think I was going to do, son, that you couldn't have done?' Second, for getting out on 190. 'You might never get as close to 200 again.' It stuck in my mind, that, as the years went by. 'I hope you do,' he said. But I never did.

Graham Atkinson

He was probably the best captain we never had; he was extremely astute. He would have been a much better skipper than I was, but he had gone to Lancashire by then.

Brian Langford

1954

GEOFF LOMAX 1954 – 1962

Unruffled, unspectacular and occasionally invaluable. Here was an artisan all-round cricketer, who was known to open both the batting and the bowling for Somerset at Lord's.

After coming down from his native Lancashire, his sense of endeavour and good nature made him a popular occupant of the Taunton dressing room. He found himself, at various times, batting in almost every position in the order; he pegged away at just above medium pace, capable of his two or three wickets. In the slips he hardly ever dropped a catch.

Geoff had one wonderful match against Notts at Weston in 1958 when he virtually ensured the nine-wicket win, with bat and ball, on his own. That was where he completed his only hat-trick. There were also two centuries in his career, and hints that he could be a perky as well as an obdurate batsman.

One of his later passions was off-shore fishing.

JAMES GEOFFREY LOMAX Born Rochdale, Lancashire, 20.5.25. Died 21.5.92. RHB, RFM. Cap 1954. SFC: 211 matches; 7516 runs @ 20.76; 2 centuries; HS 104* v Sussex, Eastbourne, 1962; 1000 runs twice; HT 1298 in 1959; 235 wickets @ 35.02; BB 6-75 v Surrey, Oval, 1954; HT 50 in 1958. Lancashire 1949-53.

JIM HILTON 1954 – 1957

Perhaps he was always in the shadow of his Test-playing brother Malcolm, and yet, after two seasons with Lancashire, Jim Hilton served Somerset well. He was an extrovert North Countryman, good fun in the dressing room and useful to have around when the wicket was taking spin. At Bath, in the wake of Roy Tattersall and the boyish Brian Langford, he finished with 7-98 and was cheered off against Warwickshire. Essentially Jim was an uncomplicated off-break man, keeping the place open for when Langford was ready.

JIM HILTON Born Chadderton, Lancashire, 29.12.30. RHB, OB. SFC: 71 matches; 994 runs @ 10.68; HS 61* v Nottinghamshire, Taunton, 1955; HT 390 in 1955; 133 wickets @ 26.48; BB 7-98 v Warwickshire, Bath, 1954; HT 42 in 1954. Lancashire 1952-53.

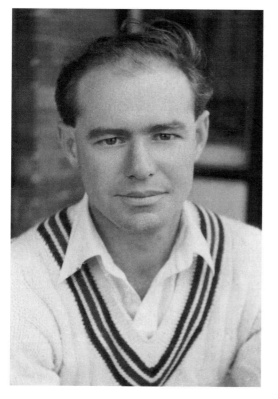

JOHN McMAHON 1954 – 1957

Once he took eight wickets in an innings for Surrey; then he did the same for Somerset. This colourful, enigmatic Australian was a thoroughly capable left-arm slow bowler, who would cannily amend his style to suit the occasion. By 1956 he was taking 100 wickets for the county and the complaints that Horace Hazell had been fired prematurely were allowed to die.

McMahon's departure from Somerset, not apparently based on his deeds with the spinning ball, was an abrupt, unforgiving matter. Team-mates, who valued his uncomplicated, reliable slow bowling, fought in vain for a reversal of the decision.

JOHN WILLIAM JOSEPH McMAHON Born Balaclava, Australia, 28.12.17. Died 8.5.2001. RHB, SLA. Cap 1954. SFC: 115 matches; 645 runs @ 6.14; HS 24 v Sussex, Frome, 1955; HT 262 in 1955; 349 wickets @ 26.11; BB 8-46 v Kent, Yeovil, 1955; 100 wickets once; HT 103 in 1956. Surrey 1947-53.

1955

Captain: G.G. Tordoff

For a fourth year Somerset propped up every other county from the gloom of the championship basement. Now it was the turn of Tordoff to take charge. Temporarily released from the Navy, the left-hander at least got his 1,000 runs and sprinted to a century against Gloucestershire. But it was generally agreed that he – like several of his predecessors – lacked the experience to skipper a county side. Maybe too much blame was heaped on his willing shoulders; patently he was let down by some of his team.

Morale was at a low ebb at times, grimly illustrated as Somerset were bowled out for 36 by Surrey and 37 by Hampshire, both debacles – as if we hadn't guessed – at Weston. Alec Bedser and Tony Lock gobbled up 19 wickets between them, with Lock completing his first hat-trick. Then, for Hampshire, Derek Shackleton came away with 14 wickets, 8-4 in just over 11 overs in the first innings. Hilton's hat-trick, in response, seemed a meagre compensation.

Somerset waited till June for their first win, which came at Frome against Sussex, thanks to McMahon's guile. The Australian slow left-arm bowler, with his varied deliveries, was always full of cunning, and in the next match at Yeovil he took 8-46 against Kent to orchestrate another rare victory.

In July, Brian Close was promoted to open the Yorkshire batting as his side set out to chase a target of 285 in three-and-a-half hours. At his most exhilarating, he belted 143 for Yorkshire to win by eight wickets. 'If only he was playing for us,' the Taunton members chorused. They had no idea how prophetic their words were to prove.

Lawrence, the club's most successful all-rounder, decided to leave. He was released from his contract at his own request after nine years of good humour and skills with ball and bat.

Stephenson continued to excel amid the wreckage of the team's constant failures; he was deservedly chosen for the MCC's 'A' tour of Pakistan, but throughout his career he suffered from the wealth of wicket-keeping talent at the highest level.

> Somerset have a hard struggle ahead, but possessing one of the largest staffs in the country – they put three teams in the field in one day last season – they will surely improve.
>
> **The Cricketer Annual**

COUNTY CHAMPIONSHIP 17th   Played 28   Won 4   Drawn 7   Lost 17

OTHER MATCHES   Played 1   Lost 1

BATTING

	M	I	NO	Runs	HS	Ave	100	50	ct	st
M.F. Tremlett	29	57	1	1838	153	32.82	2	11	25	–
P.B. Wight	29	56	3	1326	106	25.01	1	7	11	–
G.G. Tordoff	28	55	4	1132	145*	22.19	1	4	21	–
J. Lawrence	27	52	1	1128	122	22.11	1	7	19	–
J.G. Lomax	25	48	6	892	71	21.23	–	5	25	–
H.W. Stephenson	28	53	4	1034	85*	21.10	–	7	52	24
F.L. Angell	16	32	0	578	90	18.06	–	2	9	–
Yawar Saeed	24	46	2	731	64	16.61	–	3	14	–
M. Walker	8	15	0	239	100	15.93	1	–	2	–
C.F. Davey	5	10	1	132	46	14.66	–	–	2	–
J. Hilton	21	39	8	390	61*	12.58	–	1	15	–
J.W.J. McMahon	29	50	21	262	24	9.03	–	–	6	–
R. Smith	5	9	0	72	21	8.00	–	–	2	–
K.E. Palmer	3	6	1	35	12*	7.00	–	–	–	–
G.M. Tripp	3	6	0	35	13	5.83	–	–	–	–
G.L. Williams	3	6	0	30	24	5.00	–	–	4	–
B. Lobb	28	48	14	112	14	3.29	–	–	3	–

(2 matches)   B.A. Langford 41, 0, 3, 4   L. Pickles 1, 0, 1, 2
K.D. Biddulph 1, 1

(1 match)   G. Atkinson 8, 2   D.G. Hughes 2 (1 ct, 1 st)

BOWLING

	Overs	Mdns	Runs	Wkts	Ave	5wi	10wm
B. Lobb	780.3	159	2273	90	25.25	3	–
J. Lawrence	609.5	114	1917	71	27.00	5	–
M. Walker	85	15	329	12	27.41	2	–
J. Hilton	368.5	89	1019	36	28.30	2	–
J.W.J. McMahon	814.3	225	2158	75	28.77	3	–
Yawar Saeed	407.3	54	1464	43	34.04	1	–
G.G. Tordoff	108.1	24	344	9	38.22	–	–
J.G. Lomax	376	78	1073	19	56.47	–	–

K.D. Biddulph 43.2-5-148-4   M.F. Tremlett 38-6-122-1   K.E. Palmer 24-5-56-2
P.B. Wight 12-0-58-0   B.A. Langford 1-0-8-0

LEWIS PICKLES 1955 – 1958

One of the quite formidable contingent that came down from Yorkshire in that tentative post-war period. He shaped like a capable lad from those northern parts, and scored 1,000 runs in his first summer with Somerset. That kind of progress wasn't sustained, though in the second season he seemed worth the maiden hundred he desperately wanted, but didn't get, against Lancashire at Old Trafford.

LEWIS PICKLES Born Wakefield, Yorkshire, 17.9.32. RHB, OB. Cap 1956. SFC: 47 matches; 1702 runs @ 20.50; HS 87 v Lancashire, Old Trafford, 1956; 1000 runs once; HT 1137 in 1956; 1 wicket @ 65.00; BB 1-22 v Kent, Bath, 1956.

DAVID HUGHES 1955

Yet another single appearance. Often his wicket-keeping was outstanding at club level. One of the many who made it, however fleetingly, from Taunton School to the County Ground.

DAVID GARFIELD HUGHES Born Taunton, 21.5.34. RHB, WK. SFC: 1 match; 2 runs @ 2.00; HS 2 v Nottinghamshire, Taunton, 1955; 2 dismissals (1 ct, 1 st).

GRAHAM TRIPP 1955 – 1959

The runs never came as they promised to. He was a good-looking bat who always shaped so well in the Second XI and in the nets.

GRAHAM MALCOLM TRIPP Born Clevedon, Somerset, 29.6.32. RHB. SFC: 34 matches; 700 runs @ 12.72; HS 62 v Essex, Colchester, 1957; HT 217 in 1956; 0 wickets.

> Talent-wise, you'd have thought he'd have scored thousands of runs in first-class cricket. He was worth his place for fielding alone.
> Ken Biddulph

LLOYD WILLIAMS 1955

A schoolmaster at Downside, he came into the county side during the summer vacation for just one season. He was a competent bat, scored plenty of runs at club level and captained Bath CC in 1958-59.

GWYNFOR LLOYD WILLIAMS Born Kidwelly, Camarthenshire, 30.5.25. RHB. SFC: 3 matches; 30 runs @ 5.00; HS 24 v Glamorgan, Weston-super-Mare, 1955.

BRYAN LOBB 1955 – 1969

Warwickshire, for whom he played once, showed no great reluctance in letting Bryan Lobb go. No doubt they were surprised to learn, four years later, that he was Somerset's first bowler since the war to take 100 wickets in a season. He did it by yeoman labours, uncomplicated in-swing, a bit of bounce – and, invariably, with a grin on his face.

The West Country crowds respected him for his bowling, chortled at his eccentricities, which had more to do with his batting and fielding. Co-ordination was a stranger to Lobb. He loped comically down the wicket, unable to judge a single; he agonised and changed direction a dozen times, like a lanky Buster Keaton, as the ball approached him at long leg.

Away from cricket, Bryan was seldom without his pipe. He became a schoolmaster, with one eye romantically on the sports field.

BRYAN LOBB Born Birmingham, 11.1.31. Died 3.5.2000. RHB, RFM. Cap 1955. SFC: 115 matches; 624 runs @ 5.20; HS 42 v Yorkshire, Bath, 1958; HT 214 in 1957; 368 wickets @ 23.72; BB 7-43 v Middlesex, Lord's, 1958; 100 wickets once; HT 110 in 1957. Warwickshire 1953.

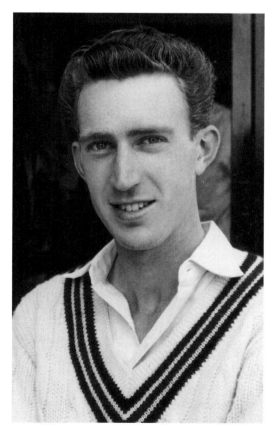

KEN BIDDULPH 1955 – 1961

Here was a bowler often asked to keep going on a placid wicket and hot afternoon, and he did so willingly. For Ken, county cricket was a wonderful alternative to a life at a desk in the Borough Treasurer's Department in Chingford. He arrived at Taunton after a spell as an *Evening News* colt at Alf Gover's Cricket School in South London, and Taunton was where he wanted to stay.

For a time he was number two to Bryan Lobb. His pace was well above mundane medium, and late in-swing earned him a fair quota of his honestly reaped wickets. Biddulph had rather misplaced pretensions when it came to his capacity for run-scoring. In his skilled post-playing role as a storyteller, he would recall Fred Trueman's words of encouragement to him as he tried to establish himself in the Somerset XI. 'Don't worry, Kenny. You'll get in that bloody team for your batting!' Biddulph also played for Durham in their pre-championship days, mainly for his bowling …

Back on the Cotswolds, he was a kindly and unstinting coach and, as the size of the congregation at his funeral demonstrated, a thoroughly popular and appreciated figure.

KENNETH DAVID BIDDULPH Born Chingford, Essex, 29.5.32. Died 7.1.03. RHB, RM. Cap 1959. SFC: 91 matches; 468 runs @ 6.78; HS 41 v Essex, Southend, 1960; HT 144 in 1959; 270 wickets @ 27.61; BB 6-30 v Combined Services, Taunton, 1959; HT 83 in 1960.

KEN PALMER 1955 – 1969

There were times when Ken Palmer gave the impression that he was carrying the cares of the world on his shoulders. In fact, on occasions he did carry the Somerset attack. His record for the county is not to be under-valued.

He was, after all, the first member of the West Country club since the war to complete the double, in 1961. By hitting the seam consistently and obtaining some swing away from the bat, he took 100 wickets four times; once he nearly ran through the whole of the Notts side at Trent Bridge. When the strip was greenish Palmer pounded away like a pugnacious terrier. That was when one could detect the challenge in his eye.

Yet he was given his first contract, as a teenager for Somerset, on the strength of his batting. He liked to open the innings then. Successive coaches Harry Parks and Horace Hazell had seen enough to recommend him. He was a ready listener, though much of the early tuition and encouragement had come from his father, who worked as a groundsman at Roundway Hospital, Devizes.

Young Kenny had actually been born in Hampshire and had gone to Southampton for a trial. His mind was set on county cricket: even as a lad his attitude was doggedly determined. He hated giving his wicket away; and he would cast a scathing glance down 22 yards when a batsman hit him for four.

His scintillating all-round form of 1961 was never quite repeated. But an unlikely Test opportunity did arise, four years later. He was doing some coaching in Johannesburg at the time, and the England bowlers touring South Africa were running into all kinds of injury scares. The call went out and Palmer was rushed to Port Elizabeth for the fifth Test. There was no romantically successful sequel, even if he was handed the new ball. His one wicket from the two innings was earned at considerable expense – and then they put him to bat at number 11. Hadn't they heard of his Devizes prowess at the top of the order?

After the playing career, though, he achieved regular Test status as an umpire.

KENNETH ERNEST PALMER Born Winchester, Hampshire, 22.4.37. RHB, RFM. Cap 1958. 1 Test 1965. SFC: 302 matches; 7567 runs @ 20.67; 2 centuries; HS 125* v Northamptonshire, Northampton, 1961; 1000 runs once; HT 1036 in 1961; Double once in 1961; 837 wickets @ 21.10; BB 9-57 v Nottinghamshire, Trent Bridge, 1963; 100 wickets 4 times; HT 126 in 1963. OD: 24 matches; 137 runs @ 9.78; 34 wickets @ 21.55; GC MoM 1. Fc umpire 1972-2002.

> To see Ken Palmer bowling in full flight is a joy to the critic and a qualm of disturbance to the batsman. His speed is below authentically fast, but his zip off the pitch, especially in his first few overs, is completely disconcerting.
>
> **A.A. Thomson**

1956

Captain: M.F. Tremlett

After all that huffing and puffing from the reactionaries, Somerset actually made the social breakthrough, largely from necessity, by appointing their first professional captain. Tremlett was to retain the position for four years, building a reputation after an understandably tentative start and modest personal form. He was arguably the best skipper in the county's history. He had a perceptive knowledge of opposing players and was a sharp tactician. In Somerset's second home game of the season, against Essex, he made a challenging declaration and won with five minutes to spare. Lobb's ten wickets from the match certainly helped. But before long there were innings defeats suffered against Gloucestershire, Hampshire and Surrey.

The trouble with Somerset was that they couldn't find a reliable opening partnership; nor did Lobb have the advantage of new-ball support. McMahon, passing 100 wickets, was the pick of the bowlers quite often, and Langford again revealed his partiality for the Bath track.

If not too much of the hoped-for success came from Aussie newcomer McCool with his leg-spin, he compensated with some superb batting. He finished near to 2,000 runs and, as he promised his chums he would, he took a century off the Australian tourists in dashing style, after a 90 in the first innings.

The Cambridge blue, Silk, arrived late in the season to score a hundred at Cardiff and, no doubt to his surprise, ended up second in the batting averages.

Some of the most memorable cricket came from the visitors. At Bath, Worcestershire's Martin Horton took 13 wickets and his only hat-trick in a fine bowling performance. Ted Dexter turned up at Taunton with Cambridge, excelling with his bold driving as he dominated the University's batting. And at Glastonbury, in Tremlett's benefit game, Denis Compton – only recently returned from his knee operation – gave a typical exhibition of panache, never wholly burdened by orthodoxy, in his 110. At the other end was Bill Edrich (89); it was, for a time, 1947 all over again.

Somerset had had so many captains over the years the players just didn't know what was going on. They had lived and played in an atmosphere of uncertainty for season after season, with disastrous results.

Maurice Tremlett took over, the county's first professional captain, and I wouldn't have taken that job had there been a life pension to go with it.

He led the side for four years. And in that time he achieved the next to impossible and turned Somerset into a cricket team. He was sneered at, moaned at, sniped at, but he shrugged it all off and got on with doing what I shall always rate as a magnificent job.

Colin McCool

COUNTY CHAMPIONSHIP   15th

Played 28   Won 4   Drawn 9   Lost 15

OTHER MATCHES

Played 2   Drawn 2

BATTING

	M	I	NO	Runs	HS	Ave	100	50	ct	st
C.L. McCool	30	53	1	1966	141	37.80	3	12	34	–
D.R.W. Silk	7	12	3	325	106*	36.11	1	–	6	–
P.B. Wight	29	52	6	1474	128*	32.04	1	8	21	–
H.W. Stephenson	24	41	3	1000	103	26.31	2	3	33	17
L. Pickles	26	48	2	1137	87	24.71	–	6	10	–
M.F. Tremlett	30	51	7	1060	106*	24.09	1	4	21	–
G. Atkinson	20	35	4	719	98	23.19	–	4	5	–
J. Hilton	8	11	6	110	39*	22.00	–	–	6	–
K.E. Palmer	7	11	4	138	42*	19.71	–	–	1	–
J.G. Lomax	28	50	1	960	99	19.59	–	6	13	–
F.G.K. Day	6	11	1	168	56*	16.80	–	1	7	4
G.M. Tripp	9	17	3	217	50	15.50	–	1	6	–
B.A. Langford	23	37	2	471	50	13.45	–	1	5	–
M. Walker	10	20	1	251	72	13.21	–	1	–	–
F.L. Angell	7	14	0	159	30	11.35	–	–	1	–
J.W.J. McMahon	30	41	15	163	17	6.26	–	–	13	–
B. Lobb	28	38	12	147	35	5.65	–	–	8	–
K.D. Biddulph	7	12	1	30	10	2.72	–	–	–	–

(1 match)   P.H. Fussell 0, 0

BOWLING

	Overs	Mdns	Runs	Wkts	Ave	5wi	10wm
J. Hilton	232.3	67	550	26	21.15	2	–
B.A. Langford	581	174	1412	57	24.77	4	1
J.W.J. McMahon	1066	319	2634	103	25.57	6	–
B. Lobb	800.2	175	2194	82	26.75	3	1
C.L. McCool	553.3	99	1658	49	33.83	3	–
K.E. Palmer	89	15	263	7	37.57	–	–
K.D. Biddulph	133.1	17	503	13	38.69	1	–
J.G. Lomax	408.4	81	1152	17	67.46	–	–
M.F. Tremlett	61.2	9	225	2	112.50	–	–

M. Walker 30-6-95-4   P.B. Wight 29.3-8-50-2   G. Atkinson 17-6-64-0
P.H. Fussell 16-3-45-0   L. Pickles 9-1-55-1   D.R.W. Silk 7-0-21-0
G.M. Tripp 1.1-0-10-0

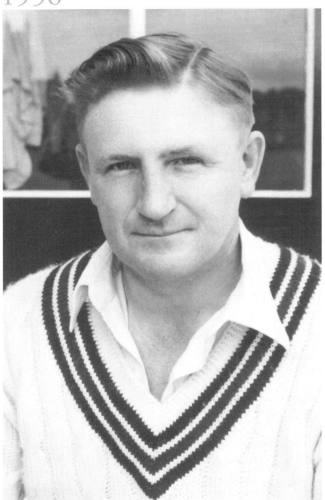

COLIN McCOOL 1956 – 1960

When he joined Somerset, to the surprise of many observers, Colin McCool was past 40; yet his influence in the half-decade which followed was to be considerable. Occasionally some of the younger pros didn't relish the way he treated them. Maybe they also resented that his salary was well in excess of their own. But their respect for his competitive approach and sheer experience was undeniable.

McCool's value to Somerset was primarily as a batsman. The way he played the slow men was much admired, and in 1956, his first campaign in Taunton, he was only just short of 2,000 runs. As for his own leg-spinners, they could be expensive, even if used judiciously to break a partnership or 'buy' wickets.

In the context of Australian cricket he was judged as a most talented all-rounder, unlucky not to be included in any of the Tests during Bradman's visit of 1948. He played some league cricket in this country and his sparring partner, Bill Alley, used to say that experience ruined Colin as a slow bowler; it tempted him to push the ball down too fast.

Sturdy, fair-skinned, a contemplative pipe-smoker in the corner of the dressing room, McCool proved an astute investment for Somerset. His hundreds were full of wristy aplomb, and his fielding in the slips was another bonus.

COLIN LESLIE McCOOL Born Sydney, Australia, 9.12.15. Died 5.4.86. RHB, LBG. Cap 1956. 14 Tests 1946-50. SFC: 138 matches; 7913 runs @ 33.81; 12 centuries; HS 169 v Worcestershire, Stourbridge, 1958; 1000 5 times; HT 1966 in 1956; 219 wickets @ 28.05; BB 8-74 v Nottinghamshire, Trent Bridge, 1958; HT 62 in 1959. New South Wales, Australia, 1939-41; Queensland, Australia, 1945-53.

In the best Somerset tradition, he was always after the bowling, and in the best Australian tradition, he always relished a fight. His five years up, he went back to Australia. 'There's no winter,' he said. 'The beer's better, and the f---ing off-spinners don't turn.'
Alan Gibson

DENNIS SILK 1956 – 1960

As Warden of Radley, Dennis Silk was one of the country's top and most respected headmasters, and after retiring to his beloved Somerset, he became president of the MCC. He's a man of gentle voice, charm and authority; and if he hadn't put education first, he'd have been unanimous choice as captain of Somerset.

The Silk personality had the right mix of leader and convivial companion, as demonstrated on his various MCC tours, for two of which, to North America and New Zealand, he was the skipper.

His reliability as a batsman and short-leg was evident from Cambridge days. Only one of his seven first-class hundreds was for Somerset, but as a vacation player he was always worth his place. So he was as a rugby man, at university, Bath and county level.

DENNIS RAOUL WHITEHALL SILK Born Eureka, California, 8.10.31. RHB, LB. Cap 1957. SFC: 33 matches; 1543 runs @ 33.54; 1 century; HS 106* v Glamorgan, Cardiff, 1956; HT 525 in 1957; 0 wickets. Cambridge University 1952-55.

A lovely bloke. He mixed well with the rest of us and, unlike most amateurs, he was worth his place in the team. Somerset would have loved him to be captain, but he was always going on to an academic life.

The greatest compliment I can pay Dennis is that the rest of the team treated him like a professional.

Brian Langford

1957

Captain: M.F. Tremlett

They used to claim that when he played league cricket at Blackpool, left-hander Alley was more popular than Stanley Matthews. His charismatic presence was quickly evident when he came to Taunton, and he was capped after only four matches. His technique was apt to veer from that of the coaching manual but he specialised excitingly in leg-side boundaries as well as making match-winning contributions as a canny seamer, a bit above medium-pace and always on a length.

Somerset climbed to eighth position. More significant than that, the team had belatedly taken on a competitive edge. Surrey, with their strongest available team, came to Weston, needing one more victory to win their sixth consecutive championship, and Somerset made it so difficult for them that they won by only three wickets with eight minutes of extra time left. Jim Laker's off-spin was decisive, and they celebrated with Bill Andrews' home-made wine.

Lobb lumbered in to deserved acclaim to become the first Somerset fast bowler since Wellard to take 100 wickets. McMahon's 81 championship victims were apparently not enough to earn him another contract – so judgment must have been influenced, whatever the facts, by considerations off the field. Langford was awarded his cap for spinning out Glamorgan. In the same match, schoolmaster Dickinson, signed from Lancashire, had opened the bowling with Lobb and taken a creditable 5-63 on his debut.

Bath threw up many cameos over the years. When Hampshire arrived there in June, Henry Horton was given run out and returned to the pavilion. But then he was called back, after the new batsman had actually taken guard. In the meantime the umpires, Paul Gibb and Harry Baldwin, had consulted and agreed that Jimmy Gray should have been the man run out. Horton resumed his innings, though not for long – this time he *was* run out.

Towards the end of the season, Somerset experimentally brought cricket back to Bristol for a friendly with Sussex at the Imperial Ground. How much support could they expect from a city where Gloucestershire had their headquarters?

The rolling green fields of Somerset seemed strange to me. It was a bit like emigrating all over again, especially as they appeared to speak in a totally foreign tongue. But I am pleased to say that it is a move I have never regretted. On the contrary, it was the best I ever made.

Bill Alley

COUNTY CHAMPIONSHIP   8th

Played 28	Won 9	Drawn 5	Lost 14

OTHER MATCHES

Played 4	Drawn 3	Lost 1

BATTING

	M	I	NO	Runs	HS	Ave	100	50	ct	st
D.R.W. Silk	9	16	3	526	79	40.46	–	5	5	–
C.L. McCool	31	54	4	1537	100*	30.74	1	10	31	–
M.F. Tremlett	31	55	3	1480	144	28.46	2	10	18	–
P.B. Wight	28	50	3	1293	88	27.51	–	8	15	–
W.E. Alley	31	58	2	1473	108	26.30	1	7	14	–
G. Atkinson	8	13	1	247	52	20.58	–	1	5	–
H.W. Stephenson	32	54	5	944	104*	19.26	1	1	51	19
K.E. Palmer	22	37	6	591	56*	19.06	–	3	18	–
L. Pickles	15	28	3	444	70	17.76	–	2	10	–
J.H. Harris	5	6	1	87	41	17.40	–	–	5	–
J.G. Lomax	15	29	0	351	36	12.10	–	–	12	–
J. Hilton	18	30	6	219	51*	9.12	–	1	11	–
B.A. Langford	25	39	4	288	31	8.22	–	–	12	–
G.M. Tripp	10	18	1	138	62	8.11	–	1	12	–
K.D. Biddulph	3	6	1	37	22	7.40	–	–	1	–
B. Lobb	30	43	9	214	30*	6.29	–	–	7	–
J.W.J. McMahon	27	40	15	90	17	3.60	–	–	17	–
T.E. Dickinson	5	7	3	11	7*	2.75	–	–	3	–

(2 matches)   C.H.M. Greetham 31, 15, 5 (1 ct)   B. Roe 47, 0*   A.G.T. Whitehead 0*, 0, 1* (1 ct)
(1 match)   R.T. Virgin 5, 14*

BOWLING

	Overs	Mdns	Runs	Wkts	Ave	5wi	10wm
P.B. Wight	58	19	145	11	13.18	1	–
T.E. Dickinson	122.4	22	321	17	18.88	1	–
B. Lobb	812.2	169	2143	110	19.48	6	1
W.E. Alley	568.1	144	1391	69	20.15	4	1
B.A. Langford	616.2	203	1422	67	21.22	4	–
J.W.J. McMahon	791.1	249	1987	86	23.10	4	–
J. Hilton	310.2	83	763	29	26.31	1	–
J.G. Lomax	128.3	18	397	13	30.53	–	–
J.H. Harris	73	12	206	6	34.33	–	–
K.E. Palmer	115.5	15	394	11	35.81	–	–
C.L. McCool	352.5	69	1087	39	37.87	1	–
A.G.T. Whitehead	55	14	119	3	39.67	–	–
K.D. Biddulph	63	11	194	4	48.50	–	–

M.F. Tremlett 28.2-4-101-4   G. Atkinson 8-1-22-0   D.R.W. Silk 5-2-23-0
B. Roe 2-0-3-0   L. Pickles 2-0-10-0   H.W. Stephenson 2-1-11-0

BILL ALLEY 1957 – 1968

Yes, of course, the craggy old leg-side spellbinder should have played for Australia. He was pencilled in for the 1948 tour of this country and would almost certainly have come, but for a ghastly accident in the nets when his jaw was broken. It coincided, more or less, with domestic bereavements. His Test aspirations were over; he came to Lancashire to play league cricket instead.

And from there, at the age of 38 (as far as one can calculate) this tough, streetwise ex-pug from Sydney surprised everyone by turning to rural Somerset. Very soon he was one of them down there; rolling a lethal ball in the skittle alleys, going out with his 12-bore, following the hounds. He also played his cricket, noisily and never less than entertainingly. He was not once going to be inhibited by convention and accepted style at the crease. He was made for the partisans and not the poets.

Bill had the unfailing eyes of a country fox. He picked up the flight of the ball quickly – and belted, this sturdy left-hander, in the rough direction of mid-wicket. Legside fielders knew it was coming but rarely stood the chance of a catch. He pulled and hooked with immense power and total disregard for the coaching manual. But the repertoire was wider than might have been thought. Many of his runs came from pugnacious chops to third man. He could produce, at times out of sheer mischief, an exquisite cover drive.

This cussed old campaigner took 134 and 95 off the Australians at Taunton. In that extraordinary 1961 summer he scored more than 3,000 runs in all first-class cricket. He never stopped smiting – or talking. Some said he spoke his mind too much, that he belly-ached too much. But he could always be, in that anti-establishment way of his, a most amusing companion. The crowds, not just in the West Country, loved him.

In addition he was the meanest of exponents of medium-paced swing and seam, while no-one remembers him putting down a catch at gully. Later, as a top umpire, his popularity was sustained, even among batsmen who were victims of his propensity for the LBW decision.

Bill became, in spirit, a Somerset man. Yet he resented the fact that the captaincy eluded him, despite promises, and that a small group of pros, upset that he had dropped Brian Langford when standing in as skipper, seemed to have ganged up against him. He was equally resentful over the imposed conditions that led to his departure, and the old welterweight bristled for a long time. Yet what a tonic he had been.

WILLIAM EDWARD ALLEY Born Sydney, Australia, 3.2.19. Died 26.11.04. LHB, RM. Cap 1957. Acting captain 1964. SFC: 350 matches; 16644 runs @ 30.48; 24 centuries; HS 221* v Warwickshire, Nuneaton, 1961; 1000 runs 10 times, incl 2000 runs once; HT 2761 in 1961; double – once in 1962; 738 wickets @ 22.03; BB 8-65 v Surrey, Oval, 1962; 100 wickets once; HT 112 in 1962. OD: 16 matches; 281 runs @ 20.07; 25 wickets @ 16.20; GC MoM 3. New South Wales, Australia, 1945-48. Fc umpire 1969-84.

He played every shot in the game when he came to us in 1957, but he kept getting out. Gradually he cut them out till in 1961 he only had three left: the dab wide of gully, the hook – he loved to hook – and the hoik over mid-wicket. The dab, the hook and the hoik, he got 3,000 runs in 1961 with those three shots.

Ken Biddulph

ROY THOMAS VIRGIN Born Taunton, 26.8.39. RHB, LB. Cap 1960. SFC: 321 matches; 15458 runs @ 28.52; 22 centuries; HS 179* v Lancashire, Old Trafford, 1971; 1000 runs 9 times, incl 2000 runs once; HT 2223 in 1970; 4 wickets @ 80.25; BB 1-6 v Lancashire, Taunton, 1969. OD: 84 matches; 1938 runs @ 25.84; 1 wicket @ 1.00; GC MoM 2. Northamptonshire 1973-77; Western Province, South Africa, 1972-73.

ROY VIRGIN
1957 – 1972

That 1970 summer belonged to Roy Virgin. There were nine hundreds, seven of them in the championship. The timing never seemed to falter with those exquisite, at times under-rated, cover drives of his. Some said his repertoire was inclined to be modest, though certainly he embraced additional forcing shots. This was noticeable in the conscious way he complemented his off-side approach with the occasional hook and improved on-driving.

Virgin was smallish, sturdy and always tidy in his batsmanship; and he looked fluent enough – at least in the view of every fellow Tauntonian – in that golden '70 summer to book himself a tour place. It didn't come; being first to 2,000 runs and one of Wisden's 'famous five' wasn't quite enough.

In 1971 his expectations were high when he was called up to stand by for the injured Geoff Boycott at Lord's in the final Test against India, but he was destined to fulfil the duties of 12th man.

Roy had grown up near the County Ground, going straight from Huish's Grammar School to the groundstaff. By the age of 20 he had been awarded his cap. Apart from the runs, he fielded well at short-leg and was a passable wicket-keeper in an emergency.

His career with Somerset ended in too many frustrations, and he surprised many by moving to Northants for five seasons, including a brief stint as captain.

CHRIS GREETHAM
1957 – 1966

'The Blond Bomber', as one or two in the team called him affectionately, could have strolled on to a film set and been mistaken for the lead. He had the looks and the presence; his appearance was invariably immaculate. As one of his contemporaries put it: 'He could dive around in the covers all day and still not have a smudge on his flannels.'

Chris was, indeed, a superb cover point, apart from being a good-looking batsman when smoothing through the off-side, and a straight, quietly nagging seamer. He would have been made for one-day cricket.

Whatever the somewhat debonair image, he was a reserved, unassuming fellow. Once he worked as a diamond sorter, teacher and, yes, film extra. After all that he was a golf club secretary in Devon, then in Jersey.

CHRISTOPHER HERBERT MILLINGTON GREETHAM Born Wargrave, Berkshire, 28.8.36. RHB, RM. Cap 1962. SFC: 205 matches; 6723 runs @ 21.97; 5 centuries; HS 151* v Combined Services, Taunton, 1959; 1000 runs twice; HT 1186 in 1963; 195 wickets @ 28.35; BB 7-56 v Glamorgan, Swansea, 1962; HT 69 in 1962. OD: 10 matches; 150 runs @ 15,00; 3 wickets @ 51.33.

Chris was modest to the point of self-effacement. He didn't seem to relax easily. But what a joy he could be! His straight drive back over the top was one of the most pleasurable things I've seen in cricket.

John Mason

ALAN WHITEHEAD
1957 – 1961

In the opinions of many, Alan Whitehead became one of our best umpires, with five Tests and 13 one-day internationals. But he suffered unfairly, some would argue, because of a moment or two of controversy. He was old-fashioned, a stickler, not prepared to be bullied.

In his five years as a slow left-arm bowler for Somerset, his appearances were intermittent and he never found the scope to build on a particularly memorable stint at Eastbourne. The county were searching for Horace Hazell's successor, and they decided that Whitehead didn't have enough variety or penetration. It was all anti-climax after making his first-class debut at 16.

ALAN GEOFFREY THOMAS WHITEHEAD Born Butleigh, Somerset, 28.10.40. LHB, SLA. SFC: 38 matches; 137 runs @ 5.70; HS 15 v Hampshire, Southampton, 1959; 67 wickets @ 34.41; BB 6-74 v Sussex, Eastbourne, 1959; HT 44 in 1959. Fc umpire 1970-2005.

TOM DICKINSON 1957

Born in Australia, he enjoyed a few matches for Lancashire and a handful more for Somerset, a reasonable mix. Dickinson was a useful bowler, well above medium pace. As a batsman of no great distinction, he was known to switch from left-hand to right in the middle of an over. Such feats of versatility behind him, he got back to teaching.

THOMAS EASTWOOD DICKINSON Born Parramatta, Australia, 11.1.31. LHB, RFM. SFC: 5 matches; 11 runs @ 2.75; HS 7* v Yorkshire, Taunton, 1957; 17 wickets @ 18.88; BB 5-36 v Glamorgan, Weston-super-Mare, 1957. Lancashire 1950-51.

BRIAN ROE
1957 – 1966

The defence was dogged, the personality amiable. 'Chico' was one of the smallest players on the circuit, causing older ladies on the West Country boundaries to feel they wanted to mother him.

In fact, he could always look after himself pretty well, especially against the fast bowlers. He relished opening the innings and worked hard for his four centuries. His team-mates valued his resolute approach. As he said, 'This isn't an easy game. Out in the middle, if a bloke can get my wicket, good luck to him. I'm there to stop him.'

In the end there was rather too much competition for places, so he opened for Devon instead. Everything he did was neat and tidy. As a club cricketer he was a prolific scorer.

BRIAN ROE Born Cleethorpes, Lincolnshire, 27.1.39. RHB. Cap 1962. SFC: 131 matches; 4859 runs @ 22.39; 4 centuries; HS 128 v Essex, Brentwood, 1962; 1000 runs 3 times; HT 1552 in 1962; 2 wickets @ 52.00; BB 1-43 v Yorkshire, Taunton, 1961. OD: 5 matches; 55 runs @ 11.00.

> He kept me going.
> His commentary, his ribbing and his jokes made a hard day much easier.
> **Ken Palmer**

1958

Captain: M.F. Tremlett

This was surely Somerset's best season so far. They had astonished the pundits – not to mention many of their own supporters – by finishing third in the championship table, and with a dozen wins to show for it. Only the mean-spirited would argue that the weather was inclined to work in their favour and that the margin of victory was not always substantial.

As captain, Tremlett was rightly given some of the credit. In truth, his tactical leadership was at times better than his batting, despite a fine century against Derbyshire at Bath. It must be admitted that Surrey came to Taunton with a weakened side. Yet they should not have gone down by six wickets. Wight opened with 175 in the first innings and was around on 45 in the second when the match was finally won.

Lomax, the Lancastrian, scored 1,000 runs for the first time with plenty of native grit when it was needed. He liked opening with Alley; two batsmen of contrasting approaches but strong on the team ethic. His 94, this time from down the order, against Yorkshire at Bath, showed Lomax's valuable, uncomplicated qualities.

Young Atkinson hit a maiden hundred against Warwickshire. McCool, who was 40 when he signed for the county, continued to parade his controlled aggression at the crease. Alley was 38 when he came West – sceptical chums implied he was older, a myth he liked to encourage – to keep the leg-side fielders busy.

At this time Somerset found they had a useful deputy wicketkeeper in Eele when Stephenson was unfit. When Lobb was unwell, Alley took his place with the new ball against Sussex and immediately seamed away to grab the first four wickets, two in his opening over, easing Somerset to their win by just eight runs.

Weston-super-Mare was as eventful as ever. Somerset came out on top in all three games. Lancashire's Tattersall, that talented adversary, took ten wickets from the match. Langford did even better, with his 9-26 in the first innings followed by six more in the second. His Clarence Park haul: 35-279.

I remember taking a second new ball one day at Taunton, and the Secretary came out after me. He stood by the gate. 'What are you doing taking a second new ball? That's another thirty bob. We can't afford that.'

It was worse when I first started at Somerset. I remember going along to the office to get a ball, and I had to sign for it. And it wasn't a new ball, either. That was my ball, I was responsible for it. I'd take it home and polish it up every evening. By the middle of July it was getting a bit tatty. So I went to see if there was any chance of another one. 'Another?' he said. 'You've only had that this summer.'

Ken Biddulph

COUNTY CHAMPIONSHIP   3rd   Played 28   Won 12   Drawn 9   Lost 7

OTHER MATCHES   Played   1   Lost 1

BATTING

	M	I	NO	Runs	HS	Ave	100	50	ct	st
G. Atkinson	7	12	1	425	164	38.63	1	1	5	–
P.B. Wight	29	54	4	1549	175	30.98	3	5	12	–
C.L. McCool	29	53	1	1490	169	28.65	2	8	35	–
D.R.W. Silk	9	15	2	291	77	22.38	–	2	5	–
W.E. Alley	29	54	2	1158	89	22.26	–	8	20	–
J.G. Lomax	29	53	3	1096	94*	21.92	–	5	34	–
M.F. Tremlett	29	52	5	870	118	18.51	1	4	21	–
H.W. Stephenson	12	21	3	287	35	15.94	–	–	18	5
L. Pickles	4	8	0	118	42	14.75	–	–	1	–
K.E. Palmer	20	32	4	409	56	14.60	–	1	8	–
C.H.M. Greetham	16	29	3	376	53	14.46	–	1	10	–
L.E. Bryant	15	21	13	99	16	12.37	–	–	9	–
G.M. Tripp	6	10	1	96	43	10.66	–	–	5	–
B.A. Langford	28	42	5	388	35	10.48	–	–	17	–
P.J. Eele	17	24	6	164	30	9.11	–	–	29	6
K.D. Biddulph	12	17	10	53	14*	7.57	–	–	6	–
B. Lobb	16	24	6	135	42	7.50	–	–	3	–
B. Roe	5	9	0	64	20	7.11	–	–	2	–
A.G.T. Whitehead	3	5	3	10	7*	5.00	–	–	3	–

(2 matches)   A.C. Shirreff 15, 1*, 7, 24 (1 ct)

(1 match)   R.T. Virgin 1, 2 (1 ct)   M. Walker 4, 0

BOWLING

	Overs	Mdns	Runs	Wkts	Ave	5wi	10wm
B.A. Langford	826.3	240	2121	116	18.28	8	2
K.E. Palmer	311.5	57	830	41	20.24	2	–
B. Lobb	461.5	107	1111	51	21.78	2	–
C.L. McCool	305.2	67	872	40	21.80	2	–
W.E. Alley	483.5	109	`1161	52	22.32	3	–
J.G. Lomax	477.4	131	1124	50	22.48	1	–
L.E. Bryant	262.1	97	563	25	22.52	1	–
K.D. Biddulph	342.4	74	989	41	24.12	2	–
P.B. Wight	121.2	38	293	12	24.41	–	–

A.G.T. Whitehead 31-10-90-0   C.H.M. Greetham 13-2-59-1   M.F. Tremlett 7-2-17-0

D.R.W. Silk 1-0-3-0

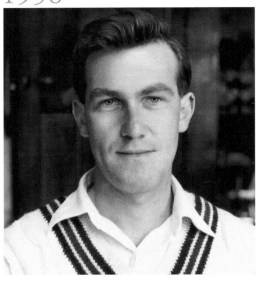

PETER EELE 1958 – 1965

Fortune was less than fair to Peter Eele. He stood by patiently and occasionally he deputised behind the stumps for Harold Stephenson. Then when he thought his turn had come, Geoff Clayton was brought in from Lancashire.

Eele, a genuine local, was a tidy and unshowy gloveman. As a left-hand bat, again without any hint of flashy tricks, he earned his one hundred.

His introvert nature was possibly not a helpful ally when twice he lost his place on the umpires' list. That kind of rejection earned him warm sympathy from plenty of his white-coated colleagues.

PETER JAMES EELE Born Taunton, 27.1.35. LHB, WK. Cap 1964. SFC: 54 matches; 612 runs @ 12.24; 1 century; HS 103* v Pakistan Eaglets, Taunton, 1963; HT 201 in 1964; 106 dismissals (87 ct, 19 st). OD: 2 matches; 10 runs @ 5.00; 2 dismissals (2 ct). Fc umpire 1981-84, 1989-90.

ERIC BRYANT 1958 – 1960

There may often have been murmurs about his bowling action but no-one complained among the clubs in Weston-super-Mare and he was thrilled to be given his chance for Somerset.

Against Gloucesteshire at Bath in 1960 he collected his highest score of 17 – and was called four times in an over. It was the end of county cricket after 22 outings for the left-arm spinner who had tried so hard to model himself on Surrey's Tony Lock.

Bryant wasn't as lucky as a previous slow bowler who had run into trouble with the more punctilious umpires. Ted Tyler, one of Somerset's Test men, survived the temporary tut-tutting and continued his career. Eric, a brooding chain-smoker, introspectively called it a day.

LEONARD ERIC BRYANT Born Weston-super-Mare, 2.6.36. Died 28.11.99. LHB, SLA. SFC: 22 matches; 133 runs @ 8.86; HS 17 v Gloucestershire, Bath, 1960; 34 wickets @ 27.73; BB 5-64 v Worcestershire, Stourbridge, 1958; HT 25 in 1958.

ALAN SHIRREFF 1958

The ex-Squadron Leader had skippered sides from the RAF and Combined Services, and no doubt some saw him as ending up captain of Somerset. He arrived as assistant secretary, with some coaching responsibilities. It was never going to work. His face didn't fit in some quarters and there was an uneasy relationship between him and skipper Maurice Tremlett. Shirreff had come by way of Cambridge, Hampshire and Kent, but he managed only two matches for Somerset, without getting a bowl.

ALEXANDER CAMPBELL SHIRREFF Born Ealing, London, 12.2.19. RHB. SFC: 2 matches; 47 runs @ 15.66; HS 24 v Essex, Taunton, 1958. Cambridge University 1939; Hampshire 1946-47; Kent 1950-56.

THE COUNTY GROUND, TAUNTON

As an impressionable schoolboy, going to watch a game at Taunton was like walking into a citadel. To me, at the time, it was an absolutely awesome place. There used to be trees down in the corner by the River Stand. We'd sit under them to eat our sandwiches and then, during the intervals for lunch and tea, we'd play our make-believe Test matches on the outfield, using a bottle for a bat and bowling with a tennis ball. I'd just dream that one day I might play there for real – and, amazingly enough, so I did.

I feel that fortune favoured me, though, in making my debut at Bath rather than Taunton. The Bath track always did something for the spinners while Taunton was a good flat wicket that suited the batsmen. If I'd started there, perhaps I'd never have been heard of again!

Brian Langford

An early memory of the ground at Taunton is of the lowing cows in the cattle market punctuating the applause from the crowd. It is the most companionable and pervasive of county grounds and, within its gregarious climate, men from origins as diverse as Sammy Woods, Len Braund, Bill Alley, Arthur Wellard, Viv Richards, Johnny Lawrence, Ian Botham, Frank Lee have become as much part of the Taunton scene as the Somerset born Harold Gimblett, Horace Hazell, Jack White, Mervyn Kitchen, Peter Denning, Colin Dredge and Bertie Buse.

It is as if they had all been drawn into the same atmosphere, like the people converging on the market from the countryside for miles around. On a July Saturday market day, cricket and the weekly visitors and shoppers all merge into a unique yet typically West Country warm, busy, relished – purely Taunton – summer's day.

John Arlott

1959

Captain: M.F. Tremlett

Down Somerset went from third to twelfth in the table. Not that it was the fault of the batsmen. Six of the team passed 1,000 runs for the season. Wight, delicate as ever in his stroke-play, scored six centuries, all of them handsome to the eye. His finest was a not-out innings of 222 against Kent, as the Australians, McCool and Alley, backed him up sturdily on the first day. Wight carried his bat with complete aplomb in an exhibition to cherish as his side moved on their way to an innings victory. He was in such good form that probably he would have gone on to 2,000 runs but for a blow on his forehead when fielding at short leg. He missed a week, then at Weston found himself suffering from double-vision.

It was at Clarence Park that the county returned to bad habits, allowing Warwickshire to roll them over for 59 in the second innings.

In his first full season, Atkinson underlined his promise with 1,000 runs. Meanwhile, the stylish Greetham enjoyed a profitable July. He scored a graceful, undefeated 151 against Combined Services and quickly followed with 104 in the match with Derbyshire at Buxton. Everything he did was neat and tidy, whether at the crease or patrolling the covers, and it was a pity that the considerable potential was never wholly fulfilled.

Yorkshire, top of the championship table, came to Bath in mid-August. Close, in particular, chose not to make things easy for Somerset. His century was typically pugnacious and then his off-breaks, perhaps under-rated, earned him six wickets. But Langford matched him with six of his own, and Yorkshire were beaten by 16 runs, their first defeat by Somerset since 1903. In the next match at the Recreation Ground, which Surrey won, it was the turn of Laker (7-59) to demonstrate how to turn the ball on a helpful pitch.

Income	£19,125
Expenditure	£28,079

Annual Account,
year ending 31 October 1959

COUNTY CHAMPIONSHIP　12th

Played 28	Won 8	Drawn 7	Lost 13

OTHER MATCHES

Played 3	Won 2	Drawn 1

BATTING

	M	I	NO	Runs	HS	Ave	100	50	ct	st
P.B. Wight	22	37	3	1874	222*	55.11	6	9	12	–
C.L. McCool	25	44	2	1697	149	40.40	4	11	28	–
W.E. Alley	29	52	4	1760	155	36.66	2	12	29	–
G. Atkinson	31	57	4	1717	119	32.39	3	11	19	–
C.H.M. Greetham	20	36	2	881	151*	25.91	2	3	8	–
M.F. Tremlett	27	45	3	1056	100	25.14	1	5	15	–
J.G. Lomax	28	53	1	1298	92	24.96	–	7	27	–
J.M. Lawrence	3	6	2	98	35	24.50	–	–	–	–
G.M. Tripp	6	11	2	214	48	23.77	–	–	6	–
R.T. Virgin	9	16	2	252	68	18.00	–	1	9	–
K.E. Palmer	19	28	7	371	52*	17.66	–	2	5	–
H.W. Stephenson	27	41	6	547	55	15.62	–	1	46	11
B.A. Langford	30	43	8	422	48	12.05	–	–	17	–
K.D. Biddulph	22	28	10	144	28	8.00	–	–	9	–
P.J. Eele	3	4	0	29	12	7.25	–	–	5	3
J.H. Harris	7	8	2	30	11	5.00	–	–	1	–
A.G.T. Whitehead	19	22	10	56	15	4.66	–	–	13	–
L.E. Bryant	4	5	1	14	6	3.50	–	–	1	–
B. Lobb	6	8	4	11	4*	2.75	–	–	–	–

(2 matches)　G.L. Keith　40, 3, 4
(1 match)　T.I. Barwell　0 (5 ct, 1 st)　H. Sully　1

BOWLING

	Overs	Mdns	Runs	Wkts	Ave	5wi	10wm
W.E. Alley	504.3	115	1289	55	23.43	1	–
K.D. Biddulph	674.2	128	1924	79	24.35	4	–
C.L. McCool	558.3	125	1587	62	25.59	3	1
J.G. Lomax	404.2	86	1114	43	25.90	1	–
J.H. Harris	114.2	27	313	12	26.08	–	–
C.H.M. Greetham	144.2	27	425	15	28.33	–	–
B.A. Langford	987.3	357	2409	83	29.02	6	–
A.G.T. Whitehead	488.1	148	1324	44	30.09	3	–
B. Lobb	158.1	32	454	15	30.26	1	–
K.E. Palmer	349.4	68	972	30	32.40	1	–
J.M. Lawrence	56	8	202	6	33.66	–	–

L.E. Bryant　44.1-14-153-4　　H. Sully　27-4-116-0　　P.B. Wight　26-4-94-0
G. Atkinson　9-1-66-0　　G.L. Keith　3-1-9-1　　M.F. Tremlett　3-1-16-0
H.W. Stephenson　1-0-3-0　　R.T. Virgin　1-0-11-0

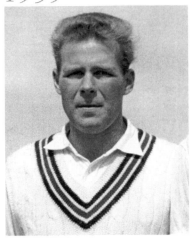

GEOFF KEITH 1959 – 1961

A tidy, stylish batsman who struggled for a place during his three years with the county. His one century was scored after he had returned to his native Hampshire. His untimely death came at the age of 38.

GEOFFREY LEYDON KEITH Born Winchester, Hampshire, 19.11.37. Died 26.12.75. RHB, OB. SFC: 15 matches; 319 runs @ 12.76; HS 48 v Gloucestershire, Bath, 1960; HT 220 in 1960; 1 wicket @ 9.00; BB 1-9 v Cambridge University, Fenner's, 1959. Hampshire 1962-67; Western Province, South Africa, 1968-69.

HAYDN SULLY 1959 – 1963

It was never going to be easy as an off-break bowler making a mark in a side which already contained the experienced Brian Langford. Sully was granted only a dozen opportunities over four years, so wisely he tried elsewhere. At Northants he took his 100 wickets in 1966, making a point or two at home.

HAYDN SULLY Born Sampford Brett, Somerset, 1.11.39. LHB, ROB. SFC: 12 matches; 98 runs @ 14.00; HS 24 v Gloucestershire, Bath, 1963; 12 wickets @ 46.41; BB 5-64 v Cambridge University, Taunton, 1961. Northamptonshire 1964-69.

MILES LAWRENCE 1959 – 1961

Eldest son of Johnny, he gave up leg-break bowling to become a most proficient league wicketkeeper. By then his championship career, extending over three seasons for Somerset, was over. Lawrence Jnr was a capable batsman, though lack of physique worked against him and his father's hopes for him were clearly not going to be fulfilled. The pair shared a marked aptitude for coaching, the son at Leeds Grammar School. Tragically Miles died at the age of 48, only four months after the death of Johnny.

JOHN MILES LAWRENCE Born Rothwell, Yorkshire, 7.11.40. Died 16.4.89. RHB, LB. SFC: 18 matches; 372 runs @ 15.50; HS 41 v Middlesex, Taunton, 1961; HT 199 in 1961; 9 wickets @ 40.33; BB 3-44 v Nottinghamshire, Taunton, 1959.

TERRY BARWELL 1959 – 1968

The technique and footwork were sound, especially against the slow bowlers. At Second XI level, with Somerset and then with Wiltshire, he revealed how proficiently he could score runs. He was a reliable fielder and, if needed, a competent wicketkeeper. In his county appearances, one or two harsh LBWs went against him to damage confidence. Later he turned successfully to teaching at Marlborough and Blundell's.

TERENCE IAN BARWELL Born Bloemhof, South Africa, 29.4.37. RHB, occ WK. Cap 1968. SFC: 43 matches; 1321 runs @ 19.71; HS 84* v Glamorgan, Weston-super-Mare, 1965; HT 410 in 1967; 9 dismissals (8 ct, 1 st). OD: 4 matches; 62 runs @ 15.50.

Terry Barwell dives for a slip catch off Middlesex's Ted Clark.
The bowler is Fred Rumsey.

1960

Captain: H.W. Stephenson

Uplifting memories may have been at a premium again. But who could ignore the match (though the bowlers may have wished they could) at Taunton with Cambridge University? The pitch, hardly for the first time, utterly befriended the batsmen, to the extent that there were three declarations and seven centuries. Poor bowling only added to the imbalance. The orgy of runs began with hundreds from Atkinson, Virgin and Wight; then came others from Cambridge's Roger Prideaux – who scored two in the match – Tony Lewis and Michael Willard. At least the statisticians were kept busy. They noted that for the first time there had been four separate three-figure opening stands. For the record, the University won by six wickets.

The summer's results made it painfully clear once more that the county badly needed another fast bowler. Medium-pace was efficient enough but lacked the penetration and fire that was a requisite at times. It didn't help that, in Stephenson's first year as captain, Somerset were too often handicapped by injuries, with Lomax and Palmer two of the casualties.

George Lambert was something of a surprise as the county's new coach, not least because of his Gloucestershire connections. McCool, about to head back to Australia after five successful years with Somerset, was going to be missed. He was 45 now, and the vigour and zest of his cutting and driving had begun to wane. Any long-term hopes of holding on to the Oxford blue Baig, as he returned to India, also had to be forgotten.

Wight had been full of fluent strokes once more, reaching 2,316 runs in all matches and beating Gimblett's 1952 record for the county in the process. Atkinson, by nature an on-side batsman, had worked diligently on extending his pleasing repertoire, while the locally born Virgin had made encouraging progress.

At the end of August, Somerset staged a championship match at Bristol's Imperial Ground for the first time. Any intentions to determine support in the area were nullified by the bad weather.

Somerset lived hand-to-mouth. Their reaction to financial difficulty was to allow a local entrepreneur to build a greyhound track around the boundary, for an annual rent of £500. Cecil Buttle, of course, was displeased with this intrusion upon his precious turf and every Friday he fought a cat-and-mouse battle, turning water hoses on and off, moving barriers, in a vain effort to avoid damage.

Peter Roebuck

COUNTY CHAMPIONSHIP 14th   Played 32   Won 5   Drawn 16   Lost 11

OTHER MATCHES   Played 2   Lost 2

BATTING

	M	I	NO	Runs	HS	Ave	100	50	ct	st
P.B. Wight	34	61	5	2316	155*	41.35	7	10	13	—
G. Atkinson	28	50	3	1895	190	40.31	5	9	19	—
D.R.W. Silk	8	13	2	401	92	36.45	—	2	1	—
J.G. Lomax	3	5	1	133	52	33.25	—	2	1	—
C.L. McCool	23	42	4	1222	131	32.15	2	6	10	—
A.A. Baig	16	28	3	721	99	28.84	—	4	11	—
R.T. Virgin	31	57	1	1453	113	25.94	1	5	16	—
W.E. Alley	26	41	7	741	110*	21.79	1	2	23	—
H.W. Stephenson	33	46	7	849	65	21.76	—	3	59	17
K.E. Palmer	19	28	4	469	54	19.54	—	2	9	—
C.H.M. Greetham	26	45	1	827	97	18.79	—	6	9	—
J.M. Lawrence	5	9	5	75	25*	18.75	—	—	2	—
B.A. Langford	33	48	12	539	68*	14.97	—	2	15	—
C.R.M. Atkinson	15	21	3	252	44*	14.00	—	—	7	—
G.L. Keith	10	18	2	220	48	13.75	—	—	5	—
G.E. Lambert	3	6	0	64	24	10.66	—	—	3	—
M.J. Kitchen	3	5	0	45	23	9.00	—	—	—	—
F.J. Herting	5	7	2	44	16*	8.80	—	—	1	—
A.G.T. Whitehead	13	17	8	65	15	7.22	—	—	3	—
K.D. Biddulph	29	31	14	118	41	6.94	—	—	13	—
L.E. Bryant	3	3	0	20	17	6.66	—	—	—	—
M.F. Tremlett	3	3	1	4	3	2.00	—	—	4	—

(2 matches)   B. Lobb 0*, 0, 0, 0 (2 ct)

(1 match)   P.J. Eele 5, 29 (2 ct, 1 st)   B. Roe 2, 0 (1 ct)   H. Sully did not bat

BOWLING

	Overs	Mdns	Runs	Wkts	Ave	5wi	10wm
K.E. Palmer	368.5	78	943	42	22.45	3	—
W.E. Alley	714	202	1628	71	22.92	5	—
K.D. Biddulph	801.2	203	2265	83	27.28	2	—
B.A. Langford	1260.2	505	2777	100	27.77	3	2
C.R.M. Atkinson	347.5	102	869	30	28.96	1	—
C.L. McCool	311.1	74	940	29	32.41	1	—
C.H.M. Greetham	330.1	87	928	24	38.66	1	—
A.G.T. Whitehead	254.3	70	733	17	43.11	—	—
L.E. Bryant	75	20	227	5	45.40	—	—
P.B. Wight	126	46	345	7	49.28	—	—
F.J. Herting	131.3	25	506	7	72.28	—	—

B. Lobb 45-6-145-4   G.E. Lambert 44.2-6-160-3   J.M. Lawrence 39-9-137-3

G. Atkinson 31-14-63-4   H. Sully 31-7-105-9   J.G. Lomax 25-2-88-2

R.T. Virgin 17-2-91-1   A.A. Baig 13-5-22-1   H.W. Stephenson 4.1-0-31-0

M.F. Tremlett 2-1-8-0

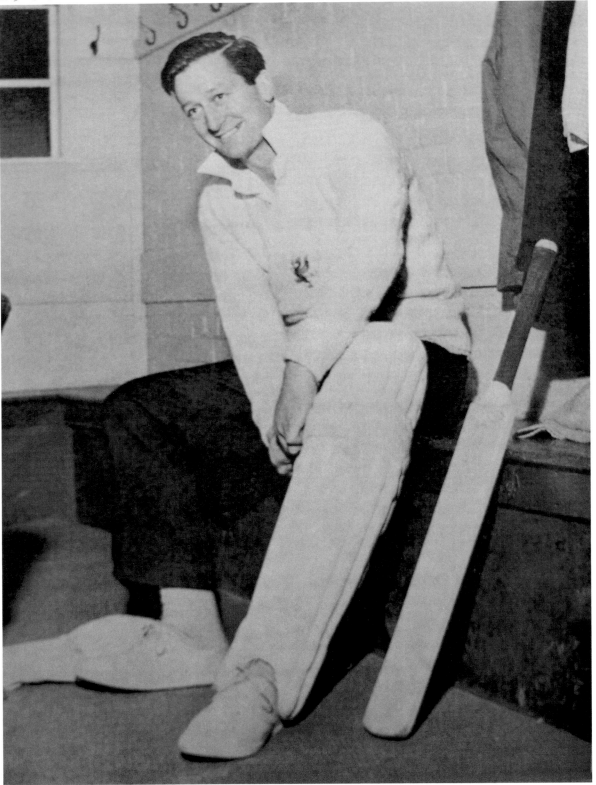

COLIN ATKINSON 1960 – 1967

The rare distinction of being captain, chairman and president of the county club reflected, in his case, intelligence and integrity – and a surprising determination for a shy and self-deprecating man. His cricket could be as competitive as anything you'd expect from a North Countryman, but he also had to work with dogged resolve to make himself into a better player than he naturally was.

He arrived at Millfield School in 1960 to teach, with the promise that he could take the summer off for cricket if Somerset wanted him. Harold Stephenson, who shared the same geographical roots, told the county to go for him. Atkinson bowled leg-breaks, was a passable middle-order bat and chased heroically in the covers, pledging himself to let nothing past. Then arthritis crept into his finger joints and he switched to seamers.

The call to take charge of the side in the mid 1960s, a period when authority was needed as well as tact, appealed to him. Whatever his traits as a private person, he relished responsibility. Under his leadership, Somerset reached the Gillette Cup Final against Kent in 1967 and finished third in the championship table the previous year.

Atkinson balanced ambition with a down-to-earth streak and basic common sense. After all, while doing research in the course of studying for a degree, he chose to earn some pocket money by playing as a pro for Northumberland.

He went on to reveal gifts as an administrator, notably evident when he followed RJO Meyer as headmaster of Millfield. The school flourished and handsome purpose-built facilities took the place of the dilapidated Nissen huts at Street. Buildings will long serve as memorials to his ability, a new pavilion at Taunton offering another example. Before his untimely death he was seen additionally as an intuitive businessman in his role of chairman of HTV West.

Historically, administrative life has never been easy for Somerset cricket. As president he found himself involved in the 1979 controversy at Worcester, when Brian Rose's team were kicked out of the Benson and Hedges competition. Atkinson, seen himself as a future chairman of the TCCB, was embarrassed. 'We did wrong but I've some sympathy for the team. People went right over the top in condemning us.'

Again it was difficult for him when he chaired that traumatic meeting at Shepton Mallet on the Richards-Garner-Botham issue. Part headmaster, part lawyer, part conciliator, he played a central role and the delicately restored dignity could be largely attributed to him.

COLIN RICHARD MICHAEL ATKINSON Born Thornaby-on-Tees, Yorkshire, 23.7.31. Died 25.6.91. RHB, LBG/RM. Cap 1961. Captain 1965-67. SFC: 163 matches; 3772 runs @ 19.05; HS 97 v Warwickshire, Edgbaston, 1967; 1000 runs once; HT 1120 in 1966; 190 wickets @ 31.01; BB 7-54 v Gloucestershire, Taunton, 1962; HT 62 in 1961. OD: 12 matches; 153 runs @ 17.00; 7 wickets @ 35.14.

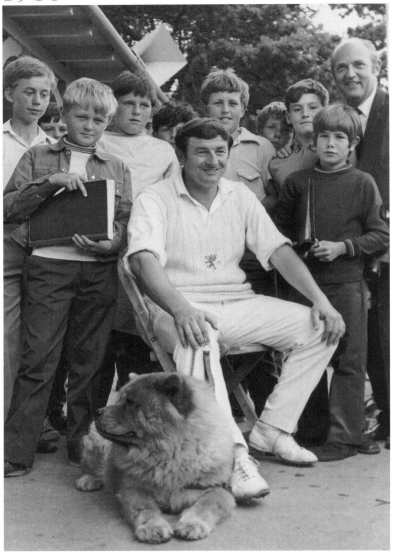

MERVYN JOHN KITCHEN Born Nailsea, Somerset, 1.8.40. LHB. Cap 1966. SFC: 352 matches; 15213 runs @ 26.41; 17 centuries; HS 189 v Pakistanis, Taunton, 1967; 1000 runs 7 times; HT 1730 in 1968; 2 wickets @ 54.50; BB 1-4 v Sussex, Taunton, 1969. OD: 172 matches; 3388 runs @ 22.43; 5 wickets @ 19.40; GC MoM 2; B&H GA 1. Fc umpire 1982-2005.

> Merv was a gritty professional, the sort you wanted in your side when the chips were down. He never ducked a challenge in his life.
>
> **Roy Virgin**

MERVYN KITCHEN
1960 – 1979

Here was the left-hander with the cheeks of a Somerset farmer and the gait which suggested that his ancestors once went to sea from Avonmouth. Crowds took to him because he was authentic Nailsea and Flax Bourton, without artifice or pretentious ambition.

Merv was best when he attacked, driving and pulling with pugnacious power. At times early on, he must have wondered whether he'd ever establish himself in the championship team. His value to the Second XI had been undeniable and, scoring more than 1,000 runs for them, he was one of the outstanding successes when they won the Minor Counties title for the first time.

Upgrading wasn't automatic and occasionally his confidence seemed to be suffering as he waited for his chance. But he practised assiduously, that village boy promise was gradually fulfilled, and Kitchen, his demeanour as uncomplicated as his style, was confirmed as a local favourite.

In 1968 he hit five hundreds, though maybe he was never fashionable enough for loftier recognition. There was some surprise when he took a year's break from the game, but back he came in 1976, and after retiring as a player he remained prominently involved as a first-class and Test umpire.

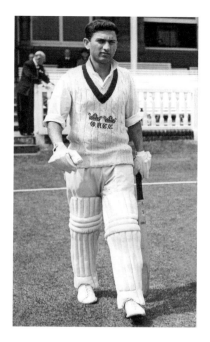

ABBAS ALI BAIG 1960 – 1962

Small, polite, neat as a choirboy. In his early days at Oxford, he decided he'd like some county cricket in the vacations. That 'League of Nations' tag at Taunton possibly influenced him. He wrote to Somerset and ended up accepting Bill Andrews' hospitality, though wisely resisting the Bacchic temptations of his host's home-made wine.

The regret is that Baig played no more than 23 matches for the county, and indeed that he failed to live up to the promise that he showed as a Test player, having begun with a hundred at Old Trafford in 1959 after being co-opted into the Indians' touring side. Once he scored a double-century at Delhi but managed only 99 for Somerset, against Gloucestershire. Those eloquent Asian wrists deserved more.

ABBAS ALI BAIG Born Hyderabad, India, 8.11.41. RHB, LB. Cap 1961. 10 Tests 1959-67. SFC: 23 matches; 1154 runs @ 30.36; HS 99 v Gloucestershire, Bristol, 1960; HT 721 in 1960; 1 wicket @ 22.00; BB 1-1 v Glamorgan, Bath, 1960. Hyderabad 1958-71; Oxford University 1959-62.

GEORGE LAMBERT 1960

It was unthinkable to some that George Lambert, a fast bowler from Gloucestershire, should have been appointed Somerset's coach in 1960. He was then 41 and played three times when Ken Biddulph and Bill Alley were unfit. In the late 1940s he was arguably the quickest bowler on the domestic circuit and was very near to a Test call. George was a Londoner, chirpy and very much a family man. Crowds at Bristol and Cheltenham loved him; his ebullience could restore morale in a depressed dressing room.

GEORGE ERNEST EDWARD LAMBERT Born Paddington, London, 11.5.18. Died 31.10.91. RHB, RFM. SFC: 3 matches; 64 runs @ 10.66; HS 24 v Middlesex, Lord's, 1960; 3 wickets @ 53.33; BB 3-55 same match. Gloucestershire 1938-57.

FRED HERTING 1960

Just seven wickets – and four of those came in one innings at Bath, where this honest left-arm seamer was surprised to find himself included.

FREDERICK JOHN HERTING Born South Ruislip, Middlesex, 25.2.40. RHB, LMF. SFC: 5 matches; 44 runs @ 8.80; HS 16* v Lancashire, Taunton, 1960; 7 wickets @ 72.28; BB 4-85 v Gloucestershire, Bath, 1960.

1961

Captain: H.W. Stephenson

The Somerset summer belonged unquestionably to Alley. Was he ever away from the crease, lambasting helpless bowlers or taking wickets by way of a change? He was the boldest, most belligerent and, partial West Country fans would say, the most brilliant batsman in the country. The Australian was the last to score 3,000 runs in a season, though his shots were not always steered through the technically approved areas. It was impossible to imagine he was 42: flushed in the face maybe, but not out of breath, and proficiently agile in the gully. In a season of such bountiful boundaries, nothing was better than his two unbeaten hundreds against Surrey at Taunton; the second took an hour and a half. It was reassuring to observe that occasionally he was also human enough to fail. At Street, he was out for 0 and 1, and only a few days later he was twice out for a duck against Glamorgan at Clarence Park. This he rapidly redressed with 117 and 50 in the match with Essex.

Frome staged its 18th and last championship match, with Hampshire beating Somerset by 18 runs, and Millfield (Street) its first and only one. The Warwickshire fixture should have been played at Glastonbury but the pitch there was being re-laid. RJO Meyer made Millfield available, maintaining the strong links with the county. Warwickshire's Jim Stewart kept hitting straight sixes, mostly at Langford's expense, on the way to his century and his team's nine-wicket victory.

Overall, despite Alley's dynamics, it had been a fluctuating season – as ever – and the lack of consistency was too often Somerset's irritating undoing.

Palmer made headway, however. He was very nearly the first player in the country to complete the double, beaten marginally by Trevor Bailey of Essex. That whippy bowling action and sensible approach to batting appeared to be putting him in line for future Test selection.

The diminutive Roe topped 1,000 runs and Langford's persevering off-spinners brought him more than 100 wickets in a side patently short of match-winning bowlers. Pearson, who had already taken all ten in an innings for Cambridge, made a few valued appearances for Somerset, impressively enough to head the county averages, even if it was accepted that his stay in the West to play cricket would not be too long.

Before the start of the season a doctor asked to see me. 'Bill, I want you to be a guinea pig,' he said. 'I want you to take three of these pills every day during the summer.' Apparently they were not on the market, and he wanted to see if they worked.

My team-mates thought it was some kind of youth preservative but, eleven centuries and 3,000 runs later, it was me who was having the last laugh.

'What's in them, Doc?' I asked at the end of the season.

'I'd like to tell you, but I can't,' he replied.

I never did know what was in those tablets.

Bill Alley

COUNTY CHAMPIONSHIP 10th   Played 32   Won 10   Drawn 7   Lost 15

OTHER MATCHES   Played 2   Won 1   Drawn 1

BATTING

	M	I	NO	Runs	HS	Ave	100	50	ct	st
W.E. Alley	32	58	11	2761	221*	56.82	10	9	25	–
A.A. Baig	6	12	1	428	93	38.90	–	3	2	–
G. Atkinson	29	53	1	2005	146	38.55	3	13	30	–
P.B. Wight	32	59	6	1660	167*	31.32	3	7	22	–
R.T Virgin	10	18	1	510	88	30.00	–	3	6	–
K.E. Palmer	32	52	12	1036	125*	25.90	1	2	21	–
C.H.M. Greetham	24	38	5	766	79	23.21	–	4	15	–
B. Roe	29	52	1	1181	102	23.15	1	6	8	–
H. Sully	5	5	2	59	20*	19.66	–	–	4	–
J.G. Lomax	29	50	1	938	71	19.14	–	6	33	–
C.R.M. Atkinson	29	42	10	587	49*	18.34	–	–	15	–
H.W. Stephenson	30	46	6	712	54*	17.80	–	2	52	9
M.J. Kitchen	6	12	0	208	45	17.33	–	–	–	–
B.A. Langford	33	44	10	474	52*	13.94	–	1	19	–
J.M. Lawrence	10	18	2	199	41	12.43	–	–	6	–
M.E. Latham	3	5	2	37	21*	12.33	–	–	2	–
P.J. Eele	4	5	0	55	39	11.00	–	–	6	–
K.D. Biddulph	16	23	14	84	18	9.33	–	–	9	–
G.L. Keith	3	6	0	52	20	8.66	–	–	6	–
G.H. Hall	4	6	3	11	6*	3.66	–	–	–	–
A.J.G. Pearson	5	1	1	2	2*	–	–	–	3	–

(2 matches)   T.I. Barwell 7, 1, 23 (1 ct)
(1 match)   A.G.T. Whitehead 5*, 0* (1 ct)

BOWLING

	Overs	Mdns	Runs	Wkts	Ave	5wi	10wm
A.J.G. Pearson	170.3	42	405	23	17.60	1	–
K.E. Palmer	965	248	2317	114	20.32	7	2
W.E. Alley	596.1	173	1414	55	25.70	–	–
B.A. Langford	1183.5	414	2976	111	26.81	6	1
H. Sully	72.3	22	238	8	29.75	1	–
K.D. Biddulph	453.5	106	1434	46	31.17	1	–
C.R.M. Atkinson	744	191	2019	62	32.56	2	–
J.G. Lomax	462	114	1223	36	33.97	–	–
C.H.M. Greetham	298.2	77	780	21	37.14	–	–
M.E. Latham	86	18	225	6	37.50	–	–
P.B. Wight	53	16	156	3	52.00	–	–
G.H. Hall	102.1	14	335	5	67.00	–	–

R.T. Virgin 23-2-96-1   B. Roe 18-1-101-2   A.G.T. Whitehead 18-8-40-3
H.W. Stephenson 14-2-76-0   J.M. Lawrence 7-0-24-0   G. Atkinson 0.5-0-1-0

MIKE LATHAM 1961 – 1962

One of the large number of bowlers, in his case a seamer rather than a spinner, to make his mark at Bath. Latham had a nice action and procured some movement, but he stayed for only two seasons with modest returns.

MICHAEL EDWARD LATHAM Born Birmingham, 14.1.39. RHB, RFM. SFC: 18 matches; 133 runs @ 14.77; HS 21* v Hampshire, Frome, 1961; 29 wickets @ 30.62; BB 5-20 v Nottinghamshire, Bath, 1962; HT 23 in 1962.

GEOFF HALL 1961 – 1965

Bespectacled Lancastrian who came south in the early 1960s to lend support to the Somerset attack. Could generate pace and once looked like a world-beater at Worksop, but suffered from a chronic lack of consistency.

GEOFFREY HAROLD HALL Born Colne, Lancashire, 1.1.41. RHB, RF. SFC: 48 matches; 90 runs @ 3.60; HS 12* v Yorkshire, Taunton, 1962; 111 wickets @ 30.85; BB 6-60 v Nottinghamshire, Worksop, 1965; HT 46 in 1962. OD: 3 matches; 2 runs @ 2.00; 8 wickets @ 13.62.

TONY PEARSON 1961 – 1963

We go to his Cambridge days (he won three blues) for his most memorable performance; at Loughborough in 1961, against Leicestershire, he took all ten wickets for 78 runs.

His obvious link with Somerset can be attributed to his schooling, and cricketing successes, at Downside. He bowled well above medium pace, possessing some natural swing, but after half a dozen spaced appearances for the county, and one fine stint against Worcestershire, Tony Pearson got on with his medical career.

ANTHONY JOHN GRAYHUST PEARSON Born Harrow, Middlesex, 30.12.41. RHB, RFM. SFC: 6 matches; 17 runs (no average); HS 15* v Kent, Gillingham, 1963; 26 wickets @ 19.50; BB 7-63 v Worcestershire, Bristol Imperial, 1961. Cambridge University 1961-63.

MORLANDS ATHLETIC GROUND, GLASTONBURY

I was born almost overlooking the ground so I retained a great affection for it. The arrival annually of county cricket in this part of Somerset was eagerly awaited and appreciated, an exciting event among the local community. The first championship match was in 1952 and Harold Gimblett chose it for his benefit. Predictably he scored a hundred on the second day.

As a ten-year-old I was proudly on the gate for the match with Glamorgan. First through was Peter Walker, and it thrilled me when he stopped to talk to me. To think that one day I'd play against him! I was then only dreaming of a first-class career, so the visit of Freddie Brown's Northants and many famous players captured my imagination.

To me the Morlands ground was a lovely place to play. It had one of the best wickets I had then seen, and it always struck me how well the ground was looked after. I have to admit it saddens me now to see all those supermarket trolleys on the adjoining fairground. But the historic Tor is still there to dominate the landscape.

At last the opportunity came to represent my county on my home ground. I had reason to be pleased with myself in 1972 when, in a John Player League match against Glamorgan, I finished with 6-25. There are many memories, going back to Alan Jones' century even before I was in the side. Nor should I forget the traditional joint dinners at the old George and Pilgrim, a great opportunity for the two teams to get together.

Support for the matches was usually encouraging, and a crowd of 5,000 for a Sunday fixture in 1967 strengthened Glastonbury's case as an out-ground capable of hosting both championship and limited-over matches. I was sorry when in 1973 Morlands went the way of so many out-grounds.

Graham Burgess

1962

Captain: H.W. Stephenson

There were no points for Somerset from their first five matches; then they appeared to take on a new urgency, winning a dozen games to finish in a commendable sixth position.

Once again Alley was the dominant figure, especially as a bowler. That deceptive medium-paced swing and unerring precision in length earned him 112 wickets. Wight remained both prolific and dependable, while Atkinson and Roe gelled at the top of the order. Atkinson pleased his mounting band of fans by passing 2,000 runs. Offsetting that was Palmer's less effective batting after the emerging skills he had shown the previous year. But Greetham was by now winning general approval for his attractive driving through the off side. He passed 1,000 runs for the first time, hinting at more generous statistics to come

Just as a second Atkinson, Colin, the Millfield schoolmaster, was making a quiet impact with his leg-spinners and googlies (7-54 in the win over Gloucestershire), a second Lomax, Ian, a racehorse owner renowned for big hitting on the cricket field, briefly made his appearance in the Somerset team. He delivered fireworks against Hampshire. His 50 came in 22 minutes, and his eventual 83 took just over an hour. Alas, Shackleton then put an end to those precocious liberties, and the county's last pair just failed to secure a famous victory.

In a notable win over Nottinghamshire at Bath, Stephenson scampered his singles while not playing with complete composure for an undefeated 147 in the first innings. Wight, attractive as ever, came along with another hundred in the second. Latham, reverting to off-cutters, was perhaps an unlikely final match-winner with his five cheap wickets. Then came Yorkshire's visit, with Wight reprising his array of strokes to compile a superb double-hundred.

At Weston, Somerset capitulated against the nagging slow left-arm accuracy of Middlesex's Colin Drybrough (6-11 in 46 balls) to go down by an innings. A week later they were then humbled again, this time by Warwickshire's Tom Cartwright, before long to be a Somerset player himself. His 8-39 was altogether too much for the home county. Roe, almost alone, stood firm.

Pleasure at the progress of Somerset has been assuaged by indignation that the selectors continue to spurn Atkinson. Perhaps there is not room for him in the team to tour Australia, but no bowler in the country will agree he is not among the leading 29 as was inferred when MCC published the list to whom availability lists were sent.

Atkinson, however, is a philosophical chap, and the years are still very much on his side.

Ron Roberts,
Playfair Cricket Monthly

COUNTY CHAMPIONSHIP   6th

OTHER MATCHES

Played 32   Won 12   Drawn 13   Lost 7

Played 2   Won 2

BATTING

	M	I	NO	Runs	HS	Ave	100	50	ct	st
P.B. Wight	30	55	9	2030	215	44.13	4	12	29	–
W.E. Alley	33	58	6	1915	155	36.82	3	12	27	–
G. Atkinson	32	61	5	2035	133	36.33	4	10	29	–
C.H.M. Greetham	30	47	4	1151	82	26.76	–	9	12	–
B. Roe	32	61	2	1552	128	26.30	2	9	8	–
H.W. Stephenson	34	47	10	919	147*	24.83	2	2	75	4
J.G. Lomax	25	43	7	865	104*	24.02	1	4	30	–
I.R. Lomax	6	12	0	267	83	22.25	–	1	2	–
B.A. Langford	34	42	11	638	54*	20.58	–	1	21	–
C.R.M. Atkinson	31	45	11	666	69	19.58	–	2	16	–
M.J. Kitchen	17	29	0	518	78	17.86	–	3	5	–
M.E. Latham	15	16	10	96	20*	16.00	–	–	8	–
K.E. Palmer	25	36	7	362	48	12.48	–	–	20	–
R.C. Kerslake	6	9	1	70	23	8.75	–	–	4	–
G.H. Hall	20	23	14	53	12*	5.88	–	–	4	–

(1 match)   A.A. Baig 0, 5   T.I. Barwell 19, 20   P.J. Eele 7, 5 (1 st)
H. Sully 14* (1 ct)

BOWLING

	Overs	Mdns	Runs	Wkts	Ave	5wi	10wm
K.E. Palmer	802.3	201	1908	94	20.29	4	–
W.E. Alley	948.1	254	2323	112	20.74	6	–
C.H.M. Greetham	559	134	1443	69	20.91	3	1
B.A. Langford	1041	370	2423	92	26.33	7	–
M.E. Latham	254	73	663	23	28.82	2	–
G.H. Hall	514	89	1566	46	34.04	–	–
C.R.M. Atkinson	518	119	1584	43	36.83	2	–
J.G. Lomax	204.1	45	564	9	62.66	–	–

P.B. Wight 24.1-8-78-4   I.R. Lomax 14-3-61-0   H. Sully 8-1-29-1
G. Atkinson 3-0-14-0

ROY KERSLAKE 1962 – 1968

The appointment of Roy Kerslake as Somerset skipper in 1968 came as a surprise. He was still a relative novice in terms of championship cricket; the unassuming manner even implied a lack of self-confidence.

On top of that, was he a good enough player in his own right, despite the credentials? In truth he could stroke the ball powerfully for a small man, could spin it notably from the off and could field as well as anyone in the side.

There was a marked resolve beneath the gentle exterior. Even then, he hated the committee politics, which later threatened to stifle him at the time the superstars were at their most super.

As chairman of the cricket committee he was accused of being too close to the players. Maybe he was, occasionally, though above all he was a fair-minded, compassionate man (accident-prone, too, as the team joked when they saw him in his latest plaster cast).

Probably he held more secrets than most concerning the Richards-Garner-Botham departures and, like the good solicitor he was, he kept them to himself.

ROY COSMO KERSLAKE Born Paignton, Devon, 26.12.42. RHB, OB. Cap 1968. Captain 1968. SFC: 52 matches; 946 runs @ 12.28; HS 55 v Essex, Bath, 1968; HT 525 in 1968; 45 wickets @ 24.04; BB 6-83 v Hampshire, Bournemouth, 1964; HT 39 in 1964. Cambridge University 1962-64.

IAN LOMAX 1962

He was seen as a gentleman farmer who trained racehorses. But his prodigious hitting for Wiltshire was equally well known. This towering Old Etonian went on the Surridge tour to Bermuda and the following year essayed county cricket. The experience kept outfielders busy, though it lasted for just half a dozen matches. In cricketing terms, this formidable amateur belonged to an earlier era.

IAN RAYMOND LOMAX Born Fulham, London, 30.7.31. Died 31.7.96. RHB, RFM. SFC: 6 matches; 267 runs @ 22.25; HS 83 v Hampshire, Taunton, 1962; 0 wickets.

MERV KITCHEN'S XI
from the years in which he played

Roy Virgin
Graham Atkinson
Greg Chappell
Brian Close (captain)
Bill Alley
Jim Parks
Ken Palmer
Kerry O'Keeffe
Tom Cartwright
Brian Langford
Fred Rumsey

You have to admit that's quite a line-up. It's so well balanced: strong on its batting and its bowling, fast and slow, and with an inspiring captain. Brian Close had many exceptional qualities. I used to marvel especially at the way he got the best out of everyone. But there was also his wisdom and knowledge of the game. He knew so much about the opposition players.

Roy and Graham provide a reassuring, nostalgic touch at the top of the order. And even if Greg Chappell wasn't around in the West Country for long, we'd seen enough of the 19-year-old to realise what a future he might have. He's my number three, mature beyond his years in those early days, and with so much natural skill for the rest of us to admire.

Then come the two left-handers, Brian Close and Bill Alley. Their inclusion is self-explanatory.

Less straightforward team selection comes when I agonise over my wicketkeeper. My choice of Jim Parks may be something of a surprise, especially as Somerset had two fine classical keepers in my day, Harold Stephenson and Geoff Clayton, followed by the talented Derek Taylor. In the end I plumped for Jim Parks, mainly because of his additional worth as a batsman.

Fred and Kenny would be my new-ball bowlers, with the impeccable Tom Cartwright and Bill Alley in reserve. And I haven't forgotten my spinners. Brian Langford would be there to turn the ball one way and Kerry O'Keeffe the other.

Now what about the 12th man? I'm going for Peter Robinson, remembering the times that Closey used to say to him: 'Go and get me a cup of tea, Robbo!'

1963

Captain: H.W. Stephenson

Rumsey arrived on a special registration from Worcestershire, where he must have felt he wasn't particularly appreciated. His presence, with those fiery left-arm deliveries, gave Somerset an added dimension. He went on to take 520 wickets for the county and play in five Tests. In his first season at Taunton his splendid tally was 102 wickets in all matches.

The pitches were greener than usual – and the big, no-nonsense Rumsey responded excitingly. Palmer did exceptionally well, too, and found himself named in the 12 for the fourth Test against the West Indians. Remarkably he took 139 wickets that summer; only Derek Shackleton and Barry Knight captured more. Against that, Alley's troublesome back restricted his bowling and Lomax had gone. Among those emerging was Kitchen, a sturdy left-hander who went on to hit 17 hundreds for the county.

Somerset ended the season, to the delight of their supporters, in third place. The eventual transfer of the championship pennant to Taunton had not been entirely out of the question. But the closing matches went against them. At the Oval, Atkinson's batting and Palmer's bowling were not enough to prevent a big win by Surrey. Then, at Hove, the weather turned against them and only five minutes play was possible on the last day. By then the title hopes were slipping away and some meaningless end-of-season crawling by Atkinson reflected the county's disappointment.

If Somerset had again planned to bank on Wight, he was out of sorts. Virgin, however, back from National Service, revealed just what he might have to offer in the coming summers. Atkinson had started in the best possible manner with 177 at headquarters, supported solidly by Roe and Virgin. Kerslake, a future captain and chairman, turned up with Cambridge and had a useful match both as a slow bowler and fighting batsman.

In the middle of August, Greetham and Stephenson, two often in a pleasant hurry, created a new record county stand for the ninth wicket, a vibrant 183 in one and three-quarter hours against Leicestershire, to prepare the way for an innings win. Not so easy was the victory over Lancashire in the following fixture, achieved on the fifth ball of the last over.

CHAMPIONSHIP TABLE
28 AUGUST

10 points for a win,

all teams play 28 matches

	Played	Won	Points
Yorkshire	26	12	134
Somerset	26	10	116
Glamorgan	27	10	114
Sussex	26	10	114
Warwickshire	25	10	114

COUNTY CHAMPIONSHIP 3rd

Played 28	Won 10	Drawn 12	Lost 6

OTHER MATCHES

Played 3	Drawn 2	Lost 1

THE KNOCK-OUT COMPETITION

Lost in First Round

BATTING

	M	I	NO	Runs	HS	Ave	100	50	ct	st
G. Atkinson	25	43	2	1454	177	35.46	2	7	15	–
W.E. Alley	25	38	2	1076	105	29.88	1	5	17	–
B. Roe	28	45	2	1235	99	28.72	–	8	8	–
C.H.M. Greetham	30	46	4	1186	141	28.23	1	6	10	–
K.E. Palmer	28	42	15	753	53	27.88	–	1	9	–
P.B. Wight	30	47	3	1074	151	24.40	1	5	22	–
R.T. Virgin	29	47	2	956	105	21.24	1	4	30	–
M.J. Kitchen	17	28	0	535	67	19.10	–	2	7	–
B.A. Langford	30	42	8	611	68	17.97	–	1	17	–
H.W. Stephenson	30	40	5	573	80	16.37	–	3	74	5
R.C. Kerslake	9	16	1	170	31	11.33	–	–	8	–
F.E. Rumsey	26	29	13	154	31	9.62	–	–	21	–
H. Sully	4	4	1	24	24	8.00	–	–	–	–
D.G. Doughty	16	19	5	82	17	5.85	–	–	4	–
G.H. Hall	5	4	1	1	1	0.33	–	–	–	–
B. Lobb	3	3	3	5	4*	–	–	–	1	–

(2 matches) C.R.M. Atkinson (2 ct) did not bat

(1 match) P.J. Eele 4, 103* C.V. Lindo 23* R.K. Paull 13
A.J.G. Pearson 15* (1 ct)

BOWLING

	Overs	Mdns	Runs	Wkts	Ave	5wi	10wm
K.E. Palmer	951.1	278	2030	126	16.11	6	2
D.G. Doughty	214.1	68	635	35	18.14	2	1
W.E. Alley	401	148	758	39	19.43	2	–
F.E. Rumsey	794.1	176	1989	102	19.50	7	2
B.A. Langford	718.2	258	1647	70	23.52	3	1
G.H. Hall	99	13	302	12	25.16	–	–
C.H.M. Greetham	402.1	94	1113	44	25.29	1	–
B. Lobb	120.1	43	262	10	26.20	–	–

R.C. Kerslake 43.3-12-144-0   P.B. Wight 43-7-136-8   A.J.G. Pearson 35-7-102-3
H. Sully 33.1-13-69-3   C.R.M. Atkinson 28-5-82-2   C.V. Lindo 26.1-5-88-8
H.W. Stephenson 1-0-4-0

DAVID DOUGHTY 1963 – 1964

He could never make up his mind whether he wanted to be a professional cricketer or a TV dramatist. His writing was done in the early hours of the morning, as he tried to land his first play. In those days, George Orwell was his literary idol.

But there was also his cricket, of course. At Alf Gover's school slow-left-armer David met Arthur Wellard and discussed a possible move to Somerset. There had already been links with several other counties, including Surrey, Leicestershire and Essex.

He had one marvellous match, snaring 11 victims, against Derbyshire at Weston. Length, and some confidence, drifted away after that.

DAVID GEORGE DOUGHTY Born Chiswick, London, 9.11.37. LHB, SLA. SFC: 17 matches; 104 runs @ 6.93; HS 22 v Australians, Taunton, 1964; 35 wickets @ 20.28; BB 6-58 v Derbyshire, Weston-super-Mare, 1963; HT 35 in 1963. OD: 1 match; 20 runs @ 20.00; 1 wicket @ 31.00.

RICHARD PAULL 1963 – 1964

He was a neat stroke-maker and a prospect. At Millfield the runs had come attractively and he shaped well in the Second XI matches for Somerset. But there were to be just half a dozen first-class outings for the county before he went off and got a blue at Cambridge.

RICHARD KENYON PAULL Born Bridgwater, 20.2.44. RHB. SFC: 6 matches; 104 runs @ 13.00; HS 21* v Sussex, Glastonbury, 1964. Cambridge University 1967.

CLEVELAND LINDO 1963

What more does any man have to do to win a contract? The Jamaican had been recommended and, after a decidedly whippy session in the Taunton nets, he was put straight into the first team against the Pakistan Eaglets. Handed the second new ball, he dismissed five tourists for one run off 21 deliveries. His figures were 8-88; but still he didn't return.

CLEVELAND VINCENT LINDO Born St Elizabeth, Jamaica, 6.6.36. RHB, RFM. SFC: 1 match; 23 runs (no average); HS 23* v Pakistan Eaglets, Taunton, 1963; 8 wickets @ 11.00; BB 8-88 same match. Nottinghamshire 1960.

FRED RUMSEY 1963 – 1968

His value to the county, whatever the whims and extrovert flourish, is seen even better at this distance. At Worcestershire Fred had done little of note, squeezed out by regular fast bowlers Jack Flavell and Len Coldwell. So he came to Somerset, on special registration, and astonished most people – especially those from his former county – by taking 100 wickets in his first Taunton-based campaign. Before long he was making five Test appearances and arguably deserving more.

Here was a real fast bowler, left-arm at that, who could make some batsmen quake. He needed to be used in shortish bursts, to be handled intelligently on and off the field, to be appreciated for the vision he often imparted to the conversation. During his six years with Somerset the girth broadened and the arm got lower. The expanse of the heart, though, seldom lessened. Rumsey and Palmer, in tandem with the new ball, gave the county hope.

The ideas kept pace with the wicked deliveries. He spoke up for professional sportsmen and was the man behind the formation of the Cricketers' Association in 1967. For a short time he helped Somerset with their public relations, before extending the role with Derbyshire. Then followed a burgeoning career in travel and corporate hospitality. It should be added that Fred liked to dine well himself.

FREDERICK EDWARD RUMSEY Born Stepney, London, 4.12.35. RFB, LF. Cap 1963. 5 Tests 1964-65. SFC: 153 matches; 766 runs @ 7.66; HS 45 v Sussex, Weston-super-Mare, 1967; HT 154 in 1963; 520 wickets @ 19.78; BB 8-26 v Hampshire, Bath, 1965; 100 wickets twice; HT 102 in 1963. OD: 15 matches; 9 runs @ 4.50; 30 wickets @ 11.36. Worcestershire 1960-62; Derbyshire 1970.

Fred was quick, much quicker than anybody before him at Somerset. And he swung it. Kenny Palmer used to say, 'We suddenly realised that some of the batsmen we played weren't quite as good as we thought they were.'
Peter Robinson

1964

Captain: H.W. Stephenson

The season was something of an anti-climax, not easy to understand because Somerset had more or less the same players available as in 1963 when they were not far off the elusive title. Only once did they sniff victory in their first six weeks, and they had to wait until July before they started to hit a semblance of form to placate restive members. Wight broke a finger and lost his touch; Roe forfeited his place, leaving Virgin to step up to partner Atkinson who was, at times, looking strangely inhibited at the wicket.

Now Stephenson was 44 and his career, especially as a nimble and intuitive wicket keeper, was coming to an end, certainly in the committee's opinion. He was struggling with injury and Alley was taking over regularly as deputy captain. But the county were missing the north-easterner's infectious approach and, despite Eele's efficiency when he took over behind the stumps, Somerset were starting their search for another experienced keeper. Amid the unrewarding matches there were meritorious performances – like Langford's display of off-spin, yet again at Bath, this time against Gloucestershire. When Nottinghamshire came to Taunton, Alley's tight bowling on the first day was significant; so was Virgin's century-making. A buoyant run, with wins against Essex, Worcestershire, Leicestershire and Sussex, only reminded Somerset what they should have been capable of achieving.

The Clarence Park pitch was at its most testing when Surrey came and were beaten by seven wickets in two days. Inevitably it was Langford in charge, claiming ten wickets from the match with the kind of loop that, in another decade, would surely have taken him into the England side. In that fixture with Surrey, 20 wickets fell on the second day.

COUNTY CHAMPIONSHIP   8th

Played 28	Won 8	Drawn 12	Lost 8

OTHER MATCHES   Played 1   Lost 1

GILLETTE CUP   Lost in Third Round

BATTING

	M	I	NO	Runs	HS	Ave	100	50	ct	st
W.E. Alley	29	47	3	1332	140	30.27	1	6	25	–
G. Atkinson	28	47	1	1207	75	26.23	–	9	18	–
T.I. Barwell	10	18	3	384	68	25.60	–	3	7	–
P.B. Wight	18	26	6	504	87	25.20	–	4	22	–
R.T. Virgin	29	49	3	1157	102	25.15	2	4	36	–
K.E. Palmer	29	42	12	734	77*	24.46	–	5	14	–
M.J. Kitchen	25	39	2	774	98	20.91	–	4	11	–
B.A. Langford	28	40	8	571	51	17.84	–	1	17	–
H.W. Stephenson	3	5	0	87	57	17.40	–	1	5	–
B. Roe	19	31	2	504	121*	17.37	1	1	7	–
C.H.M. Greetham	24	34	2	504	52	15.75	–	1	16	–
R.K. Paull	5	8	1	91	21*	13.00	–	–	–	–
P.J. Eele	26	30	13	201	23*	11.82	–	–	42	5
F.E. Rumsey	22	26	12	137	38	9.78	–	–	19	–
R.C. Kerslake	13	19	0	181	44	9.52	–	–	4	–
F.T. Willetts	3	5	0	33	16	6.60	–	–	–	–
G.H. Hall	5	3	1	2	2*	1.00	–	–	–	–

(1 match)   D.G. Doughty 22 (2 ct)   J.D. Martin 0* (1 ct)   R.T. Robinson 0, 0

BOWLING

	Overs	Mdns	Runs	Wkts	Ave	5wi	10wm
F.E. Rumsey	668	154	1518	78	19.46	3	–
B.A. Langford	972.2	379	2059	105	19.60	7	3
K.E. Palmer	956.1	271	2085	104	20.04	7	–
R.C. Kerslake	339.3	122	813	39	20.84	2	–
W.E. Alley	650.4	213	1365	64	21.32	4	–
G.H. Hall	82.2	20	218	7	31.14	–	–
P.B. Wight	65	23	162	4	40.50	–	–
C.H.M. Greetham	261.4	70	689	17	40.52	–	–

J.D. Martin 32-5-96-3   D.G. Doughty 12-0-75-0   R.T. Virgin 5.5-0-30-0
G. Atkinson 1-0-1-0

RAY ROBINSON 1964

One match, in which he didn't trouble the scorer. Better known as the Taunton and Somerset rugby player and father of England coach, Andy.

RAYMOND THOMAS ROBINSON Born Charmouth, Dorset, 15.9.40. Died 13.11.2001. RHB. SFC: 1 match; 0 runs.

TERRY WILLETTS 1964 – 1967

Went close to establishing himself both as a professional cricketer and footballer. His value, as a left-hander, was confined mostly to Somerset's Second XI, but he is well remembered for his sharp reflexes fielding close to the wicket.

FRANK TERENCE WILLETTS Born Birmingham, 20.11.39. LHB. SFC: 16 matches; 333 runs @ 11.10; HS 38 v Glamorgan, Weston-super-Mare, 1965; HT 165 in 1965. OD: 3 matches; 27 runs @ 9.00.

JOHN MARTIN 1964 – 1965

He had the fast bowler's build and picked up plenty of wickets to complement his three blues at Oxford. The good-natured story that persists is of the Minor Counties match when the Somerset seamers were hammered mercilessly in the morning session. Bill Andrews, in charge of the team, had gone to the nearby Ring o' Bells for a refresher and when he returned to the ground he said over lunch to the surprised undergraduate: 'Let's admit it, John – you were bowling some rubbish out there.' The reply was: 'But I haven't bowled yet.' To which Bill, never lost for words, came back: 'Don't argue with me!'

JOHN DONALD MARTIN Born Oxford, 23.12.41. RHB, RFM. SFC: 2 matches; 0 runs; 3 wickets @ 43.00; BB 3-59 v Hampshire, Taunton, 1964. Oxford University 1962-65.

JOHNSON PARK, YEOVIL

Here I made my tentative debut as a writer on county cricket. It was May 1951 and Notts were the visitors. My report was short, factual and grimly soulless. There was no press box as such; the row of apprentice scribes sat self-consciously in faded pre-war deckchairs. At one point I joined a queue for the autograph of an emerging celebrity: not Joe Hardstaff but John Arlott. He was positioned alongside the big, seemingly glamorous BBC outside-broadcast van.

The handsome Hardstaff made a century. For Somerset, I remember, the comically obdurate Bertie Buse found an unlikely partner in Jim Redman with a meritorious last-wicket stand to hold up Notts.

Johnson Park wasn't a pretty ground but it was the nearest to my home, and I treasured it as if it were Lord's. It had been dogged by drainage problems, the result of previously being undulating agricultural land. Yeovil's annual fixture was usually early in the season when rain was apt to limit the crowds – and drench those who hunted in vain for shelter.

Up to the final annual fixture there in 1967, there were only two wins for Somerset, a disappointing return for the loyal support in that part of the county. It was perhaps more justified as a public-relations exercise than as a source of income. But members still talk graphically of Peter Wight's exquisite 164 not out in 1962 – just as some of them were to express their surprise when the Aussie spinner John McMahon left the county abruptly, not so long after one wonderful demonstration of his cunning craft with an eight-wicket haul against Kent at Johnson Park.

The ground's demise as a county venue was probably inevitable. After two limited-overs games there – one when Brian Langford created his unbeatable record by sending down eight overs without conceding a run – Yeovil staged various one-day fixtures at the Westlands Sports ground, where a 5,000 crowd was not unknown.

David Foot

1965

Captain: C.R.M. Atkinson

Just for a fleeting, romantic moment, in early June, Somerset were on top of the championship table. By the end of the summer they were seventh. Colin Atkinson was now the captain, a choice that pleased some of the professionals, if not Alley, who had expected, reasonably enough, to be appointed after the way he had deputised for Stephenson. But Alley, his own man and loquacious by nature, was at times more loved by the crowds than fellow occupants of the dressing room. He had dropped Langford on one occasion and he was aware that not every member of the team, however much they admired his cricketing qualities, wanted him to lead them.

In some ways the new skipper was an old-style amateur. He was also a fighter, making himself a better player than he really was and he was bitterly disappointed when arthritis in his hand forced him to give up leg-spin and move on to seamers.

Injuries to Rumsey, Palmer and Wight complicated team selection. There was a new stumper, Clayton, who had left Lancashire abruptly. He possessed a strong independent streak – and outstanding talents behind the stumps. He ended the season with 85 victims and scored a maiden century after going in as night-watchman against Middlesex. In that same game Greetham fashioned an aggressive hundred as Somerset came out on top by nine wickets. Greetham was also memorably dynamic in the fixture with Cambridge at Taunton. He walked to the wicket 45 minutes before the close of play on the first day, promptly bludgeoning six sixes and seven fours in an undefeated 73; next morning he drove three more boundaries before being out seven short of his hundred.

Bath presented a travesty of a pitch and it was all over by early afternoon on the second day, Somerset beating Worcestershire by an innings. In the next match there, Hampshire were bowled out for 64 and 77. Rumsey returned 8-26 in the first innings, Alley 6-40 in the second.

One noteworthy newcomer was Groves, from Oxford University. Several of his innings were lively and good-looking, but he was never going to stay for long.

Colin Atkinson was their new captain. He was trying to smarten them up, to make Somerset very un-Somerset-like. With Bill Alley there, I think he struggled a bit.

Mick Norman,
Northamptonshire

COUNTY CHAMPIONSHIP 7th

OTHER MATCHES

GILLETTE CUP

Played 28   Won 8   Drawn 9   Lost 11

Played 2   Won 1   Drawn 1

Lost in Third Round

BATTING

	M	I	NO	Runs	HS	Ave	100	50	ct	st
G. Atkinson	30	50	5	1431	117	31.80	1	9	11	–
K.E. Palmer	10	15	5	308	83*	30.80	–	2	8	–
R.T. Virgin	29	48	2	1234	125*	26.82	2	5	29	–
T.I. Barwell	5	9	1	197	84*	24.62	–	2	4	–
M.G.M. Groves	7	13	0	305	86	23.46	–	3	7	–
C.H.M. Greetham	30	48	5	943	115*	21.93	2	3	13	–
P.B. Wight	12	21	1	429	65	21.45	–	3	8	–
W.E. Alley	29	48	6	861	110	20.50	1	3	20	–
M.J. Kitchen	13	19	0	307	80	16.15	–	2	3	–
G. Clayton	29	41	5	581	106	16.13	1	2	71	14
F.T. Willetts	6	11	0	165	38	15.00	–	–	3	–
C.R.M. Atkinson	29	36	6	426	50*	14.20	–	1	11	–
P.J. Robinson	22	27	9	217	37	12.05	–	–	16	–
B. Roe	11	15	0	172	35	11.46	–	–	4	–
B.A. Langford	29	36	8	231	31	8.25	–	–	9	–
F.E. Rumsey	21	26	7	131	42	6.89	–	–	15	–
G.H. Hall	14	15	7	23	6*	2.87	–	–	5	–

(2 matches)   R. Palmer 5*, 1*, 5

(1 match)   P.J. Eele 10 (3 ct, 3 st)   J.D. Martin did not bat

BOWLING

	Overs	Mdns	Runs	Wkts	Ave	5wi	10wm
F.E. Rumsey	622.4	180	1422	96	14.81	7	1
W.E. Alley	774	273	1525	76	20.06	1	–
K.E. Palmer	334	104	830	37	22.43	2	1
P.J. Robinson	467.2	176	1036	44	23.54	1	–
B.A. Langford	913.4	386	1890	80	23.62	5	1
C.R.M. Atkinson	402.5	141	905	38	23.81	1	–
G.H. Hall	429.4	130	1004	41	24.48	2	–

R. Palmer 48-14-138-6   C.H.M. Greetham 27-6-78-2   J.D. Martin 16-5-33-0

P.B. Wight 2-2-0-0   G. Atkinson 1-1-0-0   R.T. Virgin 1-1-0-0

PETER ROBINSON 1965 – 1978

There were too many similar bowlers at Worcestershire so Peter Robinson decided it made sense to move to Somerset, for whom he took nearly 300 first-class wickets and, with an efficient if restricted repertoire of strokes, accumulated three hundreds.

He was the nephew of Roly Jenkins, who passed on humour, wisdom and the craftsmanship of the slow bowler's trade. Peter could be relied upon to pitch the ball with precision, a nagger that batsmen forced away with difficulty.

Like many an honest and perhaps modestly rewarded bowler, he enjoyed batting and could occupy the crease with unspectacular though timely virtue. His place in the order would vary disconcertingly. He could even open the innings if necessary with doughty resolve, as he did in the 1967 Gillette final against Kent.

He was not far short of becoming a professional footballer; he played outstandingly for Worcester City, then later Taunton Town, and although he was by then well into his twenties, Bristol City once showed distinct interest.

Peter went on to guide and encourage many Second XI players and become the most conscientious of coaches for Somerset. The dry sense of fun and stream of non-malicious stories about his team-mates earned him attentive audiences, not least among the dozens of young cricketers he coached and advised with paternal skill.

PETER JAMES ROBINSON Born Worcester, 9.2.43. LHB, SLA. Cap 1966. SFC: 180 matches; 4887 runs @ 21.52; 3 centuries; HS 140 v Northamptonshire, Northampton, 1970; 1000 runs once; HT 1158 in 1970; 291 wickets @ 27.38; BB 7-10 v Nottinghamshire, Trent Bridge, 1966; HT 70 in 1966. OD: 63 matches; 964 runs @ 22.41; 8 wickets @ 12.87. Worcestershire 1963-64.

It used to leak like a sieve in the old pavilion. We had a bucket catching the drips. And an old gas fire. I've even sat in the bath with rat poison by the holes. I'm probably one of the few who's glad it's been kept. It's part of Taunton for me, that.
Peter Robinson

A square peg in a round hole, if ever there was one.
Mrs Robinson on her husband's time as the club's health and safety co-ordinator

GEOFF CLAYTON 1965 – 1967

There is a case to be made out that here was, technically, one of the best wicketkeepers to play for the county, a canny replacement for the talented Harold Stephenson. But then we come to temperament.

'Chimp' had left Lancashire in not the most cordial of circumstances. In Somerset he rarely courted popularity and certainly antagonised some by the cussed individuality of his personality.

He was never one to kowtow; team-mates and observers detected the chip that was reluctant to leave his shoulder. He was, in the modern idiom, his own man. Colin Atkinson claimed he was once so annoyed by Clayton's go-slow attitude in a match that he threatened to send him off.

In spite of all that the Lancastrian was, as all the players acknowledged readily, a fine wicket-keeper.

GEOFFREY CLAYTON Born Mossley, Lancashire, 3.2.38. RHB, WK. Cap 1965. SFC: 89 matches; 1744 runs @ 14.77; 1 century; HS 106 v Middlesex, Taunton, 1965; HT 620 in 1966; 242 dismissals (209 ct, 33 st). OD: 12 matches; 87 runs @ 12.42; 24 dismissals (22 ct, 2 st). Lancashire 1959-64.

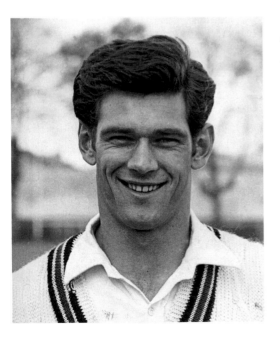

ROY PALMER 1965 – 1970

The taller brother of Ken was a useful man to have around in a one-day game, as he demonstrated with a Sunday hat-trick, the final three deliveries, against Gloucestershire at Bristol. He saved his best championship cricket for Lord's.

Once at Bath he ran into trouble for seam-picking. 'He wasn't in the same class as Ken,' joked a contemporary mischievously. Roy went on to become a successful umpire. What was that expression about poachers and gamekeepers?

ROY PALMER Born Devizes, Wiltshire, 12.7.42. RHB, RFM. Cap 1969. SFC: 74 matches; 1037 runs @ 13.29; HS 84 v Leicestershire, Taunton, 1967; HT 275 in 1968; 172 wickets @ 31.62; BB 6-45 v Middlesex, Lord's, 1967; HT 60 in 1969. OD: 43 matches; 198 runs @ 8.25; 67 wickets @ 22.31; GC MoM 2. Fc umpire 1980-.

MIKE GROVES 1965

There was a small lobby of opinion to make him captain, after Roy Kerslake and instead of Brian Langford. He had an impressive Oxford cricket pedigree behind him, associations with the Free Foresters and an amiable manner which bridged the remnants of the amateur-pro divide. An assertive batsman, lively medium-pacer and alert fielder.

MICHAEL GODFREY MELVIN GROVES Born Taihap, New Zealand, 14,1,43. RHB, RM. SFC: 7 matches; 305 runs @ 23.46; HS 86 v Derbyshire, Glastonbury, 1965. Western Province, South Africa, 1960-61; Oxford University 1963-66.

Training on the first day back, 1 April 1963
Peter Wight, Fred Rumsey, Haydn Sully, Mervyn Kitchen, Ken Palmer, Peter Eele, Chris Greetham

1966

Captain: C.R.M. Atkinson

Somerset won 13 championship matches, more than ever before in a season. They were playing with a new-found assurance; their current record was quite a talking point, nationally. They also finished in third position in the table, equalling their highest so far. Colin Atkinson had grown in authority and confidence as the skipper, passing his 1,000 runs for the first and only time to reinforce his quiet value. The balance in the team was encouraging, too. Three bowlers – Langford, Rumsey and Palmer – took more than 100 wickets.

When it was time for Bath, it was time for the spinners cannily to do their stuff on a wearing track. Langford and Robinson, off-spin and slow left-arm, took 18 wickets between them against Gloucestershire and 19 against Surrey. Among the batsmen, Kitchen was emerging usefully at number three. Against the trends at Clarence Park, Graham Atkinson and Virgin confirmed their opening status with an unbroken second-innings stand of 178 as Somerset cruised to a ten-wicket win over Sussex.

There was an aura of optimism around the boundary, traditionally in the case of Somerset a dangerous characteristic. Seam and spin succeeded in reliable rotation. Virgin kept picking up his catches close to the crease. Kitchen and Robinson were awarded their caps for discernible progress. Langford, teasingly on a length, took his 1,000th wicket, at Glastonbury. And there was a determined run in the Gillette Cup before going out in the semi-finals.

Big Fred Rumsey would have a few pints of cider in the evening, and he used to sweat profusely. I would be fielding bat-pad at short leg, and Bill Alley would be in the gully. With those great bucket hands of his. 'Look at the big tart,' Bill would say. 'He's knackered already. He's only been going three overs. Look at him there.' And Fred would start, 'Is he talking about me? What's he saying?' Bill used to call him Myrtle. 'Well bowled, Myrtle. You're going well. Keep going.' Then he'd turn to us. 'Look at him. I'll be on in three overs.'

Peter Robinson

COUNTY CHAMPIONSHIP   3rd

Played 28	Won 13	Drawn 8	Lost 7

OTHER MATCHES   Played 2   Won 1   Drawn 1

GILLETTE CUP   Lost in Semi-Final

BATTING

	M	I	NO	Runs	HS	Ave	100	50	ct	st
M.J. Kitchen	30	54	3	1422	111*	27.88	2	7	16	–
C.R.M. Atkinson	30	52	9	1120	89	26.04	–	7	11	–
G. Atkinson	30	55	2	1307	148	24.66	2	5	3	–
R.T. Virgin	30	55	1	1328	98	24.59	–	6	42	–
K.E. Palmer	29	49	10	898	118	23.02	1	2	20	–
W.E. Alley	30	51	3	1104	115	23.00	2	4	26	–
G.I. Burgess	13	21	1	406	69	20.30	–	2	7	–
P.J. Robinson	27	41	12	515	66	17.75	–	1	32	–
A. Clarkson	9	16	1	234	74*	15.60	–	1	5	–
T.I. Barwell	5	10	0	144	56	14.40	–	1	4	–
G. Clayton	30	50	5	620	63	13.77	–	2	74	10
B. Roe	4	8	0	102	32	12.75	–	–	3	–
B.A. Langford	28	37	14	222	55*	9.65	–	1	12	–
F.E. Rumsey	28	31	17	90	18*	6.42	–	–	8	–
C.H.M. Greetham	3	6	0	38	19	6.33	–	–	1	–
R. Palmer	3	4	1	11	5	3.66	–	–	–	–

(1 match)   F.T. Willetts 7, 6

BOWLING

	Overs	Mdns	Runs	Wkts	Ave	5wi	10wm
B.A. Langford	1026.4	438	1971	112	17.59	8	3
K.E. Palmer	717.1	148	1935	107	18.08	7	–
F.E. Rumsey	798	196	1889	100	18.89	4	–
W.E. Alley	519	170	1015	50	20.30	2	–
P.J. Robinson	694.3	287	1499	70	21.41	5	1
C.R.M. Atkinson	137.1	34	359	14	25.64	1	–
R. Palmer	78.4	16	241	9	26.77	–	–

G.I. Burgess 44.4-7-146-0   C.H.M. Greetham 7-3-14-2

TONY CLARKSON 1966 – 1971

Somerset and Gloucestershire fought over him when he came down from his native Yorkshire, where he played a handful of championship matches, to pursue an engineering career with Bath City Council. In the event, he integrated easily at Taunton and at times he opened the Somerset innings with considerable resolve.

Tony was able to show a straight bat or chase a Sunday League century. Later it was back to the leagues and featuring for the local clubs he used to know so well. After that he worked as an architectural and civil engineering design consultant – a title almost as long as one of his worthy innings – before returning to first-class cricket as an umpire.

ANTHONY CLARKSON Born Killinghall, Yorkshire, 5.9.39. RHB, OB. Cap 1968. SFC: 104 matches; 4378 runs @ 25.75; 2 centuries; HS 131 v Northamptonshire, Northampton, 1969; 1000 runs twice; HT 1246 in 1970; 8 wickets @ 34.37; BB 3-51 v Essex, Yeovil, 1967. OD: 50 matches; 762 runs @ 16.93; 2 wickets @ 31. Yorkshire 1963. Fc umpire 1996-.

MOST POST-WAR APPEARANCES FOR SOMERSET

First-class cricket		Limited-over cricket	
BA Langford	504	PW Denning	280
HW Stephenson	427	GD Rose	280
MF Tremlett	353	PM Roebuck	277
MJ Kitchen	352	DJS Taylor	261
WE Alley	350	RJ Harden	252
PB Wight	321	BC Rose	251
RT Virgin	321	VJ Marks	250
PM Roebuck	306	IT Botham	230
KE Palmer	302	IVA Richards	218
J Lawrence	281	RJ Turner	217
DJS Taylor	280	HR Moseley	210
VJ Marks	275	CH Dredge	209

GRAHAM BURGESS
1966 – 1979

It's hard to think that 'Budgie' could have played for any other county. He is authentic Somerset by birth and he looks like a farmer. The voice belongs unmistakably to Glastonbury and, as for the shoulders, they are broad and well made for the belting of a cricket ball.

In fact, although he could hit sixes, and often did so advantageously in the one-day matches, he could also score rapidly with the most controlled of off-drives. Yet like so many of the county's prized yeomen performers down the decades, he was apt to be inconsistent, sometimes selecting the wrong ball for the swipe.

His bowling, off the most languid of runs, in keeping with his unflurried persona, was a valued bonus. According to wicketkeeper Derek Taylor, Burgess could swing the ball both ways.

At Millfield, where his cricket was nurtured, he also played second-row for the 1st XV and took the kicks. He sampled Western League soccer as a winger, was a junior table-tennis champion and a hockey player of county potential. But cricket, for the easy-going Burgess, was the favourite sport of all. After giving up playing, he coached the boys at Monmouth and then became a first-class umpire.

GRAHAM IEFVION BURGESS Born Glastonbury, Somerset, 5.5.43. RHB, RM. Cap 1968. SFC: 252 matches; 7129 runs @ 18.90; 2 centuries; HS 129 v Gloucestershire, Taunton, 1973; HT 866 in 1970; 474 wickets @ 28.57; BB 7-43 v Oxford University, The Parks, 1975; HT 56 in 1970. OD: 207 matches; 3130 runs @ 20.06; 247 wickets @ 25.08; GC MoM 2. Fc umpire 1991-.

1967

Captain: C.R.M. Atkinson

The summer was remembered, of course, for the county's first Gillette Cup final at Lord's. It's debatable whether the showpiece occasion ever created a more convivial regional atmosphere. Somerset's supporters, joyfully and noisily in evidence among the 20,000 crowd, came in their farming smocks and war-paint. Their incessant banter was rustic and good-humoured, though not, one imagines, entirely to the liking of headquarters' haughtier and more traditional cricketing residents. For the West Country visitors, only one thing spoilt their day – Somerset lost to Kent by 32 runs. That was despite the wholehearted bowling of Alley, Palmer and Rumsey, as Kent were stopped in their tracks for a time, with six wickets going down for 21 runs.

Yet on the somewhat more mundane level of the championship, Somerset fared less well, slipping to eighth in the table. Too often they batted badly; the bowlers, so lethal the previous year, were now less effective. The county got off to an indeterminate start and never properly recovered. They had to wait till June at Bath for their first victory, against Yorkshire, who were without Brian Close, Geoff Boycott and Ray Illingworth, all on Test duty. Somerset went on to win, again at Bath, by an innings against Northants.

Atkinson's captaincy suffered, however, partly because of injury. He was to step down and return to his teaching commitments at Millfield at the end of the season. Clayton, although still keeping efficiently, was also on his way. From this unpredictable season, there remained individual feats to cherish – like the stroke-play of Tom Graveney, Alley and Basil D'Oliveira, in turn, at Glastonbury.

Somerset versus Kent, Gillette Cup, Lord's, September 2

This was a Cup Final, no mistake.

The contingent from Somerset with their pitchforks, straw and barrels of cider won the hearts of the crowd. Never before has there been such an atmosphere prevailing at Lord's as there was on this sunlit September day.

Gordon Ross,
Playfair Cricket Monthly

COUNTY CHAMPIONSHIP 8th

Played 28   Won 5   Drawn 16   Lost 7

OTHER MATCHES

Played 2   Drawn 1   Lost 1

GILLETTE CUP

Lost in Final

BATTING

	M	I	NO	Runs	HS	Ave	100	50	ct	st
W.E. Alley	28	46	4	1244	136	29.61	1	7	27	–
R.T. Virgin	30	52	2	1440	162	28.80	3	4	25	–
M.J. Kitchen	28	48	3	1279	189	28.42	2	4	15	–
T.I. Barwell	11	19	4	410	74*	27.33	–	3	13	–
P.J. Robinson	28	43	8	917	97	26.20	–	4	38	–
A. Clarkson	14	22	2	522	95	26.10	–	2	1	–
K.E. Palmer	28	45	7	893	94*	23.50	–	3	14	–
R. Palmer	12	15	2	239	84	18.38	–	1	4	–
G.I. Burgess	27	47	3	806	65	18.31	–	5	12	–
C.R.M. Atkinson	27	42	1	721	97	17.58	–	3	13	–
B.A. Langford	29	39	11	416	50*	14.85	–	1	9	–
G. Clayton	30	43	6	543	61	14.67	–	1	64	9
F.T. Willetts	6	12	0	122	29	10.16	–	–	1	–
F.E. Rumsey	29	35	17	151	45	8.38	–	–	8	–

(2 matches)   L.M.L. Barnwell 60, 0, 2 (1 ct)
(1 match)   B. Lobb 0*

BOWLING

	Overs	Mdns	Runs	Wkts	Ave	5wi	10wm
W.E. Alley	611.5	214	1166	59	19.76	2	–
K.E. Palmer	663.4	159	1709	84	20.34	5	–
G.I. Burgess	211.5	47	588	26	22.61	–	–
F.E. Rumsey	687.4	161	1739	72	24.15	5	1
R. Palmer	235.4	44	787	29	27.13	1	–
B.A. Langford	973.2	387	2101	77	27.28	4	–
P.J. Robinson	600.1	185	1730	62	27.90	3	–

A. Clarkson 34-9-114-7   C.R.M. Atkinson 28.1-6-75-1   B. Lobb 18.1-6-39-1
R.T. Virgin 8-1-46-1   M.J. Kitchen 2-0-9-0

MICHAEL BARNWELL 1967 – 1968

Nephew of John. Useful all-rounder at school and university level; not a bad footballer, either, with a blue at Cambridge. His half-dozen matches for Somerset, during which he opened the innings, never quite lived up to the warm recommendations that preceded his arrival.

LIONEL MICHAEL LOWRY BARNWELL Born Crewkerne, Somerset, 12.8.43. RHB, RM. SFC: 6 matches; 144 runs @ 16.00; HS 60 v Nottinghamshire, Trent Bridge, 1967. Cambridge University 1965-66; Eastern Province, South Africa, 1969-71.

Drink up thy Zider
Somerset supporters at the Gillette Cup Final

PETER DENNING'S XI
from the years in which he played

Sunil Gavaskar
Brian Rose
Viv Richards
Greg Chappell
Martin Crowe
Ian Botham
Derek Taylor
Ken Palmer
Tom Cartwright
Kerry O'Keeffe
Joel Garner

These players pick themselves; they are all world-class performers. Ten of them played Test cricket and the only one who didn't, wicket-keeper Derek Taylor, certainly deserved to. I reckon he would have done, too, if he had played for a more fashionable county. Maybe he should have stayed at Surrey!

One I would have liked to have included, one who might have surprised a few people, was the fast bowler David Gurr. He was a lad who never fulfilled his vast potential. Had he done so, then certainly he would have been worthy of opening the bowling with Joel Garner. He had the basic ingredients of an England player but somehow never got it together.

I was tempted to name another spinner who could bat, such as Jeremy Lloyds, whose off-breaks turned a mighty long way, but I ran out of places. Another who popped to mind was Julian Wyatt, a classy batsman who I recall taking on Malcolm Marshall, and it doesn't sit quite comfortably with me that I didn't squeeze in Brian Close, who deserves so much credit for transforming Somerset from just another county into a team genuinely contesting major prizes.

Similarly I feel a bit guilty for leaving out some of the lads who helped to break Somerset's trophy duck, the likes of Vic Marks, Peter Roebuck, Graham Burgess and Colin Dredge, while Merv Kitchen deserves a mention, too.

I realise that I might have included more home-grown players, but I have stuck to my instructions and picked the best eleven available, which made the overseas options impossible to resist.

In the end, I'm content that my fantasy team would more than hold its own against all-comers. We're talking here about fabulous cricketers, and they're all decent lads, too.

1968

Captain: R.C. Kerslake

Members were left shaking their heads as the strains and inconsistencies of the summer were finally reflected in a depressing late-season series of defeats. The descent in the championship table had continued. Too many players had patently struggled for a semblance of their true form. Injuries and illness, especially in the case of Palmer, compounded the uncertainties of team selection. And worse, some of the older players were revealing less agility in the field. Changes appeared to be on the way. But any wayward fielding was offset by the arrival of Chappell, a teenage Australian with an upright stature and neat array of shots. Just as relevant, he pleasingly patrolled the covers with a lithe presence and a safe pair of hands.

It wasn't a good time for Kerslake to take over as captain. He was injured before the opening fixture and didn't come back till June. In his quiet manner he was a popular figure. He was a sharp, proficient fielder but his qualities of leadership were apt to suffer from a nature which was too self-effacing.

Rumsey and Langford were the best of the bowlers, Kitchen and Virgin the pick of the batsmen. The versatile Robinson deservedly came up with his first hundred. But morale, in the dressing room and among the members, was understandably shaky. Changes in personnel were inevitable. Rumsey was retiring and the controversial offer of only one-day matches for Alley, coming up to 50 and still much admired around the ground, met with a snort and rapid rejection by the craggy, plain-speaking Aussie.

I always enjoyed playing against Somerset. Win, lose or draw, they neither moaned nor gloated and, a key point in any assessment, they never seemed all that averse to a glass or two.

David Green

COUNTY CHAMPIONSHIP   12th   Played 27   Won 5   Drawn 11   Lost 11

OTHER MATCHES   Played 2   Drawn 2

GILLETTE CUP   Lost in Second Round

BATTING

	M	I	NO	Runs	HS	Ave	100	50	ct	st
M.J. Kitchen	29	53	5	1730	161*	36.04	5	4	11	–
R.T. Virgin	29	53	5	1641	115*	34.18	1	11	25	–
G.S. Chappell	27	47	8	1163	148	29.82	1	7	11	–
W.E. Alley	29	49	4	1219	110	27.08	1	6	14	–
P.J. Robinson	23	33	6	718	102	26.59	1	3	30	–
A. Clarkson	10	18	0	425	82	23.61	–	4	4	–
R. Palmer	13	19	5	275	32	19.64	–	–	4	–
R.C. Kerslake	24	37	2	525	55	15.00	–	1	34	–
K.E. Palmer	16	22	1	313	76	14.90	–	3	1	–
G.I. Burgess	23	41	2	550	57	14.10	–	2	12	–
B.A. Langford	29	41	8	454	37	13.75	–	–	10	–
L.M.L. Barnwell	4	7	1	82	45*	13.66	–	–	–	–
R.A. Brooks	26	33	15	182	37	10.11	–	–	48	5
T.I. Barwell	8	13	0	116	49	8.92	–	–	4	–
F.E. Rumsey	27	29	10	103	31	5.42	–	–	7	–

(2 matches)   C.E.P. Carter 1, 0, 0, 0 (4 ct)

BOWLING

	Overs	Mdns	Runs	Wkts	Ave	5wi	10wm
F.E. Rumsey	639	156	1732	72	24.05	2	–
B.A. Langford	746.4	268	1781	70	25.44	5	–
G.S. Chappell	222.2	56	712	26	27.38	–	–
G.I. Burgess	550.3	121	1572	53	29.66	1	–
P.J. Robinson	388.5	114	1192	40	29.80	–	–
R. Palmer	271.1	60	850	28	30.35	–	–
W.E. Alley	523.5	184	1229	36	34.13	–	–
K.E. Palmer	228.1	39	790	19	41.57	–	–

R.C. Kerslake 39.4-11-125-6   M.J. Kitchen 3.3-0-27-0   R.T. Virgin 3-0-17-0
A. Clarkson 1-1-0-1

GREG CHAPPELL
1968 – 1969

What else is there to write about one of Australia's most richly talented captains? These were exploratory days with Somerset, where he came as a 19-year-old to work out for himself the vagaries of our green seamers' wickets and, in just two years, to broaden his cricketing education at the most pragmatic of universities.

If Somerset seemingly took a chance in bringing this slim, unknown lad over, he rewarded them with some astonishingly mature skills. Those who watched him at work admired his dedication and the rapidity with which he learned to avoid the pitfalls. His style was gracefully upright and Graham Burgess used to remark: 'When Greg goes out to bat, he reminds me of a captain of the Guards.'

He scored the first hundred in the Sunday League (captured on TV), at times batted as though he had been around for years, and gave up bowling spinners himself in favour of balls that moved through the air. Greg Chappell's influence rubbed off on others, and Somerset would have liked him to hang around longer.

GREGORY STEPHEN CHAPPELL Born Adelaide, South Australia, 7.8.48. RHB, RM/LB. Cap 1968. 87 Tests 1970-83. 74 LOI 1971-83. SFC: 52 matches; 2493 runs @ 30.03; 3 centuries; HS 148 v Middlesex, Weston-super-Mare, 1968; 1000 runs twice; HT 1330 in 1969; 71 wickets @ 27.70; BB 7-40 v Yorkshire, Headingley, 1969; HT 45 in 1969. OD: 17 matches; 476 runs @ 34.00; 23 wickets @ 18.43. South Australia 1966-73; Queensland, Australia, 1973-84.

Some of his ways, like going barefoot in the pavilions and his penchant for outrageous clothing, raised an eyebrow or two at Taunton, Bath and Weston, but he was recognised as basically 'a good guy'. The disappointment was great when he decided to call it a day at the end of his second season.

Peter Walker

DICKIE BROOKS 1968

One of the many who came and went in the blinking of an eye. He was signed in a hurry to take over from the enigmatic Geoff Clayton as wicket-keeper. Small and competent, he'd got a blue at Oxford and was ready to give county cricket a go. Then, after one summer, he did some serious thinking and opted for a teaching appointment at Bradfield instead. Taunton team-mates were apt, with affection, to call him 'Hollow Legs', an accolade apparently for his admired ability to sink a pint.

RICHARD ALAN BROOKS Born Edgeware, Middlesex, 14.6.43. RHB, WK. Cap 1968. SFC: 26 matches; 182 runs @ 10.11; HS 37 v Northamptonshire, Taunton, 1968; 53 dismissals (48 ct, 5 st). Oxford University 1967.

CHARLIE CARTER 1968 – 1969

Opinions varied about his talents behind the stumps but no-one in the side found him anything but a most affable team-mate; and certainly the best dressed. Those who said he had a better wardrobe than catching record offered the observation with warm-hearted good humour.

Charlie Carter was, in fact, not a bad wicket-keeper, even if he wasn't up to the exalted standard claimed by his unwavering advocate, Bill Andrews. He'd gone to Radley, then came out of the Army to try his luck at the summer game.

For a time he shared a cottage with Greg Chappell, then a fledgling pro with Somerset. Charlie was a good mixer, took the digs of the old campaigners in his stride and never for one moment complained when Hampshire paceman Butch White hit him on the head. Eventually the City offered a more pain-free and lucrative career.

CHARLES EDWARD PEERS CARTER Born Richmond, Surrey, 7.8.47. RHB, WK. SFC: 26 matches; 73 runs @ 2.92; HS 16 v Middlesex, Lord's, 1969; 53 dismissals (47 ct, 6 st). OD: 6 matches; 11 runs (no average); 9 dismissals (8 ct, 1 st).

1969

Captain: B.A. Langford

Just one championship victory out of 24 for Somerset – and that one came in the first home fixture of the season, against Hampshire. In an exciting finish, they squeezed home by two runs. Yet any hopes of building on that encouraging launch were soon shattered demoralisingly. They ended in bottom position, which they had last occupied in 1955. Team recruitment clearly now needed to be a priority, even if the debuts of two left-handers, Rose and Denning, lifted some locals' spirits.

Sadly, star batsman Chappell – who also bowled tidy medium pace – was leaving, to add to the general disappointments. A Test career was beckoning. He'd enjoyed his short stay with Somerset, despite the paucity of success. In one of his last matches he scored a handsome hundred at Clarence Park, just to remind the county what they would be missing. When he had arrived in the West Country, he had needed to sort out the demands of English pitches in early season. But his presence at the crease spurred his team-mates. They admired his strokes and, despite the lack of wins, they remained cheerful together. In Chappell's final season with Somerset, everyone used to claim that they saw his marvellous 128 not out against Surrey in the Sunday League. And maybe they did – it was on television.

One had to sympathise with Langford as he took on the captaincy. Supporters noticed how his early sense of adventure was superseded by caution, at times unnecessarily so. At least this fine off-break bowler went into the record books by sending down eight successive maidens in a Sunday League match with Essex at Yeovil. Another brave solo achievement was that of Roy Palmer, a persevering bowler, who held out for an hour without scoring to ensure a draw with Glamorgan at Glastonbury.

COUNTY CHAMPIONSHIP   17th

COUNTY CHAMPIONSHIP 17th	Played 24	Won 1	Drawn 14	Lost 9
OTHER MATCHES	Played 1			Lost 1
GILLETTE CUP	Lost in First Round			
JOHN PLAYER LEAGUE 16th	Played 16	Won 5	No Result 1	Lost 10

BATTING

	M	I	NO	Runs	HS	Ave	100	50	ct	st
M.J. Kitchen	25	45	2	1308	132	30.41	1	8	13	–
G.S. Chappell	25	45	1	1330	144	30.22	2	5	21	–
A. Clarkson	25	46	1	1191	131	26.46	1	5	2	–
R.T. Virgin	25	46	1	1170	92	26.00	–	7	20	–
P.J. Robinson	25	40	11	452	52	15.58	–	1	12	–
K.E. Palmer	15	22	5	257	37*	15.11	–	–	4	–
B.C. Rose	16	27	3	357	46	14.87	–	–	4	–
P.W. Denning	13	25	2	342	69	14.86	–	1	5	–
G.I. Burgess	22	38	1	492	62	13.29	–	1	3	–
B.A. Langford	23	36	6	391	62*	13.03	–	3	10	–
R. Palmer	24	38	10	253	40*	9.03	–	–	5	–
J.M. Galley	3	6	1	27	17	5.40	–	–	1	–
C.E.P. Carter	24	31	10	72	16	3.42	–	–	44	6
J.K. Roberts	5	7	5	3	2*	1.50	–	–	2	–

(1 match)   W.D. Buck 5, 6   D.W. Cox 0, 8 (2 ct)   J.T. Holmes 0,8 (1 ct)
B. Lobb 0   R.T.A. Windsor 0

BOWLING

	Overs	Mdns	Runs	Wkts	Ave	5wi	10wm
G.I. Burgess	529.2	123	1420	52	27.30	3	–
G.S. Chappell	432.4	92	1255	45	27.88	3	–
J.K. Roberts	135	31	401	14	28.64	–	–
K.E. Palmer	205	36	603	19	31.73	–	–
R. Palmer	619.5	130	1906	60	31.76	3	–
B.A. Langford	698.2	271	1473	42	35.07	–	–
P.J. Robinson	497.2	152	1440	39	36.92	1	–

A. Clarkson 47-12-142-0 B. Lobb 31-5-108-5   W.D. Buck 30-6-110-2
D.W. Cox 19-3-77-1   M.J. Kitchen 10-3-24-1   R.T. Virgin 4.3-1-15-1
P.W. Denning 0.2-0-4-0

BRIAN ROSE 1969 – 1987

Initially Brian Rose wasn't everyone's idea of a long-term prospect, so he went off to qualify as a teacher instead. Later, his appointment as captain didn't find favour in all quarters, but history showed him to be a sound skipper and the leader of the county in its most memorable summers when trophies at last came to Taunton.

He was in charge of a team which included players of exceptional talent and high profile, a task which could be rewarding and, on occasions, unenviable. He was a private person and was apt to carry a preoccupied expression on to the field. Tongue-in-cheek team-mates suspected aloud that he was probably just as happy doing his beloved gardening.

Rose's batting could be of high calibre. As a left-hander at the top of the order, his strokes were stylish and crisp. He belonged to Weston-super-Mare and it was appropriate that he should hit a double-century there. When Alec Bedser, the chairman of the England selectors, once came West to take a detailed look at Ian Botham, he returned home rhapsodising about Rose instead. There were nine Test appearances, but also untimely injuries in his career.

Mental pain, too, after that highly controversial Benson and Hedges match in 1979, when Somerset were dismissed from the competition for 'bending the rules'. A sensitive man, who continued to maintain that nothing illegal had been done, he was stunned by the weight of ire from the game's establishment.

Some believed that he could have proved himself a genuine all-rounder. At medium pace, with some natural swing, he once took three wickets in four balls at headquarters. But he chose to stick to his batting.

Rose was tactically sharp, as well as a reliable judge of talent. In later years, these qualities served him well as unofficial manager of the county club and as chairman of the cricket committee.

Even though he had gone off into business, seen less at Somerset matches, those who knew him best believed that the County Ground remained his spiritual home. The setting up of a review panel, on which he was joined by two other ex-captains, Roy Kerslake and Vic Marks, pointed the way towards a positive restructuring of the club, something viewed as a priority.

By the middle of the 2005 season, with results gloomy and supporters restive, Rose was announced as the new director of cricket. He'd been away from the game long enough to take a refreshing and detached view of what needed to be done and done rapidly. He wasted no time in changing attitudes. Younger players were given their heads. Simultaneously, morale lifted. Somerset won the Twenty20 Cup, no great conquest but still an indication that a new resolve was emerging, incorporating astute overseas signings and genuine encouragement of the academy material.

Rose has been given a good deal of power within the club. He is a strong man, firm of opinion in his quiet way and pleasingly imaginative. Could the next couple of years suggest an elusive formula has been found?

BRIAN CHARLES ROSE Born Dartford, Kent, 4.6.50. LHB, LM. Cap 1975. Captain 1978-83. 9 Tests 1977-81. 2 LOI 1977. SFC: 251 matches; 12342 runs @ 33.26; 23 centuries; HS 205 v Northamptonshire, Weston-super-Mare, 1977; 1000 runs 8 times; HT 1624 in 1976; 8 wickets @ 36.12; BB 3-9 v Gloucestershire, Taunton, 1975. OD: 251 matches; 5708 runs @ 27.98; 7 wickets @ 21.71; GC MoM 2; B&H GA 2.

> As a captain he was a revelation. He didn't suddenly become a domineering extrovert, but his quietly spoken words carried immense authority; he was not worried that he was younger or less famous than some of his team-mates.
>
> He wanted us to disown our reputation for being colourful, unreliable crowd-pleasers. It was important to win matches.
>
> **Vic Marks**

JOHN ROBERTS 1969 – 1970

In he came, thickset and determined, at left-arm medium over the wicket, having travelled down from the North with a nice Scouse sense of humour. After two years it was mutually decided that John was not going to be the answer to Somerset's need and he changed direction to patrol a beat for the police instead.

JOHN KELVIN ROBERTS Born Liverpool, 9.10.49. RHB, LM. SFC: 8 matches; 3 runs @ 1.00; HS 2* v Yorkshire, Headingley, 1969; 15 wickets @ 32.33; BB 4-38 same match; HT 14 in 1969. OD: 11 matches; 13 runs @ 13.00; 13 wickets @ 22.84.

TREVOR HOLMES 1969

Somerset's selection policy was apt, historically, to be bizarre. This Yorkshire-born wicketkeeper came in, to everyone's surprise, against the West Indians – on the strength of a Second XI match at Pontypridd and a typical surge of enthusiasm from coach Bill Andrews. He took one catch and that was it. The record books at Somerset are laden with illogical one-appearance careers.

JOHN TREVOR HOLMES Born Holmfirth, Yorkshire, 16.11.39. RHB, WK. 1 match; 8 runs @ 4.00; HS 8 v West Indians, Taunton, 1969; 1 dismissal (ct).

BILL BUCK 1969

Now here's a little cameo from the record books. In the same summer he played once for Hampshire, against the New Zealanders, and once for Somerset, against the West Indians. Both counties were keen to take a look at him. Buck's sum total of success with his medium-paced seamers was two wickets.

WILLIAM DALTON BUCK Born Southampton, Hampshire, 30.9.46. RHB, RM. SFC: 1 match; 11 runs @ 5.50; HS 6 v West Indians, Taunton, 1969; 2 wickets @ 55.00; BB 2-59 same match. Hampshire 1969.

LEN BEEL 1969

Was at Worcestershire, playing Second XI and Club and Ground matches, and followed Peter Robinson down to Taunton. Beel was a goalkeeper who played three Football League games for Shrewsbury Town and one for Birmingham City.

WILLIAM JOHN LEONARD BEEL Born Leominster, Herefordshire, 23.8.45. RHB, RM. OD: 1 match; 1 run (no average); 0 wickets.

DAVID COX 1969

One match, at the United Services ground, Portsmouth, and one wicket – thanks to Brian Rose's catch in the gully.

DAVID WILLIAM COX Born Oakhill, Somerset, 19.5.46. RHB, RFM. SFC: 1 match; 8 runs @ 4.00; HS 8 v Hampshire, Portsmouth, 1969; 1 wicket @ 77.00; BB 1-50 same match.

RAY WINDSOR 1969

Here was a prodigious scorer for Wellington and Taunton, who also built a substantial innings of nearly 150 for Somerset Second XI against Cornwall. Recognition was scant at the higher level, though, and he was bowled for a duck by Tony Greig on his only first-class outing.

RAYMOND THOMAS ALBERT WINDSOR Born Wellington, Somerset, 9.2.43. RHB. SFC: 1 match; 0 runs. SL: 1 match; did not bat or bowl.

JIM GALLEY 1969

Jim was born at Brislington, on the outskirts of Bristol, not far from family friend Horace Hazell. He was a terrific club cricketer who captained Lansdown for periods in the 1970s and 1980s, a stylish bat who could be both forceful and stubborn, according to the needs of his side. In the winter he played scrum-half for Bath and Somerset.

JAMES MARTYN GALLEY Born Brislington, Bristol, 4.10.45. RHB. SFC: 3 matches; 27 runs @ 5.40; HS 17 v Kent, Dover, 1969. OD: 1 match; 8 runs @ 8.00.

PETER DENNING 1969 – 1984

Dasher he was – in the way he hurtled for singles, wearing pads that usually looked too big for him. As a left-handed batsman, he made no claims as a stylist. He was proud of his Chewton carve – reasonably enough for a butcher's son – and admitted that he tended to give gully a fair chance of success.

Peter was modest about the achievements that punctuated his wholehearted career, embarrassed by compliments and ever ready to disparage his own talents. In fact, he was a fine team-mate, unselfish in the way he batted and only critical of those he felt didn't try hard enough. The gentle rebellious streak in him was demonstrated in his contempt for the wardrobe and by the length of his flaxen hair.

He was quite a paradox; on the one hand he was gruffly amusing, one of the village lads; and yet he rode with the Mendip Hunt a few times and was captain of cricket at Millfield, where Colin Atkinson detected the strong tactical sense in him.

Hidden beneath all that self-mockery were some memorable innings, both ferocious and fighting. He's there in the record books for his 310-run stand for the fourth wicket with Ian Botham – 'I leaned on my bat and let him get on with it,' Dasher would say, failing to mention that he scored 98 himself.

Frequently he opened the innings with Brian Rose. He was an exciting natural for the one-day matches, playing a prominent part in the capturing of several trophies, and he patrolled the covers with flawless vigilance.

PETER WILLIAM DENNING Born Chewton Mendip, Somerset, 16.12.49. LHB, ROB. Cap 1973. SFC: 269 matches; 11559 runs @ 28.68; 8 centuries; HS 184 v Nottinghamshire, Trent Bridge, 1980; 1000 runs 6 times; HT 1222 in 1979; 1 wicket @ 96.00; BB 1-4 v Derbyshire, Derby, 1974. OD: 280 matches; 6792 runs @ 28.06; 0 wickets. GC MoM 4; B&H GA 3.

> He was popular, stubborn, honest and inclined to regard anyone living outside his county with a mixture of pity and naked hostility.
> **Peter Roebuck**

Graham Burgess and Peter Denning open the batting in a friendly match at Wedmore.

1970

Captain: B.A. Langford

This was the summer when Virgin could do no wrong. He scored seven championship hundreds, nine altogether. His attractive batsmanship, especially through the off side, must surely have put him near to Test recognition. He was the first in the country to reach 2,000 runs, and the fans responded because he was a local boy. The support from Clarkson and Robinson shouldn't be overlooked. Kitchen had the frustrating experience of being out twice for 99.

The new acquisitions brought a difference as Somerset made modest progress away from the bottom spot. Cartwright, who had chosen to leave Warwickshire, gave his new county's bowling resources an additional dimension. Invariably there was a tempting invitation to the opposing batsman to go after him. But the deceptive medium-pace was full of movement and technical cunning. His first season with Somerset brought him 86 championship wickets and an unchallenged position at the top of the bowling averages. Whether at Bath, against Derbyshire and Leicestershire, or at Weston, where he took six for 29 against Gloucestershire, he was a master of his trade.

At times during the season, Somerset had looked in danger of sustaining their indignity at the foot of the table. But even with ten defeats, more than any other county, they eased up to 13th position. They had lacked real fire from their new-ball bowlers and certainly too many catches were put down. After reaching the semi-finals of the Gillette Cup, they should have made it harder for Lancashire by constructing a bigger total after the start given them by Virgin and Robinson. They found, however, a new and talented wicket-keeper in Taylor, signed from Surrey.

Somerset had a great appeal to me. The cricket was closer to the community than it had become at Edgbaston. And Somerset people are fairly down to earth. They're not over-impressed by flannel.

They were country people; they all had glowing, ruddy faces that stood out at away matches in early season, when most people had a pallor.

Tom Cartwright

COUNTY CHAMPIONSHIP 13th Played 24 Won 5 Drawn 9 Lost 10

GILLETTE CUP   Lost in Semi-Final

JOHN PLAYER LEAGUE   15th   Played 16   Won 5   No Result 2   Lost 9

BATTING

	M	I	NO	Runs	HS	Ave	100	50	ct	st
R.T. Virgin	24	47	0	2223	178	47.29	7	11	15	–
A. Clarkson	23	45	0	1246	105	27.68	1	8	23	–
P.J. Robinson	24	47	4	1158	140	26.93	1	9	19	–
M.J. Kitchen	24	47	4	977	99	22.72	–	6	12	–
M. Hill	17	31	1	660	65	22.00	–	3	7	–
T.W. Cartwright	24	44	9	766	63*	21.88	–	3	21	–
G.I. Burgess	24	46	4	866	67	20.61	–	4	5	–
D.J.S. Taylor	24	37	12	443	45	17.72	–	–	50	5
P.W. Denning	6	10	0	170	50	17.00	–	1	4	–
B.A. Langford	23	35	5	436	50*	14.53	–	1	16	–
R. Palmer	20	31	12	248	40*	13.05	–	–	12	–
B.C. Rose	6	10	0	73	16	7.30	–	–	4	–
A.A. Jones	22	26	11	75	19	5.00	–	–	5	–
J.K. Roberts	3	2	1	0	0*	0.00	–	–	–	–

BOWLING

	Overs	Mdns	Runs	Wkts	Ave	5wi	10wm
T.W. Cartwright	851.4	318	1891	86	21.98	6	1
G.I. Burgess	498.5	91	1667	56	29.76	3	–
P.J. Robinson	253.3	70	868	28	31.00	–	–
B.A. Langford	553	141	1634	52	31.42	3	–
A.A. Jones	470.5	79	1588	46	34.52	2	–
R. Palmer	443.5	72	1517	40	37.92	–	–

J.K. Roberts 22-3-84-1   A. Clarkson 6-1-19-0

TOM CARTWRIGHT 1970 – 1976

Cartwright came from Warwickshire, for whom he'd once hit a double-century, and ended up with Glamorgan. At Somerset he was soon topping the bowling with that unequalled medium-pace craft. Many, including the rookie Ian Botham, learned from him.

Tom hated to be thought of as merely a containing performer; he encouraged batsmen, at their peril, to go after him. He was a man of immense cricketing wisdom and we can only ask ourselves why he played no more than five times for England.

Some fuddy-duddies on the Somerset committee saw him as an argumentative Leftie. That was only partly fair. He argued, from technical strength, only when he had a personal battle of principle; and as for his radicalism, that offered a welcome second option in a game dominated by reactionary political viewpoints.

Certainly he had his differences with people. One, when Tom was asked to play at a time he claimed vehemently he wasn't fit, led to rising passions and his unscheduled departure from the club. He'd been suspended in the process. But he also had many admirers, those who rated a man who stuck to his guns and possessed an independent spirit.

He went on to be appointed national cricket coach in Wales. The words he offered were as perceptive as they were paternal.

THOMAS WILLIAM CARTWRIGHT Born Coventry, Warwickshire, 22.7.35. RHB, RM. Cap 1970. 5 Tests 1964-65. SFC: 101 matches; 2422 runs @ 18.92; 1 century; HS 127 v Essex, Leyton, 1971; HT 766 in 1970; 408 wickets @ 18.86; BB 8-94 v Derbyshire, Chesterfield, 1972; 100 wickets once; HT 104 in 1971. OD: 94 matches; 972 runs @ 15.42; 107 wickets @ 19.90; B&H GA 4. Warwickshire 1952-69; Glamorgan 1977.

He was a joy to watch as a bowler, a supreme artist, a master of accuracy, of variation, and total concentration. He did a great deal to teach our bowlers a new set of values.
Brian Close

Tom wasn't like the complaining old professionals who thought it was terrific when it rained. He wanted to do his work. He wanted to bowl his overs. He was a proud worker – but a worker all the same.
Peter Roebuck

DEREK JOHN SOMERSET TAYLOR Born Amersham, Buckinghamshire, 12.11.42. RHB, WK. Cap 1971. SFC: 280 matches; 6796 runs @ 22.42; 4 centuries; HS 179 v Glamorgan, Swansea, 1974; 1000 runs once; HT 1121 in 1975; 0 wickets; 662 dismissals (588 ct, 74 st). OD: 261 matches; 2035 runs @ 19.56; 244 runs @ 18.77; 277 dismissals (234 ct, 43 st); B&H GA 1. Surrey 1966-69; Griqualand West, South Africa, 1970-72.

DEREK TAYLOR
1970 – 1982

There are various tests for a top-notch wicketkeeper. How they get on in tandem with the off-spinner is the obvious one. But not so far behind is their ability to stand up to the best of the medium-pacers, who can make the ball 'wobble' at will. Derek Taylor's proficiency in harness with the brilliant Tom Cartwright was legendary. No-one ever remembered his putting down a catch in the process.

The sporting tragedy of Taylor's career was that there were too many great glovemen around at the same time. He earned his Test trial in 1976, but for the most time he was destined to be the country's number three. And that means nothing.

He came from Surrey Seconds and for the next dozen or so years did everything behind the stumps with a minimum of fuss. Just before he left, emigrating to Australia for a new career in insurance, he was creating a new one-day record by taking eight catches against Oxford and Cambridge in the Benson and Hedges.

His batting should never be discounted; he knew his limits and kept within them, making himself into a most adequate opener when the need was there. In the dressing room, surrounded by more volatile influences, he could be a calming creature.

He had as safe a pair of hands as anyone in the game at that time, and some of his leg-side stumpings off the medium-pace bowlers bordered on the miraculous.
Brian Close

ALLAN JONES 1970 – 1975

He's remembered for his nomadic playing career with four counties and the thunderous grunt as the ball left his grip. His 549 wickets overall were earned by honest sweat and at times exceptional pace. The successes were punctuated by tetchy exchanges with taunting spectators, who were less than sympathetic about his fielding lapses. Allan Jones surprised many observers by turning into a calm and capable first-class umpire.

ALLAN ARTHUR JONES Born Horley, Surrey, 9.12.47. RHB, RFM. Cap 1972. SFC: 118 matches; 442 runs @ 6.05; HS 27 v Northamptonshire, Taunton, 1975; 291 wickets @ 29.05; BB 9-51 v Sussex, Hove, 1972; HT 67 in 1974. OD: 113 matches; 101 runs @ 3.48; 164 wickets @ 21.94; B&H GA 1. Sussex 1966-69; Middlesex 1976-79; Glamorgan 1980-81; Northern Transvaal, South Africa, 1972-73; Orange Free State, South Africa, 1976-77. Fc umpire 1985-.

> I told him several times in the five years we played together that, if he pulled his socks up and got more consistency into his game, he was good enough to play for England.
> **Brian Close**

MAURICE HILL 1970 – 1971

Arriving at Somerset, after a lengthy, unproductive life at Notts and a brief one at Derbyshire, Maurice Hill was into his mid thirties and unable to add to his list of seven first-class hundreds. But his solid know-how was valued by younger players, particularly at a time when Somerset had just finished once more on the bottom of the table. He also struck the ball assertively, and set a consistent example either in the covers or the deep.

MAURICE HILL Born Scunthorpe, Lincolnshire, 14.9.35. RHB, LB. SFC: 22 matches; 732 runs @ 21.52; HS 65 v Northamptonshire, Taunton, 1970; HT 660 in 1970. OD: 14 matches; 197 runs @ 15.15. Nottinghamshire 1953-65; Derbyshire 1966-67.

1971

Captain: B.A. Langford

Close had arrived, not yet as captain but still to shake things up and instil more discipline among the younger pros. He'd fallen out with Yorkshire and surprised the cricket world by coming West. The Taunton culture, more relaxed and easy-going than Headingley, may have been strange to him initially. But he didn't take long to make his mark. He soared to the top of the batting averages, adapting his game to the needs of the county. There were five centuries, one of them to his undisguised satisfaction at the expense of Yorkshire.

A new breeze was blowing. Cartwright was gobbling up more than 100 wickets, the result of an impeccable length and, for the domestic circuit, unrivalled craftsmanship. He also had Taylor standing up to him. O'Keeffe, a tall, fastish Australian leg-spinner with effective variations, had been signed, too – as had Moseley, a Barbadian who had been recommended by Garfield Sobers and who was an honest, uncomplicated seamer with a decent out-swinger. By now Kitchen was opening the innings. Plenty of new thinking was going on.

Taunton, Bath and Weston-super-Mare were buzzing again. The arrival of Close and O'Keeffe, as expected, boosted the membership. Somerset's seven championship wins took them to seventh place. Six of those successes were at home; the county had the crowd behind them again. And soon Close, who hadn't missed a match and appeared free of previous injuries, would be in charge.

Somerset players were not born and reared on success – winning was not the matter of life and death to them that it was to Yorkshire players. It was a good thing in some ways, but there were times when it was a disadvantage. Because they were not used to going all out for victory as a matter of course, the players were not geared to the intensity of concentration I regarded as the norm.

Brian Close

COUNTY CHAMPIONSHIP 7th

Played 24	Won 7	Drawn 13	Lost 4

OTHER MATCHES — Played 1 — Drawn 1

GILLETTE CUP — Lost in First Round

JOHN PLAYER LEAGUE 5th — Played 16 — Won 9 — No Result 2 — Lost 5

BATTING

	M	I	NO	Runs	HS	Ave	100	50	ct	st
D.B. Close	25	41	10	1388	116*	44.77	5	6	33	–
R.T. Virgin	24	41	3	1365	179*	35.92	3	5	31	–
M.J. Kitchen	25	43	2	1325	120	32.31	2	5	9	–
A. Clarkson	23	34	7	760	69*	28.14	–	3	11	–
P.J. Robinson	13	24	3	543	112	25.85	1	1	11	–
G.I. Burgess	19	28	3	619	73	24.76	–	5	12	–
T.W. Cartwright	25	32	2	632	127	21.06	1	2	8	–
H.R. Moseley	20	20	9	219	58	19.90	–	1	7	–
K.J. O'Keeffe	25	29	7	411	58	18.68	–	1	14	–
M. Hill	5	5	1	72	27	18.00	–	–	1	–
B.A. Langford	25	28	9	304	43	16.00	–	–	7	–
D.J.S. Taylor	25	31	6	317	40	12.68	–	–	56	7
A.A. Jones	20	18	5	120	19*	9.23	–	–	5	–

(1 match)   P.W. Denning 11 (1 ct)

BOWLING

	Overs	Mdns	Runs	Wkts	Ave	5wi	10wm
T.W. Cartwright	976.4	407	1852	104	17.80	9	–
K.J. O'Keeffe	627.1	213	1738	74	23.48	6	2
H.R. Moseley	382.5	75	1042	39	26.71	1	–
B.A. Langford	422.1	110	1238	42	29.47	2	–
G.I. Burgess	289.4	55	906	29	32.24	2	1
A.A. Jones	401.4	78	1338	35	38.22	2	–

D.B. Close 32-9-124-4   P.J. Robinson 20.2-2-90-3   R.T. Virgin 1-0-10-0

BRIAN CLOSE 1971 – 1977

The enticing of Brian Close to the West was seen by Bill Andrews as his greatest achievement. Yorkshire, in the internecine ways that they made a speciality, decided to fire him. Andrews read about it and immediately picked up his pen. It was an instinctive reaction. Three times he wrote to Close, without getting a reply. Then, with a phone call or two and an invitation to stay a few days to talk things over, the move was clinched.

From the steel of Headingley to the supposedly soft-bellied aura of Taunton. It was a culture shock all round. Committee members, initially lukewarm to the proposed arrival of the Yorkshire maverick, could soon see signs of change. Some of the younger pros quaked as he shook them from their natural lethargy in the field. He stationed himself at short-leg, of course, and led by example.

There were five centuries in his first summer with Somerset, one almost inevitably against Yorkshire. Before long he was taking over from Brian Langford as skipper.

Close was full of contradictions. He'd berate a slumbering team-mate before putting his arm around the youngster's shoulders and saying: 'Don't worry, lad, I'm really a sentimental old sod.' He would lead with gritty brilliance and then make tactical decisions that lacked logic. He hated one-day cricket, while at times excelling at it. There were some edgy moments when he was at Somerset, but everyone agreed he was a timely catalyst.

DENNIS BRIAN CLOSE Born Rawdon, Yorkshire, 24.2.31. LHB, ROB/RM. Cap 1971. Captain 1972-77. 22 Tests 1949-76. 3 LOI 1972. SFC: 142 matches; 7567 runs @ 39.41; 13 centuries; HS 153 v Middlesex, Lord's, 1973; 1000 runs 5 times; HT 1388 in 1971; 74 wickets @ 34.94; BB 5-70 v Lancashire, Taunton, 1974; HT 29 in 1975. OD: 126 matches; 2658 runs @ 23.94; 41 wickets @ 22; GC MoM 1; B&H GA 1. Yorkshire 1949-70.

> He was an extraordinary man, a mixture of King Lear storming in the wilderness and Churchill defying 'em on the beaches. You could tolerate a great deal from someone who fought so hard to win.
> **Peter Roebuck**

> **On the day he was recalled to the England side, aged 45**
> We had a Sunday match at Portsmouth, and I travelled down with him. He was like a schoolboy being picked. 'You know, lad,' he said, 'it's the first year I haven't put the Tests in me diary.'
> **Peter Robinson**

1971

HALLAM MOSELEY
1971 – 1982

Around the Somerset grounds he had a cult following, especially among the mums and the schoolchildren. For years his gentle affability was a golden plus in public relations.

Hallam had been recommended to the county by Sir Garfield Sobers and, in a different decade, might have squeezed into the West Indian pace attack. The bowling action was one to be admired: he came in, spring-heeled and arm high, and the ball veered away towards the slips. Latterly the movement was less marked but the enthusiasm, as demonstrated in the sweet co-ordination of his fielding, never lessened.

A sorry misunderstanding meant that he left in the end a season before he need have done. He cherished an ambition to become a butcher, but in later years he was to be seen as a peak-capped security officer in the London area.

HALLAM REYNOLD MOSELEY Born Christchurch, Barbados, 28.5.48. RHB, RFM. Cap 1972. SFC: 205 matches; 1502 runs @ 12.41; HS 67 v Leicestershire, Taunton, 1972; HT 234 in 1972; 547 wickets @ 24.10; BB 6-34 v Derbyshire, Bath, 1975; HT 81 in 1974. OD: 210 matches; 519 runs @ 8.23; 309 wickets @ 20.03; Barbados, West Indies, 1969-72.

I was so impressed with him the first time I saw him play that I insisted on carrying his heavy bag to Taunton station.

It may not always have been easy to decipher what he was saying when he arrived, but he was the nicest guy I ever met in the game. I never once saw him lose his temper when things were going wrong, or bowl a bouncer. Everyone liked him.

Bill Andrews

KERRY O'KEEFFE 1971 – 1972

One of those overseas players, barely known when he arrived in Somerset, who went on to become a Test man, making a couple of dozen appearances for Australia during the 1970s.

Kerry O'Keeffe was a quickish leg-spinner, not easy to keep wicket to, although Derek Taylor managed it well. There was a high action and a useful top-spinner thrown in. But there was inconsistency, too, and he decided not to return to Taunton in 1973.

KERRY JAMES O'KEEFFE Born Sydney, Australia, 25.11.49. RHB, LBG. Cap 1971. 24 Tests 1971-77. 2 LOI 1977. SFC: 46 matches; 830 runs @ 20.75; HS 58 v Warwickshire, Glastonbury, 1971; HT 419 in 1972; 93 wickets @ 30.82; BB 7-38 v Sussex, Taunton, 1971; HT 74 in 1971. OD: 20 matches; 151 runs @ 18.87; 8 wickets @ 36.62. New South Wales, Australia, 1968-80.

MOST POST-WAR WICKET-KEEPING VICTIMS FOR SOMERSET

First-class cricket		Limited-over cricket	
HW Stephenson	1006	DJS Taylor	277
DJS Taylor	659	RJ Turner	248
RJ Turner	644	ND Burns	181
ND Burns	333	T Gard	70
G Clayton	242	M Burns	27
T Gard	217	G Clayton	24
WT Luckes	213	JM Parks	21
PJ Eele	105	CM Gazzard	15
RA Brooks	53	RT Virgin	13
CEP Carter	53	CEP Carter	9

1972

Captain: D.B. Close

Close, fit and feisty – and quite a martinet, it was said, to the more dreamy youngsters – was now the skipper. He hoped in vain, however, that Virgin would recapture the golden form of recent summers. The opener seemed to struggle for erstwhile confidence and was, in fact, gone by the end of the season. When it came to batting, Close relied on Kitchen and not many more. Fourteen of the county's matches were drawn; they kept their better form, and four wins, for away fixtures.

If Virgin failed, so did O'Keeffe. Conditions may have been bad for him at times, causing him to be ineffective and expensive. His meagre 18 wickets in the championship were no more than a quarter of his 1971 tally. There were not too many bonuses, but Cartwright's bowling was one, while Jones, all grunts and endeavour, showed improvement. Moseley had been out for six weeks with back trouble though he was present to excel as an unlikely batsman from down the order against Leicestershire. He saved the follow-on in the first innings and was top scorer for his team in the second. Cooper, with the build and inclinations of Colin Milburn, turned up to play one championship match and belt some attractive runs in the one-day matches.

And controversy? How could it be different with Close and Wilf Wooller facing each other. At Swansea, they clashed because of Somerset's slow scoring and delayed declaration. The Glamorgan secretary offered the St Helen's crowd their money back. Close had the last laugh – he scored a pugnacious century, and Somerset won by an innings.

> Brian Close taught Somerset how to really play cricket. Before that, I think they were playing at it a bit.
>
> **Ken Biddulph**

COUNTY CHAMPIONSHIP 11th

COUNTY CHAMPIONSHIP 11th	Played 20	Won 4	Drawn 14	Lost 2
OTHER MATCHES	Played 1		Drawn 1
GILLETTE CUP	Lost in Second Round
JOHN PLAYER LEAGUE 7th	Played 16	Won 8	No Result 1	Lost 7

BATTING

	M	I	NO	Runs	HS	Ave	100	50	ct	st
B.C. Rose	3	5	0	252	125	50.40	1	–	4	–
D.B. Close	19	31	5	1299	135	49.96	3	6	17	–
M.J. Kitchen	21	35	0	1098	156	31.37	2	4	7	–
S.G. Wilkinson	9	14	2	299	69	24.91	–	2	5	–
K.J. O'Keeffe	21	28	10	419	43*	23.27	–	–	11	–
B.A. Langford	18	22	9	285	68*	21.92	–	1	3	–
R.T. Virgin	20	34	1	707	121	21.42	2	2	15	–
P.W. Denning	20	31	3	550	54*	19.64	–	2	9	–
P.J. Robinson	3	3	0	57	55	19.00	–	1	–	–
T.W. Cartwright	21	31	3	497	93	17.75	–	3	12	–
G.I. Burgess	18	30	1	501	63	17.27	–	1	5	–
H.R. Moseley	16	18	4	234	67	16.71	–	1	11	–
D.J.S. Taylor	21	25	8	260	43	15.29	–	–	29	3
A.A. Jones	19	16	7	68	22*	7.55	–	–	8	–

(1 match)   R.C. Cooper 4,0   R.J. Clapp did not bat

BOWLING

	Overs	Mdns	Runs	Wkts	Ave	5wi	10wm
T.W. Cartwright	863	373	1827	98	18.64	6	1
A.A. Jones	437	84	1281	51	25.11	2	1
H.R. Moseley	357	73	915	33	27.72	–	–
G.I. Burgess	235.3	52	610	21	29.04	–	–
B.A. Langford	254.4	60	860	16	53.75	–	–
K.J. O'Keeffe	376.3	103	1129	19	59.42	–	–

D.B. Close 35-10-128-3   R.J. Clapp 29-3-118-3   M.J. Kitchen 9-3-19-1
P.W. Denning 8-1-25-0   B.C. Rose 2-0-5-1   S.G. Wilkinson 2-0-9-0
R.T. Virgin 1-0-5-0

RICHARD COOPER
1972

Here was the Colin Milburn of the West Country, at least in build and vigorous talent at the crease. Richard Cooper was fashioned for one-day cricket and, for a roly-poly man, was no slouch in the field or when chasing for singles.

He once scored a hundred in each innings for his native Wiltshire against Somerset Seconds, and that led to overtures from Taunton. Few club players made more runs at his lively pace.

An enigmatic figure who was never going to conform easily to the disciplines of county cricket, he was proud of his one gold award and disappointed that he made only one championship appearance. Cooper played for Wiltshire from 1969 till the time of his death, aged 44, within days of his hero, Milburn, from a similar heart attack.

RICHARD CLAUDE COOPER Born Malmesbury, Wiltshire, 9.12.45. Died 14.3.90. SFC: 1 match; 4 runs @ 2.00; HS 4 v Nottinghamshire, Trent Bridge, 1972. OD: 13 matches; 343 runs @ 28.58; 0 wickets; B&H GA 1.

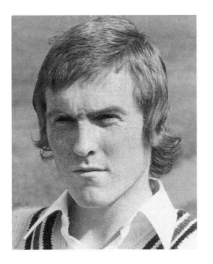

STEVE WILKINSON
1972 – 1974

Nice-looking bat without being dominant enough. Once earned an untimely rebuke from skipper Brian Close: 'You play too straight, lad.' That was after Wilkinson had played the ball back and got Close run out at the other end. Steve was around for three years, but the breakthrough proved elusive.

STEPHEN GEORGE WILKINSON Born Hounslow, Middlesex, 12.1.49. RHB, SLA. SFC: 18 matches; 452 runs @ 20.54; HS 69 v Surrey, Oval, 1972; HT 299 in 1972; 0 wickets. OD: 25 matches; 327 runs @ 16.35.

BOB CLAPP 1972 – 1977

Brian Close used to call him 'Bob Flap' because he claimed that Clapp always looked rather tense. He earned marks for endeavour as befitted a future schoolmaster, as he was at the time. His forte was the Sunday League and his name went into the record books for the most wickets in a season, when he struck 34 times in 1974.

ROBERT JOHN CLAPP Born Weston-super-Mare, 12.12.48. RHB, RM. SFC: 15 matches; 49 runs @ 4.45; HS 32 v Lancashire, Old Trafford, 1975; 25 wickets @ 29.36; BB 3-15 v Northamptonshire, Northampton, 1975; HT 8 in 1975. OD: 39 matches; 24 runs @ 3.42; 76 wickets @ 17.00.

A nice, genuine lad. He looked a world-beater in the nets, but out in the middle he couldn't relax.
Brian Close

Dodging the April showers
First day of pre-season training, April 1972
Mervyn Kitchen, Richard Cooper, Graham Burgess, Peter Denning, Derek Taylor, Roy Virgin, Peter Robinson, Brian Langford, Tom Cartwright, Allan Jones

1973

Captain: D.B. Close

Nothing too memorable about the season, although seven championship wins and only two defeats were a decent return. The weather was poor and often untimely for Somerset. Equally poor was some of the county's catching. Close at short leg, intrepid as ever, was an exception. There were three more hundreds from him but, alas, on occasions the reflexes were beginning to let him down.

So what were the more encouraging features of the season? Certainly Cartwright continued to bowl his marathon stints with uncanny precision, heading the national averages and at times, at the age of 37, appearing to carry the county's attack. Parks' arrival from Sussex was opportune. He bolstered the fragile higher order and passed his 1,000 runs. His pragmatic wicket-keeping was especially valuable in the limited-overs games. Burgess was by now making more of an impact as an all-rounder. He recorded his first hundred, quickly following up with another. Meanwhile Denning, with his occasionally unconventional batting technique and infectiously energetic qualities, won his cap, and Rose revealed genuine signs of a long-term future as an opener.

Somerset should have done better in the one-day matches. Particularly disappointing was their Gillette Cup exit to Leicestershire at Taunton. Robinson had provided the foundations for a good score and they always appeared to hold sway. But Chris Balderstone, virtually alone, had other ideas with an undefeated century.

Somerset versus Leicestershire, Gillette Cup, Taunton, July 11
Somerset 212
Leicestershire 215 for 8

We had them 58 for five, then 127 for seven. But Jim Parks got a ball on his thumb, and Closey took over the gloves. He caught a little skier: 'There you are, lad.' Then, when Allan Jones was bowling, he said, 'These gloves are too small.' And he kept without them. With Jonah, it was like red rag to a bull. He bowled faster and wider, there were byes, and in the end we lost.

It was like knocking somebody down for 14 rounds and losing in the 15th.

Peter Robinson

COUNTY CHAMPIONSHIP 10th

Played 20	Won 7	Drawn 11	Lost 2

OTHER MATCHES — Played 1 — Drawn 1

GILLETTE CUP — Lost in Second Round

BENSON & HEDGES CUP — Eliminated at Zonal Stage

JOHN PLAYER LEAGUE 11th — Played 16 — Won 5 — No Result 4 — Lost 7

BATTING

	M	I	NO	Runs	HS	Ave	100	50	ct	st
D.B. Close	21	32	5	1096	153	40.59	3	3	21	—
J.M. Parks	21	30	3	1033	155	38.25	1	7	14	—
P.W. Denning	19	28	7	649	85*	30.90	—	6	5	—
G.I. Burgess	21	31	5	752	129	28.92	2	2	6	—
M.J. Kitchen	18	31	5	738	75	28.38	—	4	5	—
D. Breakwell	21	24	5	305	46	16.05	—	—	11	—
B.C. Rose	11	16	1	240	34	16.00	—	—	4	—
P.J. Robinson	12	21	1	296	51	14.80	—	1	6	—
T.W. Cartwright	20	25	1	338	57	14.08	—	2	13	—
H.R. Moseley	20	20	8	144	20	12.00	—	—	7	—
D.J.S. Taylor	20	22	5	173	28*	10.17	—	—	41	3
S.G. Wilkinson	6	9	2	69	27	9.85	—	—	6	—
A.A. Jones	17	15	5	33	8	3.30	—	—	2	—

(2 matches)   R.J. Clapp   1,3   B.A. Langford   2, 6* (1 ct)

BOWLING

	Overs	Mdns	Runs	Wkts	Ave	5wi	10wm
T.W. Cartwright	810.4	349	1410	89	15.84	8	2
G.I. Burgess	391	93	1152	49	23.51	4	—
H.R. Moseley	504.2	130	1160	46	25.21	1	—
B.A. Langford	58	13	131	5	26.20	—	—
A.A. Jones	352	79	1089	33	33.00	1	—
D. Breakwell	274.4	66	806	20	40.30	—	—
D.B. Close	159.5	29	560	10	56.00	—	—

R.J. Clapp 42-13-107-3   P.J. Robinson 11-3-25-1   D.J.S. Taylor 3-1-10-0
J.M. Parks 2.2-1-3-0

DENNIS BREAKWELL Born Brierley Hill, Staffordshire, 2.7.48. LHB, SLA. Cap 1976. SFC: 165 matches; 3777 runs @ 21.21; 1 century; HS 100* v New Zealanders, Taunton, 1978; HT 585 in 1974; 281 wickets @ 33.22; BB 6-38 v Oxford University, The Parks, 1981; HT 47 in 1979. OD: 148 matches; 1059 runs @ 14.50; 58 wickets @ 35.53. Northamptonshire 1969-72.

DENNIS BREAKWELL
1973 – 1983

He twitched incessantly at his moustache, pulled on his fag like a nervous man in a maternity waiting-room and kept up a high-octane monologue. His value to suspect morale in the dressing room could be enormous. This chirpy-sparrow player spanned the conversational gamut; from his latest catch on the River Tone to how Somerset should go after the late-order runs.

'Breaks' had four seasons with Northants before coming to Somerset. As a left-arm bowler, he was an astute container rather than spinner. Gradually he tailored his style to meet the needs of modern cricket. Though his bowling became flatter as the seasons went on, the enthusiastic tuition to the schoolboys in his charge always advocated the virtues of old-fashioned spin.

His perky batting was not to be discounted, even if often it had to be fashioned or sacrificed in the interests of the team. His one century, against New Zealand in 1978, was quite a revelation. 'Did you see Hick's 400? Or Richards' 300? Or Breakwell's 100? All at Taunton!' friends would joke.

When he gave up playing, he became assistant coach at the county, with special responsibilities to the schools. Later he coached at King's College, Taunton.

JIM PARKS 1973 – 1976

His highest score, a double-century, was for Sussex against Somerset; and when he said a somewhat unloving farewell to Hove, it was to Taunton he headed. The West Countrymen needed him for some extra experience and to prop up the higher order. He obliged with 1,000 runs in his first season with Somerset.

Parks' continuing role as wicket-keeper was a bone of contention at Sussex. Ironically, Somerset already had the excellent Derek Taylor and Jim accepted that he was going to be required as a stumper primarily for the one-day matches.

He had met his former England colleague, Brian Close, on tour in Rhodesia and been persuaded not to give up county cricket, as seemed likely at the time, for a year or two. Those valedictory summers with Somerset were relaxed and enjoyable.

JAMES MICHAEL PARKS Born Haywards Heath, Sussex, 21.10.31. RHB, LB, WK. Cap 1973. 46 Tests 1954-68. SFC: 47 matches; 1940 runs @ 30.31; 1 century; HS 155 v Kent, Maidstone, 1973; 1000 runs once; HT 1033 in 1973; 0 wickets; 35 dismissals (35 ct). OD: 40 matches; 727 runs @ 25.06; 27 dismissals (23 ct, 4 st); B&H GA 1. Sussex 1949-72.

HIGHEST INDIVIDUAL INNINGS FOR SOMERSET SINCE THE WAR

FIRST-CLASS MATCHES

322	I.V.A. Richards	v Warwickshire	Taunton	1985
313*	S.J. Cook	v Glamorgan	Cardiff	1990
311	G.C. Smith	v Leicestershire	Taunton	2005
310	H. Gimblett	v Sussex	Eastbourne	1948
297	M.J. Wood	v Yorkshire	Taunton	2005
264	M.M. Walford	v Hampshire	Weston-super-Mare	1947
250	J. Cox	v Nottinghamshire	Trent Bridge	2004

LIMITED-OVER MATCHES

177	S.J. Cook	v Sussex (B&H)	Hove	1990
175*	I.T. Botham	v Northamptonshire (JPL)	Wellingborough	1986
162*	C.J. Tavare	v Devon (NW)	Torquay	1990
157	C. Gazzard	v Derbyshire (TSL)	Derby	2004
155*	M.D. Crowe	v Hampshire (B&H)	Southampton	1987

1974

Captain: D.B. Close

This was more like it. The spectators' smiles were back at Taunton and the outlying grounds. All they missed was the satisfaction of that elusive ultimate triumph in one of the competitions. Somerset got to second place, just two points off Leicestershire at the top of the John Player League. They reached the semi-finals of both the Benson & Hedges and the Gillette Cups. And they climbed to fifth in the championship, all of which represented notable progress.

It was all the more creditable because Cartwright, mainstay of the bowling, missed much of the season and Kitchen also struggled with fitness. That meant some experiments in the batting order. One gratifying result was the competence of Taylor, studious and unfazed, as an opening bat. Others, like fast bowler Moseley – who topped the county averages – had successful seasons. And, of course, we shouldn't forget the arrival, laden with so much promise, of two newcomers by the names of Botham and Richards. Botham, who'd taken over from his injured mentor, Cartwright, had come by way of the Lord's groundstaff. He could swing the ball and make his shots with a clean, forceful sweep of the bat: a precocious talent. Richards, the Antiguan, had been qualifying explosively with Lansdown. His Somerset debut was at Swansea in the Benson & Hedges. He made 81 not out, won the gold award and his team-mates lined up to applaud him off the field. Another great star had arrived. For this Cinderella county it was, by any standards, a transforming and indirectly historic season.

It wasn't without its ironies. Close, who had publicly criticised much about the one-day games, could still entertain the crowds by the relaxed way he participated in the batting hustle of limited-overs cricket. There were two centuries from him, and plenty of therapeutic slogging. Clapp, a teacher with capable if unexceptional prowess as a seamer, created a new record for the John Player League with 34 wickets during the summer. Another highlight was 'Dasher' Denning's hundred off fashionable Surrey in a Gillette Cup semi-final. There really were indications of exciting times ahead.

Somerset versus Hampshire, Benson & Hedges Cup, Taunton, June 12

Score with 12 overs remaining: Hampshire 182 Somerset 113 for eight

The *Sun* reporter, in difficulty with edition times and the switchboard, did a piece, asking the sports room to fill in the gaps: 'Hurrying Hampshire raced to victory over Somerset by – runs, Trevor Jesty winning the Gold award by making 79 runs and taking – wickets for – runs.'

I liked the *Sun* man, but he gave me hope that something silly would occur.

Eric Hill

Final score: Somerset 184 for nine (Botham 45)*
Gold Award: I.T. Botham

COUNTY CHAMPIONSHIP   5th

Played 20	Won 6	Drawn 10	Lost 4

OTHER MATCHES   Played 3   Drawn 2   Lost 1

GILLETTE CUP   Lost in Semi-Final

BENSON & HEDGES CUP   Lost in Semi-Final

JOHN PLAYER LEAGUE   2nd   Played 16   Won 12   No Result 2   Lost 2

BATTING

	M	I	NO	Runs	HS	Ave	100	50	ct	st
M.J. Kitchen	13	24	2	819	88	37.22	–	7	2	–
D.B. Close	23	28	7	1099	114*	35.45	1	5	23	–
I.V.A Richards	23	38	1	1223	107	33.05	2	6	18	–
D.J.S. Taylor	23	40	5	994	179	28.40	1	5	45	5
S.G. Wilkinson	3	4	1	84	32*	28.00	–	–	–	–
D. Breakwell	19	28	7	585	67	27.85	–	2	9	–
J.M. Parks	22	36	5	717	66	23.12	–	2	18	–
T.W. Cartwright	7	8	0	185	68	23.12	–	1	5	–
P.W. Denning	21	35	1	641	60	18.85	–	2	13	–
G.I. Burgess	21	33	0	588	90	17.81	–	4	19	–
I.T. Botham	18	29	3	441	59	16.96	–	1	15	–
A.A. Jones	21	24	11	103	27	7.92	–	–	4	–
H.R. Moseley	20	25	9	120	36*	7.50	–	–	9	–
B.A. Langford	14	21	7	97	18	6.92	–	–	4	–

(2 matches)   P.M. Roebuck 46, 0, 0, 8

(1 match)   B.C. Rose 14, 7   P.J. Robinson 1 (1 ct)   R.J. Clapp 0

BOWLING

	Overs	Mdns	Runs	Wkts	Ave	5wi	10wm
H.R. Moseley	661.5	198	1420	81	17.53	3	–
D.B. Close	97	30	255	13	19.61	1	–
B.A. Langford	412.1	153	937	42	22.30	3	–
T.W. Cartwright	273	130	493	22	22.40	–	–
A.A. Jones	565	122	1539	67	22.97	5	–
I.T. Botham	309	76	779	30	25.96	1	–
G.I. Burgess	437.1	114	1140	41	27.80	–	–
D. Breakwell	346.1	109	957	27	35.44	–	–
I.V.A. Richards	95	31	273	6	45.00	–	–

R.J. Clapp 7-1-24-0   J.M. Parks 5.3-3-21-0   P.W. Denning 4-1-4-0

P.J. Robinson 4-0-19-0

VIV RICHARDS 1974 – 1986

How do we measure genius? Does it have to be so soullessly perfect that it doesn't allow fallibility? Surely not. Richards made mistakes at the wicket; he would flash that Jumbo too early, as if still back at the grammar school in St John's, and give the bowler a chance. He would appear to rewrite the manuals by clipping the ball from just outside off stump through mid-wicket. He'd lapse in concentration and the thrilling instincts of the automatic pilot would let him down.

But for much of the time he ruled supreme. At Taunton, where he had arrived from his Lansdown qualification, wide-eyed and shyly charming, he regularly deposited the ball over the old pavilion roof as if he were merely golf-chipping. The wondrous eyesight in those days enabled him to pick up the flight of the ball quicker than anyone else in the game. His feet and his timing mocked any murmur of criticism at his tendency to veer from the purest orthodoxy. The rate of his scoring, never bolstered by an ugly slog, made him quickly a Somerset idol; even the forward defensive seemed to go for four.

Was it too good to last? Some misinterpreted the natural swagger in the walk. The eyes gradually became more wary, the persona seemingly more cynical. He had become a great global cricketer. But captaincy of his own country was delayed and he appeared at times to be victim of inter-island differences. The fuse had always been short – hadn't he once smashed his bat into a thousand pieces on the stone floor of the dressing room in self-rebuke and frustration? Hadn't he once jumped the boundary fence to confront a bigot?

Racial pride was his driving force. At times there were too many words in his ear, too many prejudices being awakened, too much advice being offered. Rejection by Somerset, as he saw it, was the final and cruellest ignominy. But time healed the rift. Feuds were forgotten, friendships renewed and gates were named after him at the county ground.

Now he is Sir Vivian, and we remember the acclaim he brought to modest Antigua; the effortless ferocity of his hitting; the brutally brilliant triple-hundred which caused disbelieving Warwickshire players to say, in admiration and despair, that they might as well give up the game for good; the awesome fielding; the quiet conviviality of his happier days.

After leaving Somerset, Viv had a season with Rishton in the Lancashire League and then some enjoyable years with Glamorgan.

Retirement from the game as a player brought accolades and national recognition as the chairman of selectors. It was hardly as he had hoped, and he described his two-year tenure as 'having to navigate through a war zone'. He was at times concerned about the way West Indian cricket was going, crucial of what he saw as interference by some members of the cricket board. By any standards, however, he remains a hugely iconic figure back in the Caribbean.

ISAAC VIVIAN ALEXANDER RICHARDS Born St John's, Antigua, 7.3.52. RHB, OB. Cap 1974. 121 Tests 1974-91. 187 LOI 1975-91. SFC: 191 matches; 14698 runs @ 49.82; 47 centuries; HS 322 v Warwickshire, Taunton, 1985; 1000 runs 10 times, incl 2000 runs once; HT 2161 in 1977; 96 wickets @ 44.15; BB 4-36 v Derbyshire, Chesterfield, 1986; HT 16 in 1982. OD: 218 matches; 7349 runs @ 39.94; 93 wickets @ 26.46; GC/NW MoM 4; B&H GA 6. Glamorgan 1990-93; Leeward and Combined Islands, West Indies, 1971-91; Queensland, Australia, 1976-77.

He was physically strong, supremely quick of eye and on his day – which seemed to be most days – capable of destroying any attack in the world. What struck you was the sheer size of the man, his massive presence at the crease. His shirt, buttoned down at the wrists, was worn tightly as if deliberately to display his muscular frame. He chewed gum menacingly and banged the top of his Stuart Surridge Jumbo bat handle with the palm of his hand as some sort of demonstration of his power.
John Barclay

IAN BOTHAM 1974 – 1986

To Somerset he brought glamour and controversy, monumental talents and unhappy headlines. He captained his country as well as his county, and by any standards, sporting or romantic, was at his best one of cricket's greats. He was inspirational, the most talked-about cricketer in the world. Bat in hand, he scored hundreds at a thrilling, muscular speed; even the mis-hits went for six. For the most part, he aimed straight and crisp. Then, when he snatched the ball, his out-swingers were devilishly difficult to handle. Here was an exceptional man.

Away from the field of play, the tabloids shadowed him. There was often a mutual antagonism. He created some of his own problems, and his outrage against some of the papers for their prying and treatment of him lost credibility because he was himself being paid a hefty cheque by one of them. He was fined by the courts, admitted in court a dalliance with drugs and was suspended. He seemed thoroughly ill-advised in the choice of one manager/agent, who decked him out in fancy clothes and claimed he could turn 'Both' into a Hollywood star.

The departure from Somerset, 'in sympathy with Richards' and Garner's dismissal', has been documented ad nauseam. There was much needless disaffection over the years. Once after a dismissal at Taunton, when he was at his lowest point, he made a detour on his melancholy return to the pavilion, to offer a few explicit home truths to a carping spectator.

'Beefy' moved on to Worcestershire and then Durham. In search of an extended career, he established himself as a TV panellist; he earned a winter living from panto and popular question-and-answer stage shows based on his cricket. He acquired added charm, turning into an accomplished storyteller and mimic. But he never lost a chance of informing his audiences that he could be discounted as a member of the Peter Roebuck fan club.

His deeds are imperishable in the record books. His physical courage, whether spitting out the blood from an Andy Roberts bouncer or on one of his marvellous charity walks, is undeniable. Remember him for the matches he won on his own, the unselfish play, the 1985 sixes that went into orbit to smash Arthur Wellard's long-standing record, the frisson he created . . . and the fact that he actually did savour the stillness of the riverbank.

IAN TERENCE BOTHAM Born Heswall, Cheshire, 24.11.55. RHB, RMF. Cap 1976. Captain 1984-85. 102 Tests 1977-92. 116 LOI 1977-92. SFC: 172 matches; 8686 runs @ 36.04; 16 centuries; HS 228 v Gloucestershire, Taunton, 1980; 1000 runs twice; HT 1280 in 1985; 489 wickets @ 26.52; BB 7-61 v Glamorgan, Cardiff, 1978; HT 70 in 1977. OD: 230 matches; 5049 runs @ 30.41; 300 wickets @ 23.38; GC/NW MoM 2; B&H GA 6. Worcestershire 1987-91; Queensland, Australia, 1987-88; Durham 1992-93.

> He was one of the most receptive people I've ever worked with. He learned to swing the ball both ways in a very short time, literally in weeks, and to have control over that. People may think that life came easy to Ian as a cricketer, but he worked damn hard. He really did. I had as much admiration for him in the way that he buckled down as anybody I've ever been with.
>
> **Tom Cartwright**

PETER ROEBUCK 1974 – 1991

The history of the game of cricket is littered with the names of those who fell out of love with it. Many confined their feelings to confidants or only said so in retrospective contemplation. Peter Roebuck went public.

He got out at the age of 35, when there were plenty of runs left in him, because he argued that cricket had become too cynical and results were being manufactured. And, yes, he admitted he didn't enjoy being a foot soldier after his days as a general.

That was an honest observation on playing under Chris Tavare, just an anonymous fielder and rarely consulted by the new captain. The relationship never smouldered with antipathy but it was sterile, mutually unproductive. 'Rupert' likened it perceptively to an arts-science divide (he was arts!).

He first played for Somerset Second XI at the age of 13. Only three batsmen made more first-class runs for the county, and just two – Gimblett and Richards – scored more hundreds. Roebuck never boasted as many shots as they, admitting he could look boring because of it.

In truth, he worked hard to increase his range and was capable of emerging with the most pleasant of drives and cuts. His application made him invaluable in a crisis on difficult wickets.

He had courage, physical as well as moral, when he took on the new ball. We shall never quite discover how he failed, when England were patently looking for a grafter, to make a Test appearance or two. He was also sized up as a possible captain of his country. Was he too opinionated? Did he act on too many whims?

Introspective, cerebral, moody, self-contained: he was all these things. He was also a dependable cricketer and team man, an imaginative tactician and a county captain who refused to dispense clichés.

Because of the position he held and the views he intrepidly expressed, he took much of the flak, as a leading antagonist, when the decision was taken to fire Richards and Garner. He was physically threatened by one of the departing stars and called 'Judas' by another. But he stuck to his well-reasoned brief, as one would expect of someone with a first in law at Cambridge.

His literary skills had always been evident. Now he turned full-time to journalism, while establishing himself as a successful author with a most comprehensive and readable history of his county club among his growing number of books.

Much of his working life is now away from this country. Somerset have had many complex individuals in their dressing room. Roebuck takes his place with them. He does so, as the statistics remind us, high on the credit list as a stubborn, fighting batsman, ever loath to give his wicket away.

PETER MICHAEL ROEBUCK Born Oxford, 6.3.56. RHB, LB. Cap 1978. Captain 1986-88. SFC: 306 matches; 16218 runs @ 38.34; 31 centuries; HS 221* v Nottinghamshire, Trent Bridge, 1986; 1000 runs 9 times; HT 1702 in 1984; 45 wickets @ 54.26; BB 3-10 v Leicestershire, Weston-super-Mare, 1991; HT 11 in 1989. OD: 277 matches; 6871 runs @ 30.26; 40 wickets @ 24.85; NW MoM 2; B&H GA 2. Cambridge University 1975-77.

Roebuck is eddicated – he bats an' he writes.
He could have an England cap in his sights,
But he stands so funny – in a kind of arc,
A bit like a human question mark.

David Henry Wilson,
from his poem **Zummerzet '81**

1975

Captain: D.B. Close

Centenary year: but celebrations turned out to be thin on the ground. Maybe there were too many distractions. The club had a bank overdraft of £23,000, a worrying amount in those days. Amid talk of crisis – hardly for the first time in the county's oscillating history – some officials and committee members were full of pessimism. The centenary appeal never really took off as it should have. Insiders like Colin Atkinson were already thinking seriously about the need for an all-out president's appeal to improve, as a matter of urgency, the present suspect facilities. It had been romantically hoped that Somerset's centenary season would coincide neatly with a continuation of the markedly improved playing record of 1974. In fact, the county slipped, after a deceptively bright start, to 12th in the table.

Valid excuses could be found. Cartwright was absent for almost the whole of the season. He'd injured his bowling arm when brilliantly taking a catch at Bath. Others, among them Burgess and Moseley, were also affected by injuries. Jones, who'd left the previous year, now came back for another summer, and was needed. The brighter signs, pointing to the future, could still be seen and applauded. Botham continued to grow in stature. Richards went off to Harrogate to collect a memorable double-hundred, his highest score so far. Slocombe, revealing excellent fleetness of foot against the spinners, wasted no time in scoring his maiden century, playing for MCC against the Australians and passing 1,000 runs. Here, they were chorusing around the boundary, was a young player to watch; and they were saying the same about Roebuck, due to leave his law books for a career in county cricket

Not everyone could quite agree about Close's captaincy, his style or his tactics. The county was in complete agreement, however, that he had brought a necessary more competitive edge to the Somerset game. His own form had not suffered at all, whatever the demands of a particular match. In the field he stayed unflinchingly close to the wicket. His ageless contributions – and courage – stilled any speculation about his future role. Meanwhile he liked the way Rose was opening the innings, and the clutch of gifted young players on the point of establishing themselves in the first team. All was far from lost in centenary year – for one thing, the gates were up, as they needed to be.

The slogan of the fund is 'Put Somerset Right' and the fact is, that just 50p from everyone in Somerset would do just that.

Remember, Somerset is YOUR club, and having survived against all the odds for 100 years, we really want to make the next 100 years safe.

Harold Gimblett, launching a personal appeal fund for the club's centenary.

He hoped to raise £150,000. In the event he raised barely £5,000.

COUNTY CHAMPIONSHIP   12th

COUNTY CHAMPIONSHIP 12th	Played 20	Won 4	Drawn 8	Lost 8
OTHER MATCHES	Played 2	Won 1		Lost 1
GILLETTE CUP	Lost in Second Round			
BENSON & HEDGES CUP	Lost in Quarter-Final			
JOHN PLAYER LEAGUE 14th	Played 16	Won 5	No Result 1	Lost 10

BATTING

	M	I	NO	Runs	HS	Ave	100	50	ct	st
J.M. Parks	3	6	2	179	65	44.75	–	1	2	–
D.B. Close	21	36	6	1276	138*	42.53	1	8	14	–
I.V.A. Richards	18	32	1	1151	217*	37.12	3	3	27	–
P.M. Roebuck	7	13	5	295	81*	36.87	–	1	2	–
P.A. Slocombe	20	35	5	1087	132	36.23	2	5	13	–
P.W. Denning	21	39	2	1199	81	32.40	–	10	6	–
B.C. Rose	22	41	4	1060	115*	28.64	1	6	9	–
D.J.S. Taylor	22	41	1	1121	127	28.02	2	6	52	5
G.I. Burgess	12	18	4	326	70	23.28	–	1	5	–
I.T. Botham	22	36	4	584	65	18.25	–	2	18	–
D. Breakwell	20	28	8	278	34*	13.90	–	–	4	–
K.F. Jennings	3	6	1	63	35	12.60	–	–	3	–
H.R. Moseley	18	21	5	143	36	8.93	–	–	8	–
V.J. Marks	3	6	0	53	14	8.83	–	–	1	–
R.J. Clapp	7	10	4	42	32	7.00	–	–	1	–
A.A. Jones	19	20	7	43	10*	3.30	–	–	8	–

(2 matches)   T.W. Cartwright 0, 0, 0 (2 ct)

(1 match)   P.J. Robinson 13 (1 ct)   J.S. Hook 4*, 3

BOWLING

	Overs	Mdns	Runs	Wkts	Ave	5wi	10wm
T.W. Cartwright	49.3	24	87	5	17.40	–	–
G.I. Burgess	407.1	110	987	41	24.07	3	1
H.R. Moseley	549	132	1341	52	25.78	1	–
A.A. Jones	542.5	104	1621	59	27.47	1	–
I.T. Botham	605.3	132	1704	62	27.48	1	–
D.B. Close	290.1	87	906	29	31.24	–	–
D. Breakwell	438.1	137	1228	37	33.18	1	–
I.V.A. Richards	130	33	358	10	35.80	–	–
R.J. Clapp	114	26	346	8	43.25	–	–

K.F. Jennings 41.2-10-140-1   B.C. Rose 23-4-68-4   P.M. Roebuck 23-4-86-0

V.J. Marks 20-3-90-0   P.J. Robinson 12-3-38-1   J.S. Hook 12-3-29-0

P.W. Denning 2-0-12-0   J.M. Parks 1-0-5-0

VIC MARKS 1975 – 1989

If anyone ever ran a popularity poll of all post-war players around the counties, this farmer's son would demand a lofty place. It wasn't simply that he walked away from petty or lacerating arguments, that he always chose to put the team before the individual, or that he retained a whimsical manner and schoolboyish giggle even in taut times. Suffice to say that his generously endowed all-rounder's talents, which earned him appearances in six Tests and 34 one-day internationals, were contained in the most equable and self-effacing of personae (spelt in deference to Marks, the classical scholar).

Vic was part of Somerset's most successful and volatile team, probably the quietest member. As an off-spinner, he tweaked those Chinnock fingers teasingly. When he was punished, the shoulders hunched and the consoling ciggies helped him through the lunch or tea interval. Soon he was smiling again, if wishing privately that the Taunton boundary fence had been less embracing to insensitive batsmen.

He never much compromised his style in the one-day game and, significantly, could often be a match-winner. When it was his turn to bat, we knew he was worthy of more hundreds. He improvised when he had to, most effectively, even if appearing an ungainly runner between the wickets.

Vic earned four blues at Oxford; now the deserved accolades come from his journalism. Captaincy came to him late, when Peter Roebuck decided abruptly that he'd had enough. Marks wasn't in charge sufficiently long really for us to measure his worth in that onerous role. Man-management was no problem. He could shuffle his cards to meet a tactical challenge and was patently unselfish. But the ugly cold-steel blade of battle was not for him.

Vic helped to bring his university friend Chris Tavare and manager Jack Birkenshaw to Somerset; he was also an influence on the arrival of Jimmy Cook.

VICTOR JAMES MARKS Born Middle Chinnock, Somerset, 25.6.55. RHB, OB. Cap 1979. Captain 1988-89. 6 Tests 1982-84. 34 LOI 1980-88. SFC: 275 matches; 9742 runs @ 30.53; 4 centuries; HS 134 v Worcestershire, Weston-super-Mare, 1984; 1000 runs twice; HT 1262 in 1984; 738 wickets @ 32.88; BB 8-17 v Lancashire, Bath, 1985; HT 86 in 1984. OD: 250 matches; 3623 runs @ 23.99; 226 wickets @ 27.70; NW MoM 2; B&H GA 4. Oxford University 1975-78; Western Australia 1986-87.

> As a cricketer Vic was very much under-rated, not only by the public but also by the selectors. I felt he should have played far more cricket for England than his six Tests and 34 one-day internationals.
> Although Somerset had the big names in Viv Richards and Joel Garner, he was just as important a part of our team.
> **Ian Botham**

> He is Somerset thew and sinew, and yet he never thought that it was the only thing that mattered.
> **Peter Roebuck**

KEITH JENNINGS
1975 – 1981

His forte was in one-day matches. Tom Cartwright was his mentor. He bowled straight and economically, always a reliable container when the opposition were threatening to smash the ball around. Maybe he had too few technical wiles when it came to bowling out opponents in the championship. Team-mates rated him as a competitor, not least for his courageous fielding close to the wicket. At heart a village boy, by trade a carpenter.

KEITH FRANCIS JENNINGS Born Wellington, Somerset, 5.10.53. RHB, RM. Cap 1978. SFC: 68 matches; 521 runs @ 10.63; HS 49 v West Indians, Taunton, 1976; 96 wickets @ 35.44; BB 5-18 v Sussex, Hove, 1978; HT 40 in 1978. OD: 88 matches; 233 runs @ 9.70; 104 wickets @ 24.70; B&H GA 1.

JOHN HOOK 1975

Again, one chance only. He was around at the same time as the young Richards, Botham, Roebuck and Marks. In the case of the Weston off-spinner, only for a summer.

JOHN STANLEY HOOK Born Weston-super-Mare, 27.5.54. RHB, OB. SFC: 1 match; 7 runs @ 7.00; HS 4* v Oxford University, The Parks, 1975; 0 wickets.

PHIL SLOCOMBE
1975 – 1983

The promise was immense. A century came in his third championship match and 1,000 runs in his first season. The MCC selected him and his name was firmly pencilled in for potential Test inclusion before too long. Alas, fulfilment – and latterly even selection – was elusive.

Confidence evaporated and, probably in desperation, he became increasingly theoretical, opening his stance and forsaking some of the neater, more natural traits of the young Weston and Millfield batsman. But he never lost his exquisite footwork against the slow bowlers and could play spinners like a dream. In the end, dejected by lessening encouragement, he turned to antiques for a living.

PHILIP ANTHONY SLOCOMBE Born Weston-super-Mare, 6.9.54. RHB, RM. Cap 1978. SFC: 135 matches; 5539 runs @ 27.83; 7 centuries; HS 132 v Nottinghamshire, Taunton, 1975; 1000 runs twice; HT 1221 in 1978; 3 wickets @ 18.00; BB 1-2 v Gloucestershire, Bristol, 1982. OD: 78 matches; 829 runs @ 14.80.

Slocombe's features are not well known yet, but they should be one day. He batted for two hours twenty minutes yesterday, patiently, correctly, neatly, promisingly. He could just be ready for a tour of India when the MCC side comes to be chosen in August.
John Woodcock, The Times, on his 34* for the MCC against Leicestershire, Lord's, April 1976

1976

Captain: D.B. Close

When would Somerset eventually enjoy their first major competition success? The plaintive question was understandable. They failed by a single run to win the John Player League after an agonising final over. They lost to Glamorgan when a tie would have been enough to put them above Kent, who won in the end on run-rate. But it was still a season of merit. They had been without Richards, playing for the West Indies in this country; Cartwright was out again, the victim of a freak accident when he collided with an opponent in running a leg-bye, and Close was needed for three Tests at the age of 45. As ever, Close's influence on the county team had been undeniable. He got his 1,000 runs, he chased the drifters in the field, he inspired all his team at different times – and he deservedly picked up a decent testimonial.

As a batsman, Rose was out in front, confirming the warm predictions when first he played for the county and, at the same time, offering an eloquent answer to the few doubters about his long-term progress. His hundreds against Leicestershire, Kent and Gloucestershire, all at Taunton, were composed with genuine élan. His fellow fair-haired left-hander, Denning, scored his maiden championship century, against Glamorgan at Weston-super-Mare. Kitchen was back after a year away from the game, while Marks was reminding us of his potential. Taylor earned himself a Test trial, though there was to be no elevation. He'd made himself into an excellent wicket-keeper since leaving Surrey, complemented by his calm temperament and quiet ability as a disciplined and reliable batsman.

Somerset's bowling could have done with a little more fire and penetration, but the wickets were liberally shared around. Gurr revealed that he possessed a lovely action and natural movement. What he lacked, unfortunately, was the mental fibre to back it up. An intelligent man, he fought a dogged and losing battle to sustain accuracy and the skills that had so pleased the coaches. There was, of course, no absence of self-assurance from Botham. Wisden faithfully reports that one day he sent down no fewer than 37 overs at lively pace.

Sadly, Cartwright's days with Somerset were now over. There were differences between him and county officials over his fitness latterly, and his ability to play in a specific match. It all ended with strong words at Clarence Park, where he was wanted for a Sunday fixture. 'That's it', the bowler-craftsman said to himself. 'I like living in the West Country but I've had enough.' Soon he was on his way to Glamorgan.

Subscriptions	
Full	£7
Senior Citizen	£5
Junior	£3.50

COUNTY CHAMPIONSHIP 7th

Played 20	Won 7	Drawn 5	Lost 8

OTHER MATCHES — Played 2 Drawn 1 Lost 1

GILLETTE CUP — Lost in Second Round

BENSON & HEDGES CUP — Eliminated at Zonal Stage

JOHN PLAYER LEAGUE 2nd — Played 16 Won 10 Lost 6

BATTING

	M	I	NO	Runs	HS	Ave	100	50	ct	st
B.C. Rose	20	39	4	1624	177	46.40	4	8	11	-
D.B. Close	17	28	4	971	88	40.45	–	7	13	–
I.T. Botham	20	35	5	1022	167*	34.06	1	6	16	–
P.W. Denning	20	39	2	1082	107	29.24	1	8	7	–
D.J.S. Taylor	21	39	7	807	136	25.21	1	3	50	8
V.J. Marks	9	15	0	377	98	25.13	–	3	6	–
P.A. Slocombe	16	30	1	608	90	20.96	–	3	10	–
G.I. Burgess	22	41	6	704	79*	20.11	–	4	14	–
M.J. Kitchen	18	33	1	620	79	19.37	–	5	4	–
P.M. Roebuck	4	8	0	151	69	18.87	–	1	4	–
C.H. Dredge	7	13	7	108	24*	18.00	–	–	2	–
D. Breakwell	22	36	3	520	44	15.75	–	–	13	–
D.R. Gurr	10	14	8	83	21	13.83	–	–	–	–
K.F. Jennings	8	14	2	137	49	11.41	–	–	2	–
H.R. Moseley	20	27	11	180	40	11.25	–	–	3	–
R.J. Clapp	3	3	1	3	2*	1.50	–	–	–	–

(2 matches) T.W. Cartwright 4* (1 ct)

(1 match) T. Gard 7, 2* (3 ct, 1 st) J.M. Parks 1, 10 (1 ct) N.J. Evans 0

BOWLING

	Overs	Mdns	Runs	Wkts	Ave	5wi	10wm
H.R. Moseley	582.1	156	1440	58	24.82	3	–
I.T. Botham	563.4	104	1880	66	28.48	4	–
D.R. Gurr	282.5	55	972	34	28.58	1	–
V.J. Marks	125.1	30	385	12	32.08	1	–
G.I. Burgess	492.3	130	1414	41	34.48	–	–
T.W. Cartwright	77	32	138	4	34.50	–	–
D. Breakwell	514.3	142	1348	39	34.56	2	–
D.B. Close	162.1	36	605	15	40.33	–	–
C.H. Dredge	130	23	448	9	49.77	–	–
K.F. Jennings	172	40	527	9	58.55	–	–

R.J. Clapp 38-12-102-7 N.J. Evans 18-1-62-0 P.M. Roebuck 7-2-18-0

M.J. Kitchen 5.4-1-30-0 B.C. Rose 4-0-9-0

COLIN DREDGE 1976 – 1988

The bowling action was inclined to send coaches into apoplexy, but any apparent lack of co-ordination was offset by the size of his Somerset heart. On occasions he took the new ball, with typical resolve and visible pride, but his merits were more often evident as the reliable back-up man.

Frome never produced a better workhorse. That was where he used to play, along with his numerous brothers. Once he somehow held on to a fierce return catch from a young Lansdown adventurer, out first ball. Viv Richards was the batsman. 'Who's this beanpole?' he asked afterwards in admiration.

'Herbie' was true Somerset, authentic as the Mendips. He never imagined he'd make it as a cricket pro, starting his working life as an apprentice toolmaker, then serving the county royally before eventually returning to engineering.

He was a fair old footballer, too, and Bristol City nearly took him as a centre-forward, but he settled for the likes of Frome Town, Welton Rovers and Odd Down instead.

COLIN HERBERT DREDGE Born Frome, Somerset, 4.8.54. LHB, RMF. Cap 1978. SFC: 194 matches; 2182 runs @ 13.98; HS 56* v Yorkshire, Harrogate, 1977; HT 317 in 1982; 443 wickets @ 30.10; BB 6-37 v Gloucestershire, Bristol, 1981; HT 63 in 1980. OD: 209 matches; 464 runs @ 10.54; 253 wickets @ 25.42; GC MoM 1.

It was Roebuck, Popplewell, Marks, those university types, who held the Somerset innings together, though at the last crisis it was Dredge, the Demon of Frome, who struck out for the country bumpkins.

Alan Gibson, reporting a Somerset victory in *The Times*

TREVOR GARD 1976 – 1989

No mistaking him, the true Somerset countryman. He walked to the wicket, a little fellow with those almost comically big strides. Never without his cap; on occasions carrying the bat under his arm as if it were the 12-bore he had at home.

For a long time he waited as number-two to Derek Taylor. When it was his turn, Trevor did the wicket-keeper's job without a hint of fuss. Maybe there were technically better stumpers in the county's long history, but he didn't often put down a catch and his two legside stumpings in the Lord's final against Kent are still talked about.

Realistically, if he'd been a rather more accomplished batsman, his stay with the county might have gone on for a few more summers.

TREVOR GARD Born West Lambrook, Somerset, 2.6.57. RHB, WK. Cap 1983. SFC: 112 matches; 1389 runs @ 13.75; HS 51* v Indians, Taunton, 1979; HT 457 in 1983; 0 wickets; 217 dismissals (178 ct, 39 st). OD: 81 matches; 240 runs @ 12.00; 70 dismissals (57 ct, 13 st); NW MoM 1.

DAVID GURR 1976 – 1979

He arrived from Oxford with a dream action. Everyone seemed to forecast Test recognition for him. He had the pace and natural movement; not, alas, the mental fibre. There were just 24 first-class appearances for Somerset. By then, his length, line and overall confidence had gone completely.

The county tried everything, including psychoanalysis, to restore his innate bowling gifts. He could still pitch immaculately in the nets, but it was a cruel deception.

There was the time he simply couldn't will himself to play against the New Zealanders. In a hurry, Somerset were left to include two wicketkeepers, Taylor and Gard. When Greg Chappell was back in Taunton, having a net for a challenge competition, he was beaten repeatedly by Gurr. 'Who is this chap?' he asked. 'Is he going on tour for England?'

DAVID ROBERTS GURR Born Whitchurch, Buckinghamshire, 27.3.56. RHB, RF. SFC: 24 matches; 161 runs @ 17.88; HS 21 v Gloucestershire, Bristol, 1976; 64 wickets @ 30.48; BB 5-30 v Lancashire, Weston-super-Mare, 1976; HT 34 in 1976. OD: 11 matches; 7 runs @ 2.33; 7 wickets @ 39.57.

NICK EVANS 1976

This young clubman, another from Weston, had a solitary county game. Neither runs nor wickets to show for it, alas.

NICHOLAS JOHN EVANS Born Weston-super-Mare, 9.9.54. RHB, RM. SFC: 1 match; 0 runs; 0 wickets.

1977

Captain: D.B. Close

Surely there couldn't have been a more uplifting early-season performance than the seven-wicket win against the Aussies at Bath. Somerset had never beaten them before – and it turned out to be the only time the tourists went down in a three-day match that summer. You'd not have guessed that the pitch was flooded only days before, leading to contingency plans to switch to Taunton if necessary. Those Somerset exiles, Chappell and O'Keeffe, were now playing against their former county. In fact, Chappell stroked a fine century and so did David Hookes. Let's not forget Rose's unbeaten hundred or the way the towering newcomer from the Caribbean, Garner, caused such a buzz of excitement as he took a wicket in his opening over.

In truth it was less fun for Close. He was out for a duck in what was to be not quite the ideal farewell season for him, partly because of injury, illness and suspect form. What an influence he'd been, all the same. Somerset finished in fourth position in the championship. Botham, not always available for the county, still did enough to stamp his buoyant personality on the West Country game. So, of course, did Richards, with all that sublime timing and devastating power as the scoreboard rattled. Test careers for the two of them were already ensured. And for Rose, national recognition was on the way. Prospects were perhaps not quite as grand for the popular 'Dasher', though he crashed a hundred in each innings, in his own Chewton Mendip style, against Gloucestershire (and Procter), not long after recovering from a broken jaw.

Roebuck may have been rather more academic and circumspect in his approach. But clearly here was another to watch and quietly admire. At Clarence Park, at the expense of Surrey, he scored his maiden century for Somerset. In that same match, Richards danced past 200 and his 2,000 runs for the season. With Roebuck, who in those happier days he dubbed 'The Professor', Richards created a new fourth-wicket record stand of 251.

I badly wanted to win something for Somerset, to repay a little to the county which had given me such a warm and sincere welcome when my cricket career seemed shattered. Unfortunately, I failed in the end but we had fun – and a few near misses. I hope their memories of me are as warm as mine of Somerset and its cricket.

Brian Close

COUNTY CHAMPIONSHIP 12th

Played 21	Won 6	Drawn 11	Lost 4

OTHER MATCHES — Played 1 Won 1

GILLETTE CUP — Lost in Semi-Final

BENSON & HEDGES CUP — Eliminated at Zonal Stage

JOHN PLAYER LEAGUE 9th — Played 16 Won 6 No Result 2 Lost 8

BATTING

	M	I	NO	Runs	HS	Ave	100	50	ct	st
I.V.A. Richards	20	35	2	2161	241*	65.48	7	9	16	–
P.W. Denning	17	29	3	1032	122	39.69	3	4	8	–
B.C. Rose	19	33	2	1119	205	36.09	3	3	6	–
D.R. Gurr	6	5	4	35	16*	35.00	–	–	4	–
V.J. Marks	9	13	2	347	69	31.54	–	3	1	–
M.J. Kitchen	20	33	1	1005	143*	31.40	3	2	16	–
I.T. Botham	13	22	1	650	114	30.95	1	4	9	–
P.A. Slocombe	12	19	3	437	55*	27.31	–	2	4	–
P.M. Roebuck	6	8	2	159	112	26.50	1	–	2	–
D.J.S. Taylor	20	28	9	496	84*	26.10	–	2	51	5
D.B. Close	16	25	2	438	87	19.04	–	2	19	–
J. Garner	5	6	1	91	37	18.20	–	–	5	–
D. Breakwell	17	26	5	368	51	17.52	–	1	4	–
C.H. Dredge	20	26	7	287	56*	15.10	–	1	11	–
H.R. Moseley	14	13	10	45	10*	15.00	–	–	3	–
G.I. Burgess	13	15	2	163	32	12.53	–	–	7	–
M. Olive	3	5	1	24	15	6.00	–	–	4	–
K.F. Jennings	8	12	2	42	14	4.20	–	–	8	–

(2 matches) T. Gard 3, 0 (2 ct)

(1 match) P.J. Robinson 0* (1 ct) R.J. Clapp did not bat

BOWLING

	Overs	Mdns	Runs	Wkts	Ave	5wi	10wm
J. Garner	215.1	60	539	27	19.96	1	–
I.T. Botham	535.5	118	1648	70	23.54	4	1
H.R. Moseley	451.2	107	1089	42	25.92	–	–
G.I. Burgess	367.1	101	1043	38	27.44	1	–
D.R. Gurr	143.1	22	494	17	29.05	1	–
D. Breakwell	355	110	890	29	30.68	–	–
I.V.A. Richards	89.5	24	248	7	35.42	–	–
P.M. Roebuck	92.5	26	261	7	37.28	–	–
C.H. Dredge	464	98	1396	37	37.72	–	–
V.J. Marks	263.1	80	729	19	38.36	1	–
K.F. Jennings	139.3	41	386	8	48.25	–	–

R.J. Clapp 19.1-8-37-4 P.J. Robinson 13-3-32-3 B.C. Rose 10-1-52-0

P.A. Slocombe 3-1-14-0 D.B. Close 0.2-0-8-0

Once, on a very
slow pitch at
Chelmsford,
Graham Gooch did
pull him for three
fours in one over,
but that stands out
in my memory like
an oasis in a desert.
Trevor Bailey

For Somerset he
was pure gold.
A charming
companion and a
perfect gentleman
… until you gave
him a cricket ball
and batsmen to
bowl at.
Eric Coombes

JOEL GARNER 1977 – 1986

He was the most unplayable bowler in the world and when trophies eventually came to Somerset, they could usually be traced substantially to 'Big Bird.' Towering and fearsome, at times appearing even faster than he was, making batsmen redundant with his lethal yorker, bouncing the ball from his massive fist as if it were a yo-yo, he could win matches on his own. What with Viv Richards, the best and most murderous batsman in contemporary cricket, the brew in the West Country was more exciting and potent than it had ever been before.

The pair were never bosom pals as such, indeed occasionally Garner went into print quite critically about his West Indian skipper. But, along with Ian Botham, they headed the wondrous cast in the effervescent, thrilling, twitchy golden years of Somerset cricket.

Joel liked to sleep, to prepare his Caribbean hot-pots and to withdraw from the more arduous and frantic aspects of the county game. There was something especially sad about his involvement in the Grand Guignol that led to Shepton Mallet. He attended that fateful meeting, a silent, poignant figure; and when the rebels staged an affectionate farewell for the three departing stars, only Garner turned up.

He had come to Somerset by way of Lancashire League cricket with Littleborough; he took a wicket in his first over on his county debut against the Aussies; and he went out, by now less fit and of declining value as a three-day performer, with more of an anti-climax than the accord he deserved.

At home he did social work and some opinionated journalism. He would come back here to play club cricket at a tempo he now enjoyed. The West Country didn't lose its appeal and his popular presence was to be seen and enjoyed at Glastonbury CC for a season or two. Back home he managed the West Indies 'A' team and would also express a strong view from time to time, letting it be known that pacemen such as Brett Lee and Shoaib Akhtar wouldn't be in his World XI. In other words, sheer speed alone wasn't enough.

JOEL GARNER Born Christchurch, Barbados, 16.12.52. RHB, RF. Cap 1979. 58 Tests 1977-87. 98 LOI 1977-87. SFC: 94 matches; 1170 runs @ 18.00; HS 90 v Gloucestershire, Bath, 1981; HT 324 in 1981; 338 wickets @ 18.10; BB 8-31 v Glamorgan, Cardiff, 1977; HT 88 in 1981. OD: 128 matches; 703 runs @ 14.64; 206 wickets @ 15.15; GC/NW MoM 2; B&GA 2. Barbados, West Indies, 1975-86; South Australia 1982-83.

MARTIN OLIVE 1977 – 1981

Everyone liked the look of his batting at Millfield. He made his county debut as a teenager, exuding a stylish, promising presence at the wicket, a pleasant personality away from it. It was difficult, though, for a newcomer to break in and establish himself at that particular time. In the end he moved to Devon to work for a building society, eventfully. The premises were held up on his first day at the office.

MARTIN OLIVE Born Watford, Hertfordshire, 18.4.58. RHB. SFC: 17 matches; 467 runs @ 15.56; HS 50 v Yorkshire, Weston-super-Mare, 1980; HT 290 in 1980. OD: 1 match; 2 runs (no average).

1978

Captain: B.C. Rose

Some argued that this was Somerset's finest season so far. Yet, maddeningly, they had nothing to show for it. Their first titles had been there for the taking. Big crowds, constantly supportive, cheered prematurely. The season ended with two days of abject frustration – as on the Saturday the Gillette Cup slipped away, and on the Sunday, when only a nominal tie was needed, they failed to win the John Player League by two runs. Grown men in the Somerset dressing room cried; one smashed his bat on the stone floor. The team spirit had been marvellous; the county deserved better. Apart from the Gillette and the John Player near-triumphs, the county ended the summer fifth in the championship table and reached the Benson & Hedges semi-final. Taunton tingled like never before. The unthinkable had happened – Somerset had become one of the most glamorous counties in the country. They possessed three of the most prodigiously gifted players in the world. Their mighty natural talents enthralled spectators, not just at Taunton.

It's too easy to say nerves got at Somerset, that they finally lacked the hard edge when it was most needed. One could detect a hint of naivety, the occasional suspect judgment over a decision or a scampered run. But that has always been part of Somerset's appeal. Nothing was more clear, however, than the fact that the county had tasted hitherto unknown fame and they wanted, deserved, more of it.

Rose was now the captain, a decision that may have surprised a few people. The choice, however, was a wise one: he was one of the game's thinkers and he wanted plenty of young players around him. It may have helped that he had match-winners in his side. His was the quiet, orchestrating voice; and he was learning the onerous qualities of captaincy all the time. In that team of his, it wasn't simply the superstars who made the difference. Somerset had shaken off their years of diffidence and self-effacement. Suddenly they knew they could hold their own with the best.

That fifth place in the championship was more than a reflection on the monumental skills of two or three individuals. There was also the tidy bowling of Moseley, the progress of Dredge and Jennings, the influence of coach Robinson on the younger players. Somerset were a team on a mission.

I suppose we should not have been surprised. All through their talented but eccentric history, Somerset have been winning the matches they were bound to lose and losing the matches they were bound to win. So they still remain one of the two counties (Essex is the other) who have never won anything.

So we are saying, as we have said at the end of so many seasons, 'well tried, Somerset', and no more than that.

Alan Gibson, The Times

COUNTY CHAMPIONSHIP 5th

Played 22	Won 9	Drawn 9	Lost 4

OTHER MATCHES — Played 2 — Drawn 2

GILLETTE CUP — Lost in Final

BENSON & HEDGES CUP — Lost in Semi-Final

JOHN PLAYER LEAGUE 2nd — Played 16 — Won 11 — No Result 2 — Lost 3

BATTING

	M	I	NO	Runs	HS	Ave	100	50	ct	st
I.V.A. Richards	21	38	4	1558	118	45.82	2	10	22	–
P.A. Slocombe	23	40	8	1221	128*	38.15	3	5	12	–
B.C. Rose	24	41	5	1263	122	35.08	4	3	11	–
P.M. Roebuck	23	37	8	944	131*	32.55	1	6	10	–
D. Breakwell	16	23	5	579	100*	32.16	1	4	5	–
P.W. Denning	22	39	3	925	78*	25.69	–	5	13	–
V.J. Marks	11	18	3	304	51	20.26	–	1	6	–
M.J. Kitchen	13	20	2	359	50	19.94	–	1	12	–
I.T. Botham	10	14	0	275	86	19.64	–	1	5	–
G.I. Burgess	16	23	5	336	55	18.66	–	1	12	–
D.J.S. Taylor	23	29	5	424	78	17.66	–	2	55	9
K.F. Jennings	17	19	10	152	31*	16.88	–	–	11	–
H.R. Moseley	14	9	3	62	30	10.33	–	–	7	–
C.H. Dredge	20	19	3	148	23	9.25	–	–	6	–
D.R. Gurr	4	5	3	12	4	6.00	–	–	1	–
J. Garner	4	5	2	12	6*	4.00	–	–	2	–

(2 matches) T. Gard did not bat (2 ct)
(1 match) M. Olive 3, 1

BOWLING

	Overs	Mdns	Runs	Wkts	Ave	5wi	10wm
J. Garner	170.1	61	351	22	15.95	3	–
I.T. Botham	369.5	77	1051	58	18.12	5	–
H.R. Moseley	348.1	103	813	41	19.82	1	–
D. Breakwell	445.1	135	1007	41	24.56	1	–
K.F. Jennings	442.3	147	1041	40	26.02	1	–
C.H. Dredge	573.1	137	1473	56	26.30	2	–
D.R. Gurr	104	25	296	11	26.90	–	–
V.J. Marks	349.4	99	945	31	30.48	–	–
G.I. Burgess	363	136	890	27	32.96	1	–
I.V.A. Richards	89.5	16	268	8	33.50	–	–
P.M. Roebuck	101	28	272	4	68.00	–	–

B.C. Rose 8.2-1-31-1   P.W. Denning 7-2-25-0   P.A. Slocombe 4-1-11-0

1979

Captain: B.C. Rose

At long last, for the first time in the club's history, the uplifting sparkle of silverware had arrived in Somerset and the noisy, good-natured supporters were ecstatic. In contrast with the late, agonising stumbles 12 months earlier, this time they made sure of both the Gillette Cup and the John Player League title. They had Garner available for the whole season, never more effective than when he took those half-dozen cheap wickets in the Lord's final. Richards' mighty presence – and predictable hundred – in the same victory against Northants was another positive factor. But the season was essentially a team triumph, many players weighing in with timely contributions.

That marvellous late-summer double went a long way towards offsetting the volume of the cricket establishment's scorn over the Somerset players' ill-judged ploy against Worcestershire in the Benson & Hedges competition. The county declared after one over, having calculated, with some cynicism the critics claimed, that their action, which appeared to assure their progress to the next round, was not illegal. It was, however, against the spirit of the game in the unequivocal verdict of the authorities and Somerset were disqualified for their cerebral pains. Within the siege-like dressing room, there remained more than a hint of defiance. The apportioning of blame was blurred, as it still is today. They were tough days for Rose, in his second year as captain. In fact, the team's indiscretions were quickly forgotten; the indicted skipper went on to bat with much skill and lead his side with enthusiasm.

Team spirit, in an odd way, benefited from the incident. Somerset created club history by going 23 games without a defeat. It was a record which ended only when they were forced to put out a weakened side against Sussex in the final championship match and lost by nine wickets.

> On the Sunday after the Worcester match, we had a fantastic reception at Taunton. In fact, the whole experience strengthened the backbone of the team. We were hardened by it. It made us a lot more resolute, less like the Somerset of old.
>
> **Brian Rose**

COUNTY CHAMPIONSHIP   8th

Played 21	Won 5	Drawn 15	Lost 1

OTHER MATCHES Played 3 Won 1 Drawn 2

GILLETTE CUP Champions

BENSON & HEDGES CUP Disqualified at Zonal Stage

JOHN PLAYER LEAGUE **1st** Played 16 Won 12 No Result 1 Lost 3

BATTING

	M	I	NO	Runs	HS	Ave	100	50	ct	st
T. Gard	4	5	4	71	51*	71.00	–	1	6	3
P.M. Roebuck	23	37	10	1273	89	47.14	–	11	22	–
P.W. Denning	22	35	6	1222	106	42.13	2	7	18	–
B.C. Rose	21	33	1	1317	133	41.15	2	8	12	–
I.V.A. Richards	16	26	0	1043	156	40.11	3	4	13	–
V.J. Marks	24	33	9	894	93	37.25	–	7	8	–
C.H. Dredge	11	11	5	215	55	35.83	–	1	5	–
I.T. Botham	11	15	1	487	120	34.78	1	1	11	–
D.J.S. Taylor	20	20	10	318	50*	31.80	–	1	29	10
P.A. Slocombe	23	38	3	956	103*	27.31	1	6	8	–
D. Breakwell	24	31	9	510	54*	23.18	–	2	9	–
J. Garner	14	10	4	106	53	17.66	–	1	4	–
J.W. Lloyds	4	7	0	117	43	16.71	–	–	2	–
M.J. Kitchen	7	10	0	146	36	14.60	–	–	8	–
N.F.M. Popplewell	7	10	1	119	37	13.22	–	–	1	–
H.R. Moseley	8	5	2	25	15	8.33	–	–	1	–
K.F. Jennings	19	11	5	19	11*	3.16	–	–	9	–
D.R. Gurr	4	2	2	31	20*	–	–	–	–	–

(1 match)   M. Olive 39, 38   G.I. Burgess 9, 11

BOWLING

	Overs	Mdns	Runs	Wkts	Ave	5wi	10wm
J. Garner	393.1	127	761	55	13.83	4	–
H.R. Moseley	196.4	50	495	31	15.96	2	1
V.J. Marks	568.4	153	1581	57	27.73	4	–
D. Breakwell	567.3	193	1311	47	27.89	1	–
C.H. Dredge	251	60	759	25	30.36	–	–
K.F. Jennings	245.3	78	620	20	31.00	–	–
I.T. Botham	257.4	62	846	26	32.53	1	–
N.F.M. Popplewell	102	33	271	6	45.16	–	–
I.V.A. Richards	77.3	11	270	5	54.00	–	–
D.R. Gurr	71	17	189	2	94.50	–	–

P.M. Roebuck 6-0-22-1   J.W. Lloyds 6-3-14-0   G.I. Burgess 5-3-8-0
B.C. Rose 5-0-14-0

JEREMY LLOYDS
1979 – 1984

Some at Taunton tried hard to keep Jeremy Lloyds when he chose to move up the motorway to Gloucestershire. There came a time, one suspects, when he was no longer happy in the Somerset dressing room. He was an intelligent and complex person, probably feeling that at times he deserved more support and scope.

As a player, he was seen by many as a genuine all-rounder. Jeremy was good enough to open the innings for Somerset; he could punch most fluently off his pads when runs were needed. In addition, he was a prodigious off-spinner and the most reliable of slips.

He played in the 1983 final of the NatWest Trophy for Somerset, then did so well for his new employer that, four years later, he was named as Gloucestershire's player of the season. There were more than 10,000 runs and ten centuries in his county career. He coached in South Africa before becoming a first-class umpire in 1998 and joining the international panel from 2002.

JEREMY WILLIAM LLOYDS Born Penang, Malaya, 17.11.54. LHB, ROB. Cap 1982. SFC: 100 matches; 4036 runs @ 28.42; HS 132* v Northamptonshire, Northampton, 1982; 5 centuries; HT 981 in 1982; 133 wickets @ 34.84; BB 7-88 v Essex, Chelmsford, 1982; HT 46 in 1982. OD: 62 matches; 592 runs @ 14.43; 3 wickets @ 52.66. Gloucestershire 1985-91; Orange Free State, South Africa, 1983-88. Fc umpire 1998-.

NIGEL POPPLEWELL
1979 – 1985

His Somerset contract followed a lively, fighting innings for Cambridge when they were bowled out for fewer than 100 at Bath. For the county he was apt to be jokey, self-deprecating and under-dressed, though the appearance smartened noticeably when he was embraced by the legal profession.

His cricket, early on, was inclined to be a trifle cavalier. But the wholeheartedness was always there. He was maybe no more than a modest bowler; his fielding could be brilliant, and his batting pleasantly adaptable. He would open the innings, by then tighter in technique, and enjoyed the role even more when he was on his toes to execute the square-cut which proved most profitable to him.

Those who saw his 172 at Southend described it as exquisite. Those who witnessed his hundred in 41 minutes at Bath recalled his jocular behaviour the previous night on a narrow boat when he was playfully pushed into the Avon by Ian Botham.

The trend of the game – 'less gentle and joyful' to use his own words – brought signs of disenchantment. It was time to put on a suit and follow in his illustrious father's footsteps.

NIGEL FRANCIS MARK POPPLEWELL Born Chislehurst, Kent, 8.8.57. RHB, RM. Cap 1983. SFC: 118 matches; 4594 runs @ 28.18; 4 centuries; HS 172 v Essex, Southend, 1985; 1000 runs twice; HT 1116 in 1984; 78 wickets @ 39.60; BB 5-33 v Northamptonshire, Weston-super-Mare, 1981; HT 23 in 1983. OD: 116 matches; 2022 runs @ 24.36; 43 wickets @ 30.83; NW MoM 1; B&H GA 2. Cambridge University 1977-79.

1980

Captain: B.C. Rose

Everyone assumed the season would be something of an anti-climax. Garner and Richards were mostly committed to the West Indies tourists. Botham was fighting to overcome back problems. Rose suffered in turn from illness and injuries, and was also off playing in three Tests. In between, however, he came up with a notable century in each innings against Worcestershire. But despite the unscheduled worries over selection and the lamented absentees, Somerset still finished equal fourth in the championship, an improvement on the previous year. They were also runners-up in the John Player League, winning 11 matches, the same number as the eventual champions, Warwickshire, demonstrating again that they could adapt their game to the needs of both limited-over and championship cricket.

Somerset had signed Gavaskar for the summer. This fine player didn't much enjoy the cold and rainy days, though there were still various innings to savour – especially an August treat of 155 not out against Yorkshire. If we are to nominate specific exhibitions, however, what about Botham's splendid double-hundred off the bowling of Gloucestershire's Mike Procter and company at Taunton?

Even without their stars, Somerset found others to cover with true merit. Dredge – lean, unco-ordinated and much admired around the West Country meadows – showed his worth by heading the bowling averages. Popplewell recorded his maiden hundred; and Taylor, when not passing the test as a batsman for a crisis, confirmed what a competent wicket-keeper he was.

Taunton, for so long one of the quieter, remoter county grounds, where you could enjoy the prospect of the Quantocks (and of empty seats in the foreground) now hums with enthusiasm. The skeleton of the new pavilion is built. I am afraid it is going to do nothing for the view, but it is needed.

Alan Gibson

COUNTY CHAMPIONSHIP 4th

Played 21	Won 3	Drawn 13	Lost 5

OTHER MATCHES — Played 2   Won 1   Drawn 1

GILLETTE CUP — Lost in First Round

BENSON & HEDGES CUP — Eliminated at Zonal Stage

JOHN PLAYER LEAGUE 2nd — Played 16   Won 11   Lost 5

BATTING

	M	I	NO	Runs	HS	Ave	100	50	ct	st
I.T. Botham	11	15	0	928	228	61.86	2	5	21	–
B.C. Rose	14	20	3	841	150*	49.47	2	3	4	–
D.J.S. Taylor	20	26	9	743	59	43.70	–	5	33	4
I.V.A. Richards	4	8	0	306	170	38.25	1	1	6	–
S.M. Gavaskar	15	23	3	686	155*	34.30	2	2	5	–
N.F.M. Popplewell	14	20	6	445	135*	31.78	1	1	17	–
P.W. Denning	23	34	2	1012	184	31.62	1	5	14	–
V.J. Marks	22	32	7	765	82	30.60	–	5	11	–
J.W. Lloyds	11	16	3	388	70	29.84	–	4	7	–
P.M. Roebuck	22	35	3	866	101	27.06	1	3	11	–
D. Breakwell	12	14	3	276	73*	25.09	–	1	2	–
T. Gard	3	2	0	41	22	20.50	–	–	4	1
M. Olive	9	17	1	290	50	18.12	–	1	4	–
K.F. Jennings	11	10	4	104	21*	17.33	–	–	13	–
P.A. Slocombe	13	18	2	256	114	16.00	1	–	2	–
H.R. Moseley	17	9	4	55	16	11.00	–	–	5	–
H.I.E. Gore	11	11	5	48	22*	8.00	–	–	3	–
C.H. Dredge	20	21	5	113	21*	7.06	–	–	6	–

(1 match)   N. Russom 9

BOWLING

	Overs	Mdns	Runs	Wkts	Ave	5wi	10wm
C.H. Dredge	571.2	136	1600	63	25.39	5	–
H.R. Moseley	470.5	115	1193	40	29.82	2	–
J.W. Lloyds	264	55	899	28	32.10	2	1
I.T. Botham	263.1	69	810	25	32.40	–	–
N.F.M. Popplewell	186.5	46	587	17	34.52	–	–
K.F. Jennings	225.2	53	615	14	43.92	–	–
V.J. Marks	766.1	196	2157	46	46.89	2	–
H.I.E. Gore	253.5	66	669	14	47.78	1	–
D. Breakwell	330	101	910	18	50.55	–	–

I.V.A. Richards 30-2-110-3   P.M. Roebuck 24.2-2-113-2   N. Russom 19-7-54-0
S.M. Gavaskar 14.2-2-69-0   B.C. Rose 5-0-25-0   P.A. Slocombe 3-0-18-2
D.J.S. Taylor 2-1-1-0   P.W. Denning 1.5-0-8-0

SUNIL GAVASKAR 1980

Just a one-year Somerset contract for the masterful Indian Test opener, but there were still gems to catch. One was the way he more or less bowed out with his undefeated 155 at Clarence Park. He was really only standing in for the absent Viv Richards, though some longed in vain for him to come back.

Gavaskar viewed his English summer with detached amusement and some reservations. He huddled in his sweaters in the recesses of the old dungeon-like Taunton pavilion and read his paperbacks between innings. He hated the cold and the rain – and wasn't too sure what to make of some of the grassy wickets he found in England. The incessant travelling, as experienced by our professionals, was hardly to his liking, either.

But still it was a joy to have him around, if only briefly. Younger players learned from him, and the Somerset crowds felt privileged to see this stocky little maestro at the wicket.

SUNIL MANOHAR GAVASKAR Born Bombay, India, 10.7.49. RHB, RM. 125 Tests 1971-87. 107 LOI 1974-87. SFC: 15 matches; 686 runs @ 34.30; 2 centuries; HS 155* v Yorkshire, Weston-super-Mare, 1980; 0 wickets. OD: 16 matches; 502 runs @ 33.46. Bombay, India, 1967-87.

HUGH GORE 1980

He came in 1980 as Somerset's overseas player. His fellow Antiguan, Viv Richards, who along with Joel Garner was not available for the county that season, had recommended him. Gore was amiable and sophisticated, though carrying, it seemed, a bit of surplus weight.

As a left-arm seamer, who had played for Leeward and Combined Islands, his pace was modest medium. An injury or two punctuated his stay and he made fewer than a dozen first-class appearances for Somerset. Clearly he was never going to rank with the county's more inspired overseas captures.

HUGH EDMUND IVOR GORE Born St John's, Antigua, 18.6.53. RHB, LFM. SFC: 11 matches; 48 runs @ 8.00; HS 22* v Leicestershire, Taunton, 1980; 14 wickets @ 47.78; BB 5-66 v Surrey, Oval, 1980. OD: 4 matches; 0 runs; 4 wickets @ 15.25. Leeward and Combined Islands, West Indies, 1972-79.

NEIL RUSSOM 1980 – 1983

There was some useful form at Cambridge and, one imagined, the possibility of a county career. The considered opinion at Taunton was that, although a good-looking bat and reasonable seamer, he was one of the many who over the years suffered from being around 'at the wrong time'.

NEIL RUSSOM Born Finchley, London, 3.12.58. RHB, RMF. SFC: 4 matches; 41 runs @ 13.66; HS 12 and 12* v Worcestershire, Weston-super-Mare, 1981; 5 wickets @ 33.00; BB 2-18 same match. OD: 1 match, did not bat or bowl. Cambridge University 1979-81.

SOMERSET'S POST-WAR GROUNDS

Somerset have played first-class cricket at nine grounds since the war:

County Ground, Taunton	1946-2005
Recreation Ground, Bath	1946-2005
Clarence Park, Weston-super-Mare	1946-1996
Agricultural Showgrounds, Frome	1946-1961
Rowden Road, Wells	1946-1951
Johnson Park, Yeovil	1951-1967
Morlands Athletic Ground, Glastonbury	1952-1973
Imperial Athletic Club, Bristol	1957-1966
Millfield School, Street	1961

RESULTS

	Played	Won	Tied	Drawn	Lost
Taunton	454	114	1	202	137
Bath	140	50		47	43
Weston-super-Mare	128	35		48	45
Frome	10	5		1	4
Wells	6	1		2	3
Yeovil	12	2		7	3
Glastonbury	18	5		11	2
Bristol	9	2		5	2
Street	1				1

In the summer of 1961 Somerset played their 18 home matches on seven different grounds:

Taunton (7), Bath (4), Weston-super-Mare (3), Frome, Yeovil, Bristol and Street.

Somerset have also played limited-over cricket at:

Devonshire Road, Weston-super-Mare	1969-1970
Cricket Club, Brislington	1969-1970
Recreation Ground, Torquay	1969-1975
Westlands Sports Club, Yeovil	1971-1978
Victoria Club, Street	1975-1977

In the summer of 1969 Somerset played either first-class or limited-over cricket on eight grounds:

Taunton, Bath, Weston-super-Mare (Clarence Park), Glastonbury, Brislington, Torquay, Yeovil (Johnson Park) and Weston-super-Mare (Devonshire Road).

1981

Captain: B.C. Rose

Golden days, indeed. It was now Somerset's turn to win the Benson & Hedges Cup for the first time. They beat Surrey with more than ten overs to spare, maybe not so surprising when we recall Garner's magnificently mean 5-14 in 11 overs, followed by Richards' stunning 132 not out. It seemed appropriate that his mate, Botham, was on hand to complete the formalities with some muscular late blows to match those of his illustrious partner. For the fifth time, Somerset were runners-up in the John Player League, this time denied the title by Essex. It was hardly any wonder that they were now feared as one of cricket's finest one-day sides. They had the technique – and, of course, the players.

Once more, Garner, off whom it was so often impossible to score runs as he bounced the ball challengingly from his exceptional height, frequently looked a match-winner. He missed five championship matches and still took 88 first-class wickets. Richards simply emphasised his legendary status with nine centuries in all matches. Botham was at times away making Test appearances, yet always promised excitement and bravado whenever he was back with Somerset. Roebuck had an encouraging season; Lloyds, not to be underrated as a spinner, scored his maiden hundred, and Marks did especially well in the limited-overs matches. As for those less glamorous seamers, Dredge and Moseley, they battled away, bowled straight and minimised the liberties that batsmen might unwisely want to take with them.

Things were happening structurally at Taunton. The new, and long overdue, pavilion had appeared as a metaphor for the dramatic upsurge of success, and was officially opened by Peter May. Gates were up – and so was the membership. These were good times for Somerset. But for how much longer?

Enjoy

Joel Garner's spectacular lift; Peter Denning's fielding in the covers; Ian Botham's hitting; Viv Richards's glorious stroke-play. At Bath, the scenery, Pulteney Bridge; the restaurants in nearby Pulteney Street. At Taunton, lunch in the pub beside the ground; or the saunter up the main street to buffet lunch in The Castle Hotel.

John Arlott

COUNTY CHAMPIONSHIP 3rd

	Played 22	Won 10	Drawn 10	Lost 2

OTHER MATCHES Played 2 Won 1 Drawn 1

NATWEST BANK TROPHY Lost in Second Round

BENSON & HEDGES CUP Champions

JOHN PLAYER LEAGUE **2nd** Played 16 Won 11 Lost 5

BATTING

	M	I	NO	Runs	HS	Ave	100	50	ct	st
I.V.A. Richards	20	33	3	1718	196	57.26	7	5	18	–
I.T. Botham	10	12	1	526	123*	47.81	1	3	6	–
P.A. Slocombe	4	6	2	173	62*	43.25	–	2	1	–
P.M. Roebuck	22	34	8	1057	91	40.65	–	9	13	–
P.W. Denning	24	36	6	1087	102*	36.23	1	8	14	–
B.C. Rose	23	39	4	1005	107	28.71	1	5	21	–
D. Breakwell	12	13	2	284	58	25.81	–	3	1	–
V.J. Marks	22	30	7	589	81*	25.60	–	3	9	–
J.W. Lloyds	21	35	2	837	127	25.36	1	5	11	–
N.F.M. Popplewell	17	25	2	513	51*	22.30	–	1	20	–
J. Garner	18	18	2	324	90	20.25	–	2	10	–
D.J.S. Taylor	24	28	7	370	48*	17.61	–	–	56	6
H.R. Moseley	20	21	8	162	36*	12.46	–	–	9	–
M. Olive	3	6	0	72	19	12.00	–	–	1	–
C.H. Dredge	19	16	10	51	14	8.50	–	–	9	–

(2 matches) R.L. Ollis 20, 18, 22, 0 (1 ct) K.F. Jennings 4 (2 ct)

(1 match) N. Russom 12, 12* (1 ct)

BOWLING

	Overs	Mdns	Runs	Wkts	Ave	5wi	10wm
J. Garner	605.4	182	1349	88	15.32	7	4
C.H. Dredge	498.2	129	1286	54	23.81	2	–
H.R. Moseley	436	100	1291	49	26.34	–	–
I.T. Botham	301.5	75	1012	33	30.66	1	–
V.J. Marks	633.5	187	1528	48	31.83	2	–
N.F.M. Popplewell	194.2	42	598	18	33.22	1	–
D. Breakwell	241	44	719	19	37.84	1	–
I.V.A. Richards	185.5	38	585	13	45.00	–	–
J.W. Lloyds	144.2	29	482	10	48.20	–	–

K.F. Jennings 29-4-74-4 N. Russom 10-3-29-2 P.W. Denning 3-0-18-0
B.C. Rose 2.5-0-9-0

RICHARD OLLIS 1981 – 1985

This upright left-hander was once stranded on 99 against Gloucestershire at Bristol. Home skipper David Graveney did his best, successfully, to fiddle an extra over for the batsman, but the necessary single still eluded him. Maybe he didn't realise what was happening. He never did score a first-class century.

RICHARD LESLIE OLLIS Born Clifton, Bristol, 14.1.61. LHB, RM. SFC: 37 matches; 1016 runs @ 18.14; HS 99* v Gloucestershire, Bristol, 1983; HT 517 in 1983; 0 wickets. OD: 16 matches; 149 runs @ 16.

MOST POST-WAR RUNS FOR SOMERSET			
First-class cricket		Limited-over cricket	
PB Wight	16,965	IVA Richards	7,349
WE Alley	16,644	PM Roebuck	6,871
PM Roebuck	16,218	PW Denning	6,792
RT Virgin	15,458	RJ Harden	6,275
MJ Kitchen	15,213	BC Rose	5,708
MF Tremlett	15,195	IT Botham	5,049
IVA Richards	14,698	GD Rose	4,937
H Gimblett	14,591	PD Bowler	4,431
G Atkinson	14,468	MN Lathwell	4,399
RJ Harden	12,488	KA Parsons	4,253
HW Stephenson	12,473	M Burns	4,155
BC Rose	12,342	ME Trescothick	3,752

CLARENCE PARK, WESTON-SUPER-MARE

There are so many memories for me, a local boy. They go back to the matches when, still a schoolboy, I regularly helped to work the scoreboard. I didn't miss a ball, and the appeal of county cricket had already been firmly instilled in me. So many spectators used to arrange for their annual holidays to coincide with the matches at Clarence Park. Visiting supporters liked coming to the seaside. Later, when I was playing, eight or more of my old form-mates from school would come to watch and we'd have a party to celebrate the reunion.

Traditionally, Clarence Park had quite a reputation for the variety of its wickets, going back to the days of uncovered tracks. Competing counties could be guaranteed to have a few moans. But Surrey, in the mid-1950s when few could touch them, did bowl us out for 36. Balancing things up, Brian Langford took 9-26 against Lancashire, and 15 from the match in 1958. We never quite knew the way the games would go. That uncertainty, like the ground itself with its rows of surrounding conifers and modest facilities, could be argued to be part of Weston's unusual charm.

The uneven outfield, though, was tough for the fielding side. Clarence Park, a recreation ground after all, had hockey played on it. My sentimental regard didn't lessen, and I was particularly pleased to score a double-hundred there against Northants. My father got quite excited when I was in my 190s and kept popping his head round the sightscreen. Amusing it may have been – but a little disturbing, too. I had to stop him doing it!

The last match was played there in 1996. Despite emotional pleas and a brave local campaign, it became just another out-ground to disappear.

Brian Rose

1982

Captain: B.C. Rose

The recent propensity for winning trophies was a habit not to be given up lightly. Somerset now retained the Benson & Hedges Cup, this time holding on to it with perfunctory ease. Nottinghamshire never looked like winning. They didn't even hang around for their full allocation of 55 overs and it was an early finish. The winning margin was nine wickets. Unlike Somerset, they simply didn't seem physically or temperamentally up for it when it came to Lord's. By comparison, the erstwhile shrinking violets of the West Country were looking like champions. Marks won the gold award in the final. He did, after all, bowl Derek Randall and Clive Rice, two prized and crucial scalps. Nor should we forget his championship tally of wickets.

The championship was still the more testing and elusive of propositions for Somerset, who finished sixth in the table. They badly missed Garner as he struggled with injury. Richards, judged by his highest standards, was not quite always at his best and understandably looked a little jaded on occasion, as if the demanding schedule of county and international commitments around the calendar was getting to him. But there remained plenty to enjoy and applaud. Lloyds was awarded his cap and nearly reached 1,000 runs for the season. Opening against Northamptonshire, he thoughtfully composed a not-out century in each innings. Taylor's admirable and lengthy stint behind the wickets was now coming to an end. His skills were perhaps to be valued even more in retrospect. His retirement would finally give a chance to the patient Gard. Can there be a more frustrating occupation than that of a reserve wicket-keeper? Just ask Peter Eele.

A decision was made to re-lay the squares at Weston-super-Mare and at Bath, following recurrent murmurs about their capricious behaviour, Clarence Park in particular. It was a fair point, surely. When Somerset lost there by an innings to Middlesex, they were all out for 57 with their ten wickets crumbling in the last 46 balls of the match.

Fixture card, 29 May to 5 June

Saturday Taunton
  Somerset v Kent (1st day)

Sunday Swansea
  Glamorgan v Somerset

Monday & Tuesday Taunton
  Somerset v Kent (2nd & 3rd days)

Wednesday to Friday Swansea
  Glamorgan v Somerset

Saturday Chelmsford
  Essex v Somerset

COUNTY CHAMPIONSHIP 6th

Played 22	Won 6	Drawn 10	Lost 6

OTHER MATCHES — Played 1 — Drawn 1

NATWEST BANK TROPHY — Lost in Quarter-Final

BENSON & HEDGES CUP — Champions

JOHN PLAYER LEAGUE — 9th — Played 16 — Won 8 — Lost 8

BATTING

	M	I	NO	Runs	HS	Ave	100	50	ct	st
I.V.A. Richards	20	31	2	1324	181*	45.65	4	5	11	–
B.C. Rose	21	32	8	1090	173*	45.41	2	5	10	–
I.T. Botham	11	20	1	675	131*	35.52	1	4	5	–
N.A. Felton	8	12	0	346	71	28.83	–	3	4	–
J.W. Lloyds	23	39	3	981	132*	27.25	2	3	30	–
P.A. Slocombe	13	23	1	579	78	26.31	–	6	9	–
P.W. Denning	14	22	1	541	91*	25.76	–	3	6	–
P.M. Roebuck	22	38	2	914	90	25.38	–	10	7	–
N.F.M. Popplewell	16	24	5	451	55	23.73	–	1	8	–
V.J. Marks	19	30	3	509	67	18.85	–	4	11	–
H.R. Moseley	18	19	13	113	24*	18.83	–	–	6	–
C.H. Dredge	20	26	8	317	54*	17.61	–	1	9	–
J. Garner	10	11	5	98	40*	16.33	–	–	4	–
D.J.S. Taylor	17	26	5	334	67	15.90	–	2	41	4
T. Gard	6	5	1	37	31	9.25	–	–	8	3
M.R. Davis	9	12	2	65	21*	6.50	–	–	4	–

(2 matches) M. Bryant 6, 0 (1 ct)

(1 match) G.V. Palmer 6, 27   R.J. McCool 7, 12 (1 ct)   R.L. Ollis 1, 1 (1 ct)
N. Russom did not bat (1 ct)

BOWLING

	Overs	Mdns	Runs	Wkts	Ave	5wi	10wm
J. Garner	259.1	76	583	33	17.66	4	1
I.T. Botham	247.2	65	719	39	18.43	2	–
H.R. Moseley	320	68	985	35	28.14	2	–
V.J. Marks	661.2	193	1840	65	28.30	4	–
J.W. Lloyds	468.3	96	1463	46	31.80	3	–
C.H. Dredge	446.5	108	1214	35	34.68	–	–
M.R. Davis	144	19	481	12	40.08	–	–
I.V.A. Richards	265.3	75	671	16	41.93	–	–
N.F.M. Popplewell	94	17	320	6	53.33	–	–

P.M. Roebuck 39-4-109-1 R.J. McCool 27-2-63-0   M. Bryant 17-3-158-2
G.V. Palmer 17-3-57-0   N. Russom 16-2-64-3   P.A. Slocombe 3.2-0-10-1
D.J.S. Taylor 3-2-1-0   B.C. Rose 1-0-5-0

MARK DAVIS 1982 – 1987

High on the list of the county's 'nearly men.' Off that modest run, the pace could be deceptive, and so could the movement.

The village of Kilve, generously represented by the Davis family on the local cricket pitch, was proud of Mark's undoubted promise. He would slant the ball awkwardly across the batsman, while the slips picked up the catches.

At his best, briefly alas, his name was being mentioned in the more elevated reaches of the game. Injuries worked against him and, sadly, his county career tailed away.

After that he played some league cricket in Wales, but coach Peter Robinson hit the mark when he said: 'One of my big disappointments.'

MARK RICHARD DAVIS Born Kilve, Somerset, 26.2.62. LHB, LFM. SFC: 77 matches; 803 runs @ 14.60; HS 60* v Glamorgan, Taunton, 1984; HT 315 in 1985; 149 wickets @ 35.62; BB 7-55 v Northamptonshire, Northampton, 1984; HT 66 in 1984; OD: 59 matches; 134 runs @ 7.44; 50 wickets @ 34.54; B&H GA 1.

GARY PALMER 1982 – 1989

Did the fact that he was Ken's son work against him? It's impossible to tell. Somerset had monitored his progress enthusiastically from school to Second XI level. With fatuously premature judgement, some pundits viewed the 16-year-old and argued that here might be the next Ian Botham. Gary was a great trier, a lively bowler with an odd action and not a bad batsman, but perhaps too much was expected of him. Eventually he was squeezed out by other young bowlers, and the impetus of his career died.

GARY VINCENT PALMER Born Taunton, 1.11.65. RHB, RMF. SFC: 54 matches; 903 runs @ 15.30; HS 78 v Gloucestershire, Bristol, 1983; HT 299 in 1984; 92 wickets @ 44.64; BB 5-38 v Warwickshire, Taunton, 1983; HT 30 in 1984. OD: 83 matches; 428 runs @ 16.46; 77 wickets @ 30.48

NIGEL FELTON 1982 – 1988

Somerset's decision not to renew Nigel Felton's contract surprised some close observers. It was an emotional moment for him. Form had deserted him occasionally and he had never quite built on the words of enthusiasm that had coincided with his arrival. Maybe his studies at Loughborough, resulting in a limited season for Somerset, worked against him.

Felton was a diminutive, dogged batsman, capable of opening the innings. Like many players, he seemed to reveal a chip on his shoulder at times. His earlier relationship with Kent had been disappointing – so he clobbered the Kent bowlers for 173.

When it came to the sombre announcement that he was being sacked by Somerset, he wiped the tears away and showed his best form for months, with a determined hundred against Gloucestershire. They nearly took him on, but instead he went to Northants, with whom he thrived for half a decade.

NIGEL ALFRED FELTON Born Guildford, Surrey, 24.10.60. LHB. Cap 1986. SFC: 108 matches; 4987 runs @ 28.82; 8 centuries; HS 173* v Kent, Taunton, 1983; 1000 runs twice; HT 1094 in 1987; 0 wickets. OD: 62 matches; 1269 runs @ 24.40; 0 wickets; NW MoM 1. Northamptonshire 1989-94.

RUSS McCOOL 1982

As he was born in the county town, while his father was playing for Somerset, it seemed logical – and sentimental – for Russell to try his luck. He, too, bowled leg-breaks and googlies; in the nets and in Second XI matches, he looked impressive. However, nothing much happened in his only championship appearance, and he returned to Australia.

RUSSELL JOHN McCOOL Born Taunton, 4.12.59. RHB, LB. SFC: 1 match; 19 runs @ 9.50; HS 12 v Derbyshire, Derby, 1982; 0 wickets.

MICHAEL BRYANT 1982

He took the new ball with Colin Dredge against Northants in 1982 and claimed Wayne Larkins as one of his two victims. That was the extent of his success as a first-class cricketer. They breed plenty of capable players in Cornwall and Bryant was one of them, a quickish bowler whose feats had attracted Somerset's attention. But he had a minor no-ball problem and never quite made the necessary transition.

MICHAEL BRYANT Born Camborne, Cornwall, 5.4.59. RHB, RFM. SFC: 2 matches; 6 runs @ 3.00; HS 6 v Essex, Chelmsford, 1982; 2 wickets @ 79.00; BB 1-29 v Northamptonshire, Northampton, 1982.

1983

Captain: B.C. Rose

Whatever the relative slump in the championship – only three wins and down to tenth position – Somerset had no intention of bidding farewell to the glamour of appearing as victors in a final. This time it was the NatWest Trophy and they beat Kent by 24 runs. Not that they were always confident of winning. Richards was out to the last ball before lunch after a lively half-century and there were fears that Somerset had not scored enough runs. But tight bowling by Garner, Botham and Marks made it harder for Kent, while two agile leg-side stumpings by the inexperienced Gard increased his county's hopes. There had been excitement and anxiety in the semi-final against Middlesex. The sides finished with their scores level but Somerset went through because they had lost fewer wickets. Another reason for that appearance in the final had been a dazzling captain's innings of 96 not out by Botham.

Yet again, Somerset finished second in the John Player League, the sixth time they'd been runners-up. They had actually garnered the same number of points as Yorkshire, who won the title because of their greater number of away wins.

As for the championship, there were some valid excuses for the modest form. For a time, Botham and Marks were away on World Cup duty, just like Richards and Garner, and the injuries to others such as Rose and Moseley compounded the selection strains. The county played from necessity under four different captains. Wilson, recruited from Surrey to reinforce the bowling, was another injury victim. It was better news when Felton shook off suspect assurance for a memorable maiden century, when Popplewell seemed to be building on his all-round qualities, not least his fielding, and when Denning was rattling up the runs in the Sunday matches. At Bath, Popplewell chased to his century off 41 balls, still not the fastest of the summer. In addition, there was early if brief evidence of Roebuck's potential as a thinking skipper.

Four Lord's victories, two great competitors		
	I.V.A. Richards	J. Garner
Gillette Cup 1979	117	10.3 overs, 6 for 29
Benson & Hedges Cup 1981	132*	11 overs, 5 for 14
Benson & Hedges Cup 1982	51*	8.1 overs, 3 for 13
NatWest Bank Trophy 1983	51	9 overs, 2 for 15

COUNTY CHAMPIONSHIP 10th

COUNTY CHAMPIONSHIP 10th Played 24	Won 3	Drawn 14	Lost 7
OTHER MATCHES Played 1		Drawn 1	
NATWEST BANK TROPHY Champions			
BENSON & HEDGES CUP Eliminated at Zonal Stage			
JOHN PLAYER LEAGUE 2nd Played 16	Won 10	No Result 3	Lost 3

BATTING

	M	I	NO	Runs	HS	Ave	100	50	ct	st
I.V.A. Richards	12	20	4	1204	216	75.25	5	3	6	–
I.T. Botham	10	13	0	570	152	43.84	2	1	7	–
P.M. Roebuck	22	38	5	1235	106*	37.42	1	9	9	–
J.G. Wyatt	6	12	2	352	82*	35.20	–	3	1	–
N.A. Felton	7	12	1	376	173*	34.18	1	1	2	–
J.W. Lloyds	21	35	2	901	100	27.30	1	4	12	–
J. Garner	10	16	6	265	44	26.50	–	–	10	–
R.L. Ollis	13	22	2	517	99*	25.85	–	3	3	–
N.F.M. Popplewell	24	39	3	886	143	24.61	1	4	21	–
V.J. Marks	16	25	3	524	44*	23.81	–	–	5	–
P.W. Denning	21	36	3	758	99	22.96	–	4	6	–
B.C. Rose	8	9	0	184	52	20.44	–	1	2	–
T. Gard	25	33	4	457	51	15.75	–	2	42	8
P.H.L. Wilson	11	11	7	60	25	15.00	–	–	3	–
P.A. Slocombe	11	17	2	224	66	14.93	–	1	5	–
C.H. Dredge	21	26	5	296	50	14.09	–	1	10	–
G.V. Palmer	10	13	2	119	78	10.81	–	1	8	–
M.R. Davis	14	17	5	125	20*	10.41	–	–	5	–
S.C. Booth	10	12	5	24	9	3.42	–	–	7	–

(2 matches) D. Breakwell 55*, 4, 13
(1 match) N. Russom 8

BOWLING

	Overs	Mdns	Runs	Wkts	Ave	5wi	10wm
J. Garner	277	74	708	35	20.22	1	–
C.H. Dredge	492.3	126	1323	48	27.56	2	–
J.W. Lloyds	358.1	98	1079	35	30.82	1	–
G.V. Palmer	208.3	40	630	20	31.50	1	–
I.T. Botham	119.3	28	388	12	32.33	1	–
V.J. Marks	572.3	179	1620	50	32.40	3	–
P.H.L. Wilson	248.3	45	837	25	33.48	–	–
N.F.M. Popplewell	232	38	786	23	34.17	–	–
M.R. Davis	240.4	43	873	25	34.92	–	–
I.V.A. Richards	188	61	462	12	38.50	–	–
S.C. Booth	286.2	85	849	21	40.42	–	–

D. Breakwell 49-17-121-4   N. Russom 5-1-18-0   P.M. Roebuck 5-0-25-0
P.A. Slocombe 2-1-1-0   R.L. Ollis 1-0-2-0   B.C. Rose 1-0-6-0
T. Gard 0.2-0-8-0

JULIAN WYATT
1983 – 1989

His heart belonged to Somerset and, a season or two after he was released, he was back officially as schools coach. Julian was a farmer's son, who worked ceaselessly to iron out technical flaws.

In fact, he was neat and conscientious, whether at the crease or darting around in the field. There were attractive, unflurried strokes which he brought out discriminately during his three centuries. He had plenty of courage, too, as demonstrated in a notable innings against the West Indian pacemen.

JULIAN GEORGE WYATT Born Paulton, Somerset, 19.6.63. RHB, RM. SFC: 69 matches; 2789 runs @ 25.35; 3 centuries; HS 145 v Oxford University, The Parks, 1985; HT 816 in 1985; 3 wickets @ 32.33; BB 1-0 v Sussex, Hove, 1984. OD: 43 matches; 723 runs @ 19.02.

HUGH WILSON
1983 – 1984

The cruel, unreasonable moment of truth came for Hugh Wilson on the day he was inexplicably left out of the NatWest quarter-final side to face Kent. He had arrived by way of Surrey, big of build, brisk of pace, and probably deserved more overs from Somerset.

PETER HUGH L'ESTRANGE WILSON Born Guildford, Surrey, 17.8.58. RHB, RFM. SFC: 15 matches; 60 runs @ 10.00; HS 25 v Gloucestershire, Bristol, 1983; 30 wickets @ 33.76; BB 4-77 v Gloucestershire, Bath, 1983; HT 25 in 1983. OD: 13 matches; 11 runs (no average); 14 wickets @ 31.28. Surrey 1978-82; Northern Transvaal, South Africa, 1979-80.

STEVE BOOTH   1983 – 1985

For some years Somerset searched for another slow left-armer, and a few shrewd judges thought they had found him in Steve Booth. An authentic Yorkshireman who never wanted to be taken off, he was not a big spinner of the ball but his flight impressed the purists. In the end Booth was pushed too far, too soon, and he remains a classic case of the over-exposed slow bowler who lost both confidence and control.

STEPHEN CHARLES BOOTH Born Leeds, Yorkshire, 30.10.63. RHB, SLA. SFC: 33 matches; 202 runs @ 10.63; HS 42 v Derbyshire, Taunton, 1984; 87 wickets @ 36.31; BB 4-26 v Middlesex, Lord's, 1983; HT 38 in 1984.

COUNTY CHAMPIONSHIP 1946-2005 PERCENTAGE OF MATCHES WON		
1	Surrey	36.5
2	Yorkshire	34.9
3	Middlesex	34.5
4	Essex	29.5
5	Warwickshire	29.3
6	Worcestershire	29.0
7	Kent	28.3
8	Lancashire	28.3
9	Northamptonshire	27.7
10	Gloucestershire	27.5
11	Hampshire	27.4
12	Leicestershire	24.9
13	Sussex	24.7
14	Derbyshire	24.5
15	Glamorgan	24.3
16	Somerset	24.1
17	Nottinghamshire	21.7
18	Durham	17.7

TROPHIES WON 1946-2005 County Championship & Limited Over		CC	LO	Total
1	Surrey	11½	7	18½
2	Lancashire	½	16	16½
3	Middlesex	8	7	15
	Warwickshire	5	10	15
5	Yorkshire	9½	5	14½
6	Essex	6	8	14
7	Kent	2½	10	12½
8	Worcestershire	5	5	10
9	Gloucestershire	–	9	9
	Hampshire	2	7	9
	Leicestershire	3	6	9
12	Somerset	–	7	7
13	Glamorgan	3	3	6
	Nottinghamshire	3	3	6
	Sussex	1	5	6
16	Northamptonshire	–	3	3
17	Derbyshire	–	2	2
18	Durham	–	–	–

(On three occasions the championship was shared)

1984

Captain: I.T. Botham

This was the season when Martin Crowe, the stylish and gifted New Zealander, arrived at Taunton. It took him a few weeks to work out the demands and peculiarities of our pitch conditions; then he began to make a considerable impact, so much so that his introduction to county cricket brought him 1,769 championship runs alone. He made them with authority and handsome, orthodox stroke-play. How Somerset needed him – the West Indies superstars were on tour and not available. Crowe was a serious young man, an instant influence in the dressing room, and someone with stimulating tactical ideas on how the game should be played.

Marks was now the vice-captain. He passed 1,000 runs for the first time and wasn't far short of the double, taking 86 wickets. When it came to August, he revealed new batting strengths that brought him three championship centuries and much praise. If it was Marks' most profitable season, so it was for Roebuck and Popplewell, the latter assuming new disciplines at the crease. The left-arm swing bowler, Davis, had worked diligently on correcting a few technical defects and now he was rewarded with 66 first-class wickets

Rose had handed over the captaincy to Botham, who was often absent, needed by England instead. Some familiar players like Slocombe, once so richly promising, had disappeared, leaving many to wonder why he hadn't achieved more, despite his natural ability to play the spinners as well as anyone in the club. Wilson left and Lloyds, uneasy about his lack of opportunities, made the short trip to Gloucestershire. Several of the younger players weren't making the expected progress.

Despite a few heavy defeats in the championship, that final position of seventh wasn't really so bad. But when, the faithful were asking a trifle sceptically, would that reassuring practice of collecting trophies be resumed?

COUNTY CHAMPIONSHIP 7th

Played 24	Won 6	Drawn 11	Lost 7

OTHER MATCHES — Played 2, Won 1, Lost 1

NATWEST BANK TROPHY — Lost in Quarter-Final

BENSON & HEDGES CUP — Lost in Quarter-Final

JOHN PLAYER LEAGUE 13th — Played 16, Won 5, No Result 2, Lost 9

BATTING

	M	I	NO	Runs	HS	Ave	100	50	ct	st
P.W. Denning	5	8	3	338	90	67.60	–	3	2	–
M.D. Crowe	25	41	6	1870	190	53.42	6	11	28	–
V.J. Marks	24	34	10	1262	134	52.58	3	6	16	–
P.M. Roebuck	24	37	1	1702	159	47.27	7	4	4	–
J.W. Lloyds	20	30	10	812	113*	40.60	1	5	22	–
N.F.M. Popplewell	22	36	2	1116	133	32.82	1	7	27	–
I.T. Botham	11	15	1	444	90	31.71	–	4	2	–
B.C. Rose	20	33	4	856	123	29.51	1	4	5	–
S.J. Turner	5	6	3	75	27*	25.00	–	–	12	3
J.G. Wyatt	16	28	0	666	103	23.78	1	3	8	–
M.R. Davis	19	14	6	178	60*	22.25	–	1	6	–
N.A. Felton	14	24	1	499	101	21.69	1	3	5	–
G.V. Palmer	16	20	2	299	73*	16.61	–	1	15	–
S.C. Booth	12	14	7	100	42	14.28	–	–	13	–
C.H. Dredge	21	26	8	214	25*	11.88	–	–	12	–
T. Gard	21	24	5	209	26	11.00	–	–	48	10
R.L. Ollis	6	12	1	112	22	10.18	–	–	8	–
P.H.L. Wilson	4	2	0	0	0	0.00	–	–	1	–

(1 match) M.S. Turner 0, 1

BOWLING

	Overs	Mdns	Runs	Wkts	Ave	5wi	10wm
I.T. Botham	230.2	51	691	33	20.93	1	–
M.R. Davis	500.4	108	1569	66	23.77	4	1
V.J. Marks	808	231	2233	86	25.96	5	1
C.H. Dredge	533	125	1534	53	28.94	–	–
M.D. Crowe	435	101	1353	44	30.75	1	–
S.C. Booth	408.4	117	1172	38	30.84	–	–
P.H.L. Wilson	56	14	176	5	35.20	–	–
G.V. Palmer	320.3	56	1231	30	41.03	–	–
N.F.M. Popplewell	125.3	30	370	8	46.25	–	–
J.W. Lloyds	240.2	69	697	14	49.78	–	–

M.S. Turner 29-8-85-0 P.M. Roebuck 10.2-5-18-0 J.G. Wyatt 3-1-4-1
N.A. Felton 0.1-0-4-0

MARTIN DAVID CROWE Born Auckland, New Zealand, 22.9.62. RHB, RMF. 77 Tests 1982-96. 143 LOI 1982-96. SFC: 48 matches; 3984 runs @ 59.46; 14 centuries; HS 206* v Warwickshire, Edgbaston, 1987; 1000 runs twice; HT 1870 in 1984; 44 wickets @ 33.02; BB 5-66 v Leicestershire, Grace Road, 1984; HT 44 in 1984. OD: 44 matches; 1476 runs @ 36.00; 31 wickets @ 28.03; NW MoM 1; B&H GA 3. Auckland, New Zealand, 1979-83; Central Districts, New Zealand, 1983-90; Wellington, New Zealand, 1990-95.

Crowe had a messianic streak, an urge to uplift those around him, and in Somerset's floundering young players he found a group plainly in need of such work.

Peter Roebuck

MARTIN CROWE
1984 – 1988

His arrival from New Zealand as an unknown 21-year-old, to deputise while Viv Richards and Joel Garner were otherwise engaged, was a revelation. After a tentative start, in which he got used to greenish conditions and seemed a trifle sensitive to kindly criticism, he showed everyone his worth.

During that 1984 summer, Crowe scored nearly 2,000 runs, invariably building his innings with all the proficiency of an experienced architect who aimed for handsome, aesthetic standards. The stroke-play was clean; the technique that of an infinitely older batsman.

Off the field he was a thoroughly serious young man, full of enthusiasm for the game, strong on etiquette and good behaviour. He encouraged some of the county's promising fledglings to meet him and talk – about cricket. It was something new. Here, observers were beginning to remark, was Somerset's next captain, but because of the limitation on overseas players, the theories about his ability to lead the county were not based on practicality.

Sometimes he was compared favourably to Richards. That was silly, and mischievous. In fact, both men were outstanding, but very different.

When Crowe returned to Somerset in 1987, in the wake of Viv's traumatic departure, it was noted that the New Zealander was a changed man; tougher in his ways, shorn of that endearing, earlier innocence. He was still a fine, classical batsman but eventually illness and back trouble caused him to return to his native land.

MURRAY TURNER 1984 – 1986

He was a lively and successful club cricketer in the Taunton area, his progress having been monitored from early schooldays. But in the end there were no more than a dozen first-class matches for his efforts. Instead Murray joined the RAF, where he found renewed scope for runs and, more significantly for a quickish bowler, wickets.

MURRAY STEWART TURNER Born Shaftesbury, Dorset, 27.1.64. RHB, RFM. SFC: 12 matches; 144 runs @ 18.00; HS 24* v Warwickshire, Taunton, 1985; 15 wickets @ 52.53; BB 4-74 same match. OD: 17 matches; 91 runs @ 13.00; 14 wickets @ 41.21.

SIMON TURNER 1984 – 1985

From the same talented Weston-super-Mare family as Robert, Simon displayed the same eagerness (only a few years earlier) to try his luck as a county cricketer, and like his young brother, he was a wicket-keeper of thoroughly sound ability. However, he was offered only a handful of appearances when Trevor Gard was injured.

SIMON JONATHAN TURNER Born Cuckfield, Sussex, 28.4.60. LHB, WK. SFC: 6 matches; 84 runs @ 28.00; HS 27* v Glamorgan, Taunton, 1984; 19 dismissals (14 ct, 5 st). OD: 8 matches; 23 runs @ 11.50; 3 dismissals (1ct, 2 st).

MOST POST-WAR WICKETS FOR SOMERSET

First-class cricket		Limited-over cricket	
BA Langford	1390	HR Moseley	309
KE Palmer	837	IT Botham	300
J Lawrence	791	GD Rose	298
WE Alley	738	CH Dredge	253
VJ Marks	738	GI Burgess	247
AR Caddick	648	VJ Marks	226
GD Rose	588	AR Caddick	214
HL Hazell	559	J Garner	206
HR Moseley	547	PS Jones	166
FE Rumsey	520	AA Jones	164
IT Botham	489	NA Mallender	148
GI Burgess	474	KA Parsons	123

1985

Captain: I.T. Botham

Somerset's history is laden with paradoxes but not too many compare with what happened during this miserable, confusing season. It was the summer when Botham, not too often available for the county, savaged opposing bowlers by scoring hundreds off 76 balls, twice, and then plundering another in a mere 50 deliveries. He created a new record for the number of sixes (80) in a season for Somerset. It was also the year that Richards pulverised Warwickshire with his innings of 322, so brilliantly brutal that one established Edgbaston player, in awe of Richards' might, said he would be giving up the game and looking for a new occupation. Between them, Botham and Richards, partners in astonishing power, bludgeoned 3,116 runs.

And yet 1985 was the summer, too, when Somerset – despite collecting more batting points than any other county – ended up on the bottom of the championship table, a demoralising position they last embarrassingly held in 1969. Their painfully solitary victory, which came expansively by an innings at Bath, was against Lancashire. Marks took 8-17 in the second innings and 11 wickets from the match.

Much went wrong that wasn't of Somerset's making. The injuries mounted with unrelenting regularity. Botham, who had chosen to give up the captaincy – Roebuck took over for 12 months – was able to play in only 11 championship matches, during which he captured just 11 wickets. Garner, never fully fit, took a mere 31. The support bowling too often looked limp and ineffective. There was Rose's broken arm, Wyatt's arm injury (he still compiled his maiden hundred) and Gard's concussion. Dredge and Roebuck were other untimely casualties

What was left for the loyal fans to cheer? Popplewell had touched his best form with his 172 at Southend but he would soon be gone to pursue a less frenetic career amid his law books. Too many players were failing to live up to their initial promise. At committee level, one could detect signs of apprehension.

Most sixes in a first-class season

80	I.T. Botham	Somerset	1985
66	A.W. Wellard	Somerset	1935
57	A.W. Wellard	Somerset	1936
57	A.W. Wellard	Somerset	1938
51	A.W. Wellard	Somerset	1933
49	I.V.A. Richards	Somerset	1985

The highest by a non-Somerset player is 48

COUNTY CHAMPIONSHIP 17th

COUNTY CHAMPIONSHIP 17th	Played 24	Won 1	Drawn 16	Lost 7
OTHER MATCHES	Played 3		Drawn 2	Lost 1
NATWEST BANK TROPHY	Lost in Quarter-Final			
BENSON & HEDGES CUP	Eliminated at Zonal Stage			
JOHN PLAYER LEAGUE 1st	Played 16	Won 5	No Result 5	Lost 6

BATTING

	M	I	NO	Runs	HS	Ave	100	50	ct	st
I.T. Botham	13	19	5	1280	152	91.42	5	7	9	–
I.V.A Richards	19	24	0	1836	322	76.50	9	6	9	–
P.M. Roebuck	22	33	5	1255	132*	44.82	2	7	10	–
J.C.M. Atkinson	6	5	1	167	79	41.75	–	1	–	–
N.F.M. Popplewell	18	30	2	1064	172	38.00	1	7	10	–
N.A. Felton	18	27	0	922	112	34.14	1	7	3	–
J.G. Wyatt	17	26	0	816	145	31.38	2	2	7	–
R.E. Hayward	9	12	3	278	100*	30.88	1	1	3	–
V.J. Marks	26	34	5	885	82	30.51	–	7	8	–
R.J. Harden	12	17	5	366	107	30.50	1	1	9	–
B.C. Rose	5	9	1	196	81*	24.50	–	1	2	–
M.S. Turner	10	12	6	143	24*	23.83	–	–	2	–
M.R. Davis	18	20	6	315	40*	22.50	–	–	8	–
C.H. Dredge	15	13	7	124	31	20.66	–	–	7	–
G.V. Palmer	8	11	3	164	45*	20.50	–	–	2	–
P.A.C. Bail	5	9	2	127	78*	18.14	–	1	–	–
R.L. Ollis	15	20	1	325	55	17.10	–	1	6	–
S.C. Booth	11	8	3	78	28	15.60	–	–	13	–
T. Gard	26	26	4	294	47	13.36	–	–	31	7
J. Garner	15	11	3	92	22	11.50	–	–	4	–
A.P. Jones	3	4	2	3	1*	1.50	–	–	1	–
R.V.J. Coombs	4	3	0	1	1	0.33	–	–	–	–

(1 match) S.A.R. Ferguson 8 S.J. Turner 9* (2 ct, 2 st)

BOWLING

	Overs	Mdns	Runs	Wkts	Ave	5wi	10wm
R.V.J. Coombs	93	27	268	16	16.75	1	–
J. Garner	295.4	75	739	31	23.83	1	–
V.J. Marks	812.4	197	2421	72	33.62	4	2
C.H. Dredge	317.4	73	929	25	37.16	1	–
I.T. Botham	154.4	31	521	13	40.07	–	–
S.C. Booth	390.2	112	1138	28	40.64	–	–
M.S. Turner	185.5	30	648	13	49.84	–	–
M.R. Davis	366	60	1249	24	52.04	–	–
I.V.A Richards	183	48	494	7	70.57	–	–
G.V. Palmer	167	19	683	7	97.57	–	–
J.C.M. Atkinson	65	9	250	2	125.00	–	–

A.P. Jones 37-4-142-3   N.F.M. Popplewell 27.5-2-157-0   P.M. Roebuck 16-3-47-0
R.J. Harden 12.3-5-33-2   J.G. Wyatt 10-0-59-1   P.A.C. Bail 4-2-4-0
R.L. Ollis 4-1-8-0   B.C. Rose 1-0-8-0

RICHARD HAYWARD 1985

They rushed the left-hander back from New Zealand to help prop up an injury-ravaged Somerset side in 1985. He obliged with a neat hundred against Cambridge University, but managed only nine matches before being squeezed out when the county were back to full strength. Previously he had made 13 appearances for Hampshire.

RICHARD EDWARD HAYWARD Born Hillingdon, Middlesex, 15.2.54. LHB, LM. SFC: 9 matches; 278 runs @ 30.88; 1 century; HS 100* v Cambridge University, Taunton, 1985. OD: 8 matches; 106 runs @ 26. Hampshire 1981-82; Central Districts, New Zealand, 1982-85.

ANDREW JONES 1985

Just three matches, three runs and three wickets. He had looked a useful prospect as a seam bowler.

ANDREW PAUL JONES Born Southampton, Hampshire, 22.9.64. RHB, RMF. SFC: 3 matches; 3 runs @ 1.50; HS 1* v Nottinghamshire, Taunton, 1985, and v Glamorgan, Taunton, 1985; 3 wickets @ 47.33; BB 1-9 v Glamorgan, Taunton, 1985. OD: 1 match; 3 runs @ 3.00; 1 wicket @ 16.75.

ROY SULLY 1985

Useful local cricketer who shaped well at Second XI level. His sole Sunday League appearance still came as something of a surprise. Played football for Western League sides including Taunton Town and Barnstaple.

ROYSTON CYRIL JOHN SULLY Born Taunton, 10.4.51. RHB, RM. OD: 1 match; 2 runs @ 2.00; 0 wickets.

JON ATKINSON 1985 – 1990

The Somerset debut, at Weston, couldn't have been more romantic. He arrived at Clarence Park to watch the match with Northants – and found he was playing. His name wasn't even on the scorecard. But his parents were there to applaud and, from the other end of the wicket, so did Ian Botham. Atkinson, just 17, showed not a flicker of nerves as he hit three sixes and 11 fours in a handsome, intrepid innings of 79. It gave false hopes. He continued to strike the ball well, but less consistently. His bowling lost some of the control shown in schooldays. He captained Cambridge and really had enough talent to come up with a better playing record. Was he inhibited by the presence of his dad Colin, a captain and president of the club?

JONATHON COLIN MARK ATKINSON Born Butleigh, Somerset, 10.7.68. RHB, RMF. SFC: 14 matches; 422 runs @ 28.13; HS 79 v Northamptonshire, Weston-super-Mare, 1985 (debut); HT 184 in 1989; 4 wickets @ 107.00; BB 2-80 v Indians, Taunton, 1986. OD: 8 matches; 85 runs @ 17.00; 1 wicket @ 16.00. Cambridge University 1988-90.

PAUL BAIL 1985 – 1986

Might Somerset have persevered longer with him? County cricket is strewn with a thousand such imponderables. We won't forget his 174 in the 1986 Varsity match – or the June morning the previous summer against Warwickshire. Paul opened for Somerset and soon retired with a blow to the helmet. Nigel Felton went next ball. And then Viv Richards took over, with an incomparable 322. Bail, by nature a tidy, unspectacular stroke-maker, was content to watch.

PAUL ANDREW CLAYTON BAIL Born Burnham-on-Sea, Somerset, 23.6.65. RHB, OB. SFC: 7 matches, 229 runs @ 22.90; HS 78* v Kent, Canterbury, 1985; 0 wickets. OD: 2 matches; 22 runs @ 11.00. Cambridge University 1986-88.

SIMON FERGUSON 1985

Essentially a Second XI player who struck the ball well, Ferguson also played club games for Staplegrove while he was at Taunton in 1985. Later he played good-class cricket in the London area. Once he rang coach Peter Robinson and declared: 'We've got a bowler with us you'd do well to have to look at.' It turned out to be Andy Caddick.

SIMON ALEXANDER ROSS FERGUSON Born Lagos, Nigeria, 13.5.61. RHB, RM. SFC: 1 match; 8 runs @ 8.00; HS 8 v Middlesex, Weston-super-Mare, 1985.

ROBERT COOMBS 1985 – 1986

On the evidence of a wet Weston wicket, where he took five impressive scalps against Middlesex on his debut, some local pundits were convinced that here was the left-arm spinner the county had consistently searched for. He was a student at Exeter, had played for Dorset and been considered by Hampshire. But enthusiasm for him lessened and Robert's career lasted only for an unlucky 13 matches.

ROBERT VINCENT JEROME COOMBS Born Barnet, Hertfordshire, 20.7.59. RHB, SLA. SFC: 13 matches; 32 runs @ 5.33; HS 18 v Gloucestershire, Bristol, 1986; 32 wickets @ 34.75; BB 5-58 v Middlesex, Weston-super-Mare (debut).

1985
RICHARD HARDEN 1985 – 1998

There is always especial joy among the aficionados at headquarters when a genuine Somerset lad turns up. Harden's stance didn't please every purist; nor did his penchant for the sweep. But from the age of 19 his promise was evident.

The exterior was inclined to be a trifle dour, though he could suddenly parade the crispest of strokes to complement the workmanlike construction of an innings. Somerset made him vice-captain as if trying him out for more elevated honours in the future. Meanwhile the high scores were growing and the Test selectors checked his progress periodically.

But he came to the conclusion that there really was no guaranteed future for him in the West Country. He moved to Yorkshire for two seasons, though a broken finger and other untimely injuries worked against him. He married a girl from New Zealand and that was where he emigrated.

RICHARD JOHN HARDEN Born Bridgwater, 16.8.65. RHB, SLA. Cap 1989. SFC: 233 matches; 12488 runs @ 38.90; 28 centuries; HS 187 v Nottinghamshire, Taunton, 1992; 1000 runs 7 times; HT 1460 in 1990; 16 wickets @ 56.18; BB 2-24 v Hampshire, Taunton, 1986; HT 6 in 1990. OD: 252 matches; 6275 runs @ 30.91; 0 wickets; NW MoM 1. Central Districts, New Zealand, 1987-88; Yorkshire 1999-2000.

A Somerset man who revels in every victory and in defeat has a pint. His gait in the field and his meticulous recollection of how many runs he has scored in the season is increasingly reminiscent of Mervyn Kitchen.

Vic Marks

IAN BOTHAM'S XI (or XII)
from the years in which he played

Mervyn Kitchen
Brian Rose
Viv Richards
Brian Close (captain)
Ian Botham
Peter Denning
Vic Marks
Tom Cartwright
Derek Taylor
Joel Garner
Colin Dredge
Hallam Moseley

Back with Viv and Joel again, what a prospect! It's my excuse for including myself. But this team brings back so many warm memories. Remember, it covered the years when Somerset had their first exciting sniff of silverware. Yes, heady days, a turning point in Somerset's history.

I've picked 12 players and have put them into only flexible batting order. That will depend, like the final selection, on the conditions.

Naturally I'm giving the captaincy to Closey. He'd have plenty of ideas and theories, would lead as ever from the front and would no doubt station himself fearlessly at short-leg. He had a big influence on me – and so, of course, did Tom Cartwright, who did much to encourage my bowling when others were telling me to stick to batting.

There are plenty of local voices in my side. Dasher Denning would be parading his Chewton Mendip carves and dear old Dredgy would again be demonstrating that you don't necessarily need a pretty bowling action to take vital wickets. He was an uncomplicated and wholehearted bowler, as was Hallam Moseley, who would surely have made a few Test appearances if there hadn't been so many excellent fast bowlers around in the Caribbean at that time.

No doubt I'd still try to match Viv by putting balls into the car park. That light-hearted competitive edge between us was part of the appeal of those days. Taking another look at my team, I must say that we have a reassuringly strong line-up of bowlers. We'd leave Big Joel to soften up the batsmen before Tom got to work with all that craft and guile.

1986

Captain: P.M. Roebuck

At one stage Somerset were fourth in the championship table, though they still finished one from the bottom. Events at the end of the year grimly overshadowed the cricket, however. The county staggered through by far the worst constitutional crisis in its undulating history. The decision not to renew the contracts of Richards and Garner was described variously as brave, logical, naive and absurd. Many saw it as the great betrayal. They tore up their membership, knowing that Botham, long-standing friend and fellow icon of the West Indians, would also leave out of sympathy for their abrupt dismissal. Alongside the destructive controversy were the rumours of imbalance in the dressing room.

The sentimental backlash was enormous. Then came the abrasive special general meeting at the Shepton Mallet showground, where there was a motion of no-confidence in the committee. It was defeated by 1,828 votes to 798, leading inevitably to allegations of a manoeuvred victory for the county's establishment. The whole affair, especially the initial decision not to retain the two overseas players, was handled badly, with an appalling lack of diplomacy. The vociferous, unforgiving rebels, as they were called, now targeted Roebuck with their volume of criticism and resentment. But Crowe was a decisive factor in the whole ugly argument. The county had retained his registration after the considerable impression he had made when standing in for the West Indians. Now other counties were showing an interest in him, and many on the committee didn't want him to slip away. The result was that Richards, Garner and Botham sadly left, while Crowe signed a three-year contract

Somerset had never known such deep-seated divisions. The antagonisms persisted for a long time, while Botham went on to Worcestershire and Richards to Glamorgan. In time, the rifts blissfully were healed. At Taunton, a stand was named after Botham and gates after Richards.

As for the cricket that preceded the public antipathy, Roebuck proved a good captain and consistent batsman, Richards hammered a century off 48 balls at the expense of Glamorgan, and Harden announced his arrival with two hundreds, passing his 1,000 runs. Botham, missing in June and July because of a TCCB ban, was still around enough to continue piling up the sixes in his final Somerset season.

All we ask now, in cheerful resilience, is that the sun continues to shine, the sixes still bounce reverentially off the tombstones in St James' churchyard … and that the apple juice keeps its especial West Country fizz.

The last words of David Foot's 1986 history of Somerset cricket

COUNTY CHAMPIONSHIP 16th

Played 23	Won 3	Drawn 13	Lost 7

OTHER MATCHES — Played 2 — Drawn 2

NATWEST BANK TROPHY — Lost in Second Round

BENSON & HEDGES CUP — Eliminated at Zonal Stage

JOHN PLAYER LEAGUE 6th — Played 16 — Won 8 — No Result 2 — Lost 6

BATTING

	M	I	NO	Runs	HS	Ave	100	50	ct	st
P.M. Roebuck	22	35	8	1288	221*	47.70	4	5	12	–
I.T. Botham	12	19	1	804	139	44.66	2	4	8	–
V.J. Marks	25	36	12	1057	110	44.04	1	7	9	–
R.J. Bartlett	6	9	2	307	117*	43.85	1	–	4	–
B.C. Rose	14	23	5	784	129	43.55	2	3	3	–
I.V.A. Richards	18	28	1	1174	136	43.48	4	5	19	–
R.J. Harden	22	36	3	1093	108	33.12	2	6	12	–
N.A. Felton	23	37	3	1030	156*	30.29	3	5	8	–
J.J.E. Hardy	19	29	0	863	79	29.75	–	8	12	–
J.C.M. Atkinson	4	6	2	71	16*	17.75	–	–	–	–
J. Garner	18	15	4	182	47	16.54	–	–	8	–
M.R. Davis	9	8	4	63	21*	15.75	–	–	2	–
J.G. Wyatt	4	6	0	81	40	13.50	–	–	–	–
C.H. Dredge	17	21	3	227	40	12.61	–	–	7	–
T. Gard	20	25	6	228	36	12.00	–	–	30	6
R.V.J. Coombs	9	6	3	31	18	10.33	–	–	3	–
M.D. Harman	3	5	2	27	15	9.00	–	–	1	–
N.S. Taylor	16	18	6	107	24*	8.91	–	–	2	–
R.J. Blitz	5	5	0	33	18	6.60	–	–	8	–
G.V. Palmer	4	6	0	31	17	5.16	–	–	1	–

(2 matches) P.A.C. Bail 55, 47, 0

(1 match) N.J. Pringle 10, 11   D.J. Foster 0   M.S. Turner did not bat

BOWLING

	Overs	Mdns	Runs	Wkts	Ave	5wi	10wm
J. Garner	419	95	1091	47	23.21	1	–
C.H. Dredge	389	83	1151	35	32.88	–	–
V.J. Marks	744.5	198	2121	59	35.94	2	1
N.S. Taylor	342.2	62	1222	29	42.13	–	–
I.T. Botham	285.1	61	961	22	43.68	1	–
R.J. Harden	54	5	208	4	52.00	–	–
R.V.J. Coombs	256.5	58	844	16	52.75	–	–
I.V.A. Richards	161	32	500	9	55.55	–	–
M.R. Davis	167.3	21	631	11	57.36	–	–
G.V. Palmer	81	9	290	5	58.00	–	–
M.D. Harman	60.3	12	149	1	149.00	–	–

J.C.M. Atkinson 34-7-132-2   P.M. Roebuck 24-3-120-1   M.S. Turner 15-3-55-2

B.C. Rose 11-0-57-2   N.J. Pringle 10-0-48-0   D.J. Foster 5-0-29-0

N.A. Felton 1-0-3-0   J.J.E. Hardy 1-0-5-0

JON HARDY 1986 – 1990

Perhaps basically too amiable and easy-going for the unrelenting world of county cricket. Nor did a history of illness and injury help. He started with Hampshire, won his cap with Somerset and then had a brief, barren year with Gloucestershire.

Tall, slim and, at times, most attractive against the fast bowlers, he ran into a few technical problems and was a repeated, occasionally unlucky, LBW victim. The Kenya-born left-hander remained an elegant but unfulfilled performer.

JONATHAN JAMES EAN HARDY Born Nakaru, Kenya, 2.10.60. LHB. Cap 1987. SFC: 87 matches; 3675 runs @ 27.63; 1 century; HS 119 v Gloucestershire, Taunton, 1987; 1000 runs once; HT 1089 in 1987; 0 wickets. OD: 63 matches; 1417 runs @ 25.30; NW MoM 1. Hampshire 1984-85; Western Province, South Africa, 1987-90; Gloucestershire 1991.

RAYNER BLITZ 1986

Arrived partly on the recommendation of Peter Roebuck, who had seen him keeping wicket in Australia. Small and agile, with ability to accumulate runs in Second XI cricket. Stayed a single season.

RAYNER JOHN BLITZ Born Watford, Hertfordshire, 25.3.68. RHB, WK. SFC: 5 matches; 33 runs @ 6.60; HS 18 v Hampshire, Bournemouth, 1986; 8 dismissals (8 ct). OD: 2 matches; 1 run @ 1.00; 1 dismissal (1 ct).

NICK TAYLOR 1986

So disappointed that he had been released by Surrey, where coach Geoff Arnold had changed his fast bowler's action for the better, Taylor went off to Australia with no thoughts of any more cricket. He returned, with fresh hopes at Somerset, yet only to last for one season.

Team-mates found him an individualist. He had acting aspirations; he'd done sporadic film work in Australia, had worked as a model, squash coach, waiter and bouncer. But what he wanted most of all was to follow successfully the career of his father, Ken, the Yorkshire and England player, especially after starting with two years on the staff of his home county.

NICHOLAS SIMON TAYLOR Born Holmfirth, Yorkshire, 2.6.63. RHB, RFM. SFC: 16 matches; 107 runs @ 8.91; HS 24* v Gloucestershire, Taunton, 1986; 29 wickets @ 42.13; BB 4-40 v Essex, Taunton, 1986. OD: 18 matches; 42 runs @ 8.40; 29 wickets @ 20.72. Yorkshire 1982-83; Surrey 1984-85.

NICK PRINGLE 1986 – 1991

Was it basically a lack of self-confidence? Or even a lack of opportunities? The promise, going back to Taunton School days, had been evident enough. He had a neat technique and was a nimble fielder. When he left Somerset, the understandable hope was that he might find another county, but it never happened.

NICHOLAS JOHN PRINGLE Born Weymouth, Dorset, 20.9.66. RHB, RMF. SFC: 27 matches; 707 runs @ 16.83; HS 79 v Warwickshire, Edgbaston, 1987; HT 347 in 1987; 5 wickets @ 110.20; BB 2-35 v Glamorgan, Weston-super-Mare, 1987. OD: 12 matches; 97 runs @ 10.77; 0 wickets.

RICKY BARTLETT 1986 – 1992

You can't do better than start with a hundred. That was what Ricky Bartlett did at Oxford, ensuring a place in the county record books and generating premature excitement. He was cursed with a nervous temperament, though. Never able completely to shake himself free of pre-innings tensions, was he asked to bat too high in the order? A product of Taunton School, cradle of so much cricketing talent over the generations, he was as sad as many of the locals when his Somerset career ended in 1992. Bartlett brilliantly patrolled the covers and the outfield, to underline his value in the one-day matches, but it was not enough.

RICHARD JAMES BARTLETT Born Ash Priors, Somerset, 8.10.66. RHB, OB. SFC: 50 matches; 1797 runs @ 24.28; 2 centuries; HS 117* v Oxford University, The Parks, 1986; 4 wickets @ 36.25; BB 1-9 v Glamorgan, Taunton, and v Yorkshire, Scarborough, both 1988. OD: 60 matches; 1251 runs @ 21.94.

MARK HARMAN 1986 – 1987

Maybe this capable off-spinner was unlucky to find himself competing with Vic Marks. He was a quiet young man, with a natural ability to turn the ball, and he was a valuable fighter with the bat. But, realistically, he accepted that there would be no scope with Somerset, moving on to Kent for a couple of seasons instead. In the end he decided it made more sense to opt for an accountant's ledger.

MARK DAVID HARMAN Born Aylesbury, Buckinghamshire, 30.6.64. RHB, OB. SFC: 9 matches; 121 runs @ 13.44; HS 41 v Kent, Bath, 1987; 8 wickets @ 64.75; BB 2-38 v Hampshire, Weston-super-Mare, 1987. OD: 3 matches; 2 runs @ 1.00; 1 wicket @ 91.00. Kent 1988-89.

DAREN FOSTER 1986 – 1989

The frame was slim but he found he could take batsmen by surprise with his deceptively whippy deliveries. Daren was a Haringey graduate but failed to acquire that additional measure of control that would have turned him into a genuine county seamer. An easy-going temperament may have lessened his progress.

He hoped in vain for more scope at Somerset; then at Glamorgan, his next county, he again struggled to establish himself despite the natural skills which still shone through intermittently.

DAREN JOSEPH FOSTER Born Tottenham, London, 14.3.66. RHB, RFM. SFC: 28 matches; 126 runs @ 8.40; HS 20 v Hampshire, Southampton, 1988; 49 wickets @ 45.10; BB 4-46 v Worcestershire, Worcester, 1988; HT 28 in 1988. OD: 27 matches; 13 runs @ 4.33; 19 wickets @ 43.05. Glamorgan 1991-92.

1987

Captain: P.M. Roebuck

After the disruptions and all the strong words at Shepton Mallet, there was a decided new look about the Somerset side this season. Would it bring, anxious members were asking, an accompanying new sense of ambition and verve? Famous names, all three mesmeric performers, were going to be missed. Gone with them was the frisson of excitement that they brought to the County Ground. How was the club going to compensate? Brian Rose, now the development officer, was sent off on a domestic recruitment campaign. As a result, Jones arrived from Sussex, Mallender from Northants, Graham Rose from Middlesex and Burns from Essex.

Crowe, meanwhile, was making a welcome return, however unfortunate the circumstances of his innocent involvement over Somerset's overseas registration. His influence, on and off the field, was rapid. He encouraged the younger players. As for his cricket, it was again characterised by the neatness and discernment of his shots. He was first in the country to reach 1,000 runs, and to total 2,000 in all competitions. His stylish presence helped to make up for what the county had lost in triple stardom. The news that New Zealand needed him for what turned out to be an abortive tour of Sri Lanka caused Somerset to search for a temporary replacement. They maintained their envied record in overseas recruitment by signing Steve Waugh, who played in four championship matches and compiled two excellent centuries.

These were, all the same, testing days for Somerset as in effect they started building again almost from scratch. The restructured team might have been bereft of the sheer majesty and might of the three departing international cricketers, but team spirit had not seriously suffered. Roebuck, whatever the personal crises that dogged him over the radical shake-up, responded well as skipper. His batting, too, revealed an additional repertoire of shots as if he were determined not to be dubbed a slowcoach. Somerset reached the quarter-finals of the Benson & Hedges Cup and showed marked improvement in some of their Sunday League matches. They would, no doubt, like to air-brush the fact that they went out in the first round of the NatWest Trophy to Buckinghamshire.

> When you cut down three huge trees, you can plant some saplings.
> **Martin Crowe**

COUNTY CHAMPIONSHIP 11th Played 24 Won 2 Drawn 19 Lost 3

NATWEST BANK TROPHY — Lost in First Round

BENSON & HEDGES CUP — Lost in Quarter-Final

REFUGE ASSURANCE LEAGUE 4th Played 16 Won 8 No Result 4 Lost 4

BATTING

	M	I	NO	Runs	HS	Ave	100	50	ct	st
S.R. Waugh	4	6	3	340	137*	113.33	2	1	4	–
M.D. Crowe	18	29	5	1627	206*	67.79	6	6	15	–
P.M. Roebuck	16	29	5	1199	165*	49.95	5	4	15	–
J.J.E. Hardy	24	40	2	1089	119	28.65	1	7	8	–
N.A. Felton	24	41	0	1094	110	26.68	1	5	18	–
N.D. Burns	24	35	7	729	100*	26.03	1	4	44	6
V.J. Marks	22	31	6	635	63*	25.40	–	2	9	–
G.D. Rose	18	23	4	470	95	24.73	–	1	10	–
R.J. Harden	19	30	6	568	59	23.66	–	2	9	–
J.G. Wyatt	8	13	2	250	58*	22.72	–	1	2	–
N.J. Pringle	11	18	1	347	79	20.41	–	2	1	–
G.V. Palmer	14	16	4	234	68	19.50	–	1	4	–
N.A. Mallender	15	17	9	131	20*	16.37	–	–	6	–
M.D. Harman	6	8	2	94	41	15.66	–	–	7	–
B.C. Rose	3	4	0	60	31	15.00	–	–	1	–
D.J. Foster	5	3	1	25	16	12.50	–	–	3	–
A.N. Jones	23	21	8	114	15	8.76	–	–	8	–
M.R. Davis	8	8	1	57	23*	8.14	–	–	4	–

(1 match) R.J. Bartlett 0 R.G. Woolston 0

BOWLING

	Overs	Mdns	Runs	Wkts	Ave	5wi	10wm
N.A. Mallender	351	61	1129	46	24.54	1	–
G.D. Rose	314.4	56	976	38	25.68	1	–
A.N. Jones	517.1	85	1800	63	28.57	3	1
V.J. Marks	778.5	203	2155	70	30.78	3	–
S.R. Waugh	112	22	348	11	31.63	–	–
D.J. Foster	111.5	10	490	13	37.69	–	–
G.V. Palmer	316	54	1162	29	40.06	–	–
M.R. Davis	153.5	25	505	11	45.90	–	–
M.D. Harman	131	35	369	7	52.71	–	–
N.J. Pringle	93	14	341	4	85.25	–	–

R.G. Woolston 43-10-107-2 M.D. Crowe 33-8-100-0 P.M. Roebuck 13-1-54-0
R.J. Harden 2-0-8-0

1987

NEIL BURNS 1987 – 1993

He took over from Trevor Gard, and was a decidedly promising wicket-keeper whose career, because of competition, seemed to be going nowhere at Essex. Somerset had been consciously looking for a stumper who could also score runs, and Burns fulfilled that criterion. Quickly he won his cap and, from perky middle-order, the left-hander proved his ability and occasionally pulled out a gem of an innings.

The withdrawal of Brian Rose and Martin Crowe from the county scene in the late 1980s disappointed Burns. After all, they had been the two who had the greatest influence on him when he came to Taunton. He was linked speculatively at times with other counties and a return to Essex was mentioned.

Burns was always a player of noteworthy ambition but form and, more significantly, favour deserted him in the late summer of 1993. He lost his place and sensed that his future was in jeopardy. However, his aspirations extended to his business life and he concentrated on a flourishing PR and marketing company with sporting orientation.

Despite his leading the Second XI to success, Somerset released him at the end of 1993. He was to re-emerge as a Leicestershire player and at Grace Road 'played some of the best cricket of my life.'

When the county decided not to keep him he sought legal redress over the terms of his employment in what many in the game saw as a landmark case, especially concerning the last year of a contract. The hearing went on for four days 'and they showed the white flag on the fifth.' He continues to run a sports management business, is chief executive of London County Cricket Club (founder W G Grace) and assists with the coaching and development of players at Oxford University.

NEIL DAVID BURNS Born Chelmsford, Essex, 19.9.65. LHB, WK. Cap 1987. SFC: 150 matches; 5207 runs @ 30.09; 5 centuries; HS 166 v Gloucestershire, Taunton, 1990; HT 951 in 1990; 0 wickets; 333 dismissals (303 ct, 30 st). OD: 154 matches; 1678 runs @ 19.51; 181 dismissals (152 ct, 29 st). Essex 1986; Leicestershire 2000-02.

Neil Burns photographs (left to right) Adrian Jones, Neil Mallender and Graham Rose

GRAHAM ROSE
1987 – 2002

He arrived in 1987 as Somerset recruited anxiously, attempting to fill the gaps left by the famous. The shoulders were broad, the stride was long, making him appear more Creech St Michael than Tottenham St Venables, his natural winter habitat.

The unquestionable promise of the all-rounder was not immediately fulfilled but, with that height and thrust, his bowling could carry deceptive pace and bounce on good days. There were plenty of these, and he could be a match-winner.

But it was his batting that, with the right persuasion and in the right circumstances, could also transform a match. He could drive hard, high and straight. The century off 36 balls at Torquay in the NatWest set a new record for the competition. Here was a Londoner capable of sustaining the ever-appreciated big-hitting Somerset tradition.

These days he works as a civil servant for the Ministry of Defence.

GRAHAM DAVID ROSE Born Tottenham, London, 12.4.64. RHB, RMF. Cap 1988. SFC: 244 matches; 8644 runs @ 31.20; 11 centuries; HS 191 v Sussex, Taunton, 1997; 1000 runs once; HT 1000 in 1990; 588 wickets @ 29.83; BB 7-47 v Nottinghamshire, Taunton, 1996; HT 63 in 1997. OD: 280 matches; 4937 runs @ 24.32; 298 wickets @ 28.67; B&H GA 4. Middlesex 1985-86.

As one of the few genuine all-rounders in the game, it is a shame that Graham's many productive years with bat and ball could not have coincided in the same season, as I am sure this would have produced higher honours.
David Graveney, Spring 1997
G.D. Rose in 1997: 852 runs @ 50.11, 63 wickets @ 24.80

ADRIAN JONES 1987 – 1990

They didn't come more volatile. Usually the face was flushed and intensely competitive. Meaningful stares and oaths earned him fines as he manifested his temporary wrath at umpires like Ray Julian and Mervyn Kitchen. He started with Sussex and went back there after four years with Somerset, who failed to woo him with another lengthy contract.

No-one doubted Jones' heart as a pace bowler. He could be moody; but gentle, too, off the field. Significantly he built up a warm relationship with the spectators at long-leg.

There were some valid worries about his fitness and troublesome left knee when he came to the West Country. In fact, despite the pounding he gave his legs and back, he sustained an excellent fitness record with Somerset. The challenge to do well was just as evident on the hockey or rugby field.

ADRIAN NICHOLAS JONES Born Woking, Surrey, 22.7.61. LHB, RFM. Cap 1987. SFC: 88 matches; 530 runs @ 12.32; HS 43* v Leicestershire, Taunton, 1989; 245 wickets @ 30.72; BB 7-30 v Hampshire, Southampton, 1988; HT 71 in 1989. OD: 79 matches; 177 runs @ 11.06; 119 wickets @ 24.01; B&H GA 2. Sussex 1981-86 and 1991-93; Border, South Africa, 1981-82.

STEVE WAUGH 1987 – 1988

He followed Martin Crowe, as Somerset sustained their envied reputation for enticing talented overseas players. As a batsman he could effortlessly adapt his approach to the needs of the team. The style offered more fluent off-side shots than one sees from many Australians. Matches were for winning; the stern expression on the face revealed his philosophy for the game.

Waugh was in tremendous form for Somerset in 1988, heading the national averages and showing why one or two pundits at home were already comparing him with Stan McCabe. The tranquillity of the West Country suited his temperament, making him a more relaxed batsman.

Yet how many then imagined he would go on to become the most successful Test captain of all time, leading Australia to victory in 41 matches out of 57? He played in 168 Tests during an international career of 19 years. His retirement came with an innings of 80 at Sydney in January 2004.

There were many highlights, including the 1999 World Cup triumph against Pakistan. Paradoxically, alongside that competitive, even ruthless nature, was a sensitive man: photographer, writer (he spurned the use of a ghost), charity worker and a skipper who persuaded his players to appreciate the customs and cultures of other countries.

STEPHEN RODGER WAUGH Born Sydney, Australia, 2.6.65. RHB, RMF. Cap 1988. 168 Tests 1985-2004. 325 LOI 1986-2002. SFC: 19 matches; 1654 runs @ 78.76; 8 centuries; HS 161 v Kent, Canterbury, 1988; 1000 runs once; HT 1314 in 1988; 14 wickets @ 29.14; BB 3-48 v Surrey, Oval, 1987. OD: 17 matches 750 runs @ 57.69; 8 wickets @ 37.75; B&H GA 1. New South Wales, Australia, 1984-2004; Kent 2002.

NEIL MALLENDER
1987 – 1994

Test recognition, when it came in 1992, was hardly expected. Twice Mallender had been put on alert while on his customary playing-coaching stint in New Zealand. But it must have appeared increasingly to him as if his chance at the highest level would never arrive. When it did, he bowled as well as any of the more established England players – though he was never selected again.

'Ghost' – it's that pale complexion and fair hair – was highly regarded on the domestic circuit; to employ a cliche of the trade, he was the definitive honest workhorse. He bowled straight and he hit the seam.

Yorkshire, his native county, let him slip away. Later, when he was ready to leave Northants, Brian Rose, then Somerset team manager and needing urgently to recruit additional bowlers, flew out to New Zealand to persuade Mallender to come back West, where he'd once attended Yeovil Grammar School, excelling at rugby and cricket. Incidentally, there weren't many better golfers who played cricket for a living.

Mallender was to become a thoughtful and respected first-class umpire and international panellist.

NEIL ALAN MALLENDER Born Kirk Sandall, Yorkshire, 13.8.61. RHB, RFM. Cap 1987. 2 Tests 1992. SFC: 118 matches, 1461 runs @ 17.81; HS 87* v Sussex, Hove, 1990; HT 270 in 1994; 329 wickets @ 25.78; BB 7-61 v Derbyshire, Taunton, 1987; HT 51 in 1990. OD: 136 matches; 500 runs @ 14.70; 148 wickets @ 28.87. Northamptonshire 1980-86, 1995-96; Otago, New Zealand, 1983-93. Fc umpire 1999-.

BOB WOOLSTON 1987

One of the many tried as a left-arm spinner. He came via the Lord's ground staff, claiming two wickets as his fleeting reward.

ROBERT GEORGE WOOLSTON Born Enfield, Middlesex, 23.5.68. RHB, SLA. SFC: 1 match; 0 runs; 2 wickets @ 53.50; BB 2-70 v Derbyshire, Taunton, 1987.

1988

Captain: P.M. Roebuck

Those expectations of another run-laden summer for Crowe were not met. He had been seen as the inspiration for a re-emergent Somerset. Illness came first and then, far more seriously, he was warned to take a complete rest from cricket because of back trouble. Home he went and the Somerset officials were left shaking their heads in frustration. He played no more than four championship matches, still long enough for his admirers to see exquisite centuries at Worcester and Old Trafford.

To their credit, the county had re-signed Steve Waugh, and now it was his turn to dominate the Somerset batting. During June he hardly seemed to be away from the crease as he scored 1,000 runs from all matches. Just like Crowe had done, Waugh excelled at Bath, though in his own more pragmatic style. Predictably he topped the county's batting averages by some distance and was the only player to reach 1,000 runs. As a bonus, he had a major bearing on the side's good run in the Sunday matches

Overall, though, Somerset were apt to show their inexperience, not recovering from a poor start to the season. Roebuck, one of a number of injured players, was below his best. He chose to step down as skipper and Marks was his successor. There were goodbyes: to Dredge, who latterly had wrestled with injury; to Brian Rose, who moved away from cricket for a post in industry; to Tony Brown, the county secretary leaving for a job at Lord's. The exit of batsman Felton was more poignant: the announcement that he wasn't being retained coincided with his eighth and best century for the county. Maybe Somerset should have realised in early May that it was not going to be their season. That was when Graeme Hick scored 405 for Worcestershire at Taunton.

One consolation for cricket enthusiasts is that Peter may now have more time to write about the game; another may be that I will have less.

Vic Marks, on inheriting the captaincy from Peter Roebuck

COUNTY CHAMPIONSHIP   11th   Played 22   Won 5   Drawn 11   Lost 6

OTHER MATCHES		Played 1		Lost 1

NATWEST BANK TROPHY — Lost in Second Round

BENSON & HEDGES CUP — Eliminated at Zonal Stage

REFUGE ASSURANCE LEAGUE   12th   Played 16   Won 6   No Result 1   Lost 9

BATTING

	M	I	NO	Runs	HS	Ave	100	50	ct	st
S.R. Waugh	15	24	6	1314	161	73.00	6	4	20	–
M.D. Crowe	5	9	1	487	136*	60.87	2	2	4	–
R.J. Harden	6	11	1	295	78	29.50	–	3	3	–
N.A. Felton	14	27	2	720	127	28.80	1	4	7	–
P.M. Roebuck	12	19	3	454	112*	28.37	1	1	6	–
N.D. Burns	23	34	7	708	133*	26.22	1	2	57	2
J.J.E. Hardy	22	39	3	927	97	25.75	–	6	23	–
R.J. Bartlett	18	29	3	648	102*	24.92	1	2	12	–
V.J. Marks	23	31	2	719	68	24.79	–	3	8	–
J.G. Wyatt	15	26	1	578	69	23.12	–	3	9	–
N.J. Pringle	8	15	4	244	54	22.18	–	1	8	–
G.D. Rose	20	25	6	385	69*	20.26	–	1	11	–
D.J. Foster	13	14	9	72	20	14.40	–	–	–	–
C.H. Dredge	3	6	0	82	37	13.66	–	–	–	–
N.A. Mallender	16	19	6	157	44	12.07	–	–	8	–
A.N. Jones	20	21	8	130	38	10.00	–	–	8	–
M.W. Cleal	9	12	1	97	19	8.81	–	–	2	–
H.R.J. Trump	8	10	1	62	48	6.88	–	–	7	–

(2 matches)   T.J.A. Scriven 7, 4
(1 match)   G.V. Palmer 0, 23

BOWLING

	Overs	Mdns	Runs	Wkts	Ave	5wi	10wm
N.A. Mallender	411.1	108	969	47	20.61	1	–
G.D. Rose	504.5	116	1526	57	26.77	1	–
H.R.J. Trump	258	70	653	23	28.39	–	–
M.W. Cleal	168	25	582	20	29.10	–	–
V.J. Marks	862.5	222	2214	76	29.13	5	1
A.N. Jones	512	86	1658	55	30.14	1	–
D.J. Foster	299.3	46	1044	28	37.28	–	–
C.H. Dredge	68.5	20	225	3	75.00	–	–
T.J.A. Scriven	96	25	237	3	79.00	–	–

R.J. Bartlett 30-4-145-4   P.M. Roebuck 28.4-2-106-1   S.R. Waugh 23-5-60-3
G.V. Palmer 18.2-2-54-1   R.J. Harden 16-1-61-0   N.J. Pringle 13-1-40-1
J.G. Wyatt 10-4-34-1   N.A. Felton 0.5-0-8-0   J.J.E. Hardy 0.3-0-12-0

MATTHEW CLEAL 1988 – 1991

Authentic Yeovil, so he was to be seen inevitably, foolishly, as Botham's understudy. He had his moment of deserved glory, with four wickets against the West Indians, but the likeable, easy-going Matthew, who showed a valued aptitude in helping schoolboy players, was never going to be quite fast enough, and injury further frustrated his aspirations.

MATTHEW WILLIAM CLEAL Born Yeovil, 23.7.69. RHB, RMF. SFC: 15 matches; 165 runs @ 9.16; HS 30 v Leicestershire, Taunton, 1989; 26 wickets @ 34.96; BB 4-41 v West Indians, Taunton, 1988 (debut); HT 20 in 1988. OD: 17 matches; 103 runs @ 17.16; 5 wickets @ 92.60.

TIM SCRIVEN 1988 – 1989

Did well enough for Bucks against Somerset for the West Country club to show interest. Some wondered whether the county's search for a slow left-arm spinner had ended with this tall newcomer's arrival. Alas, three matches only.

TIMOTHY JOHN ADAM SCRIVEN Born High Wycombe, Buckinghamshire, 15.12.65. RHB, SLA. SFC: 3 matches; 11 runs @ 5.50; HS 7 v Derbyshire, Weston-super-Mare, 1988; 7 wickets @ 56.00; BB 2-67 v Lancashire, Taunton, 1989.

BEST BOWLING FIGURES FOR SOMERSET SINCE THE WAR

FIRST-CLASS MATCHES

INNINGS

9-26	B.A. Langford	v Lancashire	Weston-super-Mare	1958
9-32	A.R. Caddick	v Lancashire	Taunton	1993
9-51	A.A. Jones	v Sussex	Hove	1972
9-52	K.E. Palmer	v Nottinghamshire	Trent Bridge	1963

MATCH

15-54	B.A. Langford	v Lancashire	Weston-super-Mare	1958
15-78	E.P. Robinson	v Sussex	Weston-super-Mare	1951
15-101	A.W. Wellard	v Worcestershire	Bath	1947

LIMITED-OVER MATCHES

8-66	S.R.G. Francis	v Derbyshire (C&G)	Derby	2004
7-15	R.P. Lefebvre	v Devon (NW)	Torquay	1990
7-24	Mushtaq Ahmed	v Ireland (B&H)	Taunton	1997
6-24	I.V.A. Richards	v Lancashire (JPL)	Old Trafford	1983
6-25	G.I. Burgess	v Glamorgan (JPL)	Glastonbury	1972

HARVEY TRUMP 1988 – 1997

During his year with Somerset, David Graveney was an enthusiastic admirer of Harvey Trump, seeing him as an off-spinner with the natural aggression of a fast bowler. He could be intense and competitive, revealed in the way he took those return catches.

The promise was noted in Millfield days. He captained the county at various school levels and represented England as an Under-15 all-rounder. His introduction to first-class cricket came as a part-timer while he completed his studies. Against Gloucestershire he took seven wickets in each innings.

His father, a schoolmaster, captained Devon. Harvey, who taught history and PE himself, had the resolve for further progress. But the arrival of Mushtaq Ahmed worked against Trump up to a point, limiting his opportunities in 1993.

The summers that followed were apt to be frustrating ones. He made 13 championship appearances in 1995, with 32 hard-earned wickets, but the Pakistani Test star, the other slow bowler and a potential match-winner, took nearly three times as many. The next year Trump, invariably a 'thinking' cricketer, was allotted only three championship outings.

Away from the game, he proved himself a decent hockey player and, something of a rarity among professional sportsmen, a qualified lifeguard.

By 1998 it was back to full-time teaching at King's, Taunton, a career he followed conscientiously while always willing to impart to the boys a summer anecdote or snippet of cricketing knowledge.

HARVEY RUSSELL JOHN TRUMP Born Taunton, 11.10.68. RHB, OB. Cap 1994. SFC: 106 matches; 991 runs @ 12.54; HS 48 v Nottinghamshire, Taunton, on debut 1988; HT 276 in 1994; 242 wickets @ 38.76; BB 7-52 (twice) v Gloucestershire, Gloucester, 1992; HT 51 in 1991. OD: 122 matches; 177 runs @ 7.37; 107 wickets @ 35.95; NW MoM 1.

1989

Captain: V.J. Marks

This was a summer that left one searching for high points. At least the inspired signing of Cook, from Transvaal, coinciding with the arrival of Tavare, from Kent, went some way towards offsetting the disappointments of a nondescript first-class season which lowered Somerset to 14th position in the championship, with only four wins. The county did reserve some of their better performances for home matches: the first-round defeat of Essex in the NatWest Trophy, with centuries by Roebuck and Tavare, briefly lifted spirits and hopes. It turned out to be a deceptive prelude.

Cook proved a fine capture, even if the news of his appointment came as something of a surprise initially in Taunton. His shots were never extravagant but he placed them with great, intuitive skill and was rarely, whatever his neat, controlled technique, a slow scorer. Quickly settling in England, he topped 3,000 runs in all matches and 2,000 in the championship. The quiet, unassuming personality was liked by the Somerset crowds. He decisively headed the county's batting averages, though Tavare's contribution, in his distinctively circumspect style, shouldn't be overlooked.

Marks, as captain, seemed often to have a better time with the bat than the ball and some of his wickets were earned expensively. It came as a blow to the club, and the supporters who had always taken to this farmer's son, when it was discovered that he was retiring to essay a new career in journalism. He would no doubt have liked to leave after being in charge of a more consistent, upwardly mobile team. The bowling of Rose and Mallender had been hindered by injury, and it was Jones who took most wickets, sometimes with a vociferous demeanour. Harden was not far short of his 1,000 runs, suggesting that the earlier high hopes for the local boy had not been misplaced. Jack Birkenshaw had been brought in as cricket manager, to back up Peter Anderson's appointment as chief executive.

On Trevor Gard and Dennis Breakwell

Rumour has it that they shared a sponsored bat for nine seasons and Doris recently sold it in our shop as brand new.

Peter Anderson, writing in their benefit brochure

COUNTY CHAMPIONSHIP 14th

COUNTY CHAMPIONSHIP 14th	Played 22	Won 4	Drawn 12	Lost 6
OTHER MATCHES	Played 1		Drawn 1	
NATWEST BANK TROPHY	Lost in Second Round			
BENSON & HEDGES CUP	Lost in Semi-Final			
REFUGE ASSURANCE LEAGUE 10th	Played 16	Won 7	Tied 1	Lost 8

BATTING

	M	I	NO	Runs	HS	Ave	100	50	ct	st
S.J. Cook	23	41	4	2241	156	60.56	8	8	13	–
P.M. Roebuck	22	37	3	1399	149	41.14	5	6	8	–
V.J. Marks	20	32	12	822	89*	41.10	–	4	7	–
C.J. Tavare	21	38	2	1341	153	37.25	1	9	18	–
R.J. Harden	20	34	6	969	115*	34.60	3	2	10	–
N.D. Burns	21	31	5	760	90	29.23	–	4	45	6
J.C.M. Atkinson	4	7	0	184	53	26.28	–	1	1	–
J.J.E. Hardy	13	23	4	435	65	22.89	–	2	6	–
G.D. Rose	16	20	7	258	50*	19.84	–	1	4	–
A.N. Jones	23	23	10	186	43*	14.30	–	–	8	–
N.A. Mallender	18	18	4	186	48*	13.28	–	–	8	–
R.J. Bartlett	11	19	0	228	54	12.00	–	1	10	–
J.G. Wyatt	3	4	0	46	23	11.50	–	–	–	–
M.W. Cleal	6	7	0	68	30	9.71	–	–	2	–
H.R.J. Trump	14	15	2	94	31*	7.23	–	–	6	–
N.J. Pringle	5	9	1	50	12*	6.25	–	–	5	–
D.J. Foster	9	8	1	29	11*	4.14	–	–	1	–

(2 matches) T. Gard 0, 40 (2 ct)

(1 match) P.D. Unwin 4*   T.J.A. Scriven did not bat

BOWLING

	Overs	Mdns	Runs	Wkts	Ave	5wi	10wm
G.D. Rose	418.2	104	1143	47	24.31	–	–
N.A. Mallender	514.5	121	1389	50	27.78	3	1
A.N. Jones	603.2	119	2014	71	28.36	2	–
P.M. Roebuck	141	35	347	11	31.54	–	–
H.R.J. Trump	416	93	1125	25	45.00	–	–
V.J. Marks	843.5	245	2252	47	47.91	1	–
M.W. Cleal	95.4	19	327	6	54.50	–	–
D.J. Foster	179	21	647	8	80.87	–	–

T.J.A. Scriven 43.1-8-155-4   P.D. Unwin 36-6-115-5   N.J. Pringle 26-2-122-0

R.J. Harden 23.3-4-89-0   J.C.M. Atkinson 13-3-46-0   J.J.E. Hardy 1.4-0-6-0

JIMMY COOK 1989 – 1991

No-one recognised Jimmy Cook when he first turned up at Taunton. Indeed, his was a name hardly known in this country. He was 36, had never played in a Test match because of South Africa's domestic politics, and was now Somerset's overseas cricketer.

A tall, rather solemn figure, with old-fashioned standards when it came to matters of courtesy, he relished the unlikely bonus of first-class cricket afforded him in England. Because of duties at home, it was not certain how long he would stay here.

In the event, the runs kept coming, and he was with Somerset for three bountiful summers. He occupied the crease with a minimum of movement; there was no extrovert flourish in his stroke-making. His placement was his forte, so he maintained a decent pace with twos and threes. The boundaries, often apparently effortless, were dignified calculations – they were seldom struck.

His triple-century at Sophia Gardens was a perfectly controlled entity, almost unmemorable in terms of dynamics. Jimmy pulled on his moustache between overs, allowing himself no outward emotion. There was an overwhelming serenity at the core of the temperament.

When at last South Africa resumed Test cricket, he was virtually overlooked. The rebuff must have hurt. Somerset have persuaded some richly gifted overseas players to join them; Jimmy Cook is there with the best.

STEPHEN JAMES COOK Born Johannesburg, South Africa, 31.7.53. RHB. Cap 1989. 3 Tests 1992-93. 4 LOI 1991-93. SFC: 71 matches; 7604 runs @ 72.41; 28 centuries; HS 313* v Glamorgan, Cardiff, 1990; 2000 runs 3 times; HT 2755 in 1991; 2 wickets @ 34.00; BB 2-25 v Derbyshire, Taunton, 1990. OD: 71 matches; 3048 runs @ 45.49; B&H GA 2. Transvaal, South Africa, 1972-95.

Jimmy Cook with Vic Marks

A thoroughly nice fellow. Unlike some other top batsmen I could mention, he is very quiet, almost unassuming at the crease and is quite happy to share a joke or two with the labouring bowlers.
Jonathan Agnew

7500 first-class runs in three consecutive seasons for one team			
7896	T.W. Hayward	Surrey	1904-06
7630	K.S. Ranjitsinhji	Sussex	1899-1901
7604	S.J. Cook	Somerset	1989-91
7509	C.P. Mead	Hampshire	1926-28

Unlike the others on this list, Jimmy Cook also played limited-over cricket, taking his grand total in three years for Somerset to 10,652 runs.

1989

CHRIS TAVARE 1989 – 1993

He was not an ostentatious express train. It was not his style to court popularity with flamboyant liberties. Indeed, some would say that Somerset have had few more introverted skippers. During the course of an innings there was hardly ever a flicker of emotion, not once a nuance of levity. It is possible that he was not a bundle of uninhibited fun in the dressing room.

Bad psychology and a meanness of spirit on the part of some of those in charge at Kent meant he was ready to leave. The invitation to Somerset came primarily from his pal, Vic Marks. Down in the West Country, from where his wife hailed after all, there was going to be need of an experienced captain. Tavare was never a man for rash decisions; he chose to come, first as a player and only later as skipper. That phlegmatic exterior masked a sharp tactical sense. He may have spurned risk and too many flights of imagination but he could be a calculating competitor.

There was also ample paradox in his batting. The popular image suggested the obdurate occupant of the crease. In truth, he could emerge as a most fluent and crisp stroke-maker. Note his success-rate in one-day matches; he was capable of pushing the score along comfortably without the hint of a wanton blow.

But the summer of 1993 brought him meagre success. The technical assuredness and concentration lessened. Quiet and dignified as ever, he announced his retirement and became a teacher, returning to his old school in Sevenoaks.

CHRISTOPHER JAMES TAVARE Born Orpington, Kent, 27.10.54. RHB, RM. Cap 1989. Captain 1990-93. 31 Tests 1980-89. 29 LOI 1980-84. SFC: 102 matches; 6365 runs @ 43.00; 13 centuries; HS 219 v Sussex, Hove, 1990; 1000 runs 4 times; HT 1638 in 1990; 0 wickets. OD: 109 matches; 3465 runs @ 38.50; 0 wickets; NW MoM 1; B&H GA 3. Kent 1974-88; Oxford University 1975-77.

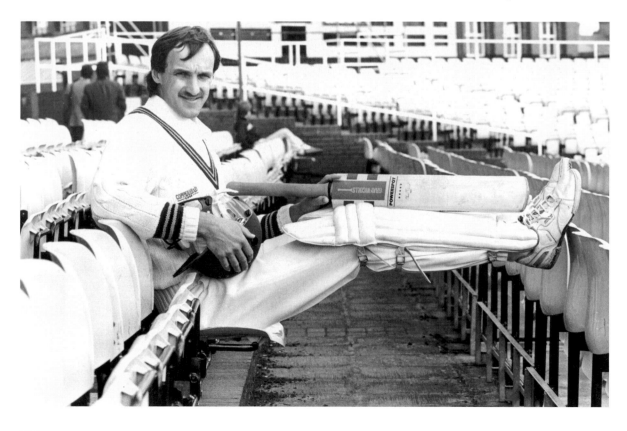

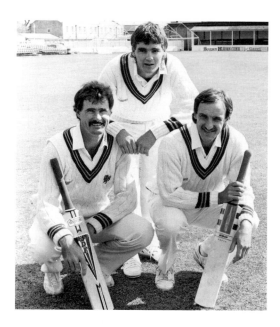

Jimmy Cook, Paul Unwin, Chris Tavare

PAUL UNWIN 1989

Over here on a cricketing exchange scheme, he made his surprise sole entry into English first-class cricket, against the Australians when Vic Marks was not available.

PAUL DAVID UNWIN Born Waipawa, New Zealand, 9.6.67. RHB, OB. SFC: 1 match; 4 runs (no average); HS 4 * v Australians, Taunton, 1989; 5 wickets @ 23.20; BB 3-73 same match. Central Districts, New Zealand, 1986-93; Canterbury, New Zealand, 1993-94.

VIC MARKS' XI
from the years in which he played

Marcus Trescothick
Jimmy Cook
Viv Richards
Brian Close
Brian Rose
Ian Botham
Rob Turner
Tom Cartwright
Mushtaq Ahmed
Joel Garner
Andrew Caddick

It's hard to keep the imports out. I disqualified M. Crowe and S. Waugh only on the basis that they didn't play that often (likewise Gavaskar, Ponting and G. Smith) and Alley because he finished too long ago. I toyed with Blackwell – rather than Rose – but decided we have enough bowling.
Close, of course, would captain the side, whether invited to or not.

1990

Captain: C.J. Tavare

Cook again excelled at the crease, reinforcing his gentle influence as vice-captain. He was the first in the country to reach 1,000 and 2,000 runs; in May he travelled to Cardiff's Sophia Gardens to score an undefeated 313. At the other end was Tavare (120), who decided to declare on the daunting total of 535-2, when Cook was only nine runs short of Richards' record-breaking 322 for the county. Are 'outsiders' less sentimental about such things?

There were plenty of big scores to savour on a surfeit of flat pitches. Rose and Harden, in particular, showed marked improvement. The former's ability to exercise those broad shoulders at the expense of wayward bowlers was much enjoyed and might more often have been a welcome asset. As ever, Somerset remained entertaining and fallible. They finished 15th in the championship, seemingly an unjust position in a season when ten other counties lost more matches. The prospects had certainly looked bright as they started off in April with a ten-wicket win over Gloucestershire. The sixth-wicket stand of Burns (166) and Rose (85) made all the difference, though praise was due also to Lefebvre, the enthusiastic Dutchman making his championship debut, Mallender and Jones, who carved up the wickets between them.

Somerset reached the semi-finals of the Benson & Hedges Cup for the second year running. Hayhurst, who had come from Lancashire to the West Country, was one of several to demonstrate positive form in the one-day matches.

On a summer in which Somerset won most batting points and the TCCB reduced the seam on the ball

If we were given trophies for batting entertainment, we'd have been the winners by the end of July.

But spare a thought for our bowlers, who toiled with balls which many a mongrel dog would refuse to play with.

Jack Birkenshaw, Team Manager

COUNTY CHAMPIONSHIP   15th

COUNTY CHAMPIONSHIP 15th	Played 22	Won 3	Drawn 15	Lost 4

OTHER MATCHES — Played 2 — Drawn 1 — Lost 1

NATWEST BANK TROPHY — Lost in Second Round

BENSON & HEDGES CUP — Lost in Semi-Final

REFUGE ASSURANCE LEAGUE   8th — Played 16 — Won 8 — Lost 8

BATTING

	M	I	NO	Runs	HS	Ave	100	50	ct	st
S.J. Cook	24	41	7	2608	313*	76.70	9	11	10	–
R.J. Harden	24	31	7	1460	104*	60.83	3	12	18	–
C.J. Tavare	24	32	4	1638	219	58.50	3	12	16	–
A.N. Hayhurst	22	35	8	1559	170	57.74	4	8	9	–
G.D. Rose	24	29	11	1000	97*	55.55	–	8	13	–
P.M. Roebuck	18	28	5	1134	201*	49.30	2	6	7	–
N.D. Burns	24	34	10	951	166	39.62	1	5	43	1
J.J.E. Hardy	9	16	5	361	91	32.81	–	1	6	–
N.A. Mallender	20	10	3	177	87*	25.28	–	1	3	–
A.N. Jones	22	9	5	100	41	25.00	–	–	6	–
I.G. Swallow	23	17	7	187	32	18.70	–	–	12	–
R.P. Lefebvre	17	16	3	214	53	16.46	–	1	8	–
H.R.J. Trump	7	5	1	11	4*	2.75	–	–	3	–
J.C. Hallett	3	1	0	0	0	0.00	–	–	–	–

(2 matches)   G.T.J. Townsend 0, 0*, 15, 6 (3 ct)
(1 match)   R.J. Bartlett 73, 12

BOWLING

	Overs	Mdns	Runs	Wkts	Ave	5wi	10wm
N.A. Mallender	553.2	116	1585	51	31.07	2	–
A.N. Jones	572.4	92	2055	56	36.69	2	–
G.D. Rose	571.4	99	1951	53	36.81	1	–
J.C. Hallett	65.5	9	238	6	39.66	–	–
R.P. Lefebvre	506.1	137	1281	31	41.32	1	–
R.J. Harden	67	6	276	6	46.00	–	–
H.R.J. Trump	164	41	520	9	57.77	–	–
A.N. Hayhurst	321.2	50	1087	17	63.94	–	–
I.G. Swallow	689.1	161	2174	34	63.94	–	–
P.M. Roebuck	182.3	42	529	8	66.12	–	–

C.J. Tavare 17.2-0-162-0   S.J. Cook 8-0-42-2   N.D. Burns 0.3-0-8-0

ROLAND LEFEBVRE 1990 – 1992

Should Somerset have made greater efforts to hold on to Roland Lefebvre? He could be a bonny fighter, especially suited to the one-day matches.

It was unusual for the county to have a Dutchman in their side. Off the field he tended aching limbs, as a qualified physiotherapist, and manipulated the ivories, as a more than passable pianist.

His tight medium pace was not easy to score off; his batting, certainly, was not to be disparaged, as his century at Clarence Park proved. But 1992 was a cruel year for Roland, as he struggled to recover and re-stake his claims after suffering injury through a misjudged jape, in which he was the innocent victim, on tour.

After leaving Somerset he became a popular and capable member of the successful Glamorgan side in 1993 before drifting out of the game.

ROLAND PHILIPPE LEFEBVRE Born Rotterdam, Holland, 7.2.63. RHB, RMF. Cap 1991. SFC: 36 matches; 650 runs @ 20.96; 1 century; HS 100 v Worcestershire, Weston-super-Mare, 1991; HT 366 in 1991; 54 wickets @ 45.40; BB 5-30 v Gloucestershire, Taunton, 1990; HT 31 in 1990. OD: 49 matches; 37 runs @ 17.13; 58 wickets @ 28.46. Holland 1983-90; Glamorgan 1993-95; Canterbury, New Zealand, 1990-91.

IAN SWALLOW 1990 – 1991

Any off-spinner who had been brought in to do what Vic Marks had done so well for so long was going to be subjected to unfair comparisons. Ian Swallow had hoped in vain that his career, which had only flickered with his native Yorkshire, would now be encouragingly relaunched. He was, in fact, a competent slow bowler and one suitably praised at times by coach Jackie Birkenshaw. But the county came to the conclusion that he wasn't going to take enough wickets.

IAN GEOFFREY SWALLOW Born Barnsley, Yorkshire, 18.12.62. RHB, OB. SFC: 27 matches; 254 runs @ 21.16; HS 41* v Glamorgan, Taunton, 1991; HT 187 in 1990; 42 wickets @ 60.19; BB 3-43 v Sussex, Taunton, 1991; HT 34 in 1990. OD: 26 matches; 112 runs @ 14.00; 12 wickets @ 64.00. Yorkshire 1983-89.

JEREMY HALLETT 1990 – 1995

His name generated early excitement. Somerset had carefully monitored his impressive schoolboy progress. They liked his temperament and competitive streak as an all-rounder. The generous prophecies gained weight when he was nominated Man of the Series on the 1989-90 Young England tour to Australia.

Hallett was one of Somerset's numerous graduates from Millfield; later he became captain at Durham University. Sadly he became one of the many to promise much but then drift away. Still, that maiden century against Middlesex at Taunton remained one to savour.

JEREMY CHARLES HALLETT Born Yeovil, 18.10.70. RHB, RMF. SFC: 16 matches; 285 runs @ 21.92; 1 century; HS 111* v Middlesex, Taunton, 1995; HT: 229 in 1995; 24 wickets @ 47.58; BB 4-59 v Kent, Canterbury, 1994; HT 12 in 1991. OD: 25 matches; 73 runs @ 12.16; 20 wickets @ 40.35.

GARETH TOWNSEND 1990 – 1992

Clinched his contract on the strength of some impressive scoring in a Second XI match. He was described as a battler, capable of occupying the crease, and with the equable temperament you'd expect from a Devonian. Solid ability was always there; but promotion did not come easily and he was released in 1992.

GARETH TERENCE JOHN TOWNSEND Born Tiverton, Devon, 28.6.68. RHB. SFC: 12 matches; 414 runs @ 20.70; HS 53 v Sri Lankans, Taunton, 1991; HT 272 in 1992. OD: 6 matches; 224 runs @ 37.33.

PERRY RENDELL 1990

He did well at times in Second XI matches and, as an all-rounder, for Weston-super-Mare. His only promotion for the county came in 1990 when his seamers brought him two wickets – plus a decent catch to dismiss Jayasuriya – in a one-day match with the Sri Lankans.

PERRY JOHN RENDELL Born Weston-super-Mare, 20.1.70. RHB, RM. OD: 1 match; did not bat; 2 wickets @ 23.00. Combined Universities 1991.

ANDREW NEIL HAYHURST Born Davyhulme, Manchester, 23.11.62. RHB, RM. Cap 1990. Captain 1994-96. SFC: 122 matches; 6634 runs @ 38.56; 13 centuries; HS 172* v Gloucestershire, Bath, 1991; 1000 runs 3 times; HT 1559 in 1990; 60 wickets @ 55.28; BB 3-27 v Yorkshire, Middlesbrough, 1992; HT 17 in 1990. OD: 121 matches; 2678 runs @ 33.06; 94 wickets @ 26.08; NW MoM 2; B&H GA 2. Lancashire 1985-89; Derbyshire 1997.

ANDY HAYHURST
1990 – 1996

When this all-rounder was signed from Lancashire, Somerset's then manager, Jackie Birkenshaw, confided that he saw him as a potential captain of his new county, and so it proved.

He made an early impact, doing well enough to win his cap and ensure that his first-class career was finally taking off. Part of the trouble at Old Trafford had been undue concentration on his medium-paced bowling, swinging the ball away from the right-hander, which was all very well, but his batting suffered as a result. With Somerset he first filled the number-three position and also proved himself a dependable opener, scoring impressively through the off-side.

Indeterminate form followed by injury worked against him in 1993, but he bounced back with renewed application, an unruffled approach and several big scores.

It was not to last. His late-season exit from the team in 1996 was abrupt and not well handled. Hayhurst's form was by now disappointing and there were growing murmurs of discontent in some quarters about his captaincy.

The day following a spineless defeat at the Oval in the NatWest quarter-finals, he was dropped after arriving at the Taunton ground. 'Go off and score some runs for the Second XI,' was the demoralising advice. He left at the end of the season to join Derbyshire, mainly to look after the second team. From there he moved to Old Trafford, to be appointed in time as director of the Lancashire Cricket Board.

GRAHAM ROSE'S XI

from the years in which he played

Matthew Wood
Marcus Trescothick
Chris Tavare
Mark Lathwell
Richard Harden
Ian Blackwell
Rob Turner
Matthew Bulbeck
Richard Johnson
Mushtaq Ahmed
Andy Caddick

My side contains only one overseas player because I feel passionately that, for the good of English cricket, no more should be allowed. At the time of writing, England are strong, but in five years' time, when some counties might have anything up to five players on their books who are ineligible to represent this country in Tests, then the picture might change dramatically.

One per county is enough, and that one should be of the very highest quality. I am very much against cricketers entering our game through the European Union and Kolpak routes, because 99.9 per cent of them are not worth it. It's a crying shame when someone like Matthew Wood, who I'm delighted to include in my line-up, should have spent so much time stagnating in the second team, often a victim of the overseas situation.

Despite my self-imposed limitation, I am more than happy with my side, which I think is well balanced, bats a long way down and has genuine wicket-taking quality throughout the attack. Certainly I would back my seam bowlers to take the top four or five wickets, leaving Mushy to winkle out the rest, then Blackie would come into the mix in the second innings. I thought about Vic Marks, but in the end there just wasn't a place.

Overall it's a combination which could be in contention for trophies, one which could give most other Somerset fantasy teams a run for their money.

Modesty forbade that I should consider myself for selection; that would be for other people to judge.

1991

Captain: C.J. Tavare

Depressingly, Somerset were down at the bottom again. Where did supporters look for glimpses of compensation? The most unlikely statistic was that only the champions, Essex, accumulated more batting points. Sadness abounded. The prolific Cook was in his third and final season for Somerset. Roebuck, after a county career full of unsung virtues, was retiring. Graveney, who had surprised many by decamping from Gloucestershire to join their traditional rivals for a summer, was now moving on to captain Durham.

All, in different ways, had made an impact. Cook had taken his place among Somerset's international heroes. Those 7,604 first-class runs contained 28 hundreds, his performances not so much spectacularly memorable, more composed works of art. Twice he scored two centuries in a match. He has gone into the county's record books on sheer uncomplicated merit. As for Graveney, the stay was short and at times profitable. Noticeably, Trump blossomed under the left-arm spinner's tutelage.

There were exciting prospects, too. The towering New Zealander, Caddick, had taken 96 wickets for the Second XI and was ready to make his notable entry to first-class cricket. And what about this young Lathwell, whose progress had been monitored so eagerly for several years? Somerset reached the quarter-finals of the NatWest Trophy before being knocked out by a mere five runs by the more fancied Warwickshire. Hayhurst had a fine, if unavailing match; he followed up his five wickets with 91 not out. When it came to the last game of the season, Somerset's resourceful 403 in the second innings at Taunton failed narrowly to bring them a championship win, again against Warwickshire. The margin: five runs. Maiden centuries for Rose and Lefebvre were other bonuses during this frustrating campaign.

Somerset has been wonderful to me, the people so kind and helpful. When I first said I was coming here, Clive Rice said I couldn't have picked a better place. And he was right.

Jimmy Cook

244

COUNTY CHAMPIONSHIP   17th

	Played 22	Won 2	Drawn 15	Lost 5

OTHER MATCHES — Played 2 — Drawn 1 — Lost 1

NATWEST BANK TROPHY — Lost in Quarter-Final

BENSON & HEDGES CUP — Eliminated at Zonal Stage

REFUGE ASSURANCE LEAGUE   8th — Played 16 — Won 7 — No Result 2 — Lost 7

BATTING

	M	I	NO	Runs	HS	Ave	100	50	ct	st
S.J. Cook	24	42	8	2755	210*	81.02	11	8	16	–
C.J. Tavare	23	37	7	1601	183	53.36	5	7	20	–
R.J. Harden	24	39	8	1355	134	43.70	3	9	21	–
G.D. Rose	15	20	3	590	106	34.70	2	2	8	–
A.N. Hayhurst	19	32	5	910	172*	33.70	3	1	5	–
I.G. Swallow	4	5	3	67	41*	33.50	–	–	3	–
P.M. Roebuck	17	29	3	833	101	32.03	1	5	4	–
N.D. Burns	23	34	8	808	108	31.07	1	4	35	8
R.J. Bartlett	5	7	1	177	71	29.50	–	1	3	–
K.H. MacLeay	15	21	6	417	63	27.80	–	2	5	–
R.P. Lefebvre	16	18	4	366	100	26.14	1	1	6	–
G.T.J. Townsend	3	5	0	121	53	24.20	–	1	3	–
N.A. Mallender	13	11	3	108	19	13.50	–	–	1	–
H.R.J. Trump	18	17	7	108	30*	10.80	–	–	12	–
J.C. Hallett	8	5	1	35	15	8.75	–	–	4	–
D.A. Graveney	21	14	7	59	17	8.42	–	–	10	–
D. Beal	3	2	0	1	1	0.50	–	–	1	–
A.P. van Troost	4	1	1	0	0*	–	–	–	1	–

(2 matches)   N.J. Pringle 7, 17, 1, 20 (1 ct)   M.N. Lathwell 16, 4, 43
A.R. Caddick 0 (1 ct)
(1 match)   I. Fletcher 56, 2*   G.W. White 42   R.J. Turner 18* (3 ct)

BOWLING

	Overs	Mdns	Runs	Wkts	Ave	5wi	10wm
N.A. Mallender	349.5	76	969	42	23.07	3	–
K.H. MacLeay	284.3	54	872	25	34.88	–	–
P.M. Roebuck	130	33	315	9	35.00	–	–
D.A. Graveney	708.2	153	2160	55	39.27	2	–
H.R.J. Trump	637.2	111	2113	51	41.43	4	–
G.D. Rose	323	53	1075	25	43.00	–	–
I.G. Swallow	100.1	16	354	8	44.25	–	–
A.P. van Troost	86.4	12	267	6	44.50	–	–
A.R. Caddick	64.5	13	251	5	50.20	–	–
J.C. Hallett	178.3	31	637	12	53.08	–	–
R.P. Lefebvre	365	74	1075	18	59.72	–	–
A.N. Hayhurst	205.3	32	780	11	70.90	–	–
D. Beal	71	6	320	3	106.66	–	–

M.N. Lathwell 28-9-99-1   R.J. Harden 23.5-0-122-3   G.W. White 6-1-30-1
S.J. Cook 4-0-26-0

ANDY CADDICK 1991 –

Here, on any timeless roll of honour, is one of Somerset's greatest bowlers. The statistics alone carry their own unchallengeable eloquence. He would have played more matches for Somerset, and taken many more wickets, but for the injuries to shin, foot and back that kept him out of the side, as did his commitment, as a Test bowler, to the system of central contracts.

His West Country devotees are convinced that eventually he was unreasonably snubbed by the England selectors. He played in 62 Tests, at times with spectacular results. Captains, for country or county, found it hard to get the ball off him; such was his single-minded enthusiasm. He was recalled by England, only to slip out of elevated favour again, left to wait in vain for the final summons. In retrospect, the selectors' judgment seemed to amount to a rather drastic dismissal from the international stage.

Caddick knew only one way to play – with an eager heart and competitive zeal. He believed he had more to parade at Test level and privately it hurt him when England decided to opt for a younger and supposedly fitter fast bowler. Yet in 2004 he had taken 56 first-class wickets, including five in an innings four times, after being out of the game injured for nearly 12 months.

The first Test call had come against Australia in the summer of 1993. Their batsmen have a traditional relish for attempting to ruin emerging reputations. They consciously went after Caddick and he was to discover the gulf in success-rate as he made the transition from county to international cricket. At times he was made to look ordinary, something that had never happened when, for instance, he annihilated Lancashire to take 9-32 in just 11 overs to ensure a two-day win for Somerset.

Thus, perhaps, some of the early Tests were not an unqualified success. Yet England captain Graham Gooch and the game's elder statesmen admired the temperament, the physical attributes, the resilience and self-confidence. They sensed that there would be, with added technical wisdom, plenty more to come.

They were right: everyone remembers his 5-16 from 13 overs against the West Indians at Lord's, followed by 5-14 at Headingley, with four wickets in one incredible over. In Sydney he took ten wickets against the Australians.

For Somerset, with that spring-heeled approach and an action that appeared deceptively languid, his marathon spells were remarkable as he shrugged off hints of injury. In 1998 he was acclaimed for passing 100 wickets; during the following season, his benefit year, he took 91 first-class scalps and was prepared to bowl as long as Jamie Cox needed.

A previous coach, Bob Cottam, had always enthused, a few thought prematurely, about Caddick's promise. The bowler had the height to bounce, the determination to add swing to seam, and the controlled rhythm which meant he never took too much out of himself.

The no-nonsense action, the mannerisms, the sweatbands even, all belonged to Richard Hadlee. Caddick was flattered by the comparison, though making a point that he had not deliberately imitated his fellow New Zealander. If there had been an influence, then it was really Dennis Lillee, whose tuition had been so keenly absorbed. Caddick, inclined to be dour in the Kiwi tradition, had always been a good listener.

One parent came from Liverpool, the other from Newcastle. So the allegiance to New Zealand was never obsessive, even less so when he discovered the scant encouragement being offered him at home as a young cricketer. Instead he set his sights on county cricket here, with Test recognition for his parents' country as his ultimate ambition. Some at home scoffed at such notions.

He came to England, playing club matches for Hampstead and later Clevedon as he went into a four-year qualification period. He chose Somerset and before too long it was clear that his days as a plasterer and tiler were over, even if his practical skills were gratefully used on occasions at the County Ground. Away from cricket, he's a helicopter pilot.

ANDREW RICHARD CADDICK Born Christchurch, New Zealand, 2.11.68. RHB, RFM. Cap 1992. 62 Tests 1993-2003. 54 LOI 1993-2003. SFC: 144 matches; 2496 runs @ 17.70; HS 92 v Worcestershire, Worcester, 1995; HT 322 in 1998; 702 wickets @ 24.24; BB 9-32 v Lancashire, Taunton, 1993; HT: 105 in 1998. OD: 175 matches; 504 runs @ 10.72; 224 wickets @ 26.03; NW MoM 2. TT: 10 matches; 0 runs; 7 wickets @ 37.28.

Like all proper fast bowlers he is capable of a good moan, but we at Somerset have learnt one thing. Stick the ball in his hand, and he does not want to relinquish it. We also know that he'll come to your rescue when the pipes have burst.
Vic Marks

DAVID GRAVENEY 1991

Already in his late thirties when he came to Somerset for a season, Graveney had been Gloucestershire's captain and was ready to seek pastures new. The move down the M5 from Bristol to Taunton – or in the opposite direction – hasn't always been a matter of approval for the spectators. But the Somerset crowd quite took to 'Grav', that towering, creaky-jointed figure, as he offered helpful advice to young spinners, including Harvey Trump. This elder statesman took most wickets for the county in a stay that was never going to last more than a year. His looming appointment at Durham was an open secret.

His eventual lofty status, as chairman of the Test selectors, reflected his varied skills, not least in man management. He was politically adroit, calm and sensible in public statements; a natural communicator, outstanding in the demands of public relations, ready to confide in and trust the press and TV pundits. Yet some observers seemed wary of his elevation.

It came as something of a surprise when in 2005 his name was mentioned discreetly as being on the favoured list for the then-vacant post of director of cricket and chief executive at Somerset, the responsible role later split between Brian Rose and Richard Gould.

DAVID ANTHONY GRAVENEY Born Bristol, 2.1.53. RHB, SLA. Cap 1991. SFC: 21 matches; 59 runs @ 8.42; HS 17 v Glamorgan, Taunton, 1991; 55 wickets @ 39.27; BB 7-105 v Kent, Taunton, 1991. OD: 14 matches; 23 runs (no average); 14 wickets @ 27.00. Gloucestershire 1972-90; Durham 1992-94.

DAVID BEAL 1991

The Beals are a well-known sporting family in the Glastonbury area. One member, who also played in goal for the Town side, achieved local fame by regularly crashing centuries for village teams while discarding on principle anything as sophisticated as batting gloves. David was a bowler, decidedly lively by club standards and a formidable taker of wickets for Morlands CC. Somerset had him their sights at Under-17 level and then cruelly, after being pitched straight into the first team at the start of 1991 – when Mike Gatting became one of his three victims – his back went.

DAVID BEAL Born Butleigh, Somerset, 17.7.66. RHB, RM. SFC: 3 matches; 1 run @ 0.50; HS 1 v Sussex, Hove, 1991; 3 wickets @ 106.66; BB 1-37 v Essex, Southend, 1991. OD: 6 matches; 1 run @ 0.50; 5 wickets @ 33.20

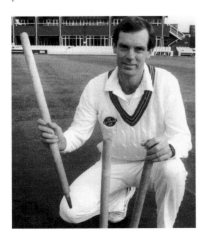

KEN MacLEAY 1991 – 1992

It looked like quite a coup when it was first announced that Ken MacLeay was coming over from Australia, for whom he played in 16 one-day internationals, to join Somerset. He had been born at Bradford-on-Avon while his father was in the Navy here, and although the family soon emigrated, it was the perfect cricketing qualification. Vic Marks, who had seen him in action for Western Australia, added his recommendations. But bowling successes proved relatively elusive and MacLeay often seemed a better bet as a batsman.

KENNETH HERVEY MacLEAY Born Bradford-on-Avon, Wiltshire, 2.4.59. RHB, RM. 16 LOI for Australia 1983-87. SFC: 27 matches; 844 runs @ 27.22; HS 74 v Warwickshire, Taunton, 1992; HT 427 in 1992; 34 wickets @ 34.79; BB 3-40 v Derbyshire, Derby, 1991; HT 25 in 1991. OD: 36 matches; 370 runs @ 17.61; 36 wickets @ 25.69. Western Australia 1981-90.

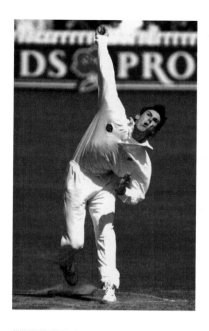

ANDRE VAN TROOST 1991 – 1998

Let no-one discount his pace or his bounce; he was 6ft 7in after all. He represented Holland – like his grandfather, who was still playing in his eighties – and came to Somerset at the same time as Roland Lefebvre.

Andre took six wickets in an innings more than once and it seemed, with the added control he strove to acquire, he was capable of making a genuine impact in this country. As for his unconventional batting, that was something else.

A conversational aside by the great West Indian opener Desmond Haynes that Van Troost was arguably the fastest bowler in the world seemed a trifle exaggerated. But at times he was very fast indeed and almost unplayable. At his best he was, without question, a match-winner.

He didn't lack ambition and news that the TCCB weren't prepared to shorten his period of qualification for England came as a big disappointment.

ADRIANUS PELRUS VAN TROOST Born Schiedam, Holland, 2.10.72. RHB, RF. Cap 1997. SFC: 67 matches; 448 runs @ 8.61; HS 35 v Lancashire, Taunton, 1993; HT 108 in 1993 and 1994; 140 wickets @ 38.70; BB 6-48 v Essex, Taunton, 1992; HT 35 in 1994. OD: 28 matches; 75 runs @ 10.71; 33 wickets @ 29.96.

GILES WHITE 1991 – 1993

Shaped well for Devon as an all-rounder. The fact that he was a leg-spinner generated added interest, but the presence of Mushtaq Ahmed made recognition for White more difficult. Ability was keenly monitored from Millfield days; then came Loughborough University.

There was little sign of headway at Somerset and he joined Hampshire, proving himself occasionally a dogged opener who several times carried his bat. The spinners brought meagre reward, despite a few tutorials from Shane Warne at the Rose Bowl. White went on to be appointed Second XI coach at Hampshire.

GILES WILLIAM WHITE Born Barnstaple, Devon, 23.3.72. RHB, LB. SFC: 1 match, 42 runs @ 42.00. HS 42 v Sri Lankans, Taunton, 1991; 1 wicket @ 30.00; BB 1-30 same match. OD: 3 matches; 41 runs @ 13.66. Hampshire 1994-2002.

IAIN FLETCHER Born Sawbridgeworth, Hampshire, 31.8.71. RHB, RM. SFC: 14 matches; 460 runs @ 24.21; HS 65* v Middlesex, Bath, 1993; HT 223 in 1993. SL: 8 matches; 72 runs @ 9.00.

IAIN FLETCHER 1991 – 1994

One of the many to arrive at Taunton by way of Millfield. He came in at the end of the 1991 season, responding with a well-made half-century at Southampton. But there was no follow-up for the stocky, punchy opener in the ensuing term, partly because on an ankle injury which kept him out when he might have made his bid.

There was more misfortune for Fletcher when he made his second appearance, two seasons after the first. Fresh from his exams in politics at Loughborough, he was played as an emergency opener at the Bath festival. He scored 65 highly competent runs before being struck by a ball from Middlesex's Neil Williams, which broke his right index finger. Once more his career was interrupted, but he had done enough to convince the county that his technique was sound and he could build an innings.

When he finished playing he turned to journalism. His reports for a Sunday paper have been perceptive, reflecting his affection for and knowledge of the game.

MARK LATHWELL 1991 – 2001

You didn't need to tell the local pundits that here was some exceptional quality. There could not have been a more self-effacing arrival at the County Ground, but the innate gifts were immediately apparent. Soon Mark was being compared with Harold Gimblett, mainly because that unforgettable entertainer, too, was an opening batsman who went for his shots. The styles varied a good deal, of course. Lathwell, perhaps, possessed more leg-side strokes, though because of his engagingly unassuming manner, he would never have claimed to equal Gimblett's sublime repertoire.

There was a thrilling inevitability about the early progress of Lathwell, this small, quite sturdy figure, from the first time he picked up a bat at Taunton. The instincts were right, if rather less so the feet. What was more, he played the ball late, like the great batsmen.

No-one at Somerset was surprised when, after his first full season, he was chosen for England 'A' in Australia – and not surprised, either, when he came up with an innings of 175 out there.

Full Test recognition came against the Australians the following summer, but it was an anti-climax. Technical flaws were exposed to a national television audience, and the so-called experts started pontificating about his inexperience; many of the comments were not constructive.

There was a notion that they might try to make him more competitive but it was always possible that, for a young man with such a delightful, easy-going temperament, it was a policy which might rebound.

Lathwell kept his thoughts to himself, though he was apt to confide to his friends that too many people had expected too much too quickly. He packed his bags for the 1993-94 'A' tour of South Africa with fingers crossed; alas, the runs did not prove plentiful.

In pleasing contrast, his double-hundred at Bath against Surrey in 1994 was full of delicious drives. In the years that followed, the outstanding innings grew less frequent, but they were always worth waiting for.

There was no cricket at all for him in 1999 because of a knee injury, but three times in 2001 he stroked his way into the nineties. These glimpses of rare skill, the kind that once earned him the writers' award as Young Cricketer of the Year, were still evident.

His heart, one felt, was never quite in it, especially the unrelenting routine of training and County Ground disciplines. The sighs at Taunton were audible when, by the end of the 2001 campaign, he had gone, despite some fervent efforts, by the chief executive Peter Anderson and others, to persuade him to change his mind.

He returned to the more gentle-paced North Devon to captain Braunton, to play darts and to see his village friends. He was instantly unburdened, doing some local coaching while he ran a car-repair business.

The tragedy of Lathwell, quite apart from his exceptional and prematurely terminated instinctive skills, was that he possessed a genuine, if under-used, cricket brain. Some saw him as a future county captain. Introvert he may have been but contributions he made to benefit brochures were both original and intelligent, with humour not far away.

MARK NICHOLAS LATHWELL Born Bletchley, Buckinghamshire, 26.12.71. RHB, RM. Cap 1992. 2 Tests 1993. SFC: 142 matches; 7988 runs @ 33.84; 10 centuries; HS 206 v Surrey, Bath, 1994; 1000 runs 4 times; HT 1230 in 1994; 13 wickets @ 55.46; BB 2-21 v Sussex, Hove, 1994. OD: 166 matches; 4399 runs @ 28.38; 1 wicket @ 193.00; NW MoM 1; B&H GA 2.

The only cricketer in modern times to be chosen for England for playing every match as though it were a village green affair.
Simon Wilde, The Times

We were only granted glimpses of what he might have achieved, but it was a privilege to see even them. I only wish his golden gifts could have come to full fruition.
Graham Rose

ROB TURNER 1991 – 2005

He may have looked big for a wicket-keeper but there was no lack of agility or intuition, qualities that surely placed him near – and unlucky to miss – international recognition, however fleeting. As it was, he found himself on standby for England's tours to the West Indies in 1997-98 and to South Africa and Zimbabwe in 1999-2000.

Rob demonstrated leadership skills for Cambridge University and Combined Universities and there must have been a time when he was strongly in the running to skipper Somerset. After making his county debut in 1991, he waited patiently for two years before taking over from Neil Burns; then the position was his for a long time.

He staked his claim unavailingly to represent his country at a point when his batting should have been a bonus. Twice he topped 1,000 runs in a season and he scored ten hundreds in a manner that was, perhaps, pragmatic rather than handsome.

He found himself stepping down at the end of the 2005 season, no doubt a year or so earlier than he would have wished. But by then Somerset's selection policy was changing. Gazzard had latterly taken over from Turner and the young Spurway was on his way up.

As a keeper, Turner was known as 'Mr Reliable'. He was thoroughly efficient, never showy. Only Stephenson and Luckes had more dismissals for Somerset. Against Surrey at Taunton in 2001, his tally of victims during the match was nine, breaking his own shared Somerset record. He was equally excellent when taking seven catches in an innings against Northants the same summer.

For more than a decade he was a reassuringly permanent fixture in the county side. Now he turned to a career in stockbroking, with maybe a little spare time to give some gentle, domestic cricketing tuition to his wife, also a wicket-keeper.

ROBERT JULIAN TURNER Born Malvern, Worcestershire, 25.11.67. RHB, WK. Cap 1994. SFC: 211 matches; 8473 runs @ 33.09; 10 centuries; HS 144 v Kent, Taunton, 1997; 1000 runs twice; HT 1217 in 1999; 0 wickets; 682 dismissals (645 ct, 37 st). OD: 226 matches; 3358 runs @ 26.23; 261 dismissals (228 ct, 33 st); B&H GA 1. TT: 6 matches; 25 runs @ 5.00; 3 dismissals (3ct). Cambridge University 1988-91.

BATH RECREATION GROUND

The Bath wicket tended to turn a bit. Len Creed, who was closely involved with the festival, brought in a groundsman who used to help out at his own club, Lansdown. This chap was an AA man. When I saw him wearing his uniform on the pitch, I suggested that he put up a sign: 'Loose clippings – please drive slowly!'

A little before that, in 1965, Somerset thought that Bath council were looking after the surface and the council thought that Somerset had it in hand. So no one touched it until two weeks before the festival, by which time the wicket was covered with long grass, weeds and flowers. The Taunton groundsman, Cecil Buttle, scythed it all down, then worked on it for a fortnight but, when the first game started, the top just went. It was hard to disagree with Wisden's verdict that it was 'a travesty of a pitch.'

Peter Robinson

1992

Captain: C.J. Tavare

Caddick instantly brought Somerset an additional dimension in attack. He could bounce the ball; he could move it off the seam. He had the necessary aggressive approach for a fast bowler. His arrival, after patient years of qualification, could be clearly detected in the county's climb to ninth position in the table. It was their highest since 1984. Membership was improving and the crowds were increasing once more. Caddick's run-up was producing the kind of frisson last generated in Somerset by Garner. Then there was Lathwell, up from North Devon, a self-effacing young man who liked to get on with it. Some pedants mumbled critically about the position of his feet. He simply played his shots instinctively. 'Just like Harold Gimblett, in a hurry before lunch', his mounting army of fans opined.

In his debut season, Caddick took 71 wickets. Lathwell went in first with Hayhurst, passed his 1,000 runs with something to spare and was partly responsible for the recaptured sniff of team success, however modest. Somerset finished the term with a reassuring rush of centuries. Tavare and Harden scored two each, with one apiece coming from Hayhurst and Turner (his maiden ton) as the county piled up the runs in the two final fixtures.

Trump had his finest moment when Somerset went to Gloucester. He ended with 14-104 from the match, including a hat-trick. More than that, Somerset were once more learning to graft as the pattern of a game took shape. They beat Gloucestershire by only 17 runs but the unflurried partnership of Hayhurst and Tavare was crucial and revealed a more astute mentality within the side. Bob Cottam was now the Director of Cricket, and the signing of Mushtaq, on a three-year contract, hinted at renewed ambition for a county which had become too used to life in the draughty basement. The elevation of Mallender to Test-match status complemented the encouraging mood.

> When I came into the first-class game, I didn't think about anything much when I batted. The pitches were so much better than those in the leagues, it was like paradise. I could get by on my eye alone.
> **Mark Lathwell**

COUNTY CHAMPIONSHIP   9th

Played 22	Won 5	Drawn 13	Lost 4

OTHER MATCHES

Played 1   Lost 1

NATWEST BANK TROPHY

Lost in Second Round

BENSON & HEDGES CUP

Lost in Semi-Final

REFUGE ASSURANCE LEAGUE   5th

Played 17   Won 9   No Result 2   Lost 6

BATTING

	M	I	NO	Runs	HS	Ave	100	50	ct	st
R.J. Turner	7	10	5	286	101*	57.20	1	1	6	–
R.J. Harden	20	33	5	1387	187	49.53	3	6	13	–
C.J. Tavare	21	32	2	1157	125	38.56	3	6	15	–
N.D. Burns	22	33	12	772	73*	36.76	–	4	42	3
M.N. Lathwell	19	33	1	1176	114	36.75	1	11	14	–
A.N. Hayhurst	23	38	2	1197	102	33.25	1	9	6	–
G.D. Rose	22	34	4	930	132	31.00	1	6	11	–
R.P. Snell	16	20	4	436	81	27.25	–	3	6	–
R.J. Bartlett	8	13	0	352	72	27.07	–	2	5	–
K.H. MacLeay	12	19	3	427	74	26.68	–	3	7	–
G.T.J. Townsend	7	13	1	272	49	22.66	–	–	4	–
A.R. Caddick	20	19	6	261	54*	20.07	–	1	6	–
R.P. Lefebvre	3	4	0	70	36	17.50	–	–	3	–
N.A. Mallender	15	18	5	182	29*	14.00	–	–	3	–
H.R.J. Trump	18	18	7	154	28	14.00	–	–	14	–
A.P. van Troost	11	9	5	42	12	10.50	–	–	3	–
A.C. Cottam	6	8	1	43	31	6.14	–	–	1	–

(1 match)   N.A. Folland 22, 82* (1 ct)   A. Payne 51*   K.A. Parsons 1, 0

BOWLING

	Overs	Mdns	Runs	Wkts	Ave	5wi	10wm
N.A. Mallender	361.4	74	1067	45	23.71	3	–
A.R. Caddick	587.4	98	1918	71	27.01	3	1
H.R.J. Trump	558	134	1584	49	32.32	2	1
K.H. MacLeay	115	28	311	9	34.55	–	–
A.P. van Troost	175.4	20	766	21	36.47	2	–
R.P. Snell	339.1	60	1194	27	44.22	–	–
G.D. Rose	392.1	84	1250	28	44.64	–	–
A.N. Hayhurst	142	30	407	9	45.22	–	–
A.C. Cottam	116.1	24	280	6	49.12	–	–
M.N. Lathwell	64	14	224	4	56.00	–	–

R.P. Lefebvre 41-11-96-5   A. Payne 27-8-71-1   R.J. Harden 3-0-31-0
C.J. Tavare 3.2-0-33-0   R.J. Turner 2.1-0-26-0

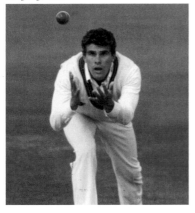

NICHOLAS ARTHUR FOLLAND Born Bristol, 17.9.63. LHB, RM. England Amateurs 1992. SFC: 31 matches; 1647 runs @ 33.61; HS 108* v Sussex, Taunton, 1993. OD: 35 matches; 988 runs @ 30.87; 0 wickets.

NICK FOLLAND 1992 – 1994

Nick Folland's pedigree as a left-hander for Devon was impressive. Had he left it too late at the age of 29 to make the transition to first-class cricket? He had the footwork and the shots and was, in the early 1990s, playing better than at any time in his career.

He had captained Devon, the Minor Counties and England amateurs in 1992, so there were obvious leadership qualities, and he managed to combine his teaching commitments at Blundell's with Somerset cricket.

The inaugural season with Somerset brought him hundreds, several good-looking innings and progress which, if not always dramatic, was solid. Never once did he look like a novice to the county scene.

Some within the Somerset dressing room saw Folland as an idealist, refreshingly free of the cynicism that was always threatening to encroach on the professional game. He loved cricket in a positive old-fashioned way; his outgoing personality was valued, and the county could have done with him longer.

But he'd sampled it, wasn't entirely at ease and got back to teaching. He became the headmaster at St Aubyn's, based at Tiverton.

ANDREW PAYNE 1992 – 1994

Here was Bob Cottam's first signing when he took over at Somerset. Cottam, as coach for the National Cricket Association, had included him in his under-17 party. Payne was rewarded with a place in the England Under-19 squad for Pakistan. He was, however, to find championship selection rare and hard-earned, despite compiling a half-century on his debut.

He caused a stir by dismissing Graham Gooch twice during a Second XI fixture. But such sporadic successes were deceptive. The hoped-for promotion didn't follow and he returned to the North Country, to settle for league cricket.

ANDREW PAYNE Born Rossendale, Lancashire, 20.10.73. RHB, RM. SFC: 4 matches; 124 runs @ 62.00; HS 51* v Gloucestershire, Taunton, 1992 on debut; 5 wickets @ 37.40; BB 2-15 v Worcestershire, Worcester, 1993. OD: 16 matches; 159 runs @ 14.45; 10 wickets @ 45.00.

RICHARD SNELL 1992

He came with the recommendations of Jimmy Cook and David Graveney, but this likeable South African Test all-rounder was never going to be the answer to Somerset's problems.

There was something a little too relaxed in his approach; he lacked the resolve for an arduous season of one-day and three-day matches. His fast-medium never brought more than three wickets in an innings.

RICHARD PETER SNELL Born Durban, South Africa, 12.9.68. RHB, RFM. 5 Tests 1992-94. 42 LOI 1991-96. SFC: 16 matches; 436 runs @ 27.25; HS 81 v Leicestershire, Grace Road, 1992; 27 wickets @ 44.22; BB 3-29 v Middlesex, Lord's, 1992. OD: 19 matches; 237 runs @ 26.33; 18 wickets @ 35.22. Transvaal, South Africa, 1988-97; Gauteng, South Africa, 1997-98.

ANDY COTTAM 1992 – 1993

Son of coach Bob Cottam – and promised no favours because of it. Slow left-arm, and a ready learner. Opportunities were rare in 1993 and he was released to join Northamptonshire, but never made his mark at Wantage Road.

ANDREW COLIN COTTAM Born Northampton, 14.7.73. RHB, SLA. SFC: 8 matches; 58 runs @ 6.44; HS 31 v Gloucestershire, Gloucester, 1992; 9 wickets @ 58.66; BB 1-1 v Gloucestershire, Gloucester, 1992. OD: 2 matches; did not bat; 0 wickets. Northamptonshire 1994.

Kevin (left) and Keith Parsons

KEITH ALAN PARSONS Born Taunton, 2.5.73. RHB, RM. Cap 1999. SFC: 120 matches; 4813 runs @ 27.82; 5 centuries; HS 193* v West Indians, Taunton, 2000; HT 821 in 1995; 95 wickets @ 45.11; BB 5-13 v Lancashire, Taunton, 2000; HT 28 in 1999. OD: 225 matches; 4812 runs @ 29.88; 133 wickets @ 35.88; C&G MoM 2. TT: 23 matches; 341 runs @ 21.31; 12 wickets @ 24.33.

KEITH PARSONS 1992 –

For too long, it seemed, he was pigeon-holed conveniently as a one-day player. In truth, he was well qualified for limited-over cricket: a thoughtful, adaptable batsman, well versed in building an innings and then accelerating at the right moment. As a change bowler of accurate medium-pace, he seldom made it easy for opposing batsmen to take liberties with him. That was all very well but his circle of supporters – and there were plenty at his native Taunton – felt he had something more to contribute as a four-day player. Privately, so did he. There was renewed recognition, in the comprehensive sense, in 2005 as Somerset revised their thinking on team composition.

Keith's first appearance came against the Pakistan tourists in 1992. A championship debut arrived the following summer but, like so many, he discovered the gulf between the Second XI and first-class cricket.

Yet there was always something of substance about him. Whether at Taunton Deane or the County Ground he was an eager learner – and against the West Indians at Taunton in 2000, characteristically unperturbed, he scored 193 not out.

Nothing was more uplifting for Keith than the manner in which he triumphed in Somerset's 2001 Cheltenham & Gloucester final against Leicestershire. The large West Country contingent at Lord's will never forget the insouciant way he rounded off his county's innings with two crucial sixes. He won the man-of-the-match award, an especial satisfaction for someone so truly Somerset. On the big stage, his calm temperament had seen him through.

KEVIN PARSONS 1992 – 1993

Worked in the county office during the winter of 1992-93 while his twin, Keith, went to New Zealand. It was a rare separation for two dedicated young players, able to show their skills and enthusiasm at the early, progressive levels.

KEVIN JOHN PARSONS Born Taunton, 2.5.73. RHB, OB. OD: 3 matches; 36 runs @ 18.00.

1993

Captain: C.J. Tavare

Somerset, buoyant and confident, got off in a rush. They won three of their first four championship matches, against Hampshire, Lancashire and Glamorgan. Lancashire were beaten in two days. Making his debut, in partnership with Lathwell, was Trescothick, who apprehensively scored four runs before being dismissed twice by Phillip DeFreitas. Such a start to the season may have offered false hopes to the county's ever-optimistic supporters, but Somerset still finished in a decidedly respectable fifth place – and with eight wins to show for it.

Mushtaq joyfully revived the art of expert leg-break bowling. His season was full of cunning and wristy trickery. His old-fashioned skills brought him 85 first-class wickets, some from his concealed googlies and other magical variants. The West Country crowds revelled in his battles with opposing batsmen. He brought the smiles back to the game. His repertoire could be rather more demanding for the wicket-keeper. Burns learned competently to cope. Towards the end of the season, Turner took over behind the stumps, ostensibly because he was said to be capable of scoring more runs.

It was Tavare's fifth and last season. He had been skipper for four of those years and done the job well for the most part. Occasionally he got his declarations slightly wrong. Didn't most captains at some time? There was speculation about who would now lead the county. John Morris and James Whitaker both seemed to be in the running. In the end it was an internal choice. Hayhurst was appointed ahead of Harden and Folland, the talented left-hander who had chosen to take a break in his teaching for a season or two.

Harden alone topped 1,000 runs. He scored three championship hundreds; Folland, Hayhurst, Lathwell and Rose contributed two each. One-day form fluctuated. Interest and discontent were the inevitable reactions to the way Somerset lost a Benson & Hedges quarter-final in a bowl-out against Derbyshire after the game had been abandoned. They were beaten by Warwickshire in a NatWest Trophy semi-final and miserably propped up all the other counties in the Sunday League. In the spirit of better times overall, nothing was more pleasing than the acceptance of life memberships by Botham, Richards and Garner, who had left the county in 1986 when Somerset seemed to be torn apart by wretched controversy.

Bob Cottam and the farmers from Box 2 celebrated Somerset's victories throughout the summer with such enthusiasm that it is perhaps a good thing, on purely medical grounds, that the team failed to win one of the major competitions.

Paul Bolton, Somerset Yearbook

COUNTY CHAMPIONSHIP   5th

Played 17	Won 8	Drawn 2	Lost	7

OTHER MATCHES

Played 1   Lost 1

NATWEST BANK TROPHY

Lost in Semi-Final

BENSON & HEDGES CUP

Lost in Quarter-Final

REFUGE ASSURANCE LEAGUE   18th

Played 17   Won 2   No Result 3   Lost 12

BATTING

	M	I	NO	Runs	HS	Ave	100	50	ct	st
R.J. Harden	18	32	3	1133	132	39.06	3	4	33	–
M.N. Lathwell	14	25	1	817	132	34.04	2	3	19	–
N.A. Folland	17	30	3	872	108*	32.29	2	4	13	–
G.D. Rose	17	29	2	865	138	32.03	2	2	10	–
A.N. Hayhurst	14	23	1	669	169	30.40	2	1	7	–
H.R.J. Trump	8	11	8	79	22*	26.33	–	–	5	–
C.J. Tavare	13	25	1	628	141*	26.16	1	2	22	–
N.A. Mallender	13	16	6	250	46	25.00	–	–	1	–
I. Fletcher	7	10	1	223	65*	24.77	–	2	1	–
N.D. Burns	13	23	2	479	102*	22.80	1	2	37	4
R.J. Turner	6	10	1	195	70	21.66	–	1	15	3
Mushtaq Ahmed	16	25	0	498	90	19.92	–	3	14	–
K.A. Parsons	5	9	1	134	63	16.75	–	1	3	–
A.R. Caddick	11	16	3	214	35*	16.46	–	–	2	–
A.P. van Troost	14	17	6	108	35	9.81	–	–	2	–
J.I.D. Kerr	7	11	3	67	19*	8.37	–	–	3	–
M.E. Trescothick	3	6	0	14	6	2.33	–	–	4	–

(2 matches)   A. Payne 17, 22* (2 ct)

BOWLING

	Overs	Mdns	Runs	Wkts	Ave	5wi	10wm
A.R. Caddick	347	81	1072	57	18.80	5	3
Mushtaq Ahmed	694.3	212	1773	85	20.85	8	3
N.A. Mallender	329.5	102	772	32	24.12	1	–
G.D. Rose	324.3	62	1090	43	25.34	3	–
J.I.D. Kerr	109.1	15	405	15	27.00	–	–
A.P. van Troost	282	49	1036	31	33.41	1	–
H.R.J. Trump	237.4	79	589	15	39.26	–	–
A.N. Hayhurst	58	19	168	3	56.00	–	–

M.N. Lathwell 25-8-73-1   A. Payne 18.2-4-62-4   K.A. Parsons 1-0-14-0
C.J. Tavare 1-0-2-0   R.J. Harden 0.3-0-0-0

photograph by John Holland

MARCUS TRESCOTHICK 1993 –

The left-hander stands tall and fearless at the top of the order, forever challenging great international pacemen to outwit him. Whatever yardstick we use, he takes his place timelessly among Somerset's finest players. And this has been achieved without ostentation. He is happy to leave the headlines to more extrovert players like Flintoff or Pietersen.

Nothing was more absurd than the murmurs of disapproval that Marcus Trescothick was fallible because he didn't move his feet enough. The glowing statistics and acclaim for the Somerset and England opening batsman discount such a superficial argument. It is true that he has never been renowned for dancing footwork. Who cares? In 2005 he was for a time the highest Test run-scorer in the world. He saved his country from embarrassment in Multan. Often he has batted inspiringly for England, with power, discrimination and minimal regard for the lofty reputations of opposing bowlers of belligerence who think they know his supposed technical weaknesses.

When he deputises as captain for an injured Vaughan, something he does with reliable competence, the words he dispenses at the nightly news conferences are inclined to be quiet and deliberately bland. He isn't a particularly emotional man – unless he has just seen his winning blow disappear out of sight beyond mid-wicket, or he's in the stand at Ashton Gate (where he has been made an honorary vice-president) for one of Bristol City's better performances.

From the age of three he had a bat in his hand. As a schoolboy he once belted more than 4,000 runs in a season, playing almost every day for anyone at Keynsham who offered him a game. He liked opening the innings, by nature giving the ball a hefty thump. Somerset encouraged him, although mildly worried about his waistline. A sensible young man, he sharpened up his fitness and became careful with his diet.

In the nets he tightened his defence. By 2000 he was making his Test debut, the kind of ascent all the more remarkable when it's remembered that in the late 1990s the runs were just not coming and he was unsure of his Somerset place. Some of his devotees were even fearing that he might search for another county in an attempt to recapture his form. But without making any sweeping changes in his batting technique, the old brio returned, the kind that brought him 1,000 runs for England Under-19, 322 in a Second XI match against Warwickshire and success in a dozen cameo innings for Somerset.

Coach Duncan Fletcher, then with Glamorgan, saw Trescothick score an exquisite hundred against his side and didn't forget when he took charge of England. The disappointment for the batsman's regional admirers was that his central contract severely limited his appearances for his county. They consoled themselves that all his great performances, like that marvellously imperishable 219 against South Africa at the Oval, also belonged in spirit to Taunton. He remains very much a local boy in some ways, with the prospect that one day – many England runs later – he will come back to captain and play full-time again for the county.

His new roll-on contract, signed early in 2006, suggests he will see out his playing career with Somerset – 'a long-term commitment', as Brian Rose describes it.

MARCUS EDWARD TRESCOTHICK Born Keynsham, 25.12.75. LHB, LM. Cap 1999. Captain 2002. 69 Tests 2000-. 114 LOI 2000-. SFC: 109 matches; 5460 runs @ 31.20; HS 190 v Middlesex, Taunton, 1999; HT 924 in 1994; 31 wickets @ 41.77; BB 4-36 v Young Australia, Taunton, 1995 (inc hat-trick). OD: 135 matches; 3815 runs @ 35.32; 48 wickets @ 25.97; NW/C&G MoM 5; B&H GA 3. TT: 3 matches; 91 runs @ 30.33.

Trescothick has never been a swaggerer; he respects the game, loves it even, and his gentle humour and self-effacing manner have made him popular wherever he's played.
Vic Marks

We just gave Mushy the ball, and he won games for us. He would bowl all day. He wasn't quite in the Shane Warne league, but he was near enough to make no odds in county cricket.

Graham Rose

MUSHTAQ AHMED 1993 – 1998

With foresight and resourcefulness, Somerset announced Mushtaq as their overseas signing for 1993, and the diminutive Pakistani brought a new dimension of pleasurable artifice to the domestic cricket scene. As the flaxen-haired Aussie, Shane Warne, confirmed, our first-class game had been denuded of wristy leg-tweakers for too long.

His first season with Somerset was an unmitigated success. A few pitches were decidedly unfavourable to him, but he made the most of them and ended the summer not so far short of 100 first-class wickets. The sheer variety of his output could be as demanding for wicket-keepers as for batsmen. His demeanour revealed that he was always enjoying himself.

At times he was the most perky of batsmen, mocking his small stature with effortless sixes out of the Taunton ground. From the days of Braund, through to schoolboy Cameron and little Lawrence, they have always appreciated cheeky leg-spinners down in the West Country.

It was a surprise to many at Somerset when he returned to the county circuit to play – with much success – for Sussex, an outstanding contributor to their championship triumph in 2003. When he came with them to Taunton, he impishly apologised for a few of his excesses in behaviour during his earlier sojourn there.

MUSHTAQ AHMED Born Sahiwal, Pakistan, 28.6.70. RHB, LBG. Cap 1993. 52 Tests 1990-. 144 LOI 1989-. SFC: 62 matches; 1272 runs @ 16.10; HS 90 v Sussex, Taunton, 1993; 289 wickets @ 26.32; BB 7-91 v Sussex, Taunton, 1993. OD: 82 matches; 564 runs @ 13.11; 97 wickets @ 25.40; NW MoM 2; B&H GA 2. Surrey 2002; Sussex 2003-; Multan 1986-91; United Bank 1987-96; Islamabad 1994-95; Lahore City1996-97; Peshawar 1998-99; Really Efficient Development Company 1999-2000; Lahore Blues 2000-01; National Bank 2001-.

JASON KERR 1993 – 2001

His first-class debut was surely one for his personal scrapbook. Brought in against the Australians, he took three wickets, including those of David Boon and century-maker Michael Slater. Kerr hailed from Lancashire and dreamed in vain of a future at Old Trafford. The medium-paced seamer went on an England Under-18 tour to India, after which he worked conscientiously on improving his game as he searched for an established place in the county side at Taunton.

He left at the end of 2001 but returned to assist with the Second XI, and to do general fitness work in his new role as assistant physiologist. In addition, his organisational ability proved handy as he helped the club beneficiaries.

JASON IAN DOUGLAS KERR Born Bolton, Lancashire, 7.4.74. RHB, RM. Cap 2001. SFC: 58 matches; 1394 runs @ 20.80; HS 80 v West Indians, Taunton, 1995; HT 381 in 1999; 113 wickets @ 40.33; BB 7-23 v Leicestershire, Taunton, 1999; HT 31 in 1999. OD: 96 matches; 542 runs @ 12.04; 109 wickets @ 29.71. Derbyshire 2002.

PETER ROBINSON'S OVERSEAS XI
1965-2005

Sunil Gavaskar
Graeme Smith
Viv Richards
Ricky Ponting
Martin Crowe
Steve Waugh (captain)
Greg Chappell
Kerry O'Keeffe
Mushtaq Ahmed
Joel Garner
Nixon McLean

If ever a selector was spoilt for choice, then it's me when I look at the batting line-up for this team. Mind you, it's a different story when I come to the seam-bowling and wicket-keeping departments.

Over the last few decades, Somerset have been blessed with a succession of world-class batsmen. When you look at my first seven, no attack on earth would look forward to bowling at them in their primes. My only worry is that in most games they wouldn't all get an innings, so perhaps I'd have to rotate the order.

It was difficult deciding who to leave out, and Jimmy Cook was unfortunate, but although he scored an enormous amount of runs, he never seemed to get many in the big games, a major factor in my decision.

My reason for playing Greg Chappell as low as seven is that all the others were established Test stars during their Somerset days, whereas Greg, brilliant though he was for us over two seasons, was still a young lad on the rise.

On the spin-bowling front, Mushy would be my first choice, then I'd add another leggy in Kerry O'Keeffe, with Graeme Smith chipping in with a bit of off-spin at need.

Pace-wise, Joel Garner was an obvious 'must', and I have made it a West Indian opening pair by picking Nixon McLean, who bowled very well during his first season at Taunton, when he was injury-free.

Beyond them there weren't many candidates, so I'd fiddle around with my medium-pacers, with Crowe, Chappell and Waugh all having to contribute.

As for the keeper, I'd have to ask Viv. He wasn't a bad fielder, after all, and I think he'd be up for the challenge!

1994

Captain: A.N. Hayhurst

At the age of 18, Trescothick – with as yet no realistic thoughts of playing for his country – made his emergent mark for Somerset. The three championship appearances the previous year had been less than promising, with only 14 runs in total from them. Now, against Hampshire in early June, he was back at the top of the order with Lathwell. He survived an early drop and went on to make 81. Soon he would be off to the West Indies as captain of England Under-19s. Confidence was high as he drove and pulled jauntily for his two first-class hundreds for Somerset. The fans were already ecstatic; here, they argued, was the county's long-term opening pair, contrasting in style, and both richly gifted.

Lathwell had a private psychological battle to wage after his premature inclusion in the Test team. He hated the fuss of it all. Happier with Somerset, it appeared, he did his best to ignore the grandiose predictions about him. Two good centuries for the county kept things more in perspective.

Hayhurst headed the batting averages. Harden, at number three, reached his 1,000 runs, even if not with the same fluency. But by August, Folland had decided he would be happier returning to academic life; it was a loss and a surprise to Somerset. He may have struggled at times to build on useful early runs, yet he possessed an attractive repertoire of strokes. The frenzy and logistics of the county game just didn't appeal sufficiently to this popular cricketer.

It was an oscillating summer for Somerset. To start with, they faltered constantly and lost their first eight competitive matches. Then came some scintillating mid-season form; the championship wins multiplied and the county looked capable of climbing up near the leaders. Hopes of another season of delights from Mushtaq, though, didn't materialise. He looked weary, as if there had been too much international cricket round the calendar. In July he was called home by Pakistan for the series against Sri Lanka. The timing couldn't have been worse; he had just beaten Worcestershire largely on his own with 12 wickets and all the signs were that the old verve was returning.

What else? Burns, now leading the Second XI, guided them to the title for the first time. Mallender, Caddick and Rose were carrying injuries. Van Troost was still striving to find the control to refine his undoubted pace.

The coarse grass has all now disappeared from the square. We've started to use a new grass seed (Elka), and the benefit of that is now being seen.

Phil Frost, Somerset's first winner of the Groundsman of the Year award

The county's pitches topped the TCCB tables of merit for both first-class and one-day matches, as they did again in 1996, 1999 and 2001.

COUNTY CHAMPIONSHIP 11th

Played 17	Won 7	Drawn 3	Lost 7

OTHER MATCHES — Played 1 — Drawn 1

NATWEST BANK TROPHY — Lost in Quarter-Final

BENSON & HEDGES CUP — Lost in First Round

REFUGE ASSURANCE LEAGUE 16th — Played 17 — Won 5 — Lost 12

BATTING

	M	I	NO	Runs	HS	Ave	100	50	ct	st
A.N. Hayhurst	18	30	6	1250	121	52.08	2	10	10	–
M.E. Trescothick	11	20	1	924	121	48.63	2	8	13	–
R.J. Harden	18	31	5	1061	131*	40.80	2	7	13	–
M.N. Lathwell	18	32	1	1230	206	39.67	2	9	10	–
M. Dimond	3	2	1	34	25*	34.00	–	–	4	–
N.A. Folland	13	22	1	671	91	31.95	–	4	6	–
N.A. Mallender	8	12	3	270	43*	30.00	–	–	1	–
G.D. Rose	16	24	2	548	121	24.90	1	2	16	–
R.J. Turner	18	27	5	537	104*	24.40	1	2	46	6
I. Fletcher	6	10	1	179	54*	19.88	–	2	3	–
P.C.L. Holloway	4	6	0	114	50	19.00	–	1	1	–
H.R.J. Trump	14	20	4	276	45*	17.25	–	–	14	–
Mushtaq Ahmed	9	14	3	168	38	15.27	–	–	4	–
A.R. Caddick	12	18	2	219	58*	13.68	–	1	5	–
K.A. Parsons	3	5	1	38	16	9.50	–	–	2	–
A.P. van Troost	14	18	6	108	33	9.00	–	–	3	–
S.C. Ecclestone	3	5	0	42	24	8.40	–	–	1	–
J.C. Hallett	3	6	1	21	10	4.20	–	–	–	–

(2 matches) V.P. Clarke 1,38, 5, 2   P.J. Bird 0*, 7, 5

(1 match) A. Payne 34   J.I.D. Kerr 1, 4 (1 ct)   B.T.P. Donelan 0

BOWLING

	Overs	Mdns	Runs	Wkts	Ave	5wi	10wm
A.R. Caddick	372.3	71	1186	51	23.25	3	–
G.D. Rose	344.1	69	1136	44	25.81	–	–
Mushtaq Ahmed	404	114	1196	45	26.57	4	1
A.N. Hayhurst	87.4	24	265	9	29.44	–	–
H.R.J. Trump	268.4	76	873	26	33.57	2	1
N.A. Mallender	193.4	51	602	16	37.62	–	–
A.P. van Troost	326.1	53	1299	34	38.20	–	–
M. Dimond	55.3	8	216	5	43.20	–	–
J.C. Hallett	53.2	15	181	4	45.25	–	–

P.J. Bird 44.5-9-166-0   M.N. Lathwell 29-4-119-3   V.P. Clarke 23-4-105-1

J.I.D. Kerr 21-3-91-0   S.C. Ecclestone 17-4-57-0   B.T.P. Donelan 15-2-59-1

A. Payne 12-2-54-0   K.A. Parsons 4-0-21-0

PIRAN HOLLOWAY 1994 – 2003

He had a Cornishman's defiant temperament and, in the words of one admirer within the club, 'would bat all day for you if that was what was needed'. The trouble was that he never felt assured of a permanent first-team place. Occasionally he would speak out, once complaining that he was competing with Andy Hayhurst for the same place and Hayhurst was being preferred because he was the captain.

Holloway was a true grafter and warmed to that commitment. Yet the small, compact left-hander was capable of exhibiting a surprising range of attacking shots in one-day games when he could prove a match-winner.

'Maybe I should have stuck to wicket keeping,' he might have thought to himself. He did the job behind the stumps competently enough at Warwickshire, the county he had joined after his promising days at Taunton School and Millfield. He was promoted rapidly at Edgbaston, learning the hard way as he kept to bowlers of the pace of Allan Donald and Gladstone Small. But he lost his place to Keith Piper, and Bob Cottam brought him down to Taunton.

Did Somerset persevere with him sufficiently? Hadn't he played for Young England for three years? Wasn't he Somerset's Young Player of the Year in 1995? Didn't he go off in 1997-98 and become the top run-scorer in Perth's A-grade cricket? That's where he's living now.

PIRAN CHRISTOPHER LAITY HOLLOWAY Born Helston, Cornwall, 1.10.70. LHB, occ WK. Cap 1997. SFC: 114 matches; 5419 runs @ 31.14; 8 centuries; HS 168 v Middlesex, Uxbridge, 1996; HT 905 in 1997; 0 wickets. OD: 97 matches; 2402 runs @ 30.40. 13 matches; 531 runs @ 40.84; NW MoM 1; B&H GA 1. Warwickshire 1988-93.

VINCE CLARKE 1994

He could bowl leg-breaks or seamers at medium pace, as he showed when he came over from Australia to play for Bridgwater and some games for Somerset Second XI. In one of only two senior appearances for the county, the six-footer hit a battling 38 against Gloucestershire at Bristol. Although born in this country, he was brought up in Australia and represented Western Australia at indoor cricket.

VINCENT PAUL CLARKE Born Liverpool, 11.11.71. RHB, RM/LB. SFC: 2 matches; 46 runs @ 11.50; HS 38 v Gloucestershire, Bristol, 1994 on debut; 1 wicket @ 105.00; BB 1-93 v Glamorgan, Swansea, 1994. OD: 7 matches; 74 runs @ 10.57; 2 wickets @ 50.00.

PAUL BIRD 1994

He could at least trade on the fact that he bowled out Brian Lara in a Sunday fixture. The early-season lift was not enough, however, to bring him more than one summer with Somerset. His genuine pace and ability to swing the ball had been evident at club level in the Bristol area. He was in the Optimists' side which won the National Cricket Association knock-out competition at Lord's in 1991. His progress with the county was not helped by a side injury, and he hoped in vain for his first championship wicket.

PAUL JAMES BIRD Born Bristol, 7.5.71. RHB, RFM. SFC: 2 matches; 12 runs @ 6.00; 0 wickets. OD: 5 matches; 4 runs @ 4.00; 3 wickets @ 43.00.

(left to right) Piran Holloway, Paul Bird, Ian Bond, Vince Clarke

SIMON ECCLESTONE 1994 – 1998

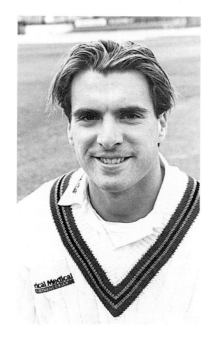

Ecclestone was born in Essex, and it was assumed that he would sample county cricket at Chelmsford. After all, he had played for Essex from Under-11 level, up to Under-19 and Second XI. But recommendations had come Somerset's way. Peter Robinson was sent to take a look, and he returned with an enthusiastic assessment.

By 1997 the left-hander was Somerset's vice-captain. That summer was his best for the county. He almost reached 1,000 runs and mischievously hammered the Oxford University team for 133, five years after gaining his blue there. In a relatively short Somerset career he scored a hundred in each of the competitions.

In every sense, here was a skipper in waiting. He had an air of authority and presence, to the extent that his team-mates dubbed him 'Major'. But they liked him, too, and knew he would always be prepared to take a chance, encouraging the opposition to go for a result.

But it was all over at the age of 27. An arthritic knee condition, a result of his rugby, curtailed his cricket, with the medical advice to forget playing full-time. It was a double blow to Somerset. It had lost not only an aggressive batsman but a future captain.

SIMON CHARLES ECCLESTONE Born Great Dunmow, Essex, 16.7.71. LHB, RM. Cap 1997. Acting captain 1997. SFC: 36 matches; 1985 runs @ 36.09; 3 centuries; HS 133 v Oxford University, Taunton, 1997; HT 951 in 1997; 11 wickets @ 40.00; BB 2-48 v Nottinghamshire, Trent Bridge, 1995; HT 11 in 1995. OD: 66 matches; 1833 runs @ 31.06; 21 wickets @ 36.33; NW MoM 1; B&H GA 1. Oxford University 1994.

MATT DIMOND 1994 – 1997

Here was a local boy, rated highly enough to go on the England Under-19 tour to the West Indies. Maybe he lacked the physical attributes for the seamer's onerous role. Yet there was nothing much wrong with his performance at Bradford where, as an eager 18-year-old, he took 4-73 in the first innings. Not only that, he helped grittily to save the follow-on when Yorkshire must have felt they had the game wrapped up. The last two wickets put on 159 with great resolve. After Rose's century came notable resistance from Mallender and last man Dimond, unbeaten on 25. In the end came a career with computers rather than cricket balls. Another case of genuine potential unfulfilled.

MATTHEW DIMOND Born Taunton, 24.9.75. RHB, RMF. SFC: 5 matches; 71 runs @ 17.75; HS 26 v Derbyshire, Derby, 1995; 6 wickets @ 52.66; BB 4-73 v Yorkshire, Bradford, 1994. OD: 4 matches; did not bat; 0 wickets.

BRAD DONELAN 1994

Here was an off-spinner who came from Sussex to Somerset. In his Hove days, he once ended a memorable bowling stint with 6-62 against Gloucestershire, totalling ten wickets from the match. He was no bad bat, either, as a confident 68 off the Hampshire bowlers illustrated. He had been on the Lord's ground staff before joining Sussex; the predictions were then encouraging. But there was to be only one appearance for Somerset. He went on to do public school coaching.

BRADLEIGH THOMAS PETER DONELAN Born Park Royal Hospital, Middlesex, 3.1.68. RHB, OB. SFC: 1 match, 0 runs; 1 wicket @ 59.00; BB 1-27 v Yorkshire, Bradford, 1994. Sussex 1989-93.

1995

Captain: A.N. Hayhurst

Somerset's form in June was that of aspiring champions, with four wins in a row. It was too good to last and the finishing position of ninth reflected another too-ordinary season. Valid excuses were easy to find. Neither Caddick nor van Troost was fit enough to play more than half a dozen matches in the championship. But it wasn't only the bowlers who struggled. The opening batsmen, Lathwell and Trescothick, were big disappointments. Finally Lathwell was dropped and something was missing from his naturally talented persona to which the fans had previously so readily warmed. There was one notable innings from Trescothick, 151 at Northampton, even if the runs were mostly elusive and he appeared to be weighed down by a few technical problems.

The most positive aspect of the summer for Somerset was the rapid influence of Bowler as a canny and experienced batsman. He had joined the club from Derbyshire where dressing-room politics were rife. Now relaxed again, he was unlucky to miss a century on his debut, to add to those he acquired at his two previous counties. The 1,619 first-class runs and six hundreds represented a formidable contribution. Harden also had a profitable season, with five centuries. Then there was a worrying gap, despite pugnacious runs from Holloway, who had come down from Warwickshire, defiant ones from Hayhurst and powerful ones from Ecclestone in so-far limited appearances.

It was heartening to have Mushtaq back parading his leg-spinner's sleight of hand. He bowled more overs than anyone else in the county game during 1995 and he was the only member of the Somerset attack to make much impact. His 92 championship wickets were an eloquent statement of undeniable craft and skill.

Somerset's first victory after following on since 1905

For Derbyshire, this was a nightmarish game with the worst end imaginable, Kim Barnett looking on, isolated and forlorn, as Peter Bowler plucked a nonchalant, one-handed slip catch. Bowler had left Derbyshire only last autumn, having fallen out terminally with Barnett, and now he had not only scored the century that turned this game on its head, he had taken over as captain of Somerset and secured a quite remarkable win.

The Times

COUNTY CHAMPIONSHIP   9th

COUNTY CHAMPIONSHIP 9th	Played 17	Won 7	Drawn 5	Lost 5
OTHER MATCHES	Played 3		Drawn 1	Lost 2
NATWEST BANK TROPHY	Lost in First Round			
BENSON & HEDGES CUP	Lost in Semi-Final			
REFUGE ASSURANCE LEAGUE 14th	Played 17	Won 5	No Result 3	Lost 9

BATTING

	M	I	NO	Runs	HS	Ave	100	50	ct	st
P.D. Bowler	19	33	3	1619	196	53.96	6	5	9	–
P.C.L. Holloway	12	22	6	863	129*	53.93	2	6	3	–
R.J. Harden	19	35	6	1429	129*	49.27	5	6	13	–
S.C. Ecclestone	7	12	2	472	81	47.20	–	3	1	–
A.N. Hayhurst	17	29	5	825	107	34.37	1	5	3	–
A.R. Caddick	6	7	0	237	92	33.85	–	2	1	–
K.A. Parsons	16	28	2	821	105	31.57	1	6	13	–
M.N. Lathwell	17	33	0	1033	111	31.30	2	5	9	–
R.J. Turner	19	30	7	717	106*	31.17	1	4	54	10
G.D. Rose	16	25	0	771	84	30.84	–	6	9	–
J.D. Batty	4	6	1	125	45*	25.00	–	–	3	–
J.I.D. Kerr	13	19	2	349	80	20.52	–	1	5	–
M.E. Trescothick	12	22	0	417	151	18.95	1	1	14	–
H.R.J. Trump	16	22	10	207	47	17.25	–	–	12	–
Mushtaq Ahmed	17	23	2	311	62*	14.80	–	1	4	–
A.P. van Troost	7	11	3	82	34	10.25	–	–	–	–

(2 matches)   J.C. Hallett 29, 42, 47, 111*
(1 match)   M. Dimond 7, 26

BOWLING

	Overs	Mdns	Runs	Wkts	Ave	5wi	10wm
A.R. Caddick	183.1	34	613	24	25.54	1	1
Mushtaq Ahmed	952	286	2821	95	29.69	7	2
S.C. Ecclestone	105	20	383	11	34.81	–	–
G.D. Rose	426	93	1402	39	35.94	1	–
A.P. van Troost	145.3	23	624	16	39.00	1	–
J.I.D. Kerr	280.1	53	1134	28	40.50	1	–
H.R.J. Trump	596.2	173	1745	40	43.62	1	–
A.N. Hayhurst	139.2	21	519	10	51.90	–	–
K.A. Parsons	105	16	458	6	76.33	–	–
J.D. Batty	111.4	13	583	7	83.28	–	–

M.E. Trescothick 33-6-143-5   M.N. Lathwell 25-5-82-2   P.D. Bowler 16.2-3-68-1
M. Dimond 14-2-70-1   J.C. Hallett 14-1-86-2   P.C.L. Holloway 2-1-12-0
R.J. Harden 1-0-17-0

PETER DUNCAN BOWLER Born Plymouth, Devon, 30.7.63. RHB, OB, occ WK. Cap 1995. Captain 1997-98. SFC: 160 matches; 9642 runs @ 41.38; 25 centuries; HS 207 v Surrey, Taunton, 1996; 1000 runs 4 times; HT 1619 in 1995; 14 wickets @ 38.57; BB 3-25 v Northamptonshire, Taunton, 1998. OD: 159 matches; 4431 runs @ 29.34; 2 wickets @ 71.50; B&H GA 1. Leicestershire 1986-87; Derbyshire 1988-94.

> The team christened me with the nickname 'Tom', thanks mainly to Bob Cottam's insistence that he had obtained my services in a raffle.
>
> **Peter Bowler**

PETER BOWLER 1995 – 2004

He was the oldest player on the circuit when, with some pangs, he retired at the end of the 2004 season. He was still able to clock up his 1,000 runs – in his case for the tenth time – and still able to impart measured words of wisdom in the dressing room. But Peter decided it was time to go, to hand over his place in the team to younger players, to accept that there was such a thing as a generation gap, and to acknowledge the reflexes weren't quite as sharp as they used to be.

He'd been a valued elder statesman around Somerset, often bringing a calming, reassuring influence to the batting order; and at the same time earning respect with his canny, competitive attitude. Something of that doubtless came from his Aussie roots. Dad had been in the Australian navy and mum was from Scotland. In 1985 he felt he should visit some of his relatives over here and maybe play a bit of club cricket as well. Leicestershire offered him a trial and suddenly visions of playing county cricket were forming in his head.

Leicestershire were to be his first county, Derbyshire his second and Somerset his third. He had the habit of signalling his arrivals in grandiose style. For Leicester and Derby he scored centuries on his debut, and he so nearly did the same for Somerset against Glamorgan, running out of partners when on 84 in the second innings. But there was a fruitful future waiting for him in the West. The runs were often plentiful and compiled with an attractive, studied composure. He wasn't one to vary the pace, swing his bat and take risks; that wasn't in his nature. His new career is going to be in law and at the crease there was the look of a vigilant, reliable solicitor about him, diligently absorbing his varied briefs while optimistically in search of a successful conclusion.

Bowler completed 45 hundreds at first-class level and appeared in five Lord's finals. As Somerset captain, he took over in mid-season from Andy Hayhurst. Then, when it was his turn to be appointed officially, back problems surfaced and his cricket suffered. Off the field he was his own man.

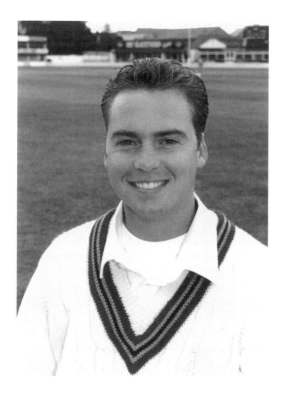

JEREMY BATTY 1995 – 1996

For the off-spinner, it appeared the perfect start. He took five wickets on his Yorkshire debut against Lancashire; what could be better? Soon he was nominated as the county's Young Player of the Year for 1991. Sadly the progress was not sustained and four years later he was on his way to Somerset, who were searching for another slow bowler.

Over two seasons in the West he made no more than 20 appearances while taking 39 wickets. His best match was against Hampshire at Taunton, where his new county won by an innings and Batty completed another of those rare, welcome five-wicket hauls. That was the time Somerset provided a dramatic prelude by dropping the captain, Andy Hayhurst, an hour before the game because of poor form. Hayhurst was released at the end of the season, and so was the unfulfilled Bradford off-spinner. Not before he revealed his worth, more than once, however, as a night-watchman.

JEREMY DAVID BATTY Born Bradford, Yorkshire, 15.5.71. RHB, OB. SFC: 20 matches; 446 runs @ 17.84; HS 45* v West Indians, Taunton, 1995; HT 321 in 1996; 39 wickets @ 55.25; BB 5-85 v Hampshire, Taunton, 1996; HT 32 in 1996. OD: 8 matches; 42 runs @ 14.00; 5 wickets @ 36.26; B&H GA 1. Yorkshire 1989-94.

MOST POST-WAR CATCHES FOR SOMERSET			
(excluding wicket-keepers)			
First-class cricket		Limited-over cricket	
RT Virgin	301	IT Botham	106
WE Alley	267	IVA Richards	97
J Lawrence	259	PW Denning	94
MF Tremlett	239	KA Parsons	82
BA Langford	224	RJ Harden	81
JG Lomax	210	CH Dredge	66
PB Wight	195	BC Rose	63
RJ Harden	183	PM Roebuck	62
PJ Robinson	168	GD Rose	62
IVA Richards	164	VJ Marks	57
H Gimblett	157	GI Burgess	51
G Atkinson	157	MJ Kitchen	51

1996

Captain: A.N. Hayhurst

Not the happiest of seasons: there were too many whispers, departures and the kind of decisions that suggested an uneasy dressing room. Hayhurst was a victim. He had already applied in vain for a post back at his native county, Lancashire. When it came to his captaincy in 1996, he was criticised often but not always, it seemed, with complete justification. He had a bad match against Surrey in the quarter-finals of the NatWest Trophy at the Oval. Somerset's tactics were at fault – and Hayhurst found himself largely shouldering the blame. Next day, for a championship match back at Taunton, he was abruptly dropped and told to go off and rediscover his form with the Second XI. It was the end of his first-class career with Somerset.

For the time being, the team was run by acting skipper Bowler, cricket chairman Brian Rose and Bob Cottam, the director of cricket. By September, however, Cottam had gone – with a year of his contract still left. His successor, officially in the role of coach, was to be Dermot Reeve, whose achievements as captain of Warwickshire had been spectacular. Another exit – accompanied by tears from the loyal Friends of Weston Cricket – was that of Clarence Park from the list of first-class arenas.

The cricket was not without merit. Mushtaq, needed elsewhere, was missed. His place went to Shane Lee, who demonstrated rapidly that he had enough good-looking shots to top the batting averages for the county. He proved a wise and valued signing, even if only for a summer.

Lathwell got his 1,000 runs and, despite some frailties, was at this point looking a slightly better prospect than Trescothick. Turner, big for a wicket-keeper, was at times surprisingly agile and once chased more than 40 yards for a memorable catch (to dismiss Reeve). Of the bowlers, Caddick had returned impressively with few signs of his shin problems. He was rewarded with a Test recall and a place on the winter tour.

COUNTY CHAMPIONSHIP 11th Played 17 Won 5 Drawn 6 Lost 6

OTHER MATCHES Played 2 Drawn 1 Lost 1

NATWEST BANK TROPHY Lost in Quarter-Final

BENSON & HEDGES CUP Eliminated at Zonal Stage

REFUGE ASSURANCE LEAGUE 5th Played 17 Won 10 No Result 1 Lost 6

BATTING

	M	I	NO	Runs	HS	Ave	100	50	ct	st
S. Lee	17	25	4	1300	167*	61.90	5	5	14	–
M.N. Lathwell	18	32	4	1224	109	43.71	2	7	13	–
P.D. Bowler	19	34	4	1228	207	40.93	2	7	5	–
P.C.L. Holloway	10	16	1	535	168	35.66	1	3	7	–
R.J. Harden	12	20	1	676	136	35.57	1	5	11	–
R.J. Turner	18	27	6	668	100*	31.80	1	3	64	3
J.I.D. Kerr	6	9	3	176	68*	29.33	–	2	–	–
K.A. Parsons	8	15	1	408	83*	29.14	–	4	2	–
S.C. Ecclestone	8	13	1	334	94	27.83	–	3	2	–
M.E. Trescothick	15	26	0	720	178	27.69	1	2	11	–
G.D. Rose	15	21	5	408	93*	25.50	–	2	8	–
A.N. Hayhurst	9	13	1	224	96	18.66	–	2	2	–
J.D. Batty	16	24	4	321	44	16.05	–	–	4	–
A.R. Caddick	14	19	5	195	38	13.92	–	–	7	–
K.J. Shine	12	15	4	121	40	11.00	–	–	5	–
A.P. van Troost	6	8	2	27	11	4.50	–	–	–	–
H.R.J. Trump	3	2	1	0	0*	0.00	–	–	3	–

(2 matches) A.C. Cottam 3, 12
(1 match) I.E. Bishop 2, 2 (1 ct)

BOWLING

	Overs	Mdns	Runs	Wkts	Ave	5wi	10wm
G.D. Rose	393.2	98	1218	50	24.36	3	1
A.R. Caddick	546.5	121	1864	67	27.82	6	3
K.J. Shine	276.3	44	1209	35	34.54	2	–
S. Lee	418.3	66	1770	40	44.25	–	–
J.D. Batty	486.4	99	1572	32	49.12	1	–
J.I.D. Kerr	131	16	586	11	53.27	–	–
A.P. van Troost	107.4	12	485	9	53.88	–	–
A.C. Cottam	89	22	248	3	82.66	–	–

H.R.J. Trump 43-10-179-4 K.A. Parsons 38-8-154-2 P.D. Bowler 31.3-2-177-3
A.N. Hayhurst 25-5-91-1 M.E. Trescothick 23-1-97-0 R.J. Harden 8-0-42-1
M.N. Lathwell 7.4-0-27-1 I.E. Bishop 7-0-29-0 P.C.L. Holloway 4.4-1-34-0
R.J. Turner 1-0-3-0

SHANE LEE 1996

Late recruitment of an overseas player can too often be a gamble. Here was one, a replacement in effect for Mushtaq Ahmed, who offered full value to Somerset. Lee may have come with a reputation more as a bowler than a batsman, but evaluation was quickly adjusted. The sage words of Aussie authorities such as two previous part-time residents of Taunton, Steve Waugh and Kerry O'Keeffe, in backing Bob Cottam's recommendation, were fully justified. Lee stayed only for a season and that was a pity. In New South Wales there was a surfeit of competition high in the batting order. Somerset, a little more appreciatively maybe, looked to him for runs and he responded with five centuries. He finished top of the batting averages. His county cap was a formality.

At home, because of his university studies – psychology was his subject – he wasn't able to accept the offered full-time scholarship place at the Australian Cricket Academy. He went part-time instead, and his promise as an all-rounder was developed, especially in the one-day games. In 1995 he made his debut for Australia in the World Series against the West Indies.

His brief career with Somerset was memorable for crisp, selective stroke-play. He saved his best for the festival crowd at Bath with an undefeated 167. He figured in a record seventh-wicket county stand with Rob Turner. Only one fact clouded the memory. Worcestershire, who had come to the match bottom of the table, won by one wicket with three balls to spare. Worse for West Country spectators, the visitors were allowed to score 449 in the demoralising (for Somerset) second innings. Medium-pacer Lee, upbeat by nature, was only one who failed to make much impact on that final frustrating day. Six years later, he turned up briefly with Worcestershire.

SHANE LEE Born Wollongong, New South Wales, Australia, 8.8.73. RHB, RFM. Cap 1996. 45 LOI 1995-2001. SFC: 17 matches; 1300 runs @ 61.90; 5 centuries; HS 167* v Worcestershire, Bath, 1996; 1000 runs once; HT 1300 in 1996; 40 wickets @ 44.25; BB 4-52 v Sussex, Hove, 1996. OD: 24 matches; 627 runs @ 34.83; 31 wickets @ 30.51; NW MoM 1. New South Wales 1992-2003; Worcestershire 2002.

KEVIN SHINE 1996 – 1998

It was no bad thing that a fast bowler who'd gone through a few technical problems himself should end up coaching others. He played for three counties – Hampshire, Middlesex and Somerset – and he readily accepts that his form fluctuated.

When he was good, he was very good. That was true when Lancashire came to Taunton in 1997. It was all over on the second day, Somerset winning with some ease. Shine took 7-43 in the first innings and ended with match figures of 11-97. Lancashire had reason to fear him. Back in 1992, in his Hampshire days, he completed career-best figures of 8-47 against them, including the hat-trick.

He argues that he was largely self-coached, adding that opportunities and wise counsel are so much better now. 'The days of having a few pints and a curry are over,' he says, and his years as Somerset's head coach were marked by a scientific approach that made ready use of visual aids and dietary advice. He is an accomplished organiser, and one of his strengths is in working one-to-one with young bowling prospects.

At the end of the 2004 season, in a surprise announcement, Somerset moved him to the newly-created post of director of development and coaching. The county went out of their way to assure any sceptics that Shine wasn't being demoted, and a year later he succeeded Troy Cooley as England's bowling coach. The appointment took some by surprise and, in view of the impressive short list, was a major compliment to him.

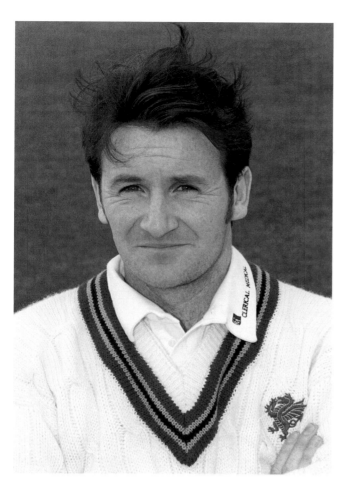

KEVIN JAMES SHINE Born Bracknell, Berkshire, 22.2.69. RHB, RFM. Cap 1997. SFC: 33 matches; 261 runs @ 9.00; HS 40 v Surrey, Taunton, 1996; HT 121 in 1996; 94 wickets @ 33.01; BB 7-43 v Lancashire, Taunton, 1997; HT 55 in 1997. OD: 11 matches; 42 runs @ 42.00; 13 wickets @ 34.38. Hampshire 1989-93, Middlesex 1994-95.

IAN BISHOP 1996

In his greenhorn days for Staplegrove, the pace suggested a possible future with Somerset for another Taunton lad with eyes focused romantically on county cricket. The truth was that he made a solitary appearance, against Pakistan, sent down seven overs and failed to take a wicket. Anxious for a second chance, he moved to Surrey, though again his appearances were limited. At times, in his matches for Devon, he demonstrated his natural skills. Like so many good club players, he found the added step into the first-class game too testing a challenge.

IAN EMLYN BISHOP Born Taunton, 26.8.77. RHB, RF. SFC: 1 match; 4 runs @ 2.00; 0 wickets. Surrey 1999-2000.

1997

Captain: P.D. Bowler

A new coach, brimming with innovative ideas and disciplines, was expected to herald an exciting era and markedly improved results. Dermot Reeve came from Edgbaston with well-intentioned plans. Just like Brian Close had done more than a quarter of a century earlier, the high-profile newcomer detected flaws in some attitudes; he managed to shake things up. So why did Somerset not progress more?

The hoped-for successes from Mushtaq failed to materialise. He took 50 championship wickets and had his good days, but the former ebullience was less evident. He looked tired, and he suffered from a recurrent knee injury. Caddick was off playing for England and made only a dozen championship appearances for Somerset. Surprisingly, they got by without him when Lancashire were beaten in two days at Taunton. The bowling honours went to Shine, who took 11 wickets in the match. He had come from Middlesex and won his cap this season. So, more controversially, did van Troost, who had been at Somerset since 1991, searching for the line and control that would have made some sense of his considerable and at times fearsome pace.

Rose, the all-rounder, had an outstanding summer. He headed the county's batting and bowling averages. It was the perfect way to augment his benefit season. The beefy stroke-play, which for years had threatened to surface more often, now gave him an average of 53. Turner, too, reminded Somerset of his worth as a batsman, quite apart from his tidy, unshowy wicket-keeping. The county leaned on him at times and, significantly, he slotted in as an opening bat of diligence.

Harden did enough to hint that this might be his best season, only for a broken finger at Bath to put a cruel end to that. Bowler searched for batting form; Ecclestone found his, hammering 123 against Kent and appearing to be lined up as a future captain.

COUNTY CHAMPIONSHIP 12th

Played 17   Won 3   Drawn 11   Lost 3

OTHER MATCHES   Played 3   Won 1   Drawn 1   Lost 1

NATWEST BANK TROPHY   Lost in Second Round

BENSON & HEDGES CUP   Lost in Quarter-Final

REFUGE ASSURANCE LEAGUE   6th   Played 17   Won 9   No Result 2   Lost 6

BATTING

	M	I	NO	Runs	HS	Ave	100	50	ct	st
R.J. Turner	17	28	7	1069	144	50.90	1	7	51	2
G.D. Rose	18	26	9	852	191	50.11	2	3	7	–
S.C. Ecclestone	13	23	2	951	133	45.28	3	4	12	–
R.J. Harden	7	11	2	395	136*	43.88	2	1	3	–
S. Herzberg	7	8	3	207	56	41.40	–	1	2	–
K.A. Parsons	10	15	3	437	74	36.41	–	3	12	–
P.C.L. Holloway	19	34	4	905	106	30.16	1	5	12	–
M.N. Lathwell	20	34	1	912	95	27.63	–	6	11	–
P.D. Bowler	16	26	1	666	123	26.64	1	5	20	–
J.I.D. Kerr	5	6	1	133	35	26.60	–	–	1	–
M. Burns	14	21	1	510	82	25.50	–	4	8	1
A.R. Caddick	13	14	2	262	56*	21.83	–	1	4	–
M.E. Trescothick	13	19	1	390	83*	21.66	–	4	6	–
Mushtaq Ahmed	14	16	2	174	33	12.42	–	–	3	–
P.S. Jones	3	5	1	26	13	6.50	–	–	3	–
K.J. Shine	18	20	5	96	18	6.40	–	–	5	–
A.P. van Troost	6	8	3	20	12*	4.00	–	–	1	–

(2 matches)   B.J. Trott 1*, 0

(1 match)   S.C.G. MacGill 7, 25   L.D. Sutton 11*, 6 (5 ct)   N.R. Boulton 1, 14
    M. Dimond 4   R.W. Sladdin did not bat

BOWLING

	Overs	Mdns	Runs	Wkts	Ave	5wi	10wm
G.D. Rose	488.5	124	1563	63	24.80	1	–
A.R. Caddick	522.5	112	1522	57	26.70	4	–
S. Herzberg	102	25	281	10	28.10	–	–
Mushtaq Ahmed	513	146	1407	50	28.14	3	–
K.A. Parsons	78.5	18	204	7	29.14	–	–
K.J. Shine	443.3	89	1678	55	30.50	3	1
J.I.D. Kerr	103	20	374	10	37.40	–	–
M. Burns	62	13	266	5	53.20	–	–
A.P. van Troost	78.5	5	496	7	70.85	–	–

P.D. Bowler 44.2-18-145-3   R.W. Sladdin 38-10-106-5   S.C.G. MacGill 36-11-123-4
P.S. Jones 31-3-165-6   B.J. Trott 27-3-128-5   M.E. Trescothick 15-3-69-1
M. Dimond 11-3-30-0   M.N. Lathwell 5-0-60-1   S.C. Ecclestone 1-1-0-0

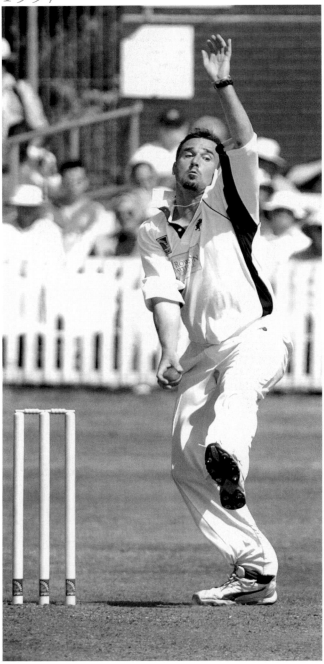

STEFFAN JONES 1997 – 2003

They used to joke about his unyielding attention to personal fitness, verging as some saw it towards a fetish. It was known that he'd converted his Taunton garage into a well-equipped gym. His own punishing routines typified his approach to professional sport. Many of his friends would have argued that his skills at rugby were equal to those on the cricket field. For a long time he tried to carry on both. There were times when, after a wearying day of numerous overs, he would chase off for an evening of rugby training.

Steffan came from the fertile rugby meadows around Llanelli and must have cherished secret wishes to play for Wales. In the end he had to be satisfied with Loughborough University, Cambridge, Swansea (a few games), Bristol, Exeter and Moseley. Because of his nature, he was an adventurous full back, prepared to take a risk as he hunted imaginatively for a way through the opposition. Occasionally he made mistakes, leaving his coach to curse.

But in everything he did, Jones was a man of passion and enthusiasm. He also had strong opinions. To quote him on cricket: 'There is too much emphasis on technique and all that rubbish. Coaches should leave players alone to develop their own methods. Flair and individualism should not be stifled.'

Some at Somerset, where he bowled fast and once, going in at number nine, hit a hundred off the New Zealanders at Taunton, saw him as too much of an individualist. But he was a loyal team man, at times shrugging off painful injuries because he was needed for a few more overs.

The successful appearance at Lord's in the C and G final gave him much pleasure. So did his nine wickets in the Varsity match. And so, we imagine, did his weekends of village cricket in West Glamorgan, where he opened the bowling with the emerging Simon Jones.

His career with Somerset tailed off in 2003, when he took a disappointing 22 wickets. Measure that against the 59 first-class wickets he took in 2001. His buoyant form in some of the limited-overs matches also seemed to belong to the past. Steffan felt it was time for a change and joined Northants, with Somerset saying they couldn't guarantee championship cricket any longer.

PHILIP STEFFAN JONES Born Llanelli, Carmarthenshire, 9.2.74. RHB, RMF. Cap 2001. SFC: 62 matches; 989 runs @ 17.98; HS 105 v New Zealanders, Taunton, 1999; HT 273 in 2003; 171 wickets @ 37.07; BB 6-110 v Warwickshire, Edgbaston, 2002; HT 59 in 2001. OD: 113 matches; 322 runs @ 11.50; 166 wickets @ 27.15. TT: 5 matches; 26 runs @ 13.00; 5 wickets @ 31.80. Cambridge University 1997; Northamptonshire 2004-.

MIKE BURNS 1997 – 2005

Mike Burns was the kind of occupant of the dressing room to give the other players the right sense of perspective. When morale was low, he told them, in effect, that they were lucky to be in employment. Once he worked as a shipyard fitter in his native Barrow. Sadly he saw the decline in the labour force; then came a few winters on the dole, no rare experience for county cricketers. Mike was used to hard manual work. When major construction was being carried out at the county ground in Taunton, he volunteered for an unglamorous labouring job. He possessed no phoney airs and graces: just a natural dry wit and honest pair of shoulders.

Brought to Somerset from Warwickshire by Dermot Reeve, he agreed with the advice that he might as well forget forever his long-cherished ambitions to be a county wicket-keeper. What chance did he have at Edgbaston as the permanent number two? 'Polish up your modest seamers instead,' he was told. And only on occasions did he need to crouch behind the stumps for Somerset. His medium pace, off that restrained run and with a natural swing away from the right-hander's bat, usefully surfaced. Ask the Leicestershire batsmen who came to the West in 2001.

For two seasons Mike captained the side. Unassumingly, he looked on it as a stop-gap measure. He was at heart one of the boys, competitive and wholehearted rather than tactically impatient to hunt out the opposition's flaws. The captaincy over recent years has at times suffered from a lack of continuity, though 'twas ever so, as any peep at the county's history reminds us.

Burns may have taken charge a trifle reluctantly, but this was not evident in his approach. He was, above all, a jobbing cricketer and proud of it. Without show he did his best to plug the gaps. He continued to talk with Cumbrian voice, ready to reminisce about his Rugby League-playing winters, and trials with Barrow and Carlisle. 'George' Burns' cricket was perhaps not made

for headlines. But don't forget his 221 against Yorkshire at Bath in 2001. It was the highest by a Somerset player on the Recreation Ground.

When it came to 2005, his benefit year, he was perhaps unlucky to be left out as Somerset decided, realistically, to opt for a more emphatic youth policy. He accepted his release graciously.

MICHAEL BURNS Born Barrow-in-Furness, Lancashire, 6.6.69. RHB, RM, occ WK. Cap 1999. Captain 2003-04. SFC: 134 matches; 7008 runs @ 34.69; 8 centuries; HS: 221 v Yorkshire, Bath, 1999; 1000 runs twice; HT 1133 in 2003; 68 wickets @ 42.11; BB 6-54 v Leicestershire, Taunton, 2001; HT 14 in 2000. OD: 179 matches; 4325 runs @ 27.54; 58 wickets @ 30.50; C&G MoM 1; B&H GA 1. TT: 9 matches; 108 runs @ 15.42; 2 wickets @ 27.50. Warwickshire 1992-96.

STEVE HERZBERG 1997

Somerset were his third county, and let's not forget first-class games for Western Australia and Tasmania. But the lofty off-spinner, who relied on bounce rather than turn, had no more than seven championship matches for Somerset. He found himself competing with Harvey Trump, though at least he got off the mark with a half-century and a wicket with his first ball for Somerset. At Worcestershire he played in the Second XI; then there were a few championship wickets for Kent. He had emigrated with his parents to Australia as a schoolboy and retained a strong Aussie accent in Somerset.

STEVEN HERZBERG Born Carshalton, Surrey, 25.5.67. RHB, OB. SFC: 7 matches; 207 runs @ 41.40; HS 56 v Surrey, Oval, 1997 on debut; 10 wickets @ 28.10; BB 3-100 v Kent, Taunton, 1997. OD: 3 matches; did not bat; 1 wicket @ 57.00. Western Australia 1991-93; Tasmania 1993-94; Kent 1995.

RICHARD SLADDIN 1997

His gentle left-arm spin brought this Yorkshireman five wickets in the second innings of his only game for Somerset, against Oxford University. Apparently Somerset were not sufficiently impressed to renew the invitation.

RICHARD WILLIAM SLADDIN Born Halifax, Yorkshire, 8.1.69. RHB, SLA. SFC: 1 match; did not bat; 6 wickets @ 17.50; BB 5-60 v Oxford University, Taunton, 1997. Derbyshire 1991-94.

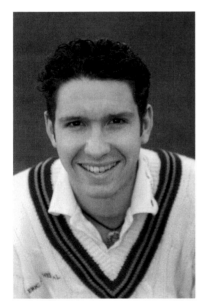

BEN TROTT 1997 – 1998

Injuries seemed to work against him in his Somerset seasons, though he was tall and brisk with a praiseworthy line and length. He found it difficult to get into the senior side and, in fact, made only one championship appearance. Other counties liked the look of him and Middlesex were among those to monitor his early promise. He played for Devon and in 2000 he joined Kent. The following season, at Tunbridge Wells, he touched the kind of new-ball form at which he had hinted often in his Somerset days. Essex went down by an innings and the boy from Wellington steamed in to take 6-13 in the second innings, and 11 wickets from the match.

BENJAMIN JAMES TROTT Born Wellington, Somerset, 14.3.75. RHB, RFM. SFC: 3 matches; 1 run @ 1.00; 7 wickets @ 26.28; BB 3-74 v Glamorgan, Taunton, 1997. OD: 1 match; did not bat; 1 wicket @ 29.00. Kent 2000-04.

NICK BOULTON 1997

This left-handed bat from South Africa went to King's School, Taunton, and Somerset decided to take a detailed look at him in the match with Pakistan 'A'. It was his only appearance at senior level.

NICHOLAS ROSS BOULTON Born Johannesburg, South Africa, 22.3.79. LHB, RM. SFC: 1 match; 15 runs @ 7.50; HS 14 v Pakistan 'A', Taunton, 1997.

LUKE SUTTON 1997 – 1998

Here was the classic case again of a capable young wicket-keeper left kicking his heels because there was no obvious prospect of forcing his way into the side by displacing Rob Turner. He was a diligent cricketer, a model of fitness, understandably impatient and eager for a fresh opportunity when it came with Derbyshire in 2000.

The pedigree was impressive: Millfield and Durham University. Sutton had captained England at Under-15 level and he went on to play for his country's Under-18s and Under-19s. Soon after his switch to Derby he was picking up the Denis Compton award for that county's most promising young player. He may have been out for a duck on his Somerset debut but his 140 against Sussex meant he was the first Derbyshire player for five years to carry his bat.

In 2004 he was appointed as Derbyshire's captain, a job he carried out with conscientious regard. At the end of 2005 he joined Lancashire.

LUKE DAVID SUTTON Born Keynsham, 6.10.76. RHB, WK. SFC: 3 matches; 41 runs @ 13.66; HS 16* v Sri Lankans, Taunton, 1998; 10 dismissals (10 ct). Derbyshire 2000-05; Lancashire 2006-.

STUART MacGILL 1997

The problem for Somerset was in being able to accommodate another overseas player. MacGill used to play for Tiverton in the Devon League and would come to the County Ground for practice. Somerset were well aware of his spinning skills and they selected him, just once, for the match with Pakistan A in 1997. He took two wickets in each innings, but it wasn't considered practicable to pursue the interest.

Meanwhile the 14-stone exponent of cunning leg-break achieved something of a reputation for his temperamental attitude during matches in Devon. There were suppressed chuckles while a few ears burned. He played for Devon in the '97 and '98 NatWest matches, spelt out the advantages of being competitive, yet at the same time clearly still liked the relatively easy-going, cream-tea philosophy that makes Devon so engaging.

Back in Australia, he would find himself in the shadows of the peerless Shane Warne, but there was scope all the same. He was the leading wicket-taker in the Test series against England in 1998-99, when he totalled 27 victims.

County cricket appealed to him. On his championship debut for Nottinghamshire in 2002 he excelled with 5-63 at Kidderminster and in the next match returned an extraordinary 14-165 against Middlesex at Trent Bridge. Doubtless there were a few sighs back at Taunton.

STUART CHARLES GLYNDWR MacGILL Born Mount Lawley, Western Australia, 25.2.71. RHB, LBG. 38 Tests 1997-. 3 LOI 1999-2000. SFC: 1 match; 32 runs @ 16.00; HS 25 v Pakistan 'A', Taunton, 1997; 4 wickets @ 30.75; BB 2-49 same match. Western Australia 1993-94; New South Wales 1996-; Nottinghamshire 2002-04.

1998

Captain: P.D. Bowler

Only ninth position in the championship – but this was still Caddick's year. He took 105 wickets, the first Somerset bowler to reach a century since Cartwright in 1971. The surprise was that Caddick's marathon stints and consistent hauls did not bring the county more than six wins. Criticised on occasion for his saturnine, defensive demeanour, he now appeared more relaxed. By any standards he had staked his claims for an elevated place in the county's record books, even if there was no place for him on the Ashes list.

Overall, Somerset were let down by their batsmen, with no-one reaching 1,000 runs for the first time since the war. Trescothick showed some improvement on his indeterminate form of recent years, but not since 1919 had Somerset's leading batsman scored as low an aggregate as his 847 runs. The captain, Bowler, was sufficiently despondent to drop himself for some one-day matches. His championship aggregate was fewer than 700. Hopes of big scores from Ecclestone proved misplaced; his knee worries didn't ease and he was able to play no more than five championship matches. That put an end to his county cricket for Somerset.

Another to leave, amid some sadness though it was not wholly a shock, was Mushtaq. It had been a non-existent season for him. The eyes were weary, the tricks and grins fewer. He was given compassionate leave because of his wife's difficult confinement back in Pakistan. In all, Somerset had to make do with a mere 14 championship wickets from him.

What else does one remember from 1998? A maiden century from Pierson, who had come from Leicestershire as a lanky off-spinner; the distinct promise of Bulbeck, arriving via the academy. Here was a left-arm bowler with a natural tendency for in-swing. Already the national coaches were keeping a paternal eye on him.

100 first-class wickets in season		
since reduction of programme in 1993		
106	C.A. Walsh	1998
105	A.R. Caddick	1998
105	A. Kumble	1995
103	Mushtaq Ahmed	2003

T.W. Cartwright (98 wickets in 1972) remains the only Somerset bowler ever to be the leading wicket-taker in an English summer.

COUNTY CHAMPIONSHIP   9th

COUNTY CHAMPIONSHIP 9th	Played 17 Won 6 Drawn 4 Lost 7	
OTHER MATCHES	Played 1 Drawn 1	
NATWEST BANK TROPHY	Lost in Second Round	
BENSON & HEDGES CUP	Eliminated at Zonal Stage	
REFUGE ASSURANCE LEAGUE 14th	Played 17 Won 6 Tied 1 No Result 2 Lost 8	

BATTING

	M	I	NO	Runs	HS	Ave	100	50	ct	st
M. E. Trescothick	18	29	2	847	98	31.37	–	6	20	–
M.N. Lathwell	12	19	0	574	106	30.21	1	5	7	–
M.P.L. Bulbeck	8	11	6	141	35	28.20	–	–	2	–
R.J. Turner	14	22	2	558	105	27.90	1	2	43	–
S.C. Ecclestone	5	7	0	186	94	26.57	–	1	4	–
M. Burns	10	17	0	450	96	26.47	–	3	16	1
P.D. Bowler	18	32	2	789	104	26.30	2	3	18	–
A.R.K. Pierson	13	20	3	438	108*	25.76	1	1	6	–
G.D. Rose	17	26	2	606	76	25.25	–	4	3	–
P.C.L. Holloway	16	28	3	624	123	24.96	1	1	7	–
A.R. Caddick	17	25	8	322	37	18.94	–	–	5	–
K.A. Parsons	14	23	1	367	101*	16.68	1	1	16	–
R.J. Harden	12	21	2	301	63	15.84	–	2	15	–
P.S. Jones	4	5	3	31	22*	15.50	–	–	–	–
Mushtaq Ahmed	6	9	1	121	37	15.12	–	–	1	–
K.J. Shine	3	5	2	44	18	14.66	–	–	–	–
G.J. Kennis	3	6	0	71	49	11.83	–	–	5	–
A.P. van Troost	5	7	1	61	23	10.16	–	–	–	–

(2 matches)   L.D. Sutton 3*, 16*, 0, 5 (5 ct)
(1 match)   B.J. Trott did not bat

BOWLING

	Overs	Mdns	Runs	Wkts	Ave	5wi	10wm
M.P.L. Bulbeck	154.4	28	609	32	19.03	–	–
A.R. Caddick	687.2	156	2082	105	19.82	10	3
G.D. Rose	480.3	132	1399	52	26.90	2	–
A.P. van Troost	118	24	415	15	27.66	–	–
Mushtaq Ahmed	136	40	411	14	29.35	–	–
M.E. Trescothick	193.3	45	654	17	38.47	–	–
A.R.K. Pierson	258.1	53	842	21	40.09	1	–
K.A. Parsons	129.2	34	412	8	51.50	–	–
K.J. Shine	57.4	10	216	4	54.00	–	–
P.S. Jones	74.5	16	245	4	61.25	–	–

P.D. Bowler 31.5-7-96-4   B.J. Trott 17-4-56-2   M. Burns 8-1-52-0
R.J. Harden 4-1-12-0

MATTHEW BULBECK
1998 – 2002

So much was expected of this talented left-arm swing bowler, who brought real variety to the Somerset attack. His early wickets included that of Brian Lara. Pundits were taking notice.

The cruel irony was that it was all over for Bulbeck by the age of 23. A serious back problem, nothing to do with the stress fractures which had limited his appearances in 2000 and 2001, ruled him out for the whole of 2003. Yet he had done so well in the previous summer, showing no obvious effects of his past injuries and recapturing that old, disconcerting movement through the air into the batsman. He took 53 championship wickets in what was a season of deceptive hope.

Here was another local boy wanting desperately to succeed, prepared to play through the pain if necessary. Medical experts told him otherwise. In 1999 he had toured New Zealand with an England Under-19 team and was tipped as a future international bowler. Now he plays as a pro in Devon, wisely concentrating on his batting, which wasn't, it should be said, at all bad at times in his curtailed county career.

MATTHEW PAUL LEONARD BULBECK Born Taunton, 8.11.79. LHB, LMF. Cap 2002. SFC: 47 matches; 821 runs @ 21.60; HS 76* v Durham, Riverside, 1999; HT 359 in 2002; 152 wickets @ 30.36; BB 6-93 v Lancashire, Taunton, 2002; HT 58 in 2002. OD: 30 matches; 117 runs @ 10.63; 30 wickets @ 33.63.

GREGOR KENNIS 1998 – 2000

Back in 1995 the insider view at the Oval was that here was a batsman to watch. He was nominated as Surrey's Second XI batsman of the year, expansively demonstrated by an innings of 258 off the Leicestershire bowlers. It was a record for a Surrey Second XI player. Alas the promise wasn't sustained and three years later he joined Somerset, only to be released at the end of the season.

By 1999 he was back again, however, this time on a summer contract. His opportunities hadn't been many but he found himself opening the innings at Taunton against the New Zealanders. He celebrated with an impressive statistical statement, scoring 175 out of a total of 554. Before that, his highest score had been 49 in 11 first-class appearances. Any hopes of relaunching an unproven career, however, were then ruined by back trouble.

GREGOR JOHN KENNIS Born Yokohama, Japan, 9.3.74. RHB, OB. SFC: 6 matches; 296 runs @ 24.66; HS 175 v New Zealanders, Taunton, 1999; HT 225 in 1999. OD: 2 matches; 27 runs @ 27.00. Surrey 1994-97.

ADRIAN PIERSON 1998 – 2000

Somerset was his third port of call, and there was still Derbyshire to come. He arrived as an off-spinner, a tall man and a thinker. Yet his batting was not to be wholly discounted. He quickly chalked up a career-best 67 against Nottinghamshire and in that same season, after going in as night-watchman and benefiting from some unlikely bowling, he reached his maiden century at Hove. He had started with Warwickshire before moving on to Leicestershire, whom he helped to win the championship in 1996, then came Somerset and Derbyshire. At Taunton, when it came to slow bowling, Harvey Trump was apt to get the vote. Dermot Reeve described Pierson as 'a good team man, ready to encourage the success of others.'

ADRIAN ROGER KIRSHAW PIERSON Born Enfield, Middlesex, 21.7.63. RHB, OB. SFC: 32 matches; 693 runs @ 21.00; HS 108* v Sussex, Hove, 1998; 41 wickets @ 47.41; BB 5-117 v Glamorgan, Cardiff, 1998. OD: 17 matches; 79 runs @ 15.80; 13 wickets @ 30.61. Warwickshire 1985-91; Leicestershire 1993-97; Derbyshire 2001.

DERMOT REEVE 1998

His reputation preceded him. He came to Somerset as director of cricket in 1997 with a brief to shake things up. Here was a proven innovator, someone full of new ideas and positive, individualistic plans to give the county a more competitive image. He demanded fitness and an increasingly energetic approach to fielding. At Warwickshire, where he'd excelled, success was a prerequisite; at Somerset, he noticed a more cosy outlook on the game. In the preparations, his words could have a cutting edge. One or two players fell by the wayside. He had been forced to retire as a player himself because of an arthritic hip. He missed the buzz of competition and couldn't resist some one-day games for his latest county.

Dermot doggedly made himself into a Test cricketer, even if some thought the recognition was fortunate. There were also 29 one-day internationals. Whether playing for his county or his country, the jaw was set; he conceded no ground and never countenanced the possibility of defeat. His self-confidence was there for all to see. He battled for his runs and that medium pace of his, so apparently innocuous from a boundary length away, carried a constant deceptive threat. His mother kept an eagle-eye on his progress. Once she took over as England's emergency scorer when Clem Driver was indisposed.

After starting with Sussex in 1983, Reeve joined Warwickshire in 1988, and he won man-of-the-match awards for both counties in NatWest finals. During his three years as skipper at Edgbaston, Warwickshire lifted six trophies.

His impact at Taunton was less assertive than some had expected. There were murmurings that he was inclined to be away from the county ground on other commitments, though this didn't conflict with his contractual obligations.

After Somerset, his enthusiasms and perceptive judgments were embraced by the TV commentary box. Also he demonstrated his fast-talking, jokey skills as an after-dinner speaker.

DERMOT ALEXANDER REEVE Born Kowloon, Hong Kong, 2.4.63. RHB, RMF. 3 Tests 1991-92. 29 LOI 1991-96. OD: 6 matches; 88 runs @ 44.00; 3 wickets @ 56.00. Sussex 1983-87; Warwickshire 1988-96

(left to right) Paul Warren, Joe Tucker, Dermot Reeve, Matthew Bulbeck, Adrian Pierson

1999

Captain: J. Cox

It had looked something of a gamble to make Tasmanian newcomer Jamie Cox the captain. He listened dutifully to senior voices and made few mistakes, though arguably one was against Gloucestershire in the NatWest final. He may have acted wrongly by inserting the opposition after winning the toss, but his debut season in county cricket was one to cherish. The 1,617 first-class runs were compiled attractively rather than flamboyantly. He was, perhaps, the principal reason that Somerset rose from ninth to fourth position in the championship table. He brought another dimension to the top-order batting, in the limited-overs matches, too. In the newly constructed National League, split into divisions, Somerset were promoted from the second flight, with 13 wins to show for it.

If Cox excelled with the bat, so did Caddick with the ball in his benefit season. He provided the most eloquent of answers to any perceived Test selection snubs. Recalled now for England – and missed by his county as a result – he took 91 first-class wickets and consistently shaped as well as any seamer in the country. Bulbeck continued to look a notable prospect in a summer when the rest of the Somerset bowling was too often less than effective.

Trescothick's 167 against Glamorgan in September could be pinpointed as the innings which fired the interest of Duncan Fletcher, the Glamorgan coach who was taking over at England.

Before long the young opener would be in the England team. Not so Turner, who seemed unreasonably ignored at the highest level. Yet he kept impeccably, accumulated more victims than any other wicketkeeper on the county scene and, as a bonus, finished the season sixth in the national batting averages.

When the New Zealanders came to Taunton, Kennis enjoyed his fleeting moment of triumph with a well-made 175 (his previous highest was 49) and Jones scored a maiden hundred. But where did things go wrong against Gloucestershire, who finished bottom of the table? First Somerset were beaten at Bath and then failed to cope with their geographical rivals in the NatWest final, not the most exciting or congenial of matches.

Christopher Ondaatje CBE, a generous benefactor to many causes, including Somerset cricket, was appointed the county's first patron. Born in Sri Lanka and educated at Blundell's School, Tiverton, he went on to become a successful investment banker and businessman in Canada until retirement and a change of direction. A £200,000 donation from him, matched by an equal sum from the Sports Council, led to the building of the County Ground's state-of-the-art school of excellence, hospitality boxes and new club shop.

Leading first-class wicketkeepers

R.J. Turner	67ct	2st	69
C.M.W. Read	59ct	2st	61
R.C. Russell	55ct	5st	60

R.J. Turner was also the leading Englishman in the batting averages.

COUNTY CHAMPIONSHIP 4th

Played 17	Won 6	Drawn 4	Lost 7

OTHER MATCHES — Played 2 — Drawn 1 — Lost 1

NATWEST BANK TROPHY — Lost in Final

BENSON & HEDGES SUPER CUP — Did not Qualify

NATIONAL LEAGUE — 2nd in Div 2 — Played 16 — Won 13 — Lost 3

BATTING

	M	I	NO	Runs	HS	Ave	100	50	ct	st
J. Cox	18	30	2	1617	216	57.75	6	6	7	–
R.J. Turner	19	27	4	1217	138*	52.91	2	10	67	2
P.D. Bowler	17	27	8	931	149	49.00	4	–	8	–
G.D. Rose	9	11	2	342	123*	38.00	1	1	2	–
M.P.L. Bulbeck	15	15	8	265	76*	37.85	–	1	1	–
G.J. Kennis	3	6	0	225	175	37.50	1	–	2	–
M.E. Trescothick	15	24	0	898	190	37.41	2	3	27	–
M. Burns	19	27	1	915	109	35.19	2	5	11	–
P.C.L. Holloway	19	32	5	869	114*	32.18	2	5	9	–
K.A. Parsons	15	21	3	499	80	27.72	–	3	12	–
I. Jones	3	4	1	78	35	26.00	–	–	–	–
P.S. Jones	9	14	3	281	105	25.54	1	–	3	–
J.I.D. Kerr	14	19	1	381	64	21.16	–	2	5	–
A.R. Caddick	13	17	5	205	44	17.08	–	–	2	–
A.R.K. Pierson	13	13	3	129	66	12.90	–	1	5	–
P.W. Jarvis	7	8	0	73	20	9.12	–	–	2	–

(1 match) Saqib Mahmood 7*, 0 (1 ct)

BOWLING

	Overs	Mdns	Runs	Wkts	Ave	5wi	10wm
A.R. Caddick	589.4	187	1488	71	20.95	4	–
M.P.L. Bulbeck	425	100	1456	51	28.54	3	1
K.A. Parsons	285.2	80	823	28	29.39	1	–
P.W. Jarvis	201.2	43	619	19	32.57	–	–
J.I.D. Kerr	305.2	68	1075	31	34.67	1	–
G.D. Rose	219.2	61	657	17	38.64	–	–
P.S. Jones	255.2	49	845	21	40.23	–	–
M. Burns	100	18	365	7	52.14	–	–
I. Jones	79.2	13	341	6	56.83	–	–
A.R.K. Pierson	271.2	52	789	13	60.69	–	–

J. Cox 49.3-6-188-4   M.E. Trescothick 38-8-127-5   P.D. Bowler 9.5-2-12-2
Saqib Mahmood 3-0-43-0

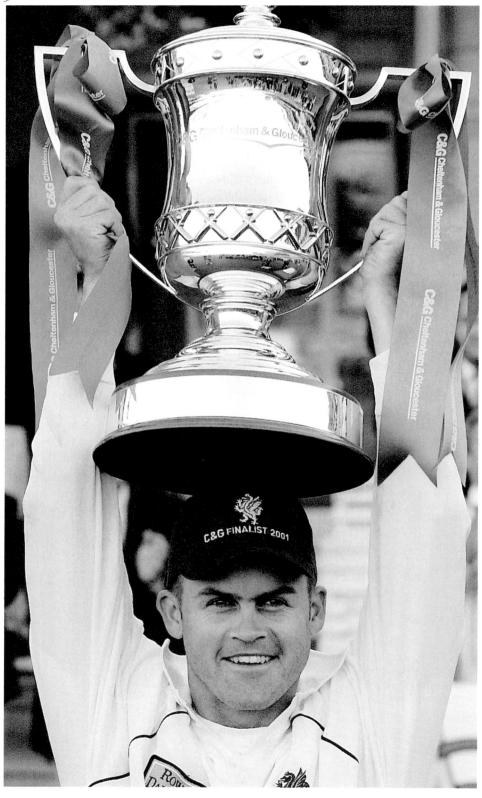

JAMIE COX 1999 – 2004

Who, a number of the Somerset faithful were asking when he first pulled into the Taunton car park in 1999, was this Jamie Cox? Whatever his emerging prowess in Tasmania, he was relatively unknown in the West Country.

But any frowns and apprehensions about his arrival were quickly superseded by expressions of appreciation as he took on the captaincy and opposing county bowlers with equal, and pleasurable, efficiency. Those who thumbed the Oz record books discovered a notable pedigree. In 1988 he'd gone with Australia Under-19 to the West Indies and the following year with Australia 'A' to Zimbabwe. He was the first young cricketer from Tasmania to attend the Australian Cricket Academy. By 1996-97, the runs were coming with an essentially neat, orthodox style that increasingly found favour in high places, where predictions were being made about his likely future as a Test player.

Cox came to Somerset to broaden his experience and play all through the year. His first season here brought him 1,617 first-class runs. There were times when he headed the national batting averages. He went off to Southampton to score a double-hundred in the first innings and another century in the second, a record for Somerset. Before leaving the county at the end of 2004, he composed a career-best 250 at Trent Bridge. The demeanour was as serene as ever.

He had captained Tasmania after David Boon and handed on to Ricky Ponting. A quiet, thoughtful man, he was a liked captain, rather than a sharply astute or adventurous one with Somerset. The team fared both particularly well and disappointingly under him. He made no excuses for poor collective form; he stuck bravely to his guns when events and tactics worked against him.

When it came to public relations skills, he was open and accessible. He went on record as saying he was 'sick to death' of the Twenty20 concept, which he found to be a shallow form of cricket while acknowledging its virtues as a crowd-puller.

Cox followed the tradition of successful and popular overseas players at Taunton. One of his valued final gestures was to recommend the recruitment, however briefly, of Ponting. Typically unassuming, he had come back himself to Somerset to cover for the Aussie skipper. In his unobtrusive way he was an enthusiast. This was illustrated when he used himself as an occasional off-spinner, surprised no doubt to pick up three Middlesex wickets in an early county fixture.

JAMIE COX Born Burnie, Tasmania, Australia, 15.10.69. RHB, OB. Cap 1999. Captain 1999-2001. SFC: 91 matches; 6688 runs @ 47.43; 17 centuries; HS: 250 v Nottinghamshire, Trent Bridge, 2004; 1000 runs 4 times; HT 1617 in 1999; 4 wickets @ 61.50; BB 3-46 v Middlesex, Taunton, 1999. OD: 110 matches; 3598 runs @ 34.26; 4 wickets @ 28.75; NW/C&G MoM 3. TT: 7 matches, 139 runs @ 23.16. Tasmania 1987-.

His simple, pure style of batting was a delight to behold. Few players have pummelled the off-side boundaries at Taunton with such elegance.

Vic Marks

PAUL JARVIS 1999 – 2000

Perhaps too much was expected of him from demanding Yorkshire fans who viewed him, unreasonably and prematurely, as a Fred Trueman successor. He was only 16 when he made his championship debut, the youngest in that county's history. Four years later he was recording his first championship hat-trick, though he had achieved that feat already in the Sunday League.

Jarvis was shortish and fast, with a skidding style which could disconcert batsmen when they looked set. England chose him for nine Tests and probably there should have been more. There were several instances when the selection processes seemed to work unfairly against him. That probably led to him joining the rebel tour of South Africa in 1989-90, a decision which brought him a three-year ban. Also he suffered more than his share of injuries. Somerset, for whom he made nine appearances and took 26 wickets, was his third county, after his native Yorkshire and Sussex.

PAUL WILLIAM JARVIS Born Redcar, Yorkshire, 29.6.65. RHB, RFM. 9 Tests 1987-93. 16 LOI 1987-93. SFC: 9 matches; 74 runs @ 8.22; HS 20 v Sussex, Taunton, 1999; HT 73 in 1999; 26 wickets @ 29.23; BB 4-21 v Oxford University, Taunton, 2000; HT 19 in 1999. OD: 33 matches; 73 runs @ 8.11; 46 wickets @ 29.06. Yorkshire 1981-93; Sussex 1994-98.

IAN JONES 1999 – 2001

Once called out of the stand at the Oval in a Sunday League match, to take over from the unwell Richard Johnson – and, with three wickets, didn't let Somerset down. Tall and naturally speedy, as they'd noticed in his days with the Durham Academy where he was actually the first to sign. But he missed the whole of the 2000 season due to ankle surgery and was released by Somerset after only three senior appearances.

IAN JONES Born Edmonton, Middlesex, 11.3.77. RHB, RFM. SFC: 3 matches; 78 runs @ 26.00; 6 wickets @ 56.83; HS 35 v Durham, Riverside, 1999; BB 3-81 v New Zealanders, Taunton, 1999. OD: 2 matches; 5 runs (no average); 4 wickets @ 16.75.

SAQIB MAHMOOD 1999

Maybe Somerset were influenced by news of his boyhood feats in London. He had once taken eight wickets for one run with his precocious leg-breaks. He also carted half-a-dozen sixes in an over in a club match. His stay in the West Country, however, was brief and unrewarded.

SAQIB MAHMOOD Born Kettering, Northamptonshire, 24.8.77. RHB, LB. SFC: 1 match; 7 runs @ 7.00; 0 wickets.

PETER ROBINSON'S HOME-GROWN XI
1965-2005

Peter Roebuck
Mark Lathwell
Chris Tavare
Bill Alley
Brian Close (captain)
Ian Botham
Ian Blackwell or Tom Cartwright
Derek Taylor
Brian Langford
Andy Caddick
Fred Rumsey

My choice of openers might surprise some observers, given that Somerset have supplied Brian Rose and Marcus Trescothick to England. But I have an exceptionally high regard for Roeby, a gutsy, muck-and-bullets kind of batsman who was responsible for plenty of match-winning innings, not all of them at Taunton.

He'd combine beautifully with Lathers, the Roundhead with the Cavalier. When Lathers was on his way up he was a joy to watch and he gave me as much pleasure as anyone. It could be argued that he under-achieved in the long run, but everyone wanted to be in their seat when he was at the crease.

I'm counting Peter Wight and Bill Alley as home-developed, though I'm picking only one of them. Because I played only briefly with Peter, I'm omitting him in favour of Chris Tavare, who was brilliant but sorely under-rated.

Bill has got to be there, and I'd put him at four, though Closey, definitely my skipper, would moan about it terribly. Certainly it would be a colourful dressing room with those two; the only problem would be that they changed in the same corner, so I don't know which one would give ground.

Next would come Both, the big lad, and then my wild card, Ian Blackwell; the two of them smacking the ball around together would be a bowlers' nightmare. If the pitch demanded an extra seamer, then I'd drop Blackie for Tom.

Langy, Caddick and Fred virtually pick themselves, but I was torn over the keeper, eventually opting for Derek's glovemanship over Rob Turner's batting, with a thought to the skills of Geoff Clayton.

Finally, if I was granted the luxury of a 13-man squad, I would add Ken Palmer, a marvellous all-rounder.

2000

Captain: J. Cox

There was not too much to cheer – but at least a listless looking West Indies side was beaten at Taunton at a time when they should have been taking advantage of serious batting practice ahead of the final Test. The margin of the win, by 269 runs, gave Somerset a late-season lift, not to mention an £11,000 cheque for being the only county to come out on top of the tourists.

It was surprising that Brian Lara and company flopped against a modest Somerset attack. Tucker was able to dine out on the fact that on his debut he had the great man caught at fine-leg second ball. Kerr, making his first senior appearance of the season, dramatically ended the match with a hat-trick. The best of the batting came from Parsons, who ran out of partners on 193.

Bowler scored five hundreds and again passed his 1,000 runs, finishing sixth in the national averages. Caddick was fifth in the bowling list, even if he and Trescothick were frequently needed by their country instead. As two match-winners, their absence was markedly felt at times. Cox shuffled his pack and did what he could. The balance wasn't right; Somerset frequently appeared in need of another seamer and spinner.

As so often happens in professional sport, second seasons can be anti-climactic. Cox failed to sustain the run total of the previous year. His three centuries were as attractive as ever but maybe some opposing bowlers believed they were beginning to work him out.

He hoped in vain to lean on Bulbeck, but the swing bowler, handicapped by a chronic back problem, played only two championship matches. Like Cox, Turner failed to live up to the stirring statistics of the previous summer. Maybe he was affected psychologically by his rejection – when surely so near to international honours – from the Test selectors. His keeping lost a little of its edge, and the runs dried up.

Somerset were about to say their farewells to Reeve and Jarvis. Reeve's unfulfilled brief had been to orchestrate the winning of a trophy or two. More encouraging, though, was a maiden century from Blackwell. The murmurs of approval could be heard all the way round the boundary.

England v Zimbabwe, The Oval

M.E. Trescothick, on debut, top-scored with 79

He looks at home at this level. He has all the shots, the talent and the mental strength to succeed.

Alec Stewart

He batted as he might in Taunton. To him the match was not a hard day at the office but an adventure, and he played in that spirit.

Peter Roebuck, Sunday Times

COUNTY CHAMPIONSHIP 5th in Div 1 Played 16   Won 2   Drawn 10   Lost 4

OTHER MATCHES			Played 2	Won 2						
NATWEST BANK TROPHY			Lost in Fourth Round							
BENSON & HEDGES CUP			Eliminated at Zonal Stage							
NATIONAL LEAGUE		6th in Div 1	Played 16	Won 7	No Result 1	Lost 8				

BATTING

	M	I	NO	Runs	HS	Ave	100	50	ct	st
P.D. Bowler	18	26	5	1305	157*	62.14	5	4	8	–
M.E. Trescothick	9	14	1	548	105	42.15	1	3	8	–
M. Burns	15	20	1	775	160	40.78	2	5	3	–
J. Cox	17	26	1	983	171	39.32	3	3	6	–
G.D. Rose	15	18	5	510	124	39.23	2	1	4	–
K.A. Parsons	15	22	3	745	193*	37.25	2	1	17	–
J.I.D. Kerr	4	5	1	116	34	29.00	–	–	–	–
I.D. Blackwell	18	23	2	582	109	27.71	1	2	6	–
A.R.K. Pierson	6	9	3	126	48	21.00	–	–	3	–
R.J. Turner	18	26	2	492	75	20.50	–	2	39	–
P.C.L. Holloway	13	20	1	377	113	19.84	1	1	9	–
M.N. Lathwell	9	14	1	257	54*	19.76	–	1	4	–
P.D. Trego	7	8	1	134	62	19.14	–	1	3	–
A.R. Caddick	3	4	1	52	21*	17.33	–	–	1	–
J.O. Grove	10	10	5	56	17	11.20	–	–	–	–
P.S. Jones	15	16	4	122	56*	10.16	–	1	4	–
M.P.L. Bulbeck	3	2	1	6	3*	6.00	–	–	–	–

(2 matches)   P.W. Jarvis 1 (1 ct)
(1 match)   J.P. Tucker 14 (1 ct)

BOWLING

	Overs	Mdns	Runs	Wkts	Ave	5wi	10wm
A.R. Caddick	114	32	294	25	11.76	3	2
J.I.D. Kerr	62	13	248	9	27.55	–	–
M. Burns	132.2	33	387	14	27.64	–	–
G.D. Rose	332.3	79	908	29	31.31	1	–
P.S. Jones	403.4	88	1294	40	32.35	1	–
P.D. Trego	165.1	34	603	18	33.50	–	–
J.O. Grove	192.5	27	733	21	34.90	1	–
K.A. Parsons	150.4	41	443	11	40.27	1	–
I.D. Blackwell	411.3	123	1010	23	43.91	–	–
A.R.K. Pierson	129	37	313	7	44.71	–	–
M.E. Trescothick	61	13	205	3	68.33	–	–

P.W. Jarvis 37.3-7-141-7   M.P.L. Bulbeck 37-9-109-7   J. Cox 14-3-35-0
J.P. Tucker 11-3-47-1   P.C.L. Holloway 2-0-4-0

PETER TREGO 2000 –

The natural ability was there and so was the self-confidence. But hopes wavered, leaving his devotees to shake their heads when scope lessened and he left, soon to join Kent. That move didn't work out for him, either, yet so much had been expected of this Weston-super-Mare boy. At Under-16 level he won Somerset's best batsman award, then before long he was off to Lilleshall with the England Under-17 squad, and he won a place in the Under-19 team against Sri Lanka.

Trego's jaunty approach could be a bonus. Apart from some fiery bowling, he was also ready to open the batting for his county, as he did against Warwickshire. What everyone remembers, though, is his innings against West Indies 'A' in 2002. He marched in at number nine and clattered a thoroughly entertaining and very nearly victorious 140. Somerset had been set 453 and they tied in an extraordinary finish.

Out of season, Trego kept goal with agility and characteristic assurance as a semi-pro for various top non-League clubs. At one of them, Chippenham, he marked his debut by netting with a free-kick taken from well within his own half.

But cricket remained his main sporting interest. After a period of indecision and limited scope, he put a frustrating contract with Kent behind him to join Middlesex, with whom he rediscovered his touch. Then, to some surprise, he re-signed for Somerset for 2006, eager to demonstrate that his swing bowling had a proper place nearer his roots.

PETER DAVID TREGO Born Weston-super-Mare, 12.6.81. RHB, RM. SFC: 14 matches; 521 runs @ 28.94; HS 140 v West Indies 'A', Taunton, 2002; HT 270 in 2002; 27 wickets @ 44.55; BB 4-84 v Yorkshire, Scarborough, 2000; HT 18 in 2000. OD: 19 matches; 118 runs @ 9.83; 14 wickets @ 35.14. Kent 2003, Middlesex 2005.

JAMIE GROVE 2000 – 2001

This wiry pace bowler had played for his country at Under-15, Under-17 and Under-19 level. Chelmsford observers quite liked the look of him but it wasn't easy breaking into the Essex side. He came to Somerset instead and could hardly have hoped for a better debut, his five wickets in an innings against Leicestershire earning encouraging comments. Not that they were the guarantee of regular first-team recognition.

Grove bowled well enough for the successful Second XI side as they clinched the runners-up place in their championship, but senior advancement at Taunton proved elusive. After Somerset, he went to Leicestershire, who may have recalled his wickets against them. But he was used mostly in limited-over matches and was released after two seasons.

JAMIE OLIVER GROVE Born Bury St Edmunds, Suffolk, 3.7.79. RHB, RMF. SFC: 14 matches; 86 runs @ 10.75; HS 19* v Surrey, Taunton, 2001; HT 56 in 2000; 27 wickets @ 45.25; BB 5-90 v Leicestershire, Leicester, 2000 on debut; HT 21 in 2000. OD: 14 matches; 9 runs @ 3.00; 13 wickets @ 39.33. Essex 1998-99, Leicestershire 2002.

JOE TUCKER 2000 – 2001

Who could possibly blame him for basking in the fact that on his debut he had Brian Lara out second ball, hooking to fine-leg? Joe had come through the Somerset Academy and gone with the England Under-19 party to South Africa in 1997-98, and New Zealand the year after. He performed diligently at Dennis Lillee's coaching school in Madras, and he was one of the quicker prospects around.

But illness and injury ruled him out for the whole of the 1999 season, then the early part of the next one, and he never regained his impetus. Tucker's wide-ranging sporting interests extended for a time to experience as a professional moto-cross rider.

JOSEPH PETER TUCKER Born Bath, 14.9.79. RHB, RFM. SFC: 2 matches; 19 runs @ 19.00; HS 14 v West Indians, Taunton, 2000; 1 wicket @ 129.00; BB 1-28, same match.

IAN BLACKWELL 2000 –

It wasn't just that Ian Blackwell batted in the spirit of Somerset's hardest hitters, he even looked like a Man o' Mendip. The girth was generous, the forearms thick, the cheeks ruddy. Blissfully, no-one tried too hard to alter or refine his technique. For his part, he heard the intermittent warnings about his amiable, carefree approach and suspect fitness, and made timely adjustments. There were reservations among the loftier echelons of the game, but he won a place in England's one-day side and in 2006 was called up for the tour of India.

Easy-going, slightly overweight or not, he lacked no support or encouragement in Somerset. The locals knew that on his day Blackwell was one of the most exciting batsmen on the circuit and the county had done well to sign him. Many were surprised when he left his native Derbyshire, where he had been making perceptible progress with his all-round cricket since he was eight.

By the age of 17 he had joined the playing staff. It was Dermot Reeve's honeyed words that convinced Blackwell Somerset were more ambitious and a better prospect for him. Reeve had liked the way the burly left-hander had

hammered 80 against Somerset in a Sunday match. He could see him as an obvious crowd-pleaser and reckoned he could step up the fitness routines. Very quickly, the newcomer was helping himself to a century in each innings against Northants, from the number-seven position.

It wasn't simply the power of Blackwell's shots but the clean manner he struck the ball. With some irony, he saved up his best at the expense of Derbyshire. Somerset had been 31-4; they ended up 409 all out, with the Chesterfield exile undefeated on 247. With Nixon McLean he created a last-wicket record stand of 163.

We must not forget Blackwell's bowling, however. That was one of the arguments in signing him because Somerset needed a slow left-arm tempter. In that role he has acquired additional skills and acts of cunning since arriving. In 2004 he took career-best figures of 7-90 against Glamorgan; not long afterwards he returned the same figures at Trent Bridge, where Somerset won by ten wickets and Blackwell was applauded for his stamina and accuracy.

His entertainment value, now allied to an increasingly more mature demeanour, showed no signs of being sacrificed in 2005. He scored the fastest hundred of the season and before the summer was over he was leading the county. One only hoped the added responsibilities would not affect his uninhibited scoring rate.

IAN DAVID BLACKWELL Born Chesterfield, Derbyshire, 10 June 1978. LHB, SLA. Cap 2001. Captain 2005-. 28 LOI 2002-. SFC: 86 matches; 5580 runs @ 45.73; 16 centuries; HS 247* v Derbyshire, Taunton, 2003; 1000 runs twice; HT 1256 in 2005; 156 wickets @ 42.39; BB 7-90 v Glamorgan, Taunton, 2004, and v Nottinghamshire, Trent Bridge, 2004; HT 36 in 2003. OD: 124 matches; 3231 runs @ 30.19; 93 wickets @ 38.44; C&G MoM 1; B&H GA 1. TT: 21 matches; 354 runs @ 20.82; 18 wickets @ 26.33. Derbyshire 1997-99.

> He hits the ball as hard as Pietersen, but he's the wrong shape. It's an image thing. He's never going to be a twig, always going to be fighting his weight. But one burst of vintage Blackie can destroy any team.
> **Graham Rose**

2001

Captain: J. Cox

This really was Somerset's finest season. They finished as championship runners-up, higher than ever before and pipped only by Yorkshire. There were times when the pennant of victory seemed to be heading for Taunton. Premature celebrations were aflame in many a West Country heart. But in the end there were 16 points between the two counties, too much ground to make up.

The extraordinary fact was that Somerset achieved so much without any stars. When trophies last came their way, they had marvellous match-winning players like Richards, Garner and Botham. Now, because of central contracts, they were mostly without Caddick and Trescothick. However you looked at it, Somerset's success was down to the team ethos.

Quite apart from the championship, they won the final of the Cheltenham & Gloucester Trophy, beating Leicestershire by 41 runs. It was the first time for 18 years that they had triumphed in a gala day at Lord's. No-one did better than Parsons, appropriately a local boy and one not even guaranteed a regular first-team place. He was in a significant stand with Turner, he hit bold and crucial last-ditch sixes and then took important wickets. The match award to him was as logical as it was sentimental.

Somerset's victory was a perfect climax to the season and a compliment to a buoyant dressing room. The influence of Kevin Shine, who had found himself taking over from Reeve as coach, should not be overlooked. His persuasive words in bringing Johnson and Dutch to the county from Middlesex had a bearing on results. The pacy Johnson, standing in for Caddick, took 62 wickets; in an eventful summer, he was called up as an England standby and then went to India. Dutch's off-breaks had their moments. He collected his maiden hundred against Essex, and he fielded well.

Also, Turner was back, keeping with his old confidence and doing it so well that he held on to a county record of seven catches in an innings against Northants. In that game Somerset's total of 650 was the second highest in their history; hundreds by Wood and Parsons, and nearly another by Lathwell, had pushed the formidable aggregate along.

What else? Certainly the under-rated Burns' double-hundred at Bath, Jones' cap for some whole-hearted bowling, and four more centuries from the endearingly forceful Blackwell.

> Winning this trophy is a monkey off our backs. Now perhaps people will talk about Parsons, Turner and Blackwell as they have revered the names of Botham, Richards and Garner.
>
> **Jamie Cox**, after winning the Cheltenham & Gloucester Trophy

COUNTY CHAMPIONSHIP **2nd** in **Div 1** Played 16 Won 6 Drawn 8 Lost 2

OTHER MATCHES	Played 1		Lost 1
C&G TROPHY	Champions		
BENSON & HEDGES CUP	Lost in Quarter-Final		

NATIONAL LEAGUE **4th in Div 1** Played 16 Won 7 Tied 1 No Result 1 Lost 7

BATTING

	M	I	NO	Runs	HS	Ave	100	50	ct	st
J. Cox	15	25	3	1264	186	57.45	1	9	6	–
M.E. Trescothick	3	4	0	216	147	54.00	1	–	3	–
I.D. Blackwell	11	17	0	839	122	49.35	4	3	5	–
M.J. Wood	7	12	0	529	122	44.08	1	4	2	–
P.D. Bowler	14	22	2	827	164	41.35	2	4	14	–
K.A. Parsons	5	8	1	254	139	36.28	1	–	5	–
M. Burns	17	28	1	961	221	35.59	1	7	13	–
M.N. Lathwell	13	21	1	702	99	35.10	–	8	9	–
R.J. Turner	17	26	3	761	115*	33.08	1	3	59	–
R.L. Johnson	13	15	3	379	68	31.58	–	2	3	–
K.P. Dutch	16	22	4	530	118	29.44	1	3	19	–
P.D. Trego	3	5	1	117	43	29.25	–	–	–	–
P.C.L. Holloway	12	21	1	567	85	28.35	–	4	3	–
J.I.D. Kerr	8	12	5	167	36	23.85	–	–	1	–
P.S. Jones	16	16	5	180	29*	16.36	–	–	3	–
M.P.L. Bulbeck	5	7	2	50	18	10.00	–	–	3	–
J.O. Grove	4	5	2	30	19*	10.00	–	–	2	–
G.D. Rose	3	4	0	25	15	6.25	–	–	–	–

(2 matches)   A.R. Caddick 0, 10*, 5*

(1 match)   Aamir Sohail 50, 36   Shoaib Akhtar 4*, 10   J.P. Tucker 5*, 0*

BOWLING

	Overs	Mdns	Runs	Wkts	Ave	5wi	10wm
A.R. Caddick	88.4	17	319	18	17.72	3	1
R.L. Johnson	463.2	89	1474	62	23.77	5	–
P.S. Jones	560	100	2015	59	34.15	1	–
K.P. Dutch	367	64	1268	35	36.22	–	–
I.D. Blackwell	291.4	72	896	20	44.80	1	–
M. Burns	138.5	23	539	12	44.91	1	–
G.D. Rose	50	15	155	3	51.66	–	–
P.D. Trego	58	11	243	4	60.75	–	–
J.I.D. Kerr	186.4	36	645	9	71.66	–	–
J.O. Grove	88.2	8	489	6	81.50	–	–
M.P.L. Bulbeck	110	6	501	4	125.25	–	–

K.A. Parsons 46-5-193-1   Shoaib Akhtar 21-3-90-3   J.P. Tucker 17-2-82-0

R.J. Turner 10-3-29-0   M.N. Lathwell 7-0-37-0   M.J. Wood 7-1-30-0

P.C.L. Holloway 4-0-19-0   Aamir Sohail 3-0-16-0   P.D. Bowler 2-0-9-0

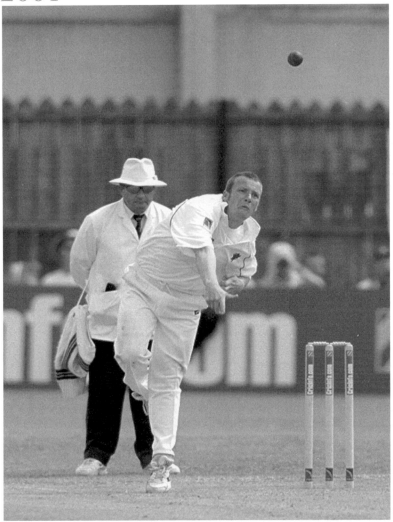

KEITH DUTCH
2001 – 2004

There were occasions in the sun when he had the appealing tendency to be a monopolist. In a single day, playing for Middlesex against Essex at Chelmsford, he scored an excellent 91 and followed up with a beguiling exhibition of off-spin to take 6-62. Yet he bettered that for Somerset, once more against Essex, this time at Taunton. He began with a maiden century for him to cherish; and as an encore he held on to three sharp catches at second slip, as well as taking four late wickets. Somerset won by an innings or, more accurately, Dutch did. At times he kept Blackwell out of the championship side.

He had come to the West Country primarily as an off-break bowler but Somerset were well aware of his capabilities as a batsman. Hadn't he once taken a double-hundred off them in a Second XI match? For several years he starred for Middlesex at that level, topping 1,000 runs in the 1996 season, and for both counties he was a useful man to have around in the one-day game.

KEITH PHILIP DUTCH Born Harrow, Middlesex, 21.3.73. RHB, OB. Cap 2001. SFC: 45 matches; 1371 runs @ 23.23; 1 century; HS 118 v Essex, Taunton, 2001; HT 530 in 2001; 77 wickets @ 38.90; BB 5-26 v Yorkshire, Scarborough, 2004; HT 35 in 2001. OD: 89 matches; 1451 runs @ 22.32; 74 wickets @ 34.70; C&G MoM 1. TT: 10 matches; 291 runs @ 32.33; 5 wickets @ 32.80. Middlesex 1993-2000.

RICHARD JOHNSON 2001 –

When still a Middlesex teenager, he demolished the Derbyshire innings on his own in stirring style, becoming the first bowler to take all ten wickets in the championship for 30 years – a feat achieved on a decent batting wicket where there were four centuries. Understandably the Lord's prophets speculated with some enthusiasm that here was an England seamer of the future. Duly Johnson was called up for England's 1995-96 tour of South Africa but back worries put an end to that, and injuries have continued to dog his career at untimely moments.

To the surprise of many, he left Middlesex for Somerset and promptly registered his presence with two five-wicket hauls, against Lancashire and Glamorgan. That delayed Test debut came in 2003 against Zimbabwe at the Riverside. The opposition may have been comparatively modest but he fired away to take a praiseworthy introductory 6-33. Johnson was ever a bowler who liked to get things under way; in that game, he struck with his third and fourth ball. He ended up man of the match and so he did in his second Test, against Bangladesh, maybe partially a kind-hearted compensation because he'd put

off his honeymoon to go there.

Originally Johnson had been selected only for the one-day commitments in Bangladesh and Sri Lanka, but he was needed to take over from the injured James Anderson for the Bangladesh first-class section before being retained for the Sri Lanka Test series, this time as replacement for the indisposed Steve Harmison. Match figures of 9-93 in the second Test at Chittagong led him to hope for extended recognition.

A lusty hitter, Johnson shouldn't be discounted with the bat, as his maiden hundred at Bristol illustrated exhilaratingly. His century against Durham in 2004 was the fastest of the season, off 63 balls, earning him the Walter Lawrence trophy.

RICHARD LEONARD JOHNSON Born Chertsey, Surrey, 29.12.74. RHB, RFM. Cap 2001. 3 Tests 2003-. 10 LOI 2003-. SFC: 58 matches; 1474 runs @ 23.39; 2 centuries; HS 118 v Gloucestershire, Bristol, 2003; HT 379 in 2001; 205 wickets @ 28.90; BB 7-43 v Hampshire, Bath, 2002; HT 62 in 2001. OD: 49 matches; 317 runs @ 14.40; 58 wickets @ 32.43. TT: 4 matches; 10 runs @ 3.33; 8 wickets @ 13.75. Middlesex 1992-2000.

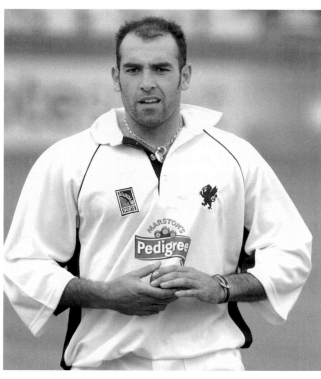

MATTHEW JAMES WOOD Born Exeter, Devon, 30.9.80. RHB, OB. Cap 2005. SFC: 58 matches; 3698 runs @ 38.52; 9 centuries; HS 297 v Yorkshire, Taunton, 2005; 1000 runs once; HT 1058 in 2005; 0 wickets. OD: 53 matches; 1189 runs @ 25.29. TT: 15 matches; 441 runs @ 29.40.

MATTHEW WOOD 2001 –

Quiet he may be by nature but there has always been a pleasing eloquence in Matthew Wood's shot selection. By 2002 he was opening the batting and composing a hundred in each innings against Surrey at Taunton. There was an audible flutter of approval around the boundary, compounded two months later when he made a thoroughly good-looking 196 against Kent. The pitch at headquarters was laden with runs that season, though this shouldn't devalue Wood's emerging batting skills in any way.

The placid temperament was what might be expected from a Devonian. Wood had played for his native county and for Exmouth CC, the progressive club chaired by his father. Down there, where the waves come up nearly to the outfield, the locals always suspected young Matthew had a first-class future, and his 71 runs on debut against Yorkshire at Bath confirmed the positive judgement.

All the odder, then, that at times Somerset seemed to show a reluctance to promote him, while acknowledging his promise. They had monitored and nurtured him, after all.

In 2005 that hesitation by past selectors was superseded by Wood's permanent, and rational, upgrading. His response was reflected in several admirable innings, including one of 297 against Yorkshire, and as another bonus he was made vice-captain.

Over the next few years his batsmanship, not to mention his steadying influence, could be an important element in Somerset's hoped-for revival.

AAMIR SOHAIL 2001

No-one quite worked out the logic of bringing him in for a guest appearance against the Australians. The Pakistan Test player opened the innings and collected an unspectacular half century. Then he was gone again.

AAMIR SOHAIL Born Lahore, Pakistan, 14.9.66. LHB, SLA. 47 Tests 1992-2000. 156 LOI 1990-2000. SFC: 1 match; 86 runs @ 43.00; 0 wickets; HS 50 v Australians, Taunton, 2001. Lahore 1983-99, Habib Bank 1987-92, Sargodha 1990-91, Allied Bank 1995-2001, Rawalpindi 1995-96, Karachi 1998-99, Lahore 2000-01.

SHOAIB AKHTAR 2001

He paid his cursory visit along with Sohail, worked up a decent speed, pulled in a few additional Pakistani spectators, took three wickets and was on his way. News that he would be playing for Somerset caused a ripple of interest, as well as a hint of scepticism. In his Test career he has created a few headlines. Not at Taunton, however.

SHOAIB AKHTAR Born Rawalpindi, Pakistan, 13.8.75. RHB, RF. 39 Tests 1997-. 124 LOI 1997-. SFC: 1 match; 14 runs @ 14.00; HS 10 v Australians, Taunton, 2001; 3 wickets @ 30.00; BB 2-9, same match. Rawalpindi 1994-99, ADBP 96-98, KRL 2001-02, Durham 2003-04, Worcestershire 2005-.

		HIGHEST POST-WAR PARTNERSHIP FOR EACH WICKET			
		(first-class cricket)			
1	278	J. Cox & P.D. Bowler	Cambridge Univ	Fenner's	1999
2	262	R.T. Virgin & M.J. Kitchen	Pakistanis	Taunton	1967
3	319	P.M. Roebuck & M.D. Crowe	Leicestershire	Taunton	1984
4	310	P.W. Denning & I.T. Botham	Gloucestershire	Taunton	1980
5	320	J.D. Francis & I.D. Blackwell	Durham UCCE	Taunton	2005
6	265	W.E. Alley & K.E. Palmer	Northamptonshire	Northampton	1961
7	279	R.J. Harden & G.D. Rose	Sussex	Taunton	1997
8	172	I.V.A. Richards & I.T. Botham	Leicestershire	Leicester	1983
	172	A.R.K. Pierson & P.S. Jones	New Zealanders	Taunton	1999
9	183	C.H. Greetham & H.W. Stephenson	Leicestershire	Weston-s-Mare	1990
	183	C.J. Tavare & N.A. Mallender	Sussex	Hove	1990
10	163	I.D. Blackwell & N.A.M. McLean	Derbyshire	Taunton	2003

2002

Captain: J. Cox

Somerset's natural progression had to be to the top spot – or so the members were convinced. They had been the runners-up in 2001 and expectations were high. Had someone forgotten the county's unrivalled reputation for unpredictability? Was there ever, during their long, variegated history, any real pattern or a semblance of consistency? True to form, Somerset mocked the heady deeds of the previous season. Relegation came with an unequivocal blow in both the championship and the Norwich Union League.

All the forecasts of belated title success disappeared rapidly. Too much cricket, especially the batting and slippery-fingered fielding, was falling short of the standards that the county had set in their dreams for the championship. At one point it was apparently so worrying that the chief executive, Peter Anderson, sent a letter of apology to all the members.

The players weren't spared; it left them smarting at what had become a public rebuke. Interviews were carried out within the club. 'You got us down – now you get us up again' was the gist of the Anderson tirade, much of which found favour with the supporters, who couldn't understand how a team could suddenly lose its verve and sense of direction.

Somerset lost their last two championship matches in two days. The players couldn't wait to get this gloomy season out of the way. Cox said he was coming back, but not as skipper. Burns, the only player to pass 1,000 runs, would take his place. Cox's batting skills, so evident in his first summer here, were badly missed when he was absent with a broken thumb. There was a solitary hundred from him.

But at least the chunky Blackwell was on hand to set the pulses racing, and clearly Wood was one for the future. Not so Trego, who crashed 140 in a glorious run-chase in a tied match against West Indies 'A'. Before long he was off to Kent and then Middlesex before his surprise return to Somerset in 2006.

By way of compensation for a generally barren season, the county reached the final of the Cheltenham & Gloucester Trophy, partly thanks to Kent's self-destructive tendencies and Somerset's own inspired fielding in the semi-finals. Then they lost by six wickets to Yorkshire.

Taunton, May 1946
Somerset v Essex
Duration: 3 days
Actual play: 17½ hours
Overs bowled: 387.3

Taunton, July 2002
Somerset v Surrey
Duration: 4 days
Actual play: 25½ hours
Overs bowled: 391.4

COUNTY CHAMPIONSHIP **8th in Div 1**

COUNTY CHAMPIONSHIP **8th in Div 1**	Played 16	Won 1	Drawn 8	Lost 7
OTHER MATCHES	Played 1		Tied 1	
C&G TROPHY	Lost in Final			
BENSON & HEDGES CUP	Eliminated at Zonal Stage			
NATIONAL LEAGUE **7th in Div 1**	Played 16	Won 5	No Result 1	Lost 10

BATTING

	M	I	NO	Runs	HS	Ave	100	50	ct	st
P.D. Trego	4	8	1	270	140	38.57	1	–	2	–
I.D. Blackwell	14	23	0	879	114	38.21	3	3	4	–
M. Burns	16	30	2	1047	99	37.39	–	9	14	–
M.J. Wood	15	28	0	971	196	34.67	3	5	5	–
P.D. Bowler	14	25	2	766	94	33.30	–	7	22	–
P.C.L. Holloway	7	13	0	428	88	32.92	–	3	4	–
J. Cox	13	25	2	724	176	31.47	1	3	6	–
R.J. Turner	16	27	4	691	83*	30.04	–	4	50	1
K.A. Parsons	15	26	2	581	68	24.20	–	4	16	–
R.L. Johnson	9	17	4	290	61	22.30	–	1	2	–
G.D. Rose	3	4	0	84	32	21.00	–	–	1	–
K.P. Dutch	16	27	3	432	74	18.00	–	2	20	–
M.P.L. Bulbeck	16	27	7	359	53*	17.95	–	1	3	–
P.S. Jones	7	8	3	76	37*	15.20	–	–	–	–
S.R.G. Francis	10	16	8	67	17	8.37	–	–	–	–
A.R. Caddick	5	8	0	53	16	6.62	–	–	2	–

(2 matches) M.E. Trescothick 0, 134, 7, 12   A.V. Suppiah 0, 21, 1, 5 (1 ct)
(1 match) W.J. Durston 26, 55 (1 ct)   N.J. Edwards 31, 27 (1 ct)
C.M. Gazzard 24, 7 (3 ct, 1st)

BOWLING

	Overs	Mdns	Runs	Wkts	Ave	5wi	10wm
R.L. Johnson	307.1	66	914	43	21.25	2	1
A.R. Caddick	247.2	53	773	34	22.73	4	–
M.P.L. Bulbeck	534	93	1940	58	33.44	1	–
S.R.G. Francis	222.3	26	947	28	33.82	1	–
I.D. Blackwell	312.5	83	830	22	37.72	1	–
K.A. Parsons	216.3	30	830	21	39.52	–	–
M. Burns	101.4	14	444	11	40.36	–	–
P.S. Jones	239.2	43	845	19	44.47	1	1
K.P. Dutch	268.3	59	852	15	56.80	–	–
P.D. Trego	63	6	357	5	71.40	–	–

G.D. Rose 30-10-95-0   A.V. Suppiah 15-4-55-3   W.J. Durston 14-0-65-1
P.D. Bowler 7-1-23-1

SIMON FRANCIS 2002 –

There were bowling bursts to earn Francis recognition from the National Academy, along with cameos for him to cherish. In 2003 at Taunton he took a hat-trick against Loughborough in that university's maiden first-class season. Watched and applauded by rather more spectators was an adept piece of fielding in a tight Cheltenham & Gloucester semi-final against Kent. He was down on the ground, but he still ran out James Golding in a spectacular and instinctive dismissal, seen as the turning point of the match.

Released by Hampshire, he came to Somerset in the hope of a regular place and the kind of figures that he always suggested he might deliver. Wickets have not come easily for him on the benign Taunton strip, though at Derby in 2004 he became only the seventh bowler in cricket history to take eight wickets in a one-day match. He was an England Under-18 hockey international and showed skills as a hockey coach.

SIMON RICHARD GEORGE FRANCIS Born Bromley, Kent, 15.8.78. RHB, RMF. SFC: 37 matches; 333 runs @ 12.33; HS 44 v Yorkshire, Taunton, 2003; HT 133 in 2003; 101 wickets @ 38.08; BB 5-42 v Glamorgan, Taunton, 2004; HT 35 in 2003. OD: 54 matches; 210 runs @ 15.00; 70 wickets @ 31.94. TT: 19 matches; 31 runs @ 6.20; 10 wickets @ 55.10. Hampshire 1997-2000

CARL GAZZARD 2002 –

This Cornishman was playing Minor Counties cricket behind the stumps at 16. He showed up well at the Somerset Academy and went with England Under-19 to Sri Lanka. In fact, he had been representing his country at virtually every age-group from Under-13.

A dislocated shoulder caused him to miss the 2001 season, and he was to learn the virtue of patience as he waited for an opportunity to take over from Rob Turner. There were times when he was played solely as a batsman in limited-overs matches.

His tendency to be an unconventional scorer eagerly inclined to sweep, allied to a bubbly presence, made him popular as well as useful. His breezy 157 against Derbyshire in the Totesport League in 2004 made the point.

CARL MATTHEW GAZZARD Born Penzance, Cornwall, 15.4.82. RHB, WK. SFC: 14 matches; 427 runs @ 26.68; HS 74 v Worcestershire, Worcester, 2005; HT 190 in 2005; 27 dismissals (26 ct, 1 st). OD: 37 matches; 817 runs @ 27.23; 36 dismissals (31 ct, 5 st). TT: 17 matches; 202 runs @ 18.36; 11 dismissals (7 ct, 4st).

NEIL EDWARDS 2002 –

He served Cornwall well when, only 16, he scored a much-praised double century for his native county's Under-19 side. Big knocks, carefully constructed, came along to boost early claims for a regular berth with Somerset. Recognition proved elusive, yet didn't he get to within three runs of a hundred for England Under-19s at Adelaide? And what about his 160 in only the tall left-hander's third championship match? That was when the statistics were rattling all round him as Somerset made 705-9, their highest total.

NEIL JAMES EDWARDS Born Treliske, Cornwall, 14.10.83. LHB, RM. SFC: 17 matches; 997 runs @ 32.16; 1 century; HS 160 v Hampshire, Taunton, 2003; HT 537 in 2004; 2 wickets @ 90.50; BB 1-16 v Derbyshire, Taunton, 2004. TT: 1 match; 1 run @ 1.00.

MICHAEL PARSONS 2002 –

No fancy seamer's tricks, no wickets from sheer pace. His valuable asset was that he bowled straight: reassuring line and length, and suggestions of movement as he worked on the rudiments of his craft. He's from Taunton, too, having played for Staplegrove and Taunton St Andrew. At county level, soon he learned something about the frustrations that come from competition. He leaned on accuracy rather than pace – would that be enough?

MICHAEL PARSONS Born Taunton, 26.11.84. RHB, RMF. SFC: 2 matches; 11 runs @ 5.50; 0 wickets. OD: 9 matches; 1 run @ 0.33; 5 wickets @ 72.40. TT: 1 match; 0 runs; 0 wickets.

WES DURSTON 2002 –

Another Millfield graduate, he brought an intelligent approach to his game as an all-rounder, an attribute he paraded in his role as Somerset's Under-19 and Second XI skipper. There was a determined half-century on his first-team debut, and other examples of decent stroke-making.

By 2005 he had established himself in the county side. At times he was needed as an off-spinner, unusually using his middle finger to impart the spin.

A nimble fielder, he created excitement by the way he ran out Lancashire's Andrew Symonds with a direct throw and little sight of the stumps in the final of the Twenty20 competition in 2005.

Durston is one of the young players to have made distinct progress under the county's revised regime; and yes, he is authentic Somerset, so much so that he was known to play village cricket for Compton Dundon alongside his father and two brothers.

WESLEY JOHN DURSTON Born Taunton, 6.10.80. RHB, OB. SFC: 12 matches; 538 runs @ 31.64; 1 century; HS 146* v Derbyshire, Derby, 2005; HT 323 in 2005; 14 wickets @ 53.85; BB 3-23 v Sri Lanka 'A', Taunton, 2004. OD: 19 matches; 354 runs @ 39.33; 8 wickets @ 42.87. TT: 18 matches; 201 runs @ 18.27; 8 wickets @ 16.37.

ARUL SUPPIAH 2002 –

He bowls useful slow left-arm but has always been seen as a better batsman. At 15 he was the youngest player to represent Malaysia, for whom his brother also plays and his mother has been known to do the scoring. His natural ability was noted and encouraged at Millfield. Then he went to Exeter University, where his stay was largely funded by the Somerset club.

Scope as a potential county cricketer was not immediately forthcoming and called for patience. But the CV was impressive: playing for England at the various levels, making his first-class debut against West Indies 'A' in 2002, confirming his wristy range for Devon.

He failed by three runs to make a hundred in the Minor Counties championship final in 2004, though by the following year he was making a stylish double-century for Devon, soon followed by a notable maiden hundred for Somerset.

His batting demonstrated a classy repertoire, while the county also liked his courteous, disciplined demeanour.

ARUL VIVASVAN SUPPIAH Born Kuala Lumpur, Malaysia, 30.8.83. RHB, SLA. SFC: 12 matches; 506 runs @ 24.09; 1 century; HS 123 v Derbyshire, Derby, 2005; HT 419 in 2005; 10 wickets @ 39.50; BB 3-46 v West Indies 'A', Taunton, 2002. OD: 14 matches; 296 runs @ 22.76; 9 wickets @ 26.11. TT: 8 matches; 45 runs @ 11.25; 1 wicket @ 5.00. Malaysia 1999-2001.

2003

Captain: M. Burns

This was Blackwell's year – certainly not Somerset's. His ferocious hitting, too well-timed and executed ever to be disparaged as slogging, provided oxygen and joy in a season laden with batting failure, wayward bowling and fielding flaws. Could this possibly have been the county which just two years before proudly took second place in the championship?

Now only Hampshire and Derbyshire were below them in Division Two. As for the National League, Scotland alone held a lower position. It added up to widespread embarrassment – and another withering reprimand from the chief executive, who sent letters to many players hinting that their future employment could be in jeopardy.

Not for the first time there had been a deceptive prelude, with three wins. Somerset then had to wait until September for the next. As head coach, Kevin Shine took more than his share of the flak. The captain, Burns, volunteered to step down from the post and there were vain attempts to persuade Surrey's Ian Ward to join the club. Caddick's foot injury meant he could play only once; and, because of his England commitments, Trescothick a mere four times. Amid such dispiriting circumstances, Bulbeck was forced to give up the game because of his back problems

Of course, there was Blackwell, all muscle and music. He passed 1,000 runs – as did Burns and Cox – although it was the thrilling method of his batsmanship that brought elation to the boundary seats. In three late matches he smashed 618 runs (with 18 sixes), climaxed by his undefeated 247 against his former county, Derbyshire. His second hundred came off 41 balls. Rightly he was chosen for the winter one-day tour of Bangladesh and Sri Lanka. For Somerset he kept superseding his career-best score and then featured in a last-wicket record stand of 163 with McLean.

Among the other paradoxes of a mostly gloomy summer, Somerset actually topped 700 runs in an innings for the first time, during which the Cornishman, Edwards, fashioned 160 in only his third championship match. Yet was the Taunton pitch altogether too generous to the batsmen?

COUNTY CHAMPIONSHIP 7th in Div 2
Played 16   Won 4   Drawn 4   Lost 8

OTHER MATCHES   Played 2   Drawn 2

C&G TROPHY   Lost in Fourth Round

TWENTY20 CUP   Eliminated at Zonal Stage

NATIONAL LEAGUE   9th in Div 2   Played 18   Won 5   No Result 1   Lost 12

BATTING

	M	I	NO	Runs	HS	Ave	100	50	ct	st
I.D. Blackwell	15	26	3	1160	247*	50.43	3	2	7	–
A.W. Laraman	13	18	5	597	148*	45.92	1	3	5	–
J. Cox	15	27	3	1087	160	45.29	3	5	10	–
N.J. Edwards	5	9	0	360	160	40.00	1	1	1	–
M.E. Trescothick	4	6	0	237	70	39.50	–	3	8	–
M. Burns	18	32	3	1133	118*	39.06	2	8	15	–
R.J. Turner	16	26	9	641	139*	37.70	1	3	65	5
P.D. Bowler	9	15	1	477	92	34.07	–	5	11	–
J.D.C. Bryant	14	24	2	658	109*	29.90	1	2	8	–
P.S. Jones	8	12	2	273	63	27.30	–	2	2	–
C.M. Gazzard	3	5	1	109	41	27.25	–	–	5	–
R.L. Johnson	10	14	3	290	118	26.36	1	–	5	–
M.J. Wood	12	23	1	536	100	24.36	1	3	1	–
T. Webley	6	11	1	208	59	20.80	–	1	3	–
G.M. Gilder	3	3	2	19	12	19.00	–	–	1	–
N.A.M. McLean	17	23	4	318	76	16.73	–	1	2	–
K.P. Dutch	7	10	0	161	61	16.10	–	1	9	–
S.R.G. Francis	10	13	2	133	44	12.09	–	–	2	–
G.M. Andrew	4	5	0	36	11	7.20	–	–	2	–

(2 matches)   P.C.L. Holloway 96, 30, 11   W.J. Durston 8, 30*, 4, 6 (4 ct)
K.A. Parsons 4, 6, 1, 2 (1 ct)
(1 match)   J.C. Hildreth 9, 0   A.V. Suppiah 16   A.R. Caddick 1

BOWLING

	Overs	Mdns	Runs	Wkts	Ave	5wi	10wm
R.L. Johnson	330.1	74	977	36	27.13	1	–
N.A.M. McLean	551.3	115	1872	65	28.80	3	–
G.M. Andrew	78	13	310	10	31.00	–	–
S.R.G. Francis	328.1	72	1179	35	33.68	–	–
I.D. Blackwell	466.4	111	1336	36	37.11	2	–
M. Burns	153.5	29	514	13	39.53	–	–
A.W. Laraman	279.5	58	979	24	40.79	–	–
P.S. Jones	204.3	27	930	22	42.27	1	–
K.P. Dutch	126.1	25	428	8	53.50	–	–

W.J. Durston 40-8-125-3   A.R. Caddick 38-8-110-7   K.A. Parsons 32.4-5-123-4
G.M. Gilder 29-2-133-1   N.J. Edwards 18.5-1-71-0   A.V. Suppiah 11-1-44-1
T. Webley 6-1-26-0   M.J. Wood 5.1-0-32-0   P.D. Bowler 4-0-8-0
J. Cox 2-0-15-0   J.D.C. Bryant 1-0-8-0

NIXON McLEAN 2003 – 2005

Nixon McLean was a product of St Vincent, and in his days for the Windward Islands he would make the ball whistle past the batsmen's rib-cages. Then his unconventional batting would scatter the doting young spectators with his beefy left-handed blows.

McLean went on to play in 19 Tests and 45 one-day internationals. He was an obvious candidate for first-class cricket in this country and signed for Hampshire in 1998 when, with straightforward pace summoned up from that wiry body, he took 62 wickets in his first season.

He appeared an astute capture at Somerset in 2003, augmenting the seam skills of Caddick and Johnson. Indeed, on paper they seemed to make up the best new-ball trio in the country. Injuries rather ruined all this, though Nixon turned in some decidedly challenging stints.

His appearance, near or at the foot of the batting order, was guaranteed at times to keep the supporters away from the bar. Nowhere was this more evident than when, with Blackwell thumping away at the other end, the pair smashed a last-wicket Somerset record stand of 163 against Derbyshire. Let no-one be uncharitable enough to recall that McLean was dropped before scoring.

His return to Taunton for the 2005 season was a late choice – and probably a mistake. He remained injury-prone and inconsistent, and had left well before the summer was over.

NIXON ALEXEI McNAMARA McLEAN Born Stubbs, St Vincent, 20.7.73. LHB, RFM. Cap 2003. 19 Tests 1997-2001. 45 LOI 1996-2003. SFC: 33 matches; 438 runs @ 13.27; HS 76 v Gloucestershire, Taunton, 2003; HT 318 in 2003; 120 wickets @ 29.21; BB 6-79 v Yorkshire, Scarborough, 2004; HT 65 in 2003. OD: 29 matches; 162 runs @ 16.20; 40 wickets @ 26.07. Hampshire 1998-99, Windward Islands 1991-2001, KwaZulu Natal 2001-.

GARY GILDER 2003

Recruited at short notice from league cricket in Durham to provide cover for injured fast bowlers, the Zimbabwean left-arm in-swinger played only three first-class matches for his new county.

He began by taking the new ball against the South Africans and captured one wicket. Then at Northampton, where Somerset lost by an innings, he was taken off after an expensive four overs. Worse was to come during the return game with Northants when he was hit on the head in the nets by his coach, Kevin Shine. It left him dazed and unable to bowl.

GARY MICHAEL GILDER Born Salisbury, Rhodesia, 6.7.74. RHB, LFM. SFC: 3 matches; 19 runs @ 19.00; HS 12 v Northamptonshire, Northampton, 2003; 1 wicket @ 133.00; BB 1-56 v South Africans, Taunton, 2003. OD: 3 matches; 9 runs (no average); 5 wickets @ 29.00. Natal/KwaZulu Natal 1994-2002.

TOM WEBLEY 2003

The schooldays at King's College, Taunton, were encouraging and then he went off to score an attractive hundred at Fenner's against Northants. But this left-hander earned only half a dozen first-class appearances. He played some Minor Counties cricket for Dorset, fearing that breakthrough at Taunton was going to be elusive.

THOMAS WEBLEY Born Bristol, 2.3.83. LHB, SLA. SFC: 6 matches; 208 runs @ 20.80; HS 59 v Hampshire, Taunton, 2003; 0 wickets.

AARON LARAMAN 2003 – 2005

As a lad he had viewed Lord's as a distant, romantic ambition. He was talented enough, though, to win his grammar school cricket cap at the age of 13. The coaches were pleased with him and he travelled on the England Under-19 tour to South Africa. For Middlesex he picked up the plaudits as reward for his four wickets on his NatWest debut. But there were too many competing for the middle-order all-rounder's job and he chose to come to Somerset.

In his first summer he hit 148 not against West Country rivals, Gloucestershire, at Taunton. No bad way to impress your new county.

The tall all-rounder may not have lived up to that, but from time to time he was a useful man to call on, with bat or ball. Hopes that he might turn into a successor to Graham Rose didn't materialise, and he accepted that his days with Somerset were numbered.

AARON WILLIAM LARAMAN Born Enfield, Middlesex, 10.1.79. RHB, RFM. SFC: 33 matches; 1019 runs @ 29.97; 1 century; HS 148* v Gloucestershire, Taunton, 2003; HT 597 in 2003; 59 wickets @ 37.61; BB 5-58 v Derbyshire, Taunton, 2004; HT 24 in 2003. OD: 22 matches; 279 runs @ 16.41; 15 wickets @ 51.66. TT: 7 matches; 35 runs @ 8.75; 9 wickets @ 16.77. Middlesex 1998-2002.

JAMES BRYANT 2003

He arrived as a British passport holder – because his father came from here – with ambitions to make a cricketing impact in this country. That meant, however, there had to be a difficult decision for him first, and he chose to abandon any private hopes he might have had of representing his native South Africa.

Playing for Eastern Province, Bryant paraded plenty of attractive strokes as he moved to 234, sharing in a new record stand for any wicket in South African domestic first-class cricket of 441. But he argued that county cricket in England, as the possible prelude to Test consideration here, was the most motivating prospect of all.

Sadly it didn't work out, even though he helped himself to a hundred in his first match for Somerset, against Loughborough University. Form was elusive and he found it was hard holding down a place. He left Somerset, romantic dreams of sporting glory in the West unfulfilled, to join Derbyshire.

JAMES DOUGLAS CAMPBELL BRYANT Born Durban, South Africa, 4.2.76. RHB, RM. SFC: 14 matches; 658 runs @ 29.90; 1 century; HS 109* v Loughborough University, Taunton, 2003 on debut; 0 wickets. OD: 9 matches; 120 runs @ 17.14. TT: 1 match, 0 runs. Eastern Province 1996-, Derbyshire 2004-.

GARETH ANDREW 2003 –

From Botham's Yeovil, Andrew, too, is an all-rounder, if of less flamboyant talents. He went with the Somerset Academy to Western Australia in 2002 and the following year with the Australian Academy to Perth. He had every reason to be satisfied with his tidy 3-14 in the second innings against Derbyshire during a match of high scoring in 2003. Similarly he gave a capable performance with bat and ball against Sri Lanka 'A' the following summer.

A local boy with a good attitude, his promise was disrupted by injury. Still, he turned in several tight one-day performances during 2005 and was the county's most successful bowler in the Twenty20 defeat of rivals Gloucestershire on an evening when more established bowlers were savaged.

GARETH MARK ANDREW Born Yeovil, 27.12.83. LHB, RMF. SFC: 11 matches; 163 runs @ 12.53; HS 44 v Sri Lanka 'A', Taunton, 2004; 28 wickets @ 35.32; BB 4-63, same match; HT 11 in 2005. OD: 28 matches; 112 runs @ 9.33; 32 wickets @ 30.62. TT: 18 matches; 49 runs @ 7.00; 19 wickets @ 21.47.

JAMES CHARLES HILDRETH Born Milton Keynes, Buckinghamshire, 9.9.84. RHB, RMF. SFC: 30 matches; 1706 runs @ 37.91; 4 centuries; HS 125* v Essex, Colchester, 2005; HT 937 in 2005; 2 wickets @ 74.50. OD: 43 matches; 970 runs @ 29.39; 0 wickets. TT: 18 matches; 359 runs @ 21.11; 10 wickets @ 19.00.

> The game's pressures do not appear to affect him. If he can develop a slightly enhanced hunger for runs, the world just might be his oyster.
>
> **David Green**

JAMES HILDRETH 2003 –

From his Millfield days as a ten-year-old, he created a buzz of expectation. Here was a true sportsman: and you could say that again. It wasn't just the hockey, tennis and squash which came with regional honours. He'd also do his stuff, with competitive zest, at rugby and soccer.

The Hildreth versatility had quickly incorporated cricket, too. Millfield has been a rich source of material for Somerset, and soon they were on his trail. At the Academy he revealed a natural, assured style, though sometimes he wondered privately why his bowling didn't generate the same attention as his batting. 'I used to look on myself as a bowler who did a bit with the bat,' he would confide. He continues to hope that his talents as a genuine all-rounder will emerge. But, of course, everyone talks with enthusiasm about his batting.

So they should. On his debut for England Under-19s he composed a highly attractive 116 and he began to be mentioned as a cricketer to watch with more than passing interest. By 2004 he was an established member of Somerset's side, there on merit and becoming in the process the third youngest to score a championship hundred for the county.

Physically he isn't especially tall and commanding. His attitude at the crease makes up for that. He has a welcome inclination to go for his shots, and they come in a wide, attractive arc. There is a maturity about him, both as a cricketer and as a young man. Here, surely, is an asset for Somerset to treasure.

One could understand the furrowed brows at Taunton when he seemed to be hesitating over a new contract at the end of the 2004 season. Northamptonshire, where there were family links, were among several counties ready to pounce.

As is so often the case, he found that second years can be anti-climactic. After all the rich promise of his first full season, runs came more reluctantly in 2005. There were still innings of brio, but not so many of them. A little of that uninhibited vigour and confidence in his stroke-play was missing.

The young cricketer got to work sorting out any technical flaws. He had a sharp cricket brain and, especially in non-championship matches, could continue to pull out a sparkling innings for the boundary faithful to savour.

MARCUS TRESCOTHICK'S XI

from the years in which he played

Mark Lathwell
Marcus Trescothick (or Graeme Smith)
Jamie Cox (captain)
Chris Tavare
Richard Harden
Ian Blackwell
Graham Rose
Rob Turner
Neil Mallender
Mushtaq Ahmed
Andrew Caddick

I'm told I can include myself and one of my reasons for doing so is, of course, to walk out again with Mark Lathwell. We were emerging together and many saw us as a long-standing opening pair for the county. Mark was so natural and free-scoring. I'm sad, like my team-mates, that he decided to leave the county game.

Jamie Cox is my captain. He had quiet leadership qualities and was a nice man. Then comes Chris Tavare, who was skipper in my first season. To me he was the perfect, unflurried number four, providing solid balance to offset some of the early aggression.

There are places in my team for Dick Harden and Neil Mallender. Dick was a big scorer for Somerset for a time, and I was sorry to see him move to Yorkshire. As for Neil, he deserved his Test recognition, however brief. He wasn't so much a swing bowler; he got his movement off the seam.

The rest of the team comes easily to me. Ian Blackwell's fastest hundred of the season in 2005 only illustrates what a destructive batsman he really is. Graham Rose takes his place among the county's best all-rounders and only just missed out on higher honours. As a bowler he could swing the ball both ways.

Rob Turner is there on unchallenged merit; Mushtaq could be a sheer genius for us. And Caddie? Well, as his record showed, he was one of the best bowlers in the world – and he'd get through the overs of *two* players to prove what an asset he was.

2004

Captain: M. Burns

Whatever the shortcomings on the field, Somerset have maintained an envied reputation in signing overseas players, even when their stays have been brief. Ponting was one of the latest to make the point. He was around for only a few weeks, but that was long enough to play three championship matches and score two memorable centuries. His residency in the West Country proved immediately influential and his international status brought a new purpose to the county's meandering form. He pulled in the crowds and coaxed lesser players. There was considerable disappointment when his transitory visit was over.

Somerset's final position was eased by a late burst which gave them four championship wins out of seven. Their season had once again been too fallible, too lacking in adventure and imagination. However did the county allow Durham to score 453 in the fourth innings to win by one wicket? Old-timers are still trying to work that out, and where to apportion the blame.

Caddick bravely battled away over the summer for 54 wickets, not enough to persuade the Test selectors to recall him. Blackwell came into his own as a steady left-arm slow bowler capable of winning a match for his side. He returned career-best figures of 7-90 against Glamorgan – and then did exactly the same at Trent Bridge. Theoretically, with a seam attack of Caddick, Johnson and McLean, there should have been more early victories, even allowing for the injuries.

At season's end Cox went back to Tasmania – though not before scoring a most attractive 250 against Nottinghamshire and leaving pleasant memories from his six years here. Also leaving was Bowler; his studied approach, acquired over 19 years on the circuit, was going to be missed.

Reassuring signs were emerging, though, of Wood, even if it was hard to understand the county's apparent reluctance initially to promote him. Hildreth, too, was shaping up with a natural facility for making strokes and taking on the bowlers. The fact that Somerset came top of the Second XI championship was another indication of better times ahead.

The new language of cricket

Our emphasis for the year has been based on 'Performance Goals' rather than 'Outcome Goals' as you do not achieve the latter without the former.

Mark Garaway
on winning the Second XI Championship

COUNTY CHAMPIONSHIP 4th in Div 2

Played 16	Won 4	Drawn 7	Lost 5

OTHER MATCHES Played 2 Won 1 Lost 1

C&G TROPHY Lost in Third Round

TWENTY20 CUP Eliminated at Zonal Stage

NATIONAL LEAGUE 8th in Div 2 Played 18 Won 6 No Result 1 Lost 11

BATTING

	M	I	NO	Runs	HS	Ave	100	50	ct	st
R.T. Ponting	3	4	1	297	117	99.00	2	1	7	–
I.D. Blackwell	11	16	2	864	131	61.71	2	6	5	–
J. Cox	13	20	1	1013	250	53.31	3	4	7	–
M.J. Wood	11	16	4	604	128*	50.33	2	3	5	–
P.D. Bowler	16	27	6	1034	187*	49.23	3	3	11	–
J.C. Hildreth	13	20	2	760	108	42.22	2	5	12	–
K.A. Parsons	3	4	1	114	55	38.00	–	1	2	–
J.D. Francis	10	16	1	554	110	36.93	2	3	6	–
M. Burns	16	22	2	733	124*	36.65	1	4	17	–
K.P. Dutch	6	8	1	248	72	35.42	–	2	2	–
N.J. Edwards	10	19	0	537	93	28.26	–	2	11	–
R.L. Johnson	15	14	2	297	101*	24.75	1	1	3	–
R.J. Turner	16	18	3	346	46	23.06	–	–	61	4
A.W. Laraman	11	11	2	186	66*	20.66	–	1	5	–
A.R. Caddick	14	14	4	204	54	20.40	–	1	5	–
S.R.G. Francis	11	10	6	46	15	11.50	–	–	6	–
N.A.M. McLean	10	11	3	61	22*	7.62	–	–	1	–

(2 matches) C.M. Gazzard 18, 35, 44* (3 ct) W.J. Durston 5, 34, 47 (8 ct)
G.M. Andrew 0, 44, 15 (2 ct) A.V. Suppiah 33, 11, 0 (1 ct)
(1 match) T.A. Hunt 1*

BOWLING

	Overs	Mdns	Runs	Wkts	Ave	5wi	10wm
K.P. Dutch	124	21	448	19	23.57	2	–
N.A.M. McLean	322.1	62	1127	43	26.20	3	1
A.W. Laraman	180.3	43	638	22	29.00	1	–
R.L. Johnson	449.5	104	1512	44	34.36	2	–
I.D. Blackwell	345.1	85	972	27	36.00	2	–
A.R. Caddick	578.5	110	2026	56	36.17	4	–
S.R.G. Francis	295.5	51	1201	33	36.39	2	–

M. Burns 44.4-7-155-3 G.M. Andrew 40-5-179-7 K.A. Parsons 37-7-183-0
J.D. Francis 36.3-9-120-2 W.J. Durston 35-6-115-4 T.A. Hunt 28-4-124-2
N.J. Edwards 25-1-110-2 A.V. Suppiah 25-1-105-4 J.C. Hildreth 17-1-76-2
R.T. Ponting 5-2-6-0 P.D. Bowler 2-1-2-0 M.J. Wood 2-0-6-0

John (right) with brother Simon

JOHN DANIEL FRANCIS Born Bromley, Kent, 13.11.80. LHB, SLA. SFC: 27 matches; 1616 runs @ 39.41; 6 centuries; HS 125* v Yorkshire, Headingley, 2005; 1000 runs once; HT 1062 in 2005; 2 wickets @ 60.00. OD: 34 matches; 838 runs @ 28.89. TT: 9 matches; 212 runs @ 35.33. Hampshire 2001-03; British Universities 2002-03.

JOHN FRANCIS 2004 –

He followed brother Simon from Hampshire in search of a more productive career, he as a batsman, his brother a bowler. Once he had been Hampshire's Young Sportsman of the Year, in 1995, and while at university he was a consistent scorer, a left-hander with a neat, calm style. The move to Somerset made sense to him, even if it surprised some at the Rose Bowl. Two centuries in his opening season for the new county confirmed his value in the higher order.

Somerset had struggled for wins over much of the 2005 campaign, and players such as Francis were clearly affected. His assets, a sound technique and considerable concentration, were put to the test. It didn't help when he was the victim of a freak accident in the field, being hit in the face by a close-range return from Matthew Wood.

But as the team appeared to gather new strengths and hopes in mid-season, so Francis shook off the grim effects of a spell which brought him six runs from five innings and took him perilously near demotion. Now, in a better climate within the club, he went on to score 1,000 runs for the first time, with four centuries, and struck knowledgeable observers as a thoroughly proficient bat.

THOS HUNT 2004

Born in Australia and brought up in this country, he had the disappointment of failing to establish himself with either Middlesex or Somerset. With some irony, he made his debut at Lord's in a one-day match against the Australians. The young seamer had only four overs but at least he took a wicket. Somerset, in need of bowling cover, gave him a one-year contract and he was offered an early chance because McLean was not yet back in England and Francis was injured. Alas, 24 overs and two expensive wickets made up his sum total of success in the West.

THOMAS AARON HUNT Born Melbourne, Australia, 19.1.82. LHB, RMF. SFC: 1 match; 1 run (no average); 2 wickets @ 62.00; BB 2-85 v Loughborough University, Taunton, 2004. OD: 1 match, 0 runs; 0 wickets. TT: 3 matches; 6 runs @ 3.00; 0 wickets.

NEIL HANCOCK 2004

He came as a short-term emergency replacement when Somerset were suddenly short of seam bowlers, a willing part-timer from Devon club cricket. There was one senior match with a solitary wicket, a couple of Twenty20s and, in truth, nothing too much to write home about apart from a whole-hearted attitude.

NEIL DAVID HANCOCK Born Casino, New South Wales, Australia, 13.4.76. RHB, RFM. OD: 1 match; 12 runs @ 12.00; 1 wicket @ 48.00. TT: 2 matches; 9 runs @ 4.50; 1 wicket @ 25.00.

RICKY PONTING 2004

Talk about an antidote. Somerset were in the doldrums again, without wins or too much visible exuberance. The chief executive, it was generally believed, was in the wings contemplating his annual withering public comment at the players' expense. 'What we need,' chairman Giles Clarke had been saying for weeks, 'is a high-profile match-winner, someone to lift the crowd as well as the club.'

Enter Ricky Ponting, who was, after all, as good as you could get. He flew in and had hardly gone through passport control before he was rushing to the ground and starting to score runs for his new county. Two centuries arrived in two innings, and suddenly there was a buzz about the place again, rather in the way there was when Viv Richards was strapping on his pads.

The pity was that Ponting was not around longer. Jamie Cox, a Tasmanian colleague, had helped to arrange the temporary switch of the Australian skipper to Taunton. It had been on the cards for some months, although a few faint-hearts feared he might never arrive. Yet for his part, he liked the idea of sampling those fleeting weeks of county cricket. Maybe he saw it as a kind of therapy after the exacting schedules of international cricket all round the world.

His introduction coincided with a heartening, overdue aura of optimism and improvement in the team. It wasn't simply his batting skills, with their instinctive brio and comprehensive technique; it was the way he galvanised the dressing room. Younger players moved closer to listen to his wisdom. By example, he got them winning again. On the field, quietly, never ostentatiously, he helped with the captaincy. Mike Burns, very much an unselfish team man, was flattered to have someone as famous and influential as Ponting in his side. He acted on the astute Aussie counsel.

The crowds took to Ponting instantly. Probably their memories went back to 2001 when the Australian tourists came to Taunton and he stood in, with serious competitive ardour, as captain for the first time, complementing his leadership by scoring 128 at a typically breezy, attractive pace.

He has been playing Test cricket since 1995, skippered his country to World Cup glory in 2003 and taken part in more than 200 limited-overs internationals. The name of Ricky Ponting is added to the list of illustrious overseas cricketers who have represented Somerset, and is not out of place.

Meanwhile, as the optimists at the County Ground hoped that somehow he might be persuaded back for 2006, he took some unfair flak, as captain, for the Australians' Ashes defeat. It was a reaction soon forgotten as his attractive innings continued to give his country weight and style.

RICKY THOMAS PONTING Born Launceston, Tasmania, Australia, 19.12.74. RHB, RM/OB. Cap 2004. 100 Tests 1995-. 237 LOI 1994-. SFC: 3 matches, 297 runs @ 99.00; 2 centuries; HS 117 v Glamorgan, Taunton, 2004; 0 wickets. OD: 4 matches, 298 runs @ 99.33. TT: 1 match, 20 runs @ 20.00. Tasmania 1992-.

2005

Captain: G.C. Smith
I.D. Blackwell

Try to forget the minimal successes of the summer. This was a time of strategic re-thinking, already beginning to take effect in the second half of the season and aiming to benefit the county club over the next few years. There had been too many low points and an inability to make some sense of days, not long ago, when Somerset were second in the table, not far off winning the championship for the first time. After that playing standards seemed to slip, along with morale.

The formation of a review panel, headed by three ex-captains – Roy Kerslake, Brian Rose and Vic Marks – was the first positive step. Then in June, Rose was appointed director of cricket. It gave him wide powers, radically to shake up the club and to initiate a new policy which appeared to give more scope and encouragement to promising young players, many from the academy. In the process, outstanding clubmen like Turner and Burns stepped aside.

Wood, now a fixture, compiled his 1,000 runs, including a marvellous 297 against Yorkshire. The former Hampshire left-hander, John Francis, after agonising over six runs in five championship innings, found a new vitality, passing 1,000 runs for the first time. Parsons was back in favour and Hildreth shook off his early-season uncertainties. All this, under new coach Mark Garaway, wasn't enough to lift Somerset up the table but team spirit seemed to be restored.

The county dared to win the Twenty20 final against Lancashire at the Oval. A 'Spirit of Cricket' award, for the way the players conducted themselves, also came to Taunton. Carrying on the prize-winning crash-bang hitting of Johnson in 2004, Blackwell now gained the Lawrence Trophy for the season's fastest century.

As part of the philosophical turnaround, Blackwell was boldly asked to take over the captaincy, with Wood as his number two.

Memorable team feats may have been rare but not famous players. Jayasuriya came briefly from Sri Lanka and struggled to get runs; Smith had time for no more than four first-class appearances, but scored a triple-hundred and made the fans regret his early departure.

The season was followed by two surprise announcements. It was revealed that Somerset would be losing Mark Garaway and Kevin Shine, both to the England set-up. Garaway, as coach, had made a pleasing impact at Taunton and was now to become England's team analyst. Then Shine was named as England's bowling coach. It represented a notable accolade for both.

I feel I've come in and been part of a new future. To walk away with a trophy ... I'll get on the plane with a really good feeling.

Graeme Smith
on winning the Twenty20 Cup

COUNTY CHAMPIONSHIP 8th in Div 2

COUNTY CHAMPIONSHIP 8th in Div 2   Played 16   Won 4   Drawn 5   Lost 7

OTHER MATCHES   Played 1   Drawn 1

C&G TROPHY   Lost in First Round

TWENTY20 CUP   Champions

TOTESPORT LEAGUE   6th in Div 2   Played 18   Won 9   No Result 1   Lost 8

BATTING

	M	I	NO	Runs	HS	Ave	100	50	ct	st
G.C. Smith	4	8	1	472	311	67.42	1	1	7	—
I.D. Blackwell	17	28	4	1256	191	52.33	3	9	5	—
M.J. Wood	13	23	1	1058	297	48.09	2	7	4	—
K.A. Parsons	8	12	3	401	94	44.55	—	2	5	—
J.D. Francis	17	31	5	1062	125*	40.84	4	5	8	—
J.C. Hildreth	16	29	4	937	125*	37.48	2	6	15	—
W.J. Durston	7	11	2	323	146*	35.88	1	—	5	—
A.V. Suppiah	7	13	0	419	123	32.23	1	2	1	—
M. Burns	9	17	1	484	87	30.25	—	2	4	—
R.J. Turner	9	13	3	277	68*	27.70	—	1	22	1
S.T. Jayasuriya	7	13	0	327	73	25.15	—	3	2	—
C.M. Gazzard	8	10	2	190	74	23.75	—	1	15	—
S.R.G. Francis	6	9	5	87	29	21.75	—	—	6	—
A.R. Caddick	11	16	3	256	54	19.69	—	1	3	—
A.W. Laraman	9	13	1	236	53	19.66	—	2	2	—
R.J. Woodman	3	4	1	54	46*	18.00	—	—	—	—
M.E. Trescothick	4	6	0	96	22	16.00	—	—	6	—
R.L. Johnson	11	15	0	218	35	14.53	—	—	5	—
G.M. Andrew	5	6	1	68	32	13.60	—	—	1	—
C.K. Langeveldt	6	6	3	38	18*	12.66	—	—	—	—
N.A.M. McLean	6	7	1	59	40	9.83	—	—	—	—

(2 matches)   M. Parsons 6*, 1, 4

(1 match)   N.J. Edwards 42   M.K. Munday did not bat

BOWLING

	Overs	Mdns	Runs	Wkts	Ave	5wi	10wm
A.R. Caddick	443.1	94	1501	54	27.79	4	1
N.A.M. McLean	123	27	507	12	42.25	—	—
C.K. Langeveldt	215.1	59	637	15	42.46	—	—
G.M. Andrew	104.5	14	500	11	45.45	—	—
S.T. Jayasuriya	56.1	7	230	5	46.00	—	—
A.W. Laraman	177	21	602	13	46.30	—	—
R.L. Johnson	287.3	52	1048	20	52.40	—	—
I.D. Blackwell	517.5	107	1569	28	56.03	—	—
K.A. Parsons	112.1	19	428	7	61.14	—	—
W. Durston	92	8	449	6	74.83	—	—
S.R.G. Francis	114.4	16	520	5	104.00	—	—
R.J. Woodman	66	11	268	2	134.00	—	—

A.V. Suppiah 43.1-8-191-2   M. Burns 40.3-5-142-3   M. Parsons 27-3-135-0

G.C. Smith 20-4-71-1   J.C. Hildreth 15-0-73-0   M.K. Munday 14-0-77-1

GRAEME SMITH 2005

Here was more glamour for Somerset as they boldly went for a big name as one of their temporary signings. The South Africa skipper was around for no more than four first-class appearances but that was long enough to make his mark in dramatic style.

Against Leicestershire at Taunton, his 311 put him behind only Richards and Cook among the county's individual record scorers. At times he took on the bowlers as though he'd never be dislodged.

Smith's attitude on and off the field bolstered Somerset. He was positive and single-minded, free with advice to younger players. The stay with the county, however brief, was much enjoyed by him, and he considered the experience to be of genuine value personally.

He'd been keen to come and sample county cricket. Jimmy Cook, who used to coach him, was one of the main contacts in encouraging the Taunton link, as had been chief executive Peter Anderson during a visit to South Africa.

Smith was remarkably mature for his age. His appointment as his country's captain, in succession to Shaun Pollock, had been clouded in controversy, but as a 22-year-old he had shown he could weather public scepticism. His strong opinions led to a frosty relationship with Michael Vaughan.

At Taunton, where he was installed instantly as skipper, he was mostly relaxed and team-mates saw few signs of that naturally dogmatic manner. He remembered warmly his first visit to the County Ground, as a member of a schoolboy touring side.

GRAEME CRAIG SMITH Born Johannesburg, South Africa, 1.2.81. LHB, OB. Cap 2005. Captain 2005. 42 Tests 2001-. 77 LOI 2001-. SFC: 4 matches; 472 runs @ 67.42; 1 century; HS 311 v Leicestershire, Taunton, 2004; 1 wicket @ 71.00. OD: 5 matches; 326 runs @ 81.50; 2 wickets @ 78.00. TT: 11 matches, 380 runs @ 38.00; 0 wickets. Gauteng 1999-2000, Western Province 2000-04, Western Province/Boland 2004-05.

CHARL LANGEVELDT 2005

One of Somerset's stopgap bowlers, albeit one with Test pedigree, he made only a handful senior appearances in 2005 before being recalled by the South African board. His pace was brisk enough to bring him 15 wickets, and he filled a hole in the bowling resources when the county were apt to look a seamer short. At home he was employed in the prison service.

CHARL KENNETH LANGEVELDT Born Stellenbosch, South Africa, 17.12.74. RHB, RFM. 6 Tests 05-. 24 LOI 01-. Cap 2005. SFC: 6 matches; 38 runs @ 12.66; HS 18* v Leicestershire, Taunton, 2005; 15 wickets @ 42.46; BB 3-67 v Leicestershire, Taunton, 2005. OD: 7 matches; 9 runs @ 4.50; 7 wickets @ 46.14. TT: 3 matches; 0 runs; 0 wickets. Boland 1997-2003, Border 2003-04, Lions 2004-

SANATH JAYASURIYA 2005

Here was another name of international repute to excite the West Country crowds and sustain the county's reputation for aiming high. But too little was seen of the wristy Sri Lankan's memorable cutting to backward point.

At times he looked strangely ill at ease in our conditions and runs came reluctantly. There was a solitary century against Australia in a limited-overs game and glimpses of his familiar stroke-making. In all, he played only seven first-class matches and a few more one-dayers for Somerset. Retrospectively it seems like a wasted opportunity.

The popular left-hander helped to raise funds while here for the Sri Lankan Tsunami Schools project of which he was a patron.

SANATH TERAN JAYASURIYA Born Matara, Sri Lanka, 30.6.69. LHB, SLA. 100 Tests 1991-. 345 LOI 1989-. SFC: 7 matches, 327 runs @ 25.15; HS 73 v Lancashire, Taunton, 2005; 5 wickets @ 46.00; BB 2-2 v. Durham, Stockton-on-Tees, 2005. OD: 9 matches; 218 runs @ 24.22; 5 wickets @ 47.20. Colombo 1988-92, Southern Province, Bloomfield 1994-.

ROBERT WOODMAN 2005 –

A local boy who played for Taunton Deane and who rose through the county's academy, he concentrated diligently on the valued craft of left-arm in-swing to complement his useful batting technique. He took a mere two wickets from three senior appearances in his 2005 debut season, including an lbw victim from his first ball against Essex, though he was only four runs short of an unbeaten half-century on his first outing. Woodman's promise earned him a place in the England Under-19 squad to tour Bangladesh and Sri Lanka.

ROBERT JAMES WOODMAN Born Taunton, 12.10.86. LHB, LMF. SFC: 3 matches; 54 runs @ 18.00; HS 46* v Worcestershire, Worcester, 2005; 2 wickets @ 134.00; BB 1-78 v Essex, Colchester, 2005. OD: 4 matches; 0 runs; 1 wicket @ 136.00. TT: 2 matches; 1 run (no average); 2 wickets @ 31.50.

MICHAEL MUNDAY 2005 –

He made his debut at Colchester in 2005 and took a wicket, if rather expensively, with his leg-spinners. He's a Cornishman who has shaped well for Oxford University.

Somerset's Peter Robinson first noted the potential when Munday was only 13. Since then he has appeared capably for Cornwall, even if his batting, at number 11, is apt to earn a modest rating.

MICHAEL KENNETH MUNDAY Born Nottingham, 22.10.84. RHB, LB. SFC: 1 match; did not bat; 1 wicket @ 77.00. Oxford University 2003-.

SAM SPURWAY 2005 –

The form of the young wicket-keeper-batsman, who played his club cricket for Ilminster, had been carefully monitored through the Academy. His chance came, with temperament successfully tested, in the inaugural international Twenty20 competition at Leicester at the end of the 2005 season. Here was one, Brian Rose argued, for the future.

SAMUEL HAROLD PATRICK SPURWAY Born Taunton, 13.3.87. LHB, WK. TT: 1 match; 15 runs (no average).

AND SO TO THE SIXTY-FIRST SUMMER

Somerset have signed three new overseas players for 2006:

CAMERON WHITE, a leg-spinner and middle-order batsman who captains Victoria and has played one-day international cricket for Australia,

DAN CULLEN, an off-spinner from South Australia, whom Shane Warne describes as 'having a bit of fire about him', and

CHARL WILLOUGHBY, a left-arm fast-medium swing bowler who has played Test cricket for South Africa and who moves to Somerset from Leicestershire.

Let us hope that the next edition of this book will be able to report their great deeds.

BIBLIOGRAPHY

The quotations in this book have been gathered from many sources. Some are from conversations with former players. Some are from newspapers and magazines: *The Times, The Cricketer, Playfair Cricket Monthly* and *Wisden Cricket Monthly*. Some are from publications produced by Somerset County Cricket Club, including yearbooks and benefit brochures. Some are from *Playfair Cricket Annual* and *Wisden Cricketers' Almanack*.

Quotations have also been drawn from the following books:

Bill Alley, *My Incredible Innings* (Pelham Books, 1969)
Bill Alley, *Standing the Test of Time* (Empire Publications, 1999)
Bill Andrews, *The Hand that Bowled Bradman* (Macdonald, 1973)
John Arlott, *Cricket in the Counties* (Saturn Press, 1950)
John Arlott, *How to Watch Cricket* (Collins Willow, 1983)
Trevor Bailey, *Wickets, Catches and the Odd Run* (Collins Willow, 1986)
John Barclay, *The Appeal of the Championship* (Fairfield Books, 2002)
Ian Botham, *Botham's Century* (Collins Willow, 2001)
Stephen Chalke, *Runs in the Memory* (Fairfield Books, 1997)
Stephen Chalke, *Caught in the Memory* (Fairfield Books, 1999)
Brian Close, *I Don't Bruise Easily* (Macdonald & Jane's, 1978)
Dickie Dodds, *Hit Hard and Enjoy It* (The Cricketer, 1976)
David Foot, *Sunshine, Sixes and Cider* (David & Charles, 1986)
David Foot, *Harold Gimblett – Tormented Genius of Cricket* (Heinemann, 1982)
Alan Gibson, *Growing up with Cricket* (George Allen & Unwin, 1985)
Frank Lee, *Cricket Lovely Cricket* (Stanley Paul, 1960)
Colin McCool, *Cricket is a Game* (Stanley Paul, 1961)
Vic Marks, *Somerset County Cricket Scrapbook* (Souvenir Press, 1984)
Douglas Miller, *Charles Palmer – More than Just a Gentleman* (Fairfield Books, 2005)
Ron Roberts, *Sixty Years of Somerset* (Westaway Books, 1952)
R.C. Robertson-Glasgow, *Cricket Prints* (Morrison & Gibb, 1943)
Peter Roebuck, *From Sammy to Jimmy* (Partridge Press, 1991)
Peter Roebuck, *Slices of Cricket* (George Allen & Unwin, 1982)
A.A. Thomson, *Vintage Elevens* (Pelham Books, 1969)
Peter Walker, *Cricket Conversations* (Pelham Books, 1978)
Norman Yardley & J.M. Kilburn, *Homes of Sport – Cricket* (Peter Garnett, 1952)